FIVE
PRESIDENTS

OTHER *NEW YORK TIMES* BESTSELLERS BY
CLINT HILL AND LISA McCUBBIN
Five Days in November
Mrs. Kennedy and Me

FIVE PRESIDENTS

*My Extraordinary Journey with Eisenhower,
Kennedy, Johnson, Nixon, and Ford*

CLINT HILL

WITH LISA McCUBBIN

GALLERY BOOKS

New York   London   Toronto   Sydney   New Delhi

G

Gallery Books
An Imprint of Simon & Schuster, Inc.
1230 Avenue of the Americas
New York, NY 10020

First Gallery Books paperback edition May 2017

GALLERY BOOKS and colophon are registered
trademarks of Simon & Schuster, Inc.

For information about special discounts for bulk purchases,
please contact Simon & Schuster Special Sales at
1-866-506-1949 or business@simonandschuster.com.

The Simon & Schuster Speakers Bureau can bring authors to your live event.
For more information or to book an event, contact the Simon & Schuster Speakers
Bureau at 1-866-248-3049 or visit our website at www.simonspeakers.com.

Interior design by Renato Stanisic

Manufactured in the United States of America

10 9 8 7 6 5

Library of Congress Cataloging-in-Publication Data

Names: Hill, Clint, author. | McCubbin, Lisa, coauthor.
Title: Five presidents : my extraordinary journey with Eisenhower, Kennedy, Johnson,
Nixon, and Ford / Clint Hill with Lisa McCubbin.
Description: New York : Gallery Books, 2016.
Identifiers: LCCN 2015050618| ISBN 9781476794136 | ISBN 9781476794174 (ebook) |
ISBN 9781476794143 (pbk.)
Subjects: LCSH: Hill, Clint. | United States. Secret Service—Officials and employees—
Biography. | Presidents—Protection—United States.
Classification: LCC HV7911.H454 A3 2016 | DDC 363.28/3092—dc23 LC record available
at http://lccn.loc.gov/2015050618

ISBN 978-1-4767-9413-6
ISBN 978-1-4767-9414-3 (pbk)
ISBN 978-1-4767-9417-4 (ebook)

This book is dedicated to the men and women
of the United States Secret Service, past and present,
who have worked tirelessly to keep the occupant of the Office
of the President of the United States in a secure environment,
through good times and bad, without regard to the political party
affiliation of the protectee. You served long, tedious hours, under
stress and in the face of danger, without complaint to ensure
continuity of our government as directed by the Constitution
and its amendments. No matter the challenges or obstacles,
you remained true to the Secret Service code of honor:
WORTHY OF TRUST AND CONFIDENCE.
I am proud to have served in your ranks.

Contents

INTRODUCTION

Walking Beside History

As a Special Agent in the United States Secret Service, I had the honor and privilege of serving five presidents—Dwight D. Eisenhower, John F. Kennedy, Lyndon B. Johnson, Richard M. Nixon, and Gerald R. Ford—three Republicans and two Democrats. From my unique vantage point, I had the rare opportunity to observe the human side of these men—the most powerful men in the world—as each dealt with the enormous responsibilities and unforeseen challenges thrust upon them, and how their individual characters and personalities affected grave decisions.

My seventeen years in the Secret Service spanned the period that encompassed the U-2 spy incident; the Cold War; the Cuban Missile Crisis; the assassinations of President John F. Kennedy, Martin Luther King Jr., and Robert F. Kennedy; the civil rights movement, riots and burning of major U.S. cities; the Vietnam War; Watergate; and the resignations of Vice President Spiro T. Agnew and President Nixon. In less than two decades, America went from being unquestionably the most respected and admired nation in the world to a country whose image had become tarnished by violence, scandal, and deceit.

It is interesting to note that of these five presidents, only Eisenhower had a normal run as president—elected by the people and serving two full terms. Kennedy was elected in 1960 by the slimmest of margins, and his term lasted just one thousand days, cut short by an assassin. Suddenly, the vice president became president. Johnson was reelected the following year, but when the demands of the office and the casualties of the Vietnam War became more than he could bear, he chose not to run for a second term. Nixon was elected in 1968, and again in 1972, but in the wake of the Watergate scandal, he became the first United States president to resign, in 1974. A year earlier, when Nixon's vice president, Spiro Agnew, resigned in disgrace, Nixon appointed Gerald Ford as vice president. Thus, upon Nixon's resignation, Ford became president, never having been elected to the office.

It was a turbulent time, and there I was, in the middle of it all.

As with our two previous books, my talented writing partner, Lisa McCubbin, and I have attempted to bring history to life through my experiences. While *Mrs. Kennedy and Me* focused on my interactions with Jacqueline Kennedy, and *Five Days in November* detailed those tragic days surrounding the assassination, the Kennedy section in this book focuses on my observations of and interactions with President Kennedy. There is unavoidably some overlap, but the recollections of my years with Eisenhower, Johnson, Nixon, and Ford are revealed here for the first time.

There is no doubt that the assassination of President Kennedy was a defining moment for me, and it would affect me on many levels for the rest of my life. I was thrust onto the pages of history, but it has often bothered me that I would be remembered solely for my actions on that one day. For there was much that led up to that moment, and much that followed.

Like the five presidents I served, there were many things that influenced the decisions I made, the actions I took, the man I became.

It has indeed been an extraordinary journey.

PART ONE

With President Eisenhower

When I was sworn into the U.S. Secret Service as a Special Agent in 1958, President Dwight D. Eisenhower was well into the second year of his second term. As the Supreme Commander of the Allied Forces in World War II, he was credited with liberating Europe, which made him a worldwide hero. General Eisenhower had entered politics as a moderate Republican and had earned the respect of the nation, with 85 percent of the country viewing him favorably. The American people trusted his judgment and leadership during a time when the threat of a nuclear attack by the Soviet Union was a very real fear for all of us.

The Eisenhower era was one of peace and prosperity. Just seven months into his term, Eisenhower had ended the Korean War, and his conservative fiscal policies led to unprecedented expansion. Having seen the numerous benefits of the autobahns in Germany, Eisenhower initiated America's interstate highway system, which created an abundance of jobs as roads and bridges were constructed across the country.

People were proud to be Americans, proud of our country, and proud of our president.

1

The Secret Dead Body

All I could think of as I stared at the dead woman lying on the bed was *How the hell are we going to get her body out of here without anyone knowing?*

There were only a few hours of darkness left, so some quick decisions had to be made. It was my first month as a Special Agent in the United States Secret Service, and I knew if I screwed this up, my career would be over before it really began.

Fortunately, I had the home telephone number of my supervisor, Earl Schoel, the Special Agent in Charge (SAIC) of the Denver Field Office, in my wallet. I walked quietly downstairs and dialed his number from the phone in the kitchen.

"Hello?" Schoel answered groggily.

"Mr. Schoel," I said, "it's Clint Hill. I'm sorry to call you in the middle of the night, but we have a situation here at the Doud residence."

Few people knew it, but President Dwight D. Eisenhower had ordered part-time Secret Service protection for his eighty-year-old mother-in-law, Mrs. Elvira Doud. There were no outright threats to the president's mother-in-law, but because she was ill and lived alone, except for a maid and a nurse, there was concern that she could be kidnapped and held for bargaining purposes. Likewise, if there was a major health problem during the night, the agents would have the means to quickly get her the help she needed and also be able to immediately notify the president and Mrs. Eisenhower.

On September 22, 1958, I was given a badge, handcuffs, holster, gun, and ammunition, and officially sworn in as a Special Agent in the United States Secret Service. I was taken out to the shooting range at the U.S. Mint in Denver to make sure I could qualify, and that was it. There was no other immediate training, except for reading the Special Agent Manual. One of my first assignments was on the midnight shift, protecting Mrs. Doud.

Mrs. Doud lived in a three-story brick home at 750 Lafayette Street in Denver, Colorado, and the protection was from seven o'clock in the evening until seven o'clock in the morning, with one agent on duty from 7:00 p.m. until 11:00 p.m., and another agent taking over from 11:00 p.m. until 7:00 a.m.

First Lady Mamie Eisenhower and her sister Mabel—whom everyone called "Mike"—had been visiting their mother over the past week and were so grateful for the agents to stay the night with her that they prepared sandwiches for us each evening and left them in the fridge. It was a very nice gesture, and they weren't so bad when Mamie made them, but when Mike got involved, let me tell you, those were the worst sandwiches I ever tasted. I never could figure out exactly what she put between the slices of white bread that tasted so bad, but it was almost inedible. The Mike and Mamie sandwiches were a running joke among the agents in the Denver office.

That particular night, I had come to work just before eleven, and the departing agent told me there had been no unusual activity. The house was quiet, with Mrs. Doud and her nurse asleep upstairs on the second floor, and the maid, Mary, in her room on the third floor.

I had been at the house for a couple of hours when I heard Mrs. Doud calling for her nurse. The nurse stayed in the bedroom adjacent to Mrs. Doud, and I assumed she would attend to her needs. A few minutes later, however, Mrs. Doud called out again, this time a bit louder. I waited a few more minutes, listening closely for any conversation upstairs, but there was just silence. When Mrs. Doud called out a third time, I realized that the nurse must be asleep.

I walked up the stairs and into Mrs. Doud's room.

"Mrs. Doud, I'm Agent Hill. Is there a problem?"

She coughed, and then said, "I've been calling for the nurse."

"She's probably asleep, ma'am," I said. "I'll go tell her you need her."

I walked into the nurse's room, and in the darkness I saw the outline of her body on the bed. I called out to her in a firm voice, but she didn't budge.

An uneasy feeling started to come over me as I walked toward the bed. I placed my hand on her shoulder and started to shake her, but her body was stiff as a board.

Oh God, I thought. *The nurse is dead.*

From the other room, Mrs. Doud called out, "Agent? Where's my nurse?"

I did not want to tell her that her nurse was dead. "Just a minute," I said as I ran up the stairs to the maid's room on the third floor.

"Mary, wake up," I whispered as I shook her. "It's Agent Hill, Mary. You need to wake up. The nurse is dead, and Mrs. Doud needs some help. You need to get up and help Mrs. Doud."

Mary sat straight up in bed, her eyes like big white marbles against the dark black of her skin opened so wide that I thought they were going to pop right out of her head.

"Oh my Lordy!" she exclaimed.

"Shh, Mary," I said. "I don't want to alarm Mrs. Doud. Please go down and see what she needs, and don't tell her the nurse is dead."

As soon as Mary went into Mrs. Doud's room, I went back into the nurse's room to try to figure out what to do. The problem was that Mrs. Eisenhower had just left Denver that morning, headed back to Washington by train. She was afraid of flying, so she always took the train. I was concerned that if the press got word that a woman had died at 750 Lafayette Street, they would assume it was Mrs. Doud. I sure as hell didn't want rumors flying and poor Mrs. Eisenhower to think her mother had died before we could clarify what actually happened.

Fortunately, when I called my supervisor, Mr. Schoel, he had a solution. He was a friend of the coroner, and he knew the coroner had a special car— not a traditional hearse, but a sedan in which the backseat had been removed and the two doors on the passenger side opened opposite each other to form an opening wide enough to get a body inside. Schoel said he would call the coroner and send him right over.

Mrs. Doud had fallen back asleep, but poor Mary was still in a state of shock as I explained what we were going to do and why we had to do it.

The coroner arrived and slowly backed the car into the driveway so that the passenger side was opposite the side door of the house leading into the kitchen. We went upstairs, wrapped the nurse in a blanket, and the two of us proceeded to haul her body downstairs. She was a hefty woman and presumably had had a heart attack, but it was clear she had been dead long before I arrived on duty. Her body was deadweight, extremely difficult to maneuver down the narrow staircase, and with every step I was privately cursing the agent who came on duty before me for not realizing there was a dead woman upstairs—or worse, for knowing the woman had died and leaving the situation to me to deal with and then do all the damn paperwork.

The coroner and I managed to get the nurse out of the house and into the car without making too much noise, and no one in the press ever knew.

Of course, when Mrs. Doud awoke that morning, she was informed that her nurse had died overnight, Mr. Schoel notified the president's staff, and I got to keep my job.

As it turned out, surreptitiously removing a dead body from the president's mother-in-law's house in the wee hours of an autumn morning in 1958 was minor-league compared to the situations I would face over the next seventeen years.

I NEVER HAD any intention of becoming a Secret Service agent. Growing up in Washburn, North Dakota, my goal was to coach athletics and teach history. I have come to realize, however, that sometimes your life takes a turn in a direction over which you have no control—and in my case, it started from the moment I was born.

When I was seventeen days old, my mother had me baptized and then, on a snowy January morning, left me on the doorstep of the North Dakota Children's Home for Adoption in Fargo. Three months later, Chris and Jennie Hill drove to Fargo with their four-year-old adopted daughter, Janice, and out of all the children at the orphanage, chose me to make their family complete.

I had a wonderful childhood. Washburn, North Dakota, is perched on the north bank of the Missouri River, about halfway between Bismarck and

Minot, and back then the population hovered around ni⌐

settled by German, Swedish, and Norwegian immigrant far⌐

had numerous churches and a couple of gas stations, but not even ⌐

light. It was the kind of close-knit community where you didn't dare ⌐

into trouble because word would get back to your parents before you could

race home and sneak in the back door. There wasn't much for a boy to do

but play sports, and that was fine with me. In high school I participated

in every competitive sport that was offered—track, football, baseball, and

basketball—and throughout the long winters, my friends and I would play

ice hockey until it was too dark to see the puck.

Our family life revolved around the Evangelical Lutheran Church where

my sister Janice played the piano and I was an altar boy. My father was the

county auditor and also served as treasurer of the church, so on Sundays he

would bring home the collection money and we would sit at the kitchen

table, counting and registering what had been offered that week while my

mother prepared dinner.

My mother was the glue that held the family together, and I rarely saw

her sitting down—she was doing laundry, tending to the vegetable garden,

canning, or cooking—and while Dad was a man of few words, he taught me

lessons I've carried with me my entire life. Always be respectful of others, no

matter who they are; live within your means and save for the future; strive to

do the best job at whatever you do; and never, ever be late.

People who have worked with me know I'm a stickler for promptness—

something that goes back to an incident that took place when I was in high

school.

My curfew was 10:00 p.m., and one night I walked in the front door at

10:08. My father was waiting for me, as he always did, and before I could

offer any explanation, he grabbed my shirt collar with both hands, lifted me

off the floor, and slammed me against the wall.

"Clinton!" he yelled. "You are late!" His eyes pierced through me with

anger and disappointment as his fists tightened around my neck. "Don't you

ever walk into this house late again!"

I honestly don't remember why I was late, but I knew that no excuse

would have made a difference. From that moment on, whether it was show-

ing up for work, meeting a friend for lunch, or coming home by curfew, rarely was I ever late again. To this day, one of the few things that causes me anxiety is to be running late.

I grew up listening to college football games on our Philco radio, and I had visions of playing football for the University of Michigan, but when the local chapter of the Lutheran Brotherhood awarded me a one-hundred-dollar scholarship to attend Concordia College in Moorhead, Minnesota, which was Lutheran-affiliated, the decision was made for me.

I took my studies seriously, but my real passion continued to be sports. I played football and baseball, and had the benefit of a wonderful football coach and mentor named Jake Christiansen. Coach Jake was already a legend at Concordia by the time I got there, and other than my parents, he had more influence on my character, ethics, and values than anyone.

I didn't have much confidence or experience with dating, but in the spring of my freshman year, I met a young lady named Gwen Brown. Gwen was a year older than me, but she was a friend of some girls who were dating some of my football buddies, and we all hung out together. Gwen grew up on a farm where the nearest town was an even smaller town than Washburn, so we had that in common, and we shared a love of music. She was a member of Concordia's elite concert choir, and I sang in an a cappella male quartet. One by one, the couples in our group got engaged, and on February 28, 1953, during my junior year and her senior year, Gwen and I got married at the Trinity Lutheran Church near the Concordia campus. We were so young—too young—but things were different in those days, and like smoking cigarettes because everybody else was doing it, we just didn't know any better.

When I graduated from Concordia in the spring of 1954, my intention was to return to North Dakota to find a job in a local high school teaching history and coaching athletics. The U.S. Army, however, had different plans for me.

No sooner did I have my degree in hand than I was notified by the draft board in McLean County, North Dakota, to report to an office in Fargo for processing and I was sworn into the U.S. Army. From there it was straight to Fort Leonard Wood, Missouri, for eight weeks of demanding physical training, along with a few written intelligence tests. Apparently, my scores on those tests gave them an indication that I had something the Army was looking for, and upon completion of basic training I was instructed to report to Fort Holabird, in Dundalk, Maryland, to attend Army Intelligence School, where I would learn how to be an agent in counterintelligence.

I had two weeks off before I needed to be at Fort Holabird, and during this time my father suffered a stroke. Fortunately, I was able to spend a few days with him, talking and reminiscing, but he died two days after I left. It was a devastating blow, and I had to come to grips with the stark realization that, at twenty-two, from that point on, there was no one to guide me—I was on my own.

I threw myself into the courses at Fort Holabird. The program was rigorous and intense, as we were taught investigative, surveillance, and interrogation techniques, and then tested by using those techniques in practical exercises. We would be assigned to interrogate someone who was suspected of committing a crime or sent on a mission to surveil a suspect around Baltimore and the surrounding area. They were real-life situations, with our professional instructors role-playing the parts of the suspects, using every con artist and thug trick in the book to try to mislead us, and I found it both fascinating and challenging.

In January 1955, after four months at Fort Holabird, I was assigned to Region IX 113th Counterintelligence Corps (CIC) Field Office in Denver, Colorado, where my work consisted mostly of running background investigations on individuals who were being considered for various security clearances in the U.S. government—up to and including "Top Secret."

Nine months after I arrived in Denver, President Eisenhower happened to be in Colorado for a golf and fishing vacation when he suffered a heart attack. He was rushed to Fitzsimons Army Hospital in Aurora, and although the White House press office termed it a "mild" heart attack, the president remained there for seven weeks. I had some investigations that required me to check records at Fitzsimons, and I ended up meeting several members of Eisenhower's Secret Service detail. Dressed in suits with white shirts and ties, the agents were resolute in their protective measures, and certainly could be intimidating if necessary, but they were at the same time courteous and respectful to the nurses, doctors, family members, and friends who had authorization to come in close contact with the president. I was impressed with their professionalism and the way they conducted themselves, and suddenly had a newfound respect for all that was required to protect the President of the United States. Still, it never entered my mind that I would ever be among their ranks.

My TOUR OF duty was scheduled to be completed in July 1956, just about the same time Gwen and I were expecting our first child. Rather than suddenly have to find a new job and possibly move just as the baby arrived, I decided it made a lot more sense to stay in the Army for at least one more year so the baby could be born in the military hospital.

On July 21, Gwen went into labor, and in the early morning hours of July 22, she delivered a baby boy. Unfortunately, there was a problem during delivery, and he had to have a blood transfusion. When I first held him in my arms, there was a white bandage on the top of his little head where they had done the transfusion, but other than that, he was absolutely perfect. We named him Chris Jeffrey Hill—Chris after my father, and Jeffrey so he could have the same CJH initials as both my father and I had. A year later, I was honorably discharged from the U.S. Army in Fort Carson, Colorado, and my intent was to return to North Dakota to find a job coaching athletics and teaching history.

For the next several weeks, I interviewed at dozens of schools all over North Dakota and Minnesota, but with no previous teaching experience, the only jobs available were in small towns, with small salaries and few benefits. The responsibility of providing for my family weighed heavily on me, and I eventually came to the conclusion that perhaps I should consider alternative careers. I reflected on my father and how he had been able to buy a home for our family, as well as put aside enough money to send both Janice and me to college, and I was determined to do the same. Even though my dad was no longer alive, I believed he was still watching me, and I wanted to make him proud. I realized I had enjoyed the investigative work in the CIC and had made a lot of connections in the Denver area, and that was probably the best place to start.

It didn't take long for me to land a job as a credit investigator with a credit company, and shortly thereafter I found a better position with the Chicago, Burlington and Quincy Railroad as a railroad detective, investigating theft and ensuring security of their facilities. One day I was driving past Fitzsimons Army Hospital, and I remembered the Secret Service agents I had met in 1955. I had no idea what it took to become an agent, but I figured I might as well give it a shot, so I drove straight to the Secret Service in Denver to find out what the possibilities might be.

I learned that there were 269 agents in the entire Secret Service organization, and rarely were there openings. Even if you could pass all the background checks and score highly on the intelligence tests, the only way you were going to get in was if an agent died or retired. It was a long shot, but I decided to fill out an application and hope for the best. I went back to work at the railroad and didn't think much more about it.

A few months later I got the phone call that would change the course of my life. It turned out that because of retirements, three openings in the Secret Service had occurred simultaneously. One of them was in Denver, and I was being considered for that position. Since I had just come out of the CIC the year before, my background check was a breeze, and on September 22, 1958, I was hired and sworn in as a Special Agent in the United States Secret Service in the Denver Field Office.

THE U.S. SECRET Service is one of the oldest law enforcement agencies in America, created in 1865. Its original mission was to investigate and prevent counterfeit currency, which was rampant after the Civil War and threatened to destabilize the country's economy. The legislation to establish the "Secret Service Division" of the United States Treasury was on Abraham Lincoln's desk the night he was assassinated, but it wasn't until after the assassination of President William McKinley in 1901 that Congress assigned the duties of presidential protection to the Secret Service. To this day, the agency has two distinct missions—investigating and preventing financial crimes, and the protection of our nation's leaders.

In the Denver office, while we had the responsibility of protecting President Eisenhower's mother-in-law, Mrs. Doud, the majority of our time was spent investigating financial crimes—counterfeiting and forged checks. However, when President Eisenhower would come to town, we dropped everything in order to assist the White House Detail—the small group of agents who protected the president and his family. I had no specialized training other than watching the detail agents and following their directions. I took mental notes of everything they did, the way they used hand and eye signals to communicate with one another, blending in with the other people around the president while simultaneously moving purposefully to create an invisible barrier of protection.

These were the guys I had met back in 1955—the best of the best—and I wanted to be one of them.

2

The White House Detail

The Secret Service today has stiff entrance requirements and consistent and rigorous training, and in order to even be considered for the White House Detail—presently called the Presidential Protective Division (PPD)—you will have to have been an agent for five to nine years, depending on the needs of the organization. When I joined the Secret Service, every new agent was sent to Washington during the first year on the job for thirty days' temporary duty on the White House Detail to determine if you were the type of agent the Secret Service wanted assigned to the White House on a permanent basis. I had been on the job in Denver for about six months when my evaluation period came around.

It was the summer of 1959, and hotter than hell. Compared to the dry, crisp air of Colorado, the Washington humidity was smothering, and from the moment I stepped off the airplane at National Airport, I was in a constant state of sticky perspiration.

The Treasury Department had negotiated cheap rates for agents to stay at a boardinghouse about two blocks from the White House, run by a woman everyone called "Ma Bouma." While Ma kept the rooms clean, it was no-frills and there was no air-conditioning—but all I could think about was that I was being given the chance of a lifetime.

I had been instructed to report to the Northwest Gate of the White House and present my credentials.

"Good morning," I said as I handed the uniformed guard my blue leather commission book, trying to sound as if walking up to the White House and expecting to be let in was perfectly natural. A wave of apprehension washed over me as he scrutinized the photo, looked at me, looked back at the photo, and then began flipping through some papers.

Finally, he handed my commission book back to me and said, "Good morning, Agent Hill. You can go in through the West Wing door. Mr. Rowley is expecting you."

As I entered the White House for the first time, my anxieties dissipated, and all I could feel was an overwhelming sense of pride. Portraits of past presidents lined the walls, gazing down on the people who were bustling around with urgency and purpose, seemingly oblivious to the history surrounding them. As I was escorted to Mr. Rowley's office, I tried to take it all in, making mental observations of every detail so the next time I saw my mother I could tell her what it was like to be inside the White House.

Fifty-year-old James J. Rowley was the Special Agent in Charge of the White House Detail and, having been in the position since Franklin D. Roosevelt was president, was highly respected by all the agents. Rowley's office, which he shared with his administrative assistant, Walter Blaschak, was just inside the West Wing lobby. Crammed into the small, windowless office were two desks facing each other in the middle of the room, while a couple of metal filing cabinets and a well-worn couch were squeezed against one wall. Standing ominously on the opposite wall was a large gun case stacked with .45-caliber Thompson submachine guns, 12-gauge shotguns, and .30-caliber carbines.

Mr. Rowley stood up from his desk as I entered the office and greeted me warmly with a smile and a firm handshake.

"Welcome to the White House, Clint," he said. "I understand you've been doing good work out there in Denver."

"Thank you, sir," I said. "It's an honor to meet you."

Mr. Rowley had an affable personality with an easy smile belied by steely eyes that could size you up in an instant, without revealing what he was thinking. The son of Irish Catholic immigrants, he had a toughness that came from being raised in the Bronx during the Depression and having to support his family after his father was killed in a job-related accident with the city of New York highway department. There was a no-nonsense air about him, and I liked him immediately.

Mr. Rowley explained that I would be assigned to a shift, and over the course of the next thirty days I would always be with an agent on that shift to witness firsthand how the detail operated. He handed me a black notebook that had metal pins holding it together so pages could easily be added or removed and said, "Here's the White House Detail manual. This should answer a lot of your questions, but certainly don't hesitate to ask anyone if there's anything you don't understand. We have no room for error or miscommunication."

Printed in silver on the cover of the manual was a Secret Service star, and beneath it: WHITE HOUSE DETAIL. In the lower right hand corner was the number 9. Mr. Rowley explained that there were a set number of copies of the manual and each one was assigned to a specific agent. Inside was detailed information about the automobiles and aircraft we used; people to be notified when the president left the White House; the protocol for arrivals and departures both domestically and internationally; the formation of motorcades for various situations; and a litany of other details that only the agents protecting the president were to know. Under no circumstances was the manual to be shared with anyone outside the detail.

By the time I left his office, the enormity of the responsibility I was about to undertake had begun to set in, and I hoped I could prove to be worthy of the trust being placed in me.

EVERY ONE OF the next thirty days was exhilarating and exhausting. There was so much information to take in, and all my training was on the job.

In that month on temporary duty, I worked midnight shifts in the pitch-black darkness at Eisenhower's Gettysburg farm and at Camp David, the nearby presidential retreat in Maryland's Catoctin Mountains; traveled to New York City as part of the White House Detail protecting President Eisenhower as he toured the Soviet Exhibition of Science, Technology, and Culture; traveled to Canada and helped secure the area for President Eisenhower and Queen Elizabeth to participate in the opening of the St. Lawrence Seaway; stood post at designated points within the White House; helped man the Secret Service follow-up car in fast-paced, police-escorted motorcades through downtown Washington; and posed as a golfer along the fairway at Burning Tree Country Club, carrying a golf bag filled with a couple of beat-up old clubs and a carbine rifle. It was an interesting and edu-cational experience, and I enjoyed every aspect of it.

I would learn later that it was not only the top-level supervisors who would determine whether I qualified to be on the White House Detail, but that the agents on my shift, my peers, would weigh in as well. At the end of the thirty days, the shift would take a vote, and I would be either in or out. It wasn't up to the president or his staff or even the chief of the Secret Service. The guys who mattered were your immediate supervisors and the agents you worked with day in and day out, and they had to be certain you were a team player—reliable, trustworthy, and willing to work in the worst of cir-cumstances without complaint. When the thirty days were up, I returned to Denver knowing I'd done my best, but not knowing if it was good enough.

Fortunately, I didn't have to wait long. Just a few weeks later, I got notifi-cation that I was being transferred from Denver to the White House Detail, effective November 1, 1959. I was bursting with pride to know that I had been accepted, but it was daunting to think of the responsibility I was about to face—the responsibility to protect the President of the United States, at all costs. To put his life before mine or anyone else's, for the good of the country.

The first order of business, however, was to find a place for Gwen, Chris, and me to live in the Washington area. My friend and fellow agent Paul Rundle had been transferred from the Denver office to the White House Detail a few months earlier, so I called him for advice.

"Don't worry, Clint," Paul said. "I'll take care of it."

Before we even left Denver, Paul and his wife, Peggy, found us a semidetached two-bedroom home for rent at 3704 South 3rd Street in Ar-lington, Virginia, which was within our budget and was an easy seven-mile commute to the White House. When we arrived with all our belongings, the Rundles had already stocked the house with food and the necessary staples, and they helped us unpack and get settled. I was grateful to Paul for making that part of the transition so easy, and when I thanked him, he said, "You're on the detail now, Clint. We take care of each other. It's what we do."

PRESIDENT DWIGHT D. Eisenhower was sixty-nine years old when I started on his protective detail. Even though he had suffered from some major health issues in the nearly seven years since he had first taken the oath of office, outwardly he appeared fit and competent, with no indication of slowing down.

I was immediately placed on one of the three shifts of agents who provide security for the president twenty-four hours a day, seven days a week, 365 days a year. He is never left alone. The day shift covered 8:00 a.m. to 4:00 p.m., the evening shift 4:00 p.m. to midnight, and the midnight shift ran from midnight to 8:00 a.m. Each shift had only nine men, and with some agents on regular days off or handling advances for an upcoming presidential trip or off-site, that meant there might be only five or six agents around the president at any given time. Depending on the president's schedule, your shift might start early or get extended because there was always a team that went ahead of the president to provide protection for arrivals, departures, and on-site posts. Rarely did you have an eight-hour day, and then every two weeks the teams rotated shifts, which meant that just as your body was getting used to a sleep pattern, you'd start a new one.

I was the new man on the job, so I worked with another agent for the first week to make sure I was completely aware of my assignments. The first step was to learn the layout of the White House and the Executive Office Building, both of which seemed like mazes to me at first, but would eventually become as familiar as my own home. Next was to be able to identify every person who had authorized access to the White House complex. There is an army of people who keep the White House running, and it was critical to be able to recognize the cooks and dishwashers as well as the housekeepers, florists, and maintenance staff. On top of all those faces, I had to learn all the cabinet and congressional members, and be able to address them by name. It was also helpful to know their state and party affiliation. Finally, there was the White House press corps. Members of the press had access to the West Wing press room and the West Wing lobby but had to be escorted anywhere else. It was a lot to take in all at once, but I felt deeply privileged to have this responsibility.

My first week on the job on the White House Detail was a real eye-opener into President Eisenhower's leadership style and how he dealt with the vast demands of the office. A typical day for President Eisenhower began with his prompt arrival in the Oval Office at 8:00 a.m. Usually his first meeting was with his staff secretary, Brigadier General Andrew J. Goodpaster, and the president's thirty-seven-year-old son, Major John Eisenhower, who worked directly for Goodpaster.

After the initial morning briefing, President Eisenhower would have one nonstop appointment after another until lunchtime. Having been a career military officer, President Eisenhower was cognizant of the clock and was adamant about staying on schedule. He was not inclined to chitchat or small talk, instead preferring to get right down to business with whomever he was meeting, and at times it seemed like the Oval Office had a revolving door, he was able to fit so many meetings into a short amount of time. The same thing was true for meetings or events outside the White House; whether it was a speech to congressional members or a ribbon-cutting ceremony, he got the job done in the time allotted, and then it was on to the next thing. What was interesting to me was to see how much the president was able to accomplish each day, yet still manage to play golf on an almost daily basis.

After the morning's meetings had concluded, usually by 12:30, he would leave the West Wing and return to the mansion for lunch, which was served promptly at 1:00 p.m. On Monday, my first day at the White House, shortly before 2:00 p.m., we drove him to the exclusive, all-male Burning Tree Country Club in Bethesda, Maryland. He played eighteen holes of golf with friends and returned to the White House around six o'clock. Wednesday, same schedule, different golf partners. Friday, same thing, until about three o'clock when a sudden rainstorm forced the halt of the game after five holes, and when it was determined that the rain was going to continue for quite some time, the president returned to the White House. No further appointments had been scheduled, so he spent the rest of the rainy afternoon in the movie theater watching a Western.

Tuesday and Thursday had similar nonstop activity until lunchtime, along with some scattered appointments in the afternoon. Still, he managed to fit in some golf practice on the South Grounds of the White House. After changing into his golf cleats in the Oval Office, he walked out the east door—leaving spike holes in the wooden floor that would remain there for years—to the three-thousand-square-foot putting green he had arranged to have installed about fifty yards outside the Oval Office. For about an hour, he alternated between putting and driving, using the White House lawn as his own private golf course.

It was a great treat for tourists walking along the south fence to see the President of the United States whacking golf balls across the lawn, while his personal valet, Sergeant John Moaney, ran back and forth retrieving them. The first time I saw Moaney fetching the golf balls, I felt sorry for him, because it seemed like a humiliating chore. However, I soon realized that no one was more devoted to President Eisenhower than his valet, who had been with him since the war, when Moaney was assigned to the general's personal staff. They had a great relationship, and it seemed like Moaney enjoyed participating in the most relaxing part of his boss's day.

The president's job does not stop on the weekends—it is round-the-clock, seven days a week. The same goes for the Secret Service. By the end of my first week, I was beginning to feel more comfortable with the protective procedures, and with President Eisenhower himself. He could be very intense, but was also quick to laugh. When it came to the agents who were around him constantly, he pretty much treated us like his troops. There were only two agents he called by name—his driver, Dick Flohr, and the Special Agent in Charge, Jim Rowley. He had no interest in learning (or need to learn) any of the rest of our names. If he needed something, he'd look at you and call out, "Hey, agent!" It was our job to protect the man, not become his personal friends.

During my second week on the White House Detail, I went on my first trip with President Eisenhower. On Thursday, November 12, we left the White House at 10:30 a.m. and flew to Augusta, Georgia, aboard the presidential aircraft, a Lockheed VC-121E Super Constellation named *Columbine III*. Three hours later, the president was teeing off the first hole at the Augusta National Golf Club.

Founded in 1933, Augusta National Golf Club is a private and very exclusive club that you have to be invited to join, and up until 2012, only men were allowed. The meticulously manicured eighteen-hole course is considered one of the most beautiful in the world, with over one hundred acres of flawless grass fairways dotted with white sand bunkers and lined by 150-year-old pine trees and countless flowering shrubs and trees. Each spring when the flowers are at their peak the best golfers in the world are invited to Augusta National to compete for the green jacket given to the winner of the Masters, one of golf's most prestigious tournaments.

There were no permanent residences along the golf course, but ten cabins had been built for the use of members, including one specifically built in 1953 for President Eisenhower. The Eisenhower Cabin was not at all rustic, as the name implies, but was an elegant four-bedroom, two-story home with a spacious front porch near the No. 10 tee, and because the Secret Service had been involved in the design of the cabin, it included special communications equipment and facilities in the basement for use by the on-duty agents when Ike was in residence.

President Eisenhower loved to play Augusta because it offered so many challenges. One in particular was a large loblolly pine standing along the 17th fairway that had become Ike's nemesis on the course. The president hit that same tree so regularly that each time he approached the 17th hole, he'd become agitated. He'd watch the flight of the ball, wincing and willing it to avoid the tree, but so often you'd hear a crack as it smacked the bark, and then immediately a burst of profanity from the president as he stormed toward his archenemy. The tree had become so problematic to him that he even lobbied the club to have it cut down. The proposal was denied, however, and instead the tree became known as the "Eisenhower Tree," much to the president's dismay.

One of the most fun things about protecting President Eisenhower on his golf outings was being around the high-profile people with whom he played—people like Cliff Roberts, a co-founder of Augusta National; Bill Robinson, chairman of the board of Coca-Cola; and the most interesting to me, Arnold Palmer.

When Palmer drove from the tee, the ball would rise and remain about three feet off the ground for about two hundred yards and then zoom upward, coming to rest near or on the green. He was amazing.

After nine holes, the group would take a break for beverages, and if Cliff Roberts was in the group, he would say, "Drinks all around . . . except for the Secret Service!" The joke got tiresome for us, but we'd smile and find our way to the water cooler at the end of the round.

I had very little experience playing golf myself—just a few times hitting balls with some borrowed clubs on the rough, prairie-grass-covered public course near Underwood, North Dakota—but over the next year on President Eisenhower's detail I would spend so much time on the Augusta National and Burning Tree courses that I could anticipate which club the president would use on every hole, and where he was most likely to slice a shot into the woods. That first trip I took to Augusta in November 1959, President Eisenhower played eighteen holes of golf every day for twelve days straight. It turned out to be a pretty good indication of how much time I'd be spending on golf courses for the duration of Ike's term.

3

The Eleven-Nation Tour

In late 1959, the most pressing issues on the international front were the recent takeover of Cuba by the Communist Fidel Castro and the conflict between the Western allies and Soviet premier Nikita Khrushchev about the future of Berlin. That first week I was at the White House, I was informed that President Eisenhower and his staff were planning a trip in December, built around a meeting in Paris between the Big Four Western allies—the United Kingdom, France, Germany, and the United States. It was an ambitious and historic journey that would encompass three continents, eleven countries, and over 22,000 miles in nineteen days. Three Boeing 707 jets had recently been acquired for the presidential fleet—the first jets available to any president—and clearly Eisenhower was determined to make good use of them.

On the evening of December 3, 1959, President Eisenhower appeared live on national television from the White House, less than an hour prior to our departure. Bidding farewell to the American people, he outlined the nature of the trip while stressing the unbreakable connection between economic stability at home and the maintenance of peace through strength around the globe. With his wire-rimmed glasses dangling casually from his right hand, the president looked straight into the camera, knowing that every American who had their television on was watching him.

"Good evening, fellow Americans," he began.

Dressed in a three-piece suit with a crisp white shirt and tie, he looked every bit the country's chief executive officer, confident and in control. He placed the glasses on his face and continued, with the soothing voice of a wise and comforting grandfather.

"I leave in just a few minutes on a three-week journey halfway around the world." Glancing intermittently at the notes on the podium in front of him, he explained to the American people the purpose for his journey to Italy, Turkey, Pakistan, Afghanistan, India, Iran, Greece, Tunisia, France, Spain, and Morocco.

"During this mission of peace and goodwill, I hope to promote a better understanding of America and to learn more of our friends abroad. In every country, I hope to make widely known America's deepest desire—a world in which all nations may prosper in freedom, justice, and peace, unmolested and unafraid. We have heard much of the phrase 'Peace and Friendship.' This phrase, in expressing the aspirations of America, is not complete. We should say instead, 'Peace and friendship in freedom.' This, I think, is America's real message to the world."

It was his mission to use his last year in office to improve America's image by convincing people around the globe that the United States was sincerely searching for a world peace formula, with no ulterior motives or aggressive designs.

For me, accompanying President Eisenhower on this international trip was beyond my wildest dreams. Other than a brief one-day visit to Canada during my temporary White House Detail assignment, I had never been anywhere outside the United States and here I was, about to embark on a historic trip visiting countries and cities I had only read about in books. In preparation, I'd been given a myriad of shots and inoculations to meet the health regulations of every country we would visit, courtesy of the White House physician's office, and was issued a diplomatic passport. Notable by its green cover embossed with gold, indicating I was an official representative of the United States government, the passport included my photograph and identification, followed by dozens of blank pages that would soon be filled with entry and exit stamps from countries all over the world.

We had four airplanes in the entourage—the presidential plane with tail number 86970, which became "Air Force One" when the president was aboard; the backup plane with tail number 86971; and two press planes— one provided by Pan American World Airways and one by Trans World

Airlines. At 8:15 p.m., the caravan of aircraft departed Andrews Air Force Base, and after a brief refueling stop in Goose Bay, Labrador, at 1:00 a.m., we flew directly to Rome, Italy.

ROME

It was raining heavily as we were attempting to land at Ciampino Airport around noon, local time. The city was filled with banners and signs greeting the American president, and despite the rain there were large, welcoming crowds at the airport and all along the motorcade route.

It worked out that my shift was on midnight rotation for the first portion of the trip, so we were immediately taken to the hotel to rest, while the day shift accompanied President Eisenhower in the motorcade through the city to an official lunch with President Giovanni Gronchi. Most of us had slept on the flight, and since our shift duty didn't begin until midnight, we realized we had the opportunity to sightsee for a few hours. So we dropped off our bags at the hotel and headed to the U.S. Embassy, where we exchanged our dollars for Italian lira.

The embassy staff wanted to do everything they could to help us, and when they offered to provide cars with drivers to show us around Rome, we readily accepted. We drove all around the city, stopping at the major tourist sights—the Trevi fountain, the Spanish Steps, the Forum—and ended up at the Colosseum, where we had a private guided tour. I had never seen structures so old or walked on streets made of cobblestone. I was struck by the blending of the modern and the ancient, to see motorbikes whizzing around contemporary office buildings standing next to two-thousand-year-old marble structures and ruins. It was a whirlwind tour, with just enough time to get a taste of Rome and to buy a few postcards before returning to the hotel to get some sleep before our shift.

President Eisenhower was staying at the four-hundred-year-old Palazzo del Quirinale, the official residence of the president of Italy, for his two nights in Rome, accompanied by his son, Major John Eisenhower, and John's wife, Barbara. Mrs. Eisenhower had elected not to come on the trip, largely, I suspected, because of her aversion to flying. A black-tie dinner and reception for nearly three thousand was held in honor of President Eisenhower at the palace that first night, and after a long day, he retired for the evening to his palatial apartment suite at around 10:30.

I quickly realized that being on the midnight shift in Rome was like drawing the lucky straw. Our duty entailed standing post while the president slept in an exceptionally secure environment, while the agents on the other two shifts were having to work twelve to fourteen hours a day covering the president's activities in this unfamiliar locale. Protecting the president in a foreign country was very different from protecting him on our own soil. Not only did very few people speak English, but also we were guests of the people of Italy and had to make sure there was a cooperative effort on the part of the Italian authorities that blended with our protective operation.

The rain continued through the night, and it was still coming down when we were relieved by the day shift. While the other shift agents covered President Eisenhower as he visited the Tomb of the Unknown Soldier and attended meetings with various Italian leaders, we on the midnight shift, once again, were able to play tourist. The president was scheduled to have an audience with His Holiness Pope John XXIII at the Vatican the following day, and as we were trying to decide where to go sightseeing, the agent who had conducted the advance with the Vatican piped up and asked if any of us would be interested in a tour there.

A few phone calls were made, and the next thing I knew we were being introduced to members of the Swiss Guard, our counterparts to the pope. Public access was limited as a result of the tight security around President Eisenhower's visit, so we were able to experience St. Peter's Basilica, the great halls of the Vatican Museum, and the glory of the Sistine Chapel almost completely by ourselves. The pièce de résistance was a tour of the back rooms of the Vatican Treasury, an area not available to the general public, which housed the priceless jewels, ornaments, and gold accumulated by the Catholic Church over the centuries.

Meanwhile, despite the inclement weather, President Eisenhower was drawing huge crowds, with Rome's streets lined with people huddled under drenched umbrellas, waving and cheering wherever he went. At one point as the presidential motorcade drove by, two hundred young student priests from a Catholic seminary broke into a chant of "We like Ike!" His visit was impacting the people of Italy exactly as he had hoped. One Italian journalist stated just how much this country thought of the American president in a local newspaper report: "He represents a moral conscience, a spiritual force. The world must be inspired by his goodwill mission."

By Sunday morning the rain had passed, and the sun shone brightly against a blue sky for President Eisenhower's last day in Rome. The clear weather brought out thousands more spectators than had been seen the previous two days, and gave President Eisenhower the opportunity to ride in an open car as he drove from the Quirinale to the Vatican. An Italian motorcycle escort paved the way for the president's convertible, and as the motorcade entered St. Peter's Square, the enormous crowd erupted into cheers, prompting the president to stand up and wave his hat in appreciation. Immediately following the services, President Eisenhower was escorted to the papal apartment on the second floor of the Vatican, where he had an audience with Pope John XXIII. The twenty-six-minute meeting was hailed as a coming together of two scions of peace, and capped off what was by all accounts a very successful visit.

ANKARA

From Rome we flew directly to Ankara, the capital of Turkey. Although Eisenhower had traveled to Ankara during the war in his capacity as Supreme Allied Commander, this was his first visit to the country as president. But more important, it was the first time any American president had ever visited the Republic of Turkey.

When we landed at Esenboga Airport, dozens of American flags flapped in the wind alongside Turkish flags, along with a large banner that said WELCOME IKE. Turkish president Celal Bayar was there to meet President Eisenhower with a full military reception, and then the two leaders climbed into a 1934 Lincoln convertible, furnished by the Turkish government, and drove the twenty miles into downtown Ankara. As the motorcade entered the Turkish capital, I could hardly believe the sight.

As far as your eyes could see, there were people. Masses of people. They lined Ataturk Boulevard, often twenty people deep on both sides, while still more waved from open windows, and up above, balconies and rooftops were packed with bodies, the majority of them waving small American flags. As the motorcycle escort came into view of the crowds, the people erupted with a roar of cheers and clapping. Overcome with gratitude, President Eisenhower stood up, took off his hat, and waved to the throngs of admirers as the motorcade proceeded through the city.

Fences had been set up on the side of the street with a strong showing of Turkish police stationed intermittently to keep the large crowds contained, but a few times groups of people would try to break through and run alongside the cars. There were banners draped across the street showing President Eisenhower and President Bayar side by side, and on one building a six-story canvas painting of Eisenhower hung down. It felt like we were in the middle of a circus parade as the crowds shouted *"Yasha! Yasha!"*—"Long Live!"— while bands played and groups of performers in traditional costumes danced and sang all the way to our destination of the Turkish government guesthouse where the presidential party would stay overnight. Estimates were that nearly 700,000 people came out to welcome President Eisenhower to Ankara. It was remarkable.

KARACHI

From Ankara we flew to the port city of Karachi, Pakistan. President Eisenhower had never visited Pakistan and was looking forward to the visit with great anticipation. As we approached our destination, there was a sudden thundering roar outside the aircraft at about 25,000 feet. A dozen U.S.-built jet fighters of the Pakistani air force were flying in formation to escort us as we landed at Mauripur Air Force Base. It was a high honor to President Eisenhower, and part of the preauthorized plan, but also a clear example of how much trust and confidence the Secret Service must place in the relationship with the host country and their security forces.

President Eisenhower was beaming as he stepped off the plane and strode down the steps to greet President Muhammad Ayub Khan, who was waiting at the bottom of the ramp. The two shook hands and began an animated conversation that indicated their genuine fondness and respect for each other, despite this being their first meeting.

Formed as an Islamic Republic just a few years earlier, Pakistan was a young country, and President Ayub Khan had only recently become its leader in a military coup. Ayub Khan had pledged a strong alliance with the United States from the outset, and Eisenhower's visit was a boost in prestige for the fifty-two-year-old Pakistani president.

After the formal arrival ceremonies at the air base, Eisenhower and Ayub Khan got into the backseat of a white open-top convertible for the motorcade into downtown Karachi. After seeing the reception for President Eisenhower in Ankara, I expected there might be a similar reception in Karachi, and there was—except that here the crowds were *twice the size*, and almost completely made up of men and boys. Everywhere you looked there were hundreds of thousands of Pakistani males dressed in long tunics and loose trousers shouting and waving as the cars rolled by.

"Eisenhower Zindabad!" they chanted. "Long Life to Eisenhower!"

In response to the tremendous outpouring of affection, President Eisenhower rose up out of his seat and stood so the people could see him better, his arms outstretched, waving with his hat in his hand. More than a million people were packed along the roadways, perched on balconies and rooftops, hanging out every window of every building, cheering and clapping for this American president.

Throughout the downtown area, the Stars and Stripes and Pakistan's green and white crescent flag waved from poles and arches, intermingled in a show of solidarity between the two nations. As the motorcade came to a halt in a broad corner square near the U.S. Embassy, thousands of Pakistanis pushed and shoved their way into the square to get a better view. With just a handful of agents covering President Eisenhower, it could have been a disastrous situation, but fortunately the Pakistani police force kept control over the people, keeping them a safe distance from the two presidents.

In front of the embassy, Eisenhower and Ayub Khan switched from the convertible to a royal-looking red and gold coach drawn by six black horses, ridden by members of the military bedecked in knee-length red jackets adorned with brass buttons. As the procession moved slowly toward the presidential residence, President Eisenhower stood erect in the carriage, grinning broadly as he waved to the exuberant crowds amid a constant roar of cheers and clapping. Secret Service agents and Pakistani security agents walked between the carriage and the mass of spectators, while Special Agent in Charge Jim Rowley rode in the carriage with the president and Ayub Khan. Even though the crowds were well behaved, the exposure of the president at such a slow speed was very precarious.

Karachi is a large port city and, at that time, it was the capital of Pakistan, and overflowing with people living in extreme poverty. Because of the poor conditions in the city and the lack of appropriate hotel accommodations, a United States ship had been brought into port to be used as the housing facility for the agents and the staff. About an hour before my shift started, we went ashore and were driven to President Ayub Khan's residence, where the president was staying. As we drove through the dark city, the car's headlights illuminated an astonishing sight. Hundreds of people were lying, unmoving, along the side of the road. The next morning when we returned to the ship, government trucks were driving slowly through the streets with workers walking alongside them, kicking the people on the side of the road to determine if they were alive or dead. We watched with horror as the workers picked up the dead bodies and threw them, like sacks of potatoes, into the backs of the trucks. Some of the trucks were piled high with dead bodies, and we realized this was most likely a daily occurrence. It was almost hard to comprehend; a real eye-opener about how fortunate we were in the United States.

By the time President Eisenhower's activities began in the morning, the bodies had all been removed, as if they were never there. Ayub Khan took great care to present his country in a good light, and had arranged nonstop events from morning until late evening for the two-night stay of his esteemed guest. There was a cricket match between Australia and Pakistan at the National Stadium, a horse show at the Polo Field, and black-tie dinners capped off with entertainment by turbaned sword dancers. At each event and all around Karachi, people waved American flags and held banners proclaiming: THANK YOU AMERICA! and WE LIKE IKE!

KABUL

After two nights in Pakistan, we were off to the neighboring country of Afghanistan. The flight to Kabul was just over an hour, and as we descended toward Bagram Airport at around 8:30 in the morning, I was struck by the harshness of the terrain. The city of Kabul was situated at nearly six thousand feet, and appeared to be a sprawling array of primitive structures that might have dated back to the time of Genghis Khan wedged into a narrow valley between the craggy, snow-covered Hindu Kush mountains.

At the time, Afghanistan was a monarchy ruled by forty-five-year-old King Mohammed Zahir Shah, and although it was a neutral country, there was mounting Soviet influence, which was exemplified by the Russian-built airstrip and paved road leading to the capital city. Eisenhower's visit was scheduled to be just six hours, with no overnight stay, and although my shift was not on duty, we had all decided to ride into the city out of pure curiosity.

The two agents who had been sent ahead to Kabul a couple of weeks earlier to do the advance had, we soon found out, been violently ill with dysentery. Both Larry Short and Paul Rundle looked like they had each lost about ten pounds, and although there wasn't much color in their faces, they handled the president's arrival with the utmost professionalism, and everything went off without a hitch. King Zahir met President Eisenhower at the airport, and after a simple ceremony, which included some children dancing in native costumes to traditional music, we set off by motorcade into downtown Kabul.

The temperature was near freezing, and yet tens of thousands of villagers lined the route from the airport to Kabul. The vast majority of the onlookers were long-bearded men dressed in ankle-length tunics with wool wraps and turbans, and you could tell from their leathered skin that life here was hard, and the people were a tough breed. It appeared that many of the tribesmen had been waiting for hours, warming themselves with small bonfires, and as our motorcade rode along the same route that had been traveled by Alexander the Great and Genghis Khan, the people waved and cheered.

President Eisenhower and King Zahir rode in the backseat of the king's 1947 Lincoln convertible, and as we entered the downtown area, the crowds got denser and denser, making it difficult for the Afghan police motorcycle riders to keep the path open for the cars following behind. Men and young boys crowded around the slow-moving motorcade, waving small American flags and throwing streamers and confetti, trying to move in closer to see President Eisenhower. The situation got so bad that Agents Jim Rowley and Dick Flohr were perched on the back fender of the car, and at times they had to physically throw overly exuberant young men back into the street as they tried to reach in and touch President Eisenhower. Fortunately, the motorcade made its way to the Chilstoon Palace, and President Eisenhower was scurried into the safety of the king's residence without any major incident.

A luncheon was held at the palace, and then a private meeting between President Eisenhower and King Zahir. Eisenhower expressed concern about the large amount of resources the Afghan king had accepted from the Soviets, but the end result of the meeting was a strengthening of the relationship between our two countries, with Eisenhower committing $145 million in U.S. aid to help build roads and a new airport in Kandahar.

Meanwhile, those of us who weren't on duty wandered around the city, curious to witness daily life in such a remote location. People filled the streets, haggling for foodstuffs from vendors selling fruits and vegetables from baskets and bins along the side of the road. One man had a couple of pigeons in a cage, and next to them a dozen rabbits, all presumably destined to become dinner, while still other vendors cooked flatbread in large cast iron skillets over open fires. Camels were a common sight, being led by their masters, their backs piled high with blankets and burlap bags stuffed to the seams. I felt like I had been transported back in time.

The downtown was a mix of rustic mud buildings, ornate mosques, and modern low-rise structures, and at the edge of the city ramshackle houses were clustered precariously on the surrounding hillsides. People greeted us with smiles and offered us food, but having seen the condition of our colleagues Rundle and Short, we didn't dare try any of the local delicacies. Our time on the ground in Kabul was just six hours, and at 2:00 p.m. we were airborne for New Delhi, India.

Of all the stops on this tour, President Eisenhower was most excited about visiting India. After the tremendous receptions he had received in Rome, Ankara, Karachi, and Kabul, we were expecting large, enthusiastic crowds, but nothing could have prepared us for what happened in New Delhi.

INDIA

I slept for the entire two-and-a-half-hour flight, and the next thing I knew it was 5:00 p.m. and we were landing at Palam Airport in New Delhi. Our plane arrived several minutes ahead of Air Force One, and I could hardly believe what I saw when I stepped off the aircraft. People were stacked twenty deep behind rope lines, and still thousands more were seated in bleachers, as if the arrival of the American president were a sporting event. There had to be nearly seventy thousand people waiting on the tarmac—more than could fill Yankee Stadium. The crowd cheered when Air Force One landed, and then, moments later, when the door opened and President Eisenhower stepped out to the top of the stairway, there was a thunderous roar. Ike broke into an enormous grin at the rousing welcome of flags waving and people clapping, cheering, and whistling.

As soon as he stepped off the ramp, he was draped with a garland of flowers that looped around his neck and hung to his shins. President Rajendra Prasad was the first to greet him, followed by Vice President Sarvepalli Radhakrishman, Prime Minister Jawaharlal Nehru, and his daughter, Indira Gandhi. The agents on shift kept their distance, allowing the president space while maintaining a carefully orchestrated envelope around him so that, should any trouble occur, they could pounce and shield him in an instant.

A small raised stage had been set up with a microphone for President Eisenhower to make a statement, and as he stepped up to the podium the crowd went wild with excitement.

"Mr. President, Mr. Prime Minister, Your Excellencies, and ladies and gentlemen," he began. "As I set foot on the soil of India I am fulfilling a cherished wish held for many years. India won its freedom and its independence through peaceful means. This in itself was a great accomplishment, and one that has challenged the admiration of the entire world . . . the only alternative to global war is peace, for the other alternative is too horrible even to mention."

At every pause, the people clapped and cheered, chanting, *"Zindabad Ike! Zindabad Ike!"* "Long Live Ike!"

A few minutes later the motorcade was under way, with President Eisenhower, Prasad, and Nehru riding in the backseat of an open-top two-door black Cadillac convertible, led by an Indian police motorcycle escort.

Since I wasn't on duty, I was assigned to a car several cars behind the presidential vehicle, and as we exited the airport, I was amazed by the sheer number of people of all ages—men, women, and children—who had come to see the American president. The streets were lined with people as far as you could see, and where there was a higher vantage point, be it a roof, a balcony, or a tree limb, those spots too were jammed with people.

We hadn't gone very far when the motorcade stopped, and I could see there was a commotion up ahead. People had broken past the police lines, filling the street so the cars and motorcycles couldn't pass. The authorities were yelling and shoving people, trying to get them to clear a pathway, but the crowd had swarmed around the presidential vehicle and there was nowhere for anyone to go. The Indian security forces had completely lost control of the situation. Suddenly, Prime Minister Nehru got out of the car and started swinging a swagger stick at the people. I could hardly believe my eyes. The Indian prime minister was hitting his own people! As people struggled to move out of the way, they began trampling each other. It was a horrifying scene, but slowly the crowd inched away, clearing enough of an opening so the vehicles could begin moving again.

The ten-mile journey from the airport to Rashtrapati Bhavan—the president's residence—took well over an hour, simply due to the overwhelming throngs. *One and a half million people* lined the route, and as a sign of respect and admiration, many were throwing handfuls of flower petals and even whole bouquets into the presidential vehicle. On several more occasions, the crowd pushed its way into the roadway, and each time, Prime Minister Nehru jumped out, swinging his swagger stick to clear the path. There was an enormous outpouring of affection, a massive crowd, yet still, despite the overwhelmingly positive nature of the people, it was on the verge of calamity, and there was always the possibility that one person, or an organized group, might have intentions of harming the president. It was intense, on-the-job training in how a crowd—even a friendly crowd—can quickly and unpredictably spiral out of control.

Even with the superb advance planning by two experienced agents, we were somewhat at the mercy of the local authorities. There is no way to predict what will happen in any given situation, so you have to be able to constantly adjust your security procedures. But it is very difficult when you have limited resources, you are in a foreign country, you are guests of that country, and they are unable to control their own people. Fortunately, the two presidents got through the crowd to their destination without any harm to either of them, but it was a priceless lesson for all of us on the detail that day. We were lucky the people were friendly. Had there been any animosity, I shudder to think what could have happened.

It had been a long, tiring day for President Eisenhower, so, shortly after arriving at Rashtrapati Bhavan, he retired to his private suite for the night.

All of the agents were given accommodations in the presidential guesthouse, and since I was still on the midnight shift, I went directly to my room. I knew I'd better use the few free hours I had before I went on duty to get some rest, so I undressed, set the alarm on my wind-up travel clock, got into bed, and promptly fell asleep.

Upon awakening to the sound of the alarm, I groggily got up, only to find that all my clothes were missing.

What the hell?

At that moment, there was a knock on the door. I grabbed a towel from the bathroom, wrapped it around my waist, and opened the door.

Standing before me was a very thin young Indian man, his arms outstretched, holding my undershorts, undershirt, dress shirt, suit coat, and pants, all freshly cleaned and pressed.

With a big smile and a British-tinged accent, he said, "Here you are, sir. Anything else I can do for you, sir?"

"Uh, no, thank you," I said as I took my clothes.

"Please don't hesitate, sir," he replied. "I am pleased to be at your service."

It turned out that he was the houseboy assigned to my room, and part of his job was to do my laundry, whether or not I requested it. I quickly learned not to leave any article of clothing lying around unless I wanted it cleaned and pressed.

We had designated security posts around the suite occupied by President Eisenhower, John, and Barbara, and throughout the night the agents on the midnight shift rotated posts every thirty minutes. In addition, members of the presidential protective unit of India had personnel in corresponding posts near each of us, presumably as our backup, but they spent most of the night chatting with each other, often loudly and with animation. We couldn't understand a word they were saying, so we simply tried to ignore them and went about our normal protective procedures.

At around two in the morning, I happened to be standing at the post immediately outside the door to the presidential suite when the president's son John came out.

"Agent," he said, "will you please get those Indian guys to stop talking? Their voices carry right into the president's bedroom and he can't get to sleep."

"Absolutely, Major Eisenhower," I said. "I'll take care of it."

I was embarrassed that we hadn't realized the noise might keep the president awake and hadn't handled the situation earlier, but I immediately confronted the Indian guards and convinced them to move farther away, and to halt all conversation. We didn't hear another word from inside the suite, so, presumably, after that the president was finally able to get some sleep.

WITH FOUR DAYS in India, once again, those of us on the midnight shift got a lucky break. When we were relieved by the day shift at eight o'clock in the morning, we had time to do a little sightseeing. While none of us knew much about Indian culture, the one thing about which we had all heard was the magnificent splendor of the Taj Mahal. Our contacts at the State Department provided us with a car and an Indian driver, so a few of us piled into the car and headed down to Agra.

At that early morning hour, the streets of New Delhi were coming alive, as shops opened and people went about their daily life. The streets were filled with people on bicycles—sometimes two or three people to one bike—riding every which way, interspersed with people walking alongside camels piled high with blankets and burlap sacks; tractors and rusty old trucks; and every so often a lone cow—sacred in India—wandering aimlessly among the chaos.

The city turned to countryside, where we rarely saw any sign of life, but then all of a sudden there would be a village, marked only by a row of outdoor produce stands and perhaps a one-pump gas station. The vast majority of the people were skeletal-thin and often barefoot, with a look of despair on their faces. Cooking was done over open fires that created heavy plumes of smoke, and when we asked our driver about the unusual stench, he told us it was from the elephant dung commonly used for fuel.

Finally we reached Agra, and the driver pulled up to a massive arched gate and parked the car.

"This is the Taj Mahal," he said. "Come, I will show you."

As we walked through the gate, suddenly the Taj Mahal was visible, and the sight was truly breathtaking. The white marble domed structure stood at the end of an extraordinary reflecting pool, like a beautiful queen staring into a mirror, oblivious of her timeless beauty. It was truly one of the most magnificent buildings I had ever seen. You couldn't help but be overcome by a sense of awe as you approached the Taj, and as we walked, our driver explained how the Mughal emperor Shah Jahan was grief-stricken when his third wife, Mumtaz Mahal, had died during the birth of their fourteenth child. He commissioned the Taj Mahal to be built as a mausoleum to honor her memory, and after fourteen years of construction, the main building was completed in 1638.

The interior of the Taj was like an art museum, filled with intricate mosaics on the ceilings, walls, and floors, all encrusted with colorful, semiprecious stones. It was a masterpiece, a timeless tribute to the woman who was the love of the emperor's life. I thought to myself, *Damn, she must have been one hell of a woman.*

Driving back to New Delhi, it was impossible not to notice the stark contrast between the splendor and riches of the ruling class—as exemplified by the Taj Mahal—and the numbing poverty of the masses. It was just one of the many times throughout this journey that made me realize how lucky I was to have been born in the United States of America.

IT WAS REALLY remarkable to me how much stamina our sixty-nine-year-old president possessed. The time change between Washington and New Delhi alone caused me a problem, but the president seemed not to be bothered at all by jet lag, and I wondered how he did it. He wanted to see as much of India as he could during his four-day visit, so the schedule was tightly packed. He was up early every morning, with one meeting, speech, or official function after another, dinners sometimes with five thousand guests, and as the guest of honor, the president always had to be on.

Sunday, December 13, was an example of how tiring, long, and complicated a day traveling with the president can be. The president arose at 6:00 a.m. and departed by car with President Prasad at 7:50 to attend services at the Protestant Church of India Cathedral. They returned to the Rashtra-pati Bhavan at 9:00 a.m., and fifteen minutes later departed for Palam Airport with Prime Minister Nehru. They flew to the city of Agra and transferred to an open-top car, so the tens of thousands of people lining the route from the airport to the Taj Mahal could get a good view of the American president.

The three-hundred-year-old "temple of love" was something President Eisenhower had yearned to see ever since first reading about it as a young boy in Kansas, and while he told Nehru it was the thing he had looked forward to most of all on this entire trip, just thirty minutes were allotted in the schedule for his private tour. Then it was back in the helicopter for a flight to Bichpuri, where they transferred to a car for a brief tour of an agricultural training center at a college before driving to the rural village of Laraonda. People lined the dirt roads and stood on the thatched roofs of mud shacks, cheering the "prince of peace" as President Eisenhower waved from the backseat of the open convertible. The village headman greeted President Eisenhower with yet another long garland of flowers, introduced him to the town councilors, and then it was back in the car to Bichpuri, where the helicopter awaited. They choppered to Agra, transferred to a small airplane, and flew back to Palam Airport in New Delhi, landing at 1:20 p.m. It had already been a full day, but by the time the president motored back to Rashtrapati Bhavan, there was just enough time for a quick bite to eat and a short rest before the evening events.

At 4:15 p.m. Prime Minister Nehru arrived at the palace to accompany President Eisenhower to the Ramlila Ground, a sprawling park that separated Old Delhi and New Delhi, for what would be Eisenhower's final public appearance in India. Fortunately, the Indian officials had learned from the near tragic arrival motorcade, as well as an incident the previous day when Indian police were forced to beat back crowds at the World Agricultural Fair, and sturdy fences had been erected around large pens in which to contain the people.

It was a wise decision, because by the time we brought President Eisenhower to the site, more than *one million people* had gathered for the farewell speech. Acres of solidly packed humanity stretched as far as I could see, and when President Eisenhower walked onto the elevated stage, the crowd broke into a roar of cheers. President Eisenhower captivated the audience with a stirring speech in which he repeatedly invoked the name of Mohandas K.

Gandhi, the leader of India's independence movement, in an effort to show the strong bond we shared in our dedication to freedom. There had never been a larger crowd assembled in the Ramlila Ground, and the fact that all these people had come to hear President Eisenhower left a lasting image in my mind about the enormous impact, and power, the President of the United States had. Because of all the great things Dwight D. Eisenhower had accomplished, both before and during his term of office, he had earned the respect of people all over the world. He was an ambassador of the highest order, instilling hope and inspiration, a true leader who reflected positively on the American people.

TEHRAN

We left India before dawn on Monday, December 14, 1959, and headed for our next stop—Tehran, Iran. This was to be only a six-hour stop, but as usual there was a lot packed into a short amount of time. It was a short flight, with just enough time to review the advance agents' report on the events and situation in Tehran.

Our shifts had rotated the day before, so for the next two weeks I would be working the 4:00 p.m. to midnight shift. There would be no more sightseeing, but that was fine with me. I much preferred being where the action was. Every country, every city, and every venue had its own challenges when it came to protecting the president, and the adrenaline was constantly flowing.

We landed at Mehrabad Airport right on schedule at 8:45 a.m. It was a frigid morning, but that hadn't deterred thousands from coming out to meet the American president. Wearing a topcoat, scarf, and hat, the president smiled broadly as he stepped off the plane, waving to the cheering crowd as he descended the steps. A band was playing, and before us was a sea of little flags flapping in the wind. Seven hundred fifty schoolchildren stood bundled in coats and hats, half of them holding American flags and the other half waving red, white, and green Iranian flags. His Imperial Majesty Mohammad Reza Pahlavi, the Shah of Iran, was waiting at the bottom of the steps with a line of Iranian dignitaries, and as Eisenhower greeted them, three cannons fired off a twenty-one-gun salute. Suddenly there was a tremendous roar overhead as a group of military jets flying in tight formation spelled out "IKE" in the crisp blue sky. After a brief welcoming ceremony, President Eisenhower and the Shah got into the backseat of the open-top Cadillac convertible provided by the Iranian government, and the motorcade was under way.

It was an impressive motorcade, with dozens of Iranian motorcycle officers in a V-formation ahead of the presidential vehicle, while our agents mixed with the Iranian protective detail in vehicles slightly to the rear on either side of the president's car. We had been given our assignments by the Agent in Charge, and as I took my position in the follow-up car, I noticed a contingent of vehicles behind us filled with Iranian soldiers carrying submachine guns. It was a bit disconcerting, but one thing I had begun to realize on this trip was how much we had to rely on, and trust, our host government's security procedures. This was their home turf.

Despite the freezing cold temperatures, more than three quarters of a million people lined the route from the airport to downtown Tehran. The crowds cheered as we drove past colorful banners celebrating Iran's friendship with the United States, and while the people were exuberant, they were kept in order by thousands of soldiers standing intimidatingly with rifles, bayonets attached, slung over their shoulders.

As we neared the city, suddenly the road turned red. Huge, intricately woven Persian rugs had been placed end to end in the street—dozens of them for hundreds of yards—creating the largest and most beautiful welcome mat you can imagine. It seemed a shame to me that the motorcycles and cars drove right over these magnificent works of art, but that is exactly what we did. Talk about rolling out the red carpet.

The destination was the Shah's palace, where the two leaders met privately for about two hours. Then President Eisenhower addressed a joint session of the Iranian Parliament, praising the people of Iran for refusing to stand on the sidelines in the free world's fight against Communism.

"I know I speak for the American people when I say we are proud to count so valiant a nation as a partner," he declared.

The members of Parliament listened intently to his every word, and at the end of his comments rose out of their seats in a standing ovation. From there it was on to an official luncheon in the Hall of Mirrors at Golestan Palace. The room was literally covered from floor to ceiling with mirrors and prisms that caught the light so that it looked like wallpaper made out of diamonds.

After lunch, there was another motorcade through the streets of Tehran back to Air Force One. On this, my first trip to Iran, there was no time for sightseeing. The overwhelming memory I have is the feeling of tension and adrenaline, scanning the massive crowds at the airport and the crowded streets of Tehran. My senses were focused on the people, not the art and architecture. That is the usual situation for an agent on duty. You may have visited some exotic place, but there is no time for exploration or enjoyment.

ATHENS

It was 4:40 p.m. local time when we landed at Hellinikon Airport outside Athens, Greece. Waiting at the foot of the ramp to greet the president were King Paul and his son Crown Prince Constantine, resplendent in their formal navy uniforms bedecked with medals, ribbons, and gold braid.

Once again, there was an elaborate arrival ceremony, which included a twenty-one-gun salute, greetings by Greek dignitaries, and an inspection of the honor guard, followed by a short speech by President Eisenhower in which he acknowledged the people of Greece and the warm friendship between our two nations.

King Paul guided President Eisenhower to the backseat of their designated car, a magnificent open-top Rolls-Royce touring sedan driven by a Greek military aide, with another Greek aide in the right-front passenger seat. It was unusual not to have one of our agents in the car with the president, but this is how the trip had been negotiated between the Greeks and our political and Secret Service advance team. Those of us on President Eisenhower's detail took our predesignated positions in convertibles directly behind the Rolls-Royce, and the motorcade got under way.

The sun had gone down, and darkness was setting in as we made our way through the streets of Athens, making it difficult to see any unusual movement or activity within the throngs of people that lined the motorcade route. People were packed shoulder to shoulder along the boulevards, waving huge flags, clapping, and cheering, and up above people hung out open windows, jamming rooftops and balconies. It was estimated that 750,000 people had come out to welcome President Eisenhower—the largest gathering ever assembled in Greece for a visiting dignitary—and to show appreciation,

President Eisenhower and King Paul both stood and waved from the back of the open car the entire length of the eight-mile route.

It felt like we were in the middle of a circus as people threw flowers and confetti, while others attempted to run into the street. Fortunately, the Greek police were out in force and were able to keep control of the excited crowd as we headed first to the Tomb of the Unknowns for a wreath-laying ceremony, and then, finally, on to the palace.

That night there was a formal dinner at the palace hosted by King Paul and Queen Frederika, and it was quite late by the time we got President Eisenhower safely into his suite. It had been a grueling twenty-two-hour day for everyone on the trip. Three countries, two flights, and five motorcades with exposure to more than one and a half million people.

THE NEXT DAY, President Eisenhower had a typically full schedule that included breakfast at the American Embassy residence, meetings with Greek prime minister Konstantinos Karamanlis, and a speech in front of the Greek Parliament. Meanwhile, the USS *Des Moines*, a heavy cruiser stationed in the Mediterranean, was waiting at anchor off the coast of Greece, its crew preparing the ship to transport the commander in chief on the next leg of his trip. The president would sail from Athens to Tunis, Tunisia; disembark in Tunis for a meeting with President Habib Ben Ali Bourguiba; and then return to the ship for a leisurely twenty-four-hour cruise to Toulon, a port city in the southeast of France. In Toulon, the president would board a private train and travel the 430 miles north to Paris.

By this point, everyone on the trip was ready for a little rest and relaxation. There was very limited space on board the *Des Moines*, so only minimal staff and a few Secret Service agents could accompany the president on this leg of the trip—which meant the majority of the presidential staff and most of the Secret Service agents would fly directly from Athens to Paris.

PARIS

We flew to Paris, and with a day and a half of free time, we were determined to make the most of it. With the assistance of the French police officers with whom we would be working once the president arrived, we had the best tour guides one could find.

The first day, we had quick visits to all the famous tourist locations—the Cathedral of Notre Dame, the Eiffel Tower, the Arc de Triomphe, and the Louvre—but one of the officers convinced us that if we wanted to experience the real Paris, we had to get up early in the morning.

"Trust me," he said as he brought his fingers to his mouth with a kiss. "You love."

When night fell, the city turned absolutely magical. Tiny white lights were strung on balconies and draped around the bare tree branches so that it looked like twinkling chandeliers were hanging along the streets and the banks of the Seine. Store windows were decorated with gingerbread houses, Christmas trees, and fake snow, while carolers sang on street corners. We had been working so hard, we had almost forgotten it was Christmastime.

The next morning, we had no idea what we were getting ourselves into, but we followed the officer's directions and found our way to Les Halles. It turned out that Les Halles was a market where the produce, cheese, and meats arrived from the countryside each day. It was before dawn, but the place was bustling with shopkeepers and farmers bargaining in French, a cigarette in one hand and a handful of francs in the other.

Our French police officer guide brought us to one particular stall and said something in French to the man behind the counter. Next thing we knew, out came individual crocks of steaming hot onion soup for each of us. A thick layer of crusty, gooey cheese was baked over the top, and the officer showed us how to dip in our spoon, twirl it around with the cheese, and then sop it all up with a piece of crusty baguette. I'll never forget the morning I had authentic French onion soup for breakfast in Les Halles.

That evening, December 18, 1959, President Eisenhower arrived in Paris at 10:30 p.m. after a nine-hour train trip from Toulon.

The purpose of this visit was a summit of the leaders of the four largest Western countries—Charles de Gaulle, Eisenhower, Prime Minister Harold Macmillan of Britain, and West German chancellor Konrad Adenauer—and was dubbed the Four Power Conference. The goal was to outline a plan for a future East-West summit with Soviet premier Nikita Khrushchev and to come up with a solid allied Western front on nuclear disarmament, unifying Germany, and the status of West Berlin, which was isolated far inside Communist East Germany.

To have the four most important people in the free world together in one place required careful choreography between the various security groups. The biggest problems I had during this visit to France were my inability to speak French and the inability of most French security officials to speak English. Relying on hand gestures to communicate became a necessity as we worked together on security matters.

The Secret Service had flown one of our own cars—a large, heavy convertible with a distinctive glass-domed roof—to transport the president in Paris. This vehicle, which we called "4-B," was a Lincoln sedan originally built in 1950 for President Harry S. Truman, but the see-through roof was actually President Eisenhower's idea. Apparently, Ike was riding in the convertible on the way back to Washington from Richmond, Virginia, in May 1954, and it started raining. The agents put the canvas roof on the car to keep the president from getting soaked, but by doing this the hundreds of spectators along the route couldn't see him. This really bothered Ike, who liked seeing the crowds, but more important, wanted them to have the opportunity to see him—especially during the presidential campaign. He suggested the car should have a glass roof for inclement weather, and the idea was turned over to the Ford Motor Company engineering group. The "all weather" top, made of four clear Plexiglas sections that fit together with aluminum bars, and which could be stored conveniently in the trunk, was delivered three months later. Additionally, a light was installed behind the center armrest so the president could be seen more clearly at night. The Secret Service had had little to do with the design, and nothing on the car was bulletproof. Indeed, President Eisenhower preferred to use the car as an open convertible whenever possible so he could stand up and be even more visible to people viewing the motorcade. Ike used the car extensively during the 1956 presidential campaign and during the 1957 Inaugural Parade, during which he stood in the open car the entire route through downtown Washington.

Here in Paris there were no grand parades or motorcades organized to generate crowds, but the eyes of the world were on the leaders' every move as they met Saturday at the Élysée Palace, de Gaulle's residence, and on Sunday at the Château de Rambouillet, thirty miles outside the city.

For me, it was a fascinating learning experience to see how heads of state and governments worked together for the betterment of all their people. I was pleased to see the respect each had for one another, knowing they all had different philosophies, but also realizing that if these men did not work together toward a common goal, the result could be the end of humanity as we knew it. They all bore heavy burdens, and took them seriously. In the end, each of the four Western leaders sent letters to Soviet premier Nikita Khrushchev inviting him to the first of a series of summit meetings to "consider international questions of mutual concern."

When President Eisenhower departed Paris the afternoon of Monday, December 21, on Air Force One, it was clear that the long days of negotiation had been arduous, but nevertheless he was pleased that they'd been able to move forward on talks with the Soviets. We still had two more stops on his peace and friendship tour, so there was no time for any of us to rest. Next stop: Madrid, Spain.

MADRID

The two-hour flight from Paris to Madrid gave me the chance to study the protective survey report for Madrid and prepare myself mentally for what challenges lay ahead. We would be landing at Torrejón Air Base and were expecting huge crowds along the motorcade route into Madrid, because this was the first time an American president had ever visited Spain, and it was not without controversy.

His Excellency Francisco Franco Bahamonde—commonly referred to as Generalissimo Franco—had been ruling by dictatorship since 1939 and was a pariah throughout Europe, for, although Spain was officially neutral in World War II, Franco did not hide his support for Nazi Germany and Fascist Italy. During his tenure, thousands of political opponents had been suppressed or killed. Because of its strategic location in defense against the Soviet Union, however, the United States had brokered a deal that allowed us to build three air bases and a naval base on Spanish soil in return for financial aid to Franco's regime. When word leaked of Eisenhower's planned tour through Asia and Europe, which originally did not include a stop in Spain, Franco took it as an insult and threatened that the future of the U.S. bases could be in jeopardy. Subsequently, the president decided to add the one-day stop in Madrid to the schedule, which, to many, appeared to be a U.S. stamp of approval on Franco's politics.

It was 4:30 in the afternoon when we landed, and there to greet President Eisenhower was the usual reception committee, headed by Generalissimo Franco himself, in full military dress. Our Secret Service car 4-B had been flown to Madrid, and although it was quite cold, with a brisk wind blowing, only the rear portion of the bubble top was in place, allowing the middle section to remain open so the two leaders could stand and wave to the crowds if they desired. The purpose of the motorcade was, after all, to allow the people of Madrid to see President Eisenhower, and in return the city had made every effort to impress. Huge canvas photos of Eisenhower were draped from arches and buildings; on the side of the tallest building in the city, lights ten stories high spelled out IKE; and a plaza had even been renamed *Plaza del Presidente Eisenhower.*

As we made our way into the city, the crowds grew larger and larger—police estimated one and a half million spectators in this city of two million—and despite the raw wind, President Eisenhower stood the entire way, his arms outstretched, his face beaming at the jubilant reception. People were hanging out windows and lined up on rooftops and balconies, waving white handkerchiefs like they were cheering on a matador in a bullring and chanting "Ee-kay! Ee-kay!"—their way of saying Ike. It was wild.

A cordon of soldiers dressed in ankle-length wool topcoats, many of them armed with submachine guns, kept the exuberant crowds in order, but still the adrenaline was running high for those of us in the follow-up car, scanning the masses of people, searching for any sign of antagonism or that lone individual who just didn't fit.

After an hour and forty-five minutes, we finally reached the Moncloa Palace, where President Eisenhower would stay the night. We got him secured in his suite and took our posts outside the doors. He had just a couple of hours to rest and get changed for the formal state dinner in his honor.

I had learned that the Europeans eat dinner much later than we Americans do, but here in Spain, dinner often didn't start until ten o'clock. The dinner for President Eisenhower was scheduled to begin at nine at another palace, the Oriente, about three miles away, so we had one shift of agents move ahead to the Oriente while one shift stayed with the president.

The Oriente Palace contains the largest square footage within its walls of any palace in Europe. With 870 windows, 240 balconies, and 44 staircases in its 1,450,000-square-foot floor area, it was immense—and impossible for us to secure on our own. We had to rely on the Spanish security forces to secure the outer perimeter, while we stationed agents only in the areas where the president would be.

It wasn't until after eleven o'clock that we finally got President Eisenhower tucked into his suite back at the Moncloa Palace, and those of us who had been on duty all day were relieved by the midnight shift.

Morning came early, as the schedule called for another rigorous day.

CASABLANCA

Every country we visited on this trip had been an eye-opening experience for me, but our seven hours on the ground in Morocco were certainly the wildest and most exotic.

It was 11:20 a.m. when we touched down at Nouasseur Air Base, a U.S. Air Force Strategic Air Command base outside Casablanca, and waiting to greet President Eisenhower was Morocco's King Mohammed V. The king wore a peaked cap and was dressed in a long, hooded, brown wool cloak, known as a burnoose, and if I hadn't been briefed, I never would have picked him out as the king, simply judging by his attire. The two leaders greeted each other warmly, and after a brief formal reception, Eisenhower and King Mohammed got into the back of a white Lincoln convertible for the motorcade into downtown Casablanca.

As we exited the air base, it felt like we were driving through a movie set for the *Arabian Nights*. The streets were lined with people of all ages, dressed in traditional Moroccan attire—women in long robes and headscarves of all colors, with white kerchiefs veiled across their faces, wailing with a shrill noise that sounded like "luh-luh-luh-luh-luh," while scraggly-bearded men, also in long robes, each with a dagger at his waist, cheered and waved. But most striking of all were the Berber tribesmen—hundreds of them—who had ridden from their villages on horseback and were galloping along the roadside, firing rifles into the air as they lined up in formation to welcome the American president.

Watching from the follow-up car as President Eisenhower stood in the open car directly in front of us, waving and holding his arms out in appreciation, I was about as tense as I had ever been. The crowd was jubilant and welcoming, but with all those rifles firing into the air, I couldn't help but imagine how quickly the situation could turn to disaster if one man decided to turn his gun on the president. It would be so easy, and there would be nothing we could do to stop it.

The motorcade stopped at the Town Hall where President Eisenhower was presented with dates and milk, followed by a luncheon at the palace and a private meeting between the leaders and their staffs. It was estimated that at least 500,000 Moroccans had come out to welcome Ike in a demonstration that surpassed anything I'd ever witnessed in my life. All the agents breathed a sigh of relief when we finally got the president back on Air Force One without incident.

Shortly after six in the evening, we were airborne, and after a brief refueling stop in Gander, Newfoundland, we touched down at Andrews Air Force Base at 11:30 p.m. on December 22, 1959. We had traveled 22,000 miles in nineteen days and visited eleven nations, and the president had appeared before millions upon millions of people who embraced him as a "prince of peace." Everyone who had been on the trip, from the staff to the press to the agents, was worn ragged, and while we were all happy to be back on American soil, there was no denying that President Eisenhower's effort had not only increased his personal popularity but also had raised the image of the United States in the eyes of all those we encountered. Diplomatically, he had strengthened relations with a number of countries, and there were high hopes that the East-West summit meeting in Paris scheduled for the spring could move the world closer to peace.

For me, personally, it had been an amazing adventure. To think that that was my first trip outside the United States. I was filled with pride and love for my country, and enormously humbled to be a Special Agent in the U.S. Secret Service. *How did this kid from North Dakota get so lucky?*

It was wonderful to see Gwen and Chris, to sleep in my own bed, and to be home in time for Christmas. I was eager to tell Gwen about everything I'd seen, but at the same time I realized that no matter how vividly I described what I had experienced, there was no way she could understand what it had really been like. I was cautious about what I shared with her—not for worry of divulging anything secret—but because the last thing I wanted was for her to get the impression that I'd been on a glamorous European holiday while she was at home taking care of all the household chores and parenting our son all on her own. So, in a way that was typical of my staunch Norwegian upbringing, I said very little.

Fortunately, Paul Rundle's wife, Peggy, had introduced Gwen to the other White House Detail wives, and the women got together regularly for bridge games and lunches at one another's apartments. Like the men on the detail, our wives developed a camaraderie because they were all in the same situation. With husbands gone for weeks at a time, they relied on one another for emotional support as well as sharing supermarket coupons, reciprocal babysitting, and casserole recipes.

I was back on duty at the White House the next day, and four days later, on Sunday, December 27, I was on a plane headed for Augusta, Georgia, where the president and Mrs. Eisenhower would spend the rest of the holidays. New Year's Eve 1959 was a quiet night at Augusta National, and for the agents it was a relief not to be going somewhere, fighting a crowd. We appreciated the lack of excitement.

On January 4, as I walked along the serene golf course carrying a bag with two old golf clubs and a .30-caliber carbine—a world away from the Berber tribesmen, the elephant-dung fires in India, and the Four Power meeting in Paris—I thought back on all I had experienced in the past year and realized I had become an eyewitness to history in the making. It was my twenty-eighth birthday, and little did I know, the history had only just begun.

4

The South American Tour

On January 5, 1960, President Eisenhower played one last round of golf at Augusta, and then we flew back to Washington. Congress was about to reconvene, and it was time for the annual State of the Union address.

All of us on the detail had well-tanned faces, having spent so many hours on the golf course in the mild Georgia weather, and that didn't go over too well with our wives, who had spent New Year's without husbands in frigid Washington temperatures. Additionally, we had just learned that President Eisenhower was so pleased with the results of the eleven-nation tour that plans were already under way for a similar trip to South America at the end of February.

President Eisenhower had spent a great deal of time working on his State of the Union speech to the American people. It was important for him to lay out the problems that faced the United States in no uncertain terms, but also to stress that he would not slow down in his quest for global peace and protection of the free world.

"Mr. President, Mr. Speaker, Members of the 86th Congress," he began. "Seven years ago I entered my present office with one long-held resolve overriding all others. I was then, and remain now, determined that the United States shall become an ever more potent resource for the cause of peace—realizing that peace cannot be for ourselves alone, but for peoples everywhere.

"First, I point out that for us, annual self-examination is made a definite necessity by the fact that we now live in a divided world of uneasy equilibrium, with our side committed to its own protection and against aggression by the other. With both sides of this divided world in possession of unbelievably destructive weapons, mankind approaches a state where mutual annihilation becomes a possibility. No other fact of today's world equals this in importance—it colors everything we say, plan, and do."

It was true. The fear of nuclear war was ever present, hovering like fog in every American's mind, and Eisenhower realized that maintaining our military strength was imperative to sustaining freedom in pursuit of world peace.

"America possesses an enormous defense power," he said, with the tone of the general who knew its capabilities. "It is my studied conviction that no nation will ever risk general war against us unless we should be so foolish as to neglect the defense forces we now so powerfully support. It is worldwide knowledge that any nation which might be tempted today to attack the United States, even though our country might sustain great losses, would itself promptly suffer a terrible destruction. But I once again assure all peoples and all nations that the United States, except in defense, will never turn loose this destructive power."

Along with our military defenses, it was critical, President Eisenhower said, to offer aid to emerging nations whose very survival depended on foreign assistance, and which at this moment were being courted by both the Western allies and the Soviets.

"If we grasp this opportunity to build an age of productive partnership with less fortunate nations and those that have already achieved a high state of economic advancement, we will make brighter the outlook for a world order based upon security, freedom, and peace. Otherwise, the outlook could be dark indeed."

He touched on his support of investing in space exploration and also urged the Democratic-controlled Congress to take under serious consideration his recommended legislation regarding civil rights. In closing, President Eisenhower referred to his eleven-nation tour.

"On my recent visit to distant lands I found one statesman after another eager to tell me of the elements of their government that had been borrowed from our American Constitution, and from the indestructible ideas set forth in our Declaration of Independence.

"By our every action we must strive to make ourselves worthy of this trust, ever mindful that an accumulation of seemingly minor encroachments upon freedom gradually could break down the entire fabric of a free society."

The speech was 100 percent Dwight D. Eisenhower, spoken from the heart and from the wisdom of an Army general who had experienced the horrors of war and whose supreme goal was not politics or power but peace and freedom.

IN LATE JANUARY, I was given my first advance security assignment outside Washington, under the tutorial of a more senior agent named Harvey Henderson. If there was one thing I had learned on Eisenhower's eleven-nation tour, it was how critically important the advance security preparations were. It was up to the advance agents to research and anticipate any possible security concerns, as well as to arrange all logistics in cooperation with the president's political and personal agenda.

We were notified by the president's staff that the president had a speaking engagement in Los Angeles, and would then be heading to Palm Springs, where he would spend a few days of golf and relaxation. The president would stay at La Quinta Country Club at the residence of George Allen—a longtime friend who also owned a neighboring farm in Gettysburg—and play golf at his favorite course in the area, the Eldorado Country Club.

The first step of the advance assignment was to check with the Protective Research Section (PRS) of the Secret Service to see if there were any threats or cases of protective interest in the Palm Springs area. Whenever a threat was made against the president—whether it was a written letter, a phone call, someone attempting to jump the White House fence, or information gathered from an informant—a case file was created and a thorough investigation was done on the individual. Each case was analyzed and then ranked according to the seriousness of the threat. Some people had grievances against the government in general and their threats would reemerge each time there was a new president, so once a case was filed, it remained open until the death of the individual.

Located in the Executive Office Building, the PRS office was our central intelligence center, and at that time, before we had computerized databases, the voluminous amount of information was kept in large metal filing cabinets, organized by case number. Additionally, there were rows of smaller cabinets that contained thousands of three-by-five cards on which threats were indexed both alphabetically and geographically.

The three-by-five cards had photos of the individual on the front and summaries of their threat history, last known location, and current status typed on the back. We carried a stack of the most serious threat cases with us at all times, using them like flash cards to memorize the faces of the individuals who were most likely to harm the president. Although there were thousands of people on our watch list, those who gave us the greatest concern were the ones we didn't know—the lone individuals or conspiratorial groups who had not yet surfaced and could show up anytime, anywhere.

Agent Henderson and I flew to Palm Springs and were met by an agent from our Los Angeles office, in whose jurisdiction Palm Springs was located. We relied heavily on the agents in the local field offices for a number of reasons, not the least of which was their knowledge of the locale and emergency medical personnel. They knew where the best hospitals were, who the best doctors and surgeons in the area were, and how to get hold of them on a moment's notice. This was always a concern whenever President Eisenhower traveled because of his history of heart attacks. But just as important were the agents' relationships with the local officials, fire departments, and law enforcement agencies, which had developed through Secret Service investigations of financial crimes.

The relationships the field agents made in the local communities were important extensions of their investigative responsibility. The investigations had them working side by side with local officials, and the better their relationships with the locals, the more cooperation we received when we came into the area with a protectee. Because we as an agency lacked sufficient resources to do the job on our own, we depended heavily on local support and assistance.

Harvey Henderson was a good ol' Southern boy whom the other agents had dubbed the "Birmingham Baron." He was a colorful character who seemed to have been plucked right off the pages of *Gone With the Wind*, complete with a syrupy drawl, but Agent Henderson had been on the detail for a number of years and had a reputation for conducting thorough advances, so I felt I was in good hands.

The president's four-night stay in Palm Springs required a great deal of preparation and manpower to ensure his security. We went directly to the Eldorado Country Club, checked in to our rooms, and met with club management to inform them of the president's upcoming visit.

"This must be kept strictly confidential," Agent Henderson told the manager. "Tell only those you need to tell for the comfort and security of the president during his stay here."

Next, we made appointments with the Office of the City Manager and the chiefs of the police and fire departments to ensure their cooperation and assistance with the president's visit. We were asking them to take personnel off regular duties to help us secure buildings and routes of travel, and any overtime or extra resources came out of their budget. It was like inviting yourself to a stranger's home and expecting them to drop everything and cater to your every desire, no matter how big or small. Fortunately, because of the trust and respect the local Secret Service agents had earned, our hosts were eager and willing to help us every step of the way.

The list of preparations seemed endless, but Henderson showed me how to systematically go through the schedule and make the necessary arrangements. We checked out the local medical facilities; arranged with the White House Army Signal Agency (WHASA), commonly referred to as "Wasa," to provide adequate, appropriate communications for the president, staff, and the Secret Service while in the Palm Springs area; checked with the Air Force to determine exactly where Air Force One would be parked at the Palm Springs airport and verified it with the airport authorities; examined the helicopter landing site at La Quinta to ensure it was adequate and safe and made arrangements for fire department coverage; arranged for vehicles from the local Ford Motor Company dealership for the presidential party, the other agents, and ourselves; mapped out the routes from one site to the next; and, finally, arranged accommodations for the agents and staff accompanying the president.

Because this was a private visit, there were no big arrival or departure ceremonies, but still, every detail had to be in place. Agent Henderson was at La Quinta with George Allen to meet the president when he arrived by helicopter promptly at 10:30 a.m., and after dropping off bags at the residence, the president was ready to hit the golf course at Eldorado. Ike played eighteen holes each day and attended lunches and dinners with friends, but had no formal public appearances. Everything went smoothly, but it wasn't until the president boarded Air Force One in Palm Springs on Monday, February 1, that I breathed a sigh of relief. It appeared to have been an enjoyable, relaxing time for the president, with no unexpected incidents, and was important on-the-job training for me.

PRESIDENTIAL ACTIVITIES AT the White House continued at the same fast, controlled pace—appointments in and out, one after the other. Never really a lapse in activity, but everything well managed with military precision. There were frequent weekend trips to Gettysburg, during which the president spent time with his son John, daughter-in-law Barbara, and the grandchildren, who lived on an adjacent farm. A group of agents was permanently assigned to Gettysburg for the protection of the grandchildren, and they had made friends with the proprietor of a nearby motel who gave them a great deal on rates, which he passed on to the rest of us when we were in town with the president. The motel seemed to have been there since the Civil War, and while it had running water, there were the bare minimum of conveniences. The rickety beds squeaked with any little movement, the walls were thin, and you could literally see outside through the cracks in the siding. With no insulation, it was miserable during the month of August when temperatures reached 90 degrees with 90 percent humidity, and in the winter, when the wind blew through the cracks, you felt like you were going to freeze to death. The best thing about the motel was that it made every other place we stayed seem posh.

SHORTLY AFTER I returned from Palm Springs, I received a letter with the presidential seal on the envelope. Inside was a formal invitation.

I am informed that
THE PRESIDENT OF THE UNITED STATES
Dwight D. Eisenhower
has invited
Clinton Hill

to accompany him on his flight to
Cape Canaveral
on
February 10, 1960
in the Presidential jet aircraft
departing from
Andrews Air Force Base

The President, by custom, is the last member of the official party to board his airplane before take-off, and the first to leave after landing. Consequently, it will be greatly appreciated if you will be in your seat, number <u>8B</u>, as marked in the diagram by <u>8:00 a.m.</u> After landing, please remain seated until the President has departed from the aircraft.

Members of the crew will be at your service, and invite you to make your desires known to them.

I hope you will enjoy your jet flight.

If additional information regarding this flight is desired, I shall be glad to be of service. My office number is National 8-1414, extension 318 or 319.

COLONEL WILLIAM G. DRAPER, USAF
Aircraft Commander

On the back of the invitation was a diagram of the interior of the aircraft with seat 8B circled.

I boarded the aircraft promptly with the other agents on my shift and found aisle seat 8B in the rear of the plane. The jet had two rows of seats immediately behind the crew; the presidential stateroom took up a large portion of the middle of the aircraft, and then there were seven rows of seats in the rear, with two seats on each side of the aisle.

Secret Service agents filled a third of the seats, and the rest were occupied by presidential staff and military advisors.

It was a short two-hour flight from Andrews Air Force Base to the Cape Canaveral landing strip, during which the agents were briefed on the schedule. Shortly after touchdown, President Eisenhower received a one-hour classified briefing on defense missile activity, and then everyone in the presidential party donned white hard hats to tour the launching complexes. As we moved with the president, we got an education in the capabilities of the various missiles—the Titan and Atlas intercontinental ballistic missiles, the Polaris submarine missile, and the Thor space rocket. The massive size of the missiles was staggering, and the warheads on these rockets were over one hundred times more powerful than the bomb dropped over Nagasaki in 1945. President Eisenhower listened intently to the engineer's briefing, and you couldn't help but realize the extraordinary burden the president felt, knowing that the decision to use these devastating weapons would be his alone. The capability for destruction was almost incomprehensible, and just being in the presence of these weapons made me understand even more fully why President Eisenhower was so intent on using the strength of his reputation during his last year in office to promote peace through freedom. We were on the ground for just three hours, then got back on Air Force One. As we flew back to Washington, everyone was silent, seemingly in contemplation of what we had just experienced.

There was an ongoing debate between the Republicans and the Democrats about our defense policies and how much money should be spent on programs like those at Cape Canaveral, and it was important to President Eisenhower to see things for himself so he could make a strong case one way or another. But one thing I observed about President Eisenhower and his dealing with political matters was that when he had an off-the-record, closed-door meeting about Top Secret national security matters, he would frequently invite representatives of both political parties. He brought them together to discuss both sides of an issue in an attempt to reach an agreeable compromise that was in the best interest of the country, not just a partisan position. It made sense, and it made me admire him as a leader.

WE HAD BEEN alerted that the president was going to make a trip to South America beginning in late February 1960. The 15,500-mile journey would take us from Puerto Rico to Brazil, Argentina, Chile, and Uruguay. Advance teams were dispatched, appropriate immunizations were administered, and file folders filled with briefing materials were distributed to everyone on the trip. Scientific analyses had been done on the drinking water in the cities we were to visit, and it was decided that it would be prudent to bring our own supply to minimize the chances of people in the presidential party becoming ill. Hundreds of cases of Poland Spring bottled water were added to the cargo list, and we were advised to use the bottled water for brushing our teeth as well as drinking. As it turned out, once again the scheduling of the trip put me in an enviable position. I would be on the midnight shift, which would give me an opportunity to see more than just airports, speech sites, and mass crowds.

We departed the morning of Monday, February 22, 1960, from Andrews Air Force Base and flew directly to Ramey Air Force Base in Puerto Rico. Jets in those days didn't have the fuel capacity or range that they do today, so it was always necessary to stop for refueling when we were traveling long distances. Ramey was a secure location for the president to stay overnight, and, perhaps more important, it had a well-maintained eighteen-hole golf course on the property with beautiful Caribbean views. By two o'clock, Ike was teeing off with press secretary James Hagerty and two Air Force colonels.

The next morning we flew to Brasília, a city that was literally being carved out of the jungle to become the new capital of Brazil. The official changeover of the capital from Rio de Janeiro to Brasília wasn't to take place for two more months, and there was still considerable construction under way, with many buildings only half completed and roads still unpaved. It was raining when we arrived, yet along with Brazil's president, Juscelino Kubitschek, there were about five thousand people who were waiting in the downpour at the airport to greet President Eisenhower.

After a very short welcoming ceremony, the two leaders got into the back of our Lincoln bubbletop convertible, which had been transported by cargo plane, and motorcaded from the airport to the center of the city. The steady rain, however, had turned the roads into muddy rivers, making it a real challenge for the drivers not to get stuck. The majority of the city's population was construction workers—about 100,000 of them—and they had been given the day off in honor of President Eisenhower's visit. Everywhere you looked there were bulldozers, graders, and dump trucks set amid walls of gravel and deep pits where foundations were being laid.

This was just a one-night stay, and after standing midnight shift at the palace, we accompanied President Eisenhower back to the airport first thing the next morning. The day shift took over aboard Air Force One, and those of us on the midnight shift flew on the backup plane to our next stop, Rio de Janeiro.

The sun was shining brightly and it was a balmy 82 degrees when we touched down at Galeão Airport at around ten o'clock the morning of February 24. After the typical arrival ceremonies, the president boarded a motor launch and traveled by boat across Guanabara Bay to the Brazilian Navy Ministry. Meanwhile, those of us on the midnight shift went straight to our hotel near the U.S. Embassy. Our hotel happened to be very close to the famed Copacabana Beach, so as soon as we checked in, Agent Larry Short and I changed into shorts and short-sleeved shirts, grabbed a couple of towels from the hotel bathroom, and headed to the beach. It was just a few days before the start of Mardi Gras, and the beach was packed with tourists and locals, scantily clad in their beachwear. We found a spot to lay down our towels and took off our shirts to join the sun worshippers and soak up the Brazilian sun.

"Here's to the midnight shift!" Larry said with a grin.

"Yeah, we sure got the luck of the draw on this one," I said.

We later learned that while we were reveling in our good fortune of being on the midnight shift, the agents on the day shift were dealing with crowds that rivaled those we'd seen in New Delhi as President Eisenhower and President Kubitschek rode in a motorcade through downtown Rio. The streets were so full of people that the motorcade had to slow to a crawl, with the agents walking alongside the car almost the entire way.

Back at Copacabana Beach, Larry Short and I had promptly fallen asleep facedown on our towels in the sand. We'd been there for at least a couple of hours, and poor Larry, with his fair complexion and light reddish hair, was burned from head to toe. Even though I'm 50 percent Norwegian, the other 50 percent, whatever it is, saved me, and my skin was lightly bronzed, not burned at all. That evening, I felt so sorry for Larry. His back, arms, and legs were covered with blisters, and he was in such pain that he had a hard time getting dressed. You could tell he was damned uncomfortable standing post all night in his suit and tie, yet he never uttered a word of complaint.

The next morning we were headed to Buenos Aires. Overnight, while we were rotating posts around the palace, we received news that five separate bombs had just exploded in Buenos Aires in what appeared to be an anti-American manifestation. Juan Perón had recently been deposed as dictator, but he still had a lot of sympathizers who did not back the new Argentine president, Arturo Frondizi. A few weeks earlier, when the president of Mexico was visiting, protestors had thrown rocks at Frondizi and his guest as they motorcaded from the airport into downtown. Knowing that the same situation could occur during President Eisenhower's visit, the advance agents worked with Argentine law enforcement to drastically tighten security for our arrival, and instead of the standard motorcade parade, President Eisenhower flew by helicopter directly from the airport to the U.S. Embassy residence, where he would be staying.

Meanwhile, hundreds of thousands of Eisenhower supporters, undeterred by the bomb blasts on the other side of the city, had gathered along the route President Eisenhower would take later that afternoon to give a speech. By the time President Eisenhower departed the embassy residence, somewhere between 750,000 and one million people were in the streets and waiting in the plaza adjacent to Casa Rosada, where the government offices were located. It was the largest reception yet on this South American tour. Special Agent in Charge Jim Rowley rode in a half-standing position in the front passenger seat of the Lincoln bubbletop 4-B, all senses alert for any indication of trouble, while President Eisenhower stood tall, directly behind him, one hand on Rowley's shoulder and waving to the exuberant crowd with his other hand. The crowd was overwhelmingly pro-Eisenhower, waving American flags and throwing flowers and confetti into the open car, with just a few protestors here and there.

Later that evening, a large group of about five hundred protestors marched toward the U.S. Embassy residence chanting "Viva Perón!" and "Go Away, Ike!" as they ripped down American flags and banners of President Eisenhower. Fortunately the Argentine police were able to corral the agitators and keep them well back from the gates of the residence.

It was the first time I'd seen any anti-American demonstrations, and it certainly was a vivid reminder of not only the need for constant vigilance, but also how reliant we were on the host country's law enforcement and their ability to control their people.

The next day the president was scheduled to fly to the seaside resort town of Mar del Plata, spend two hours on the ground, and then fly on to San Carlos de Bariloche, where he would stay at the Llao Llao Hotel. Those of us on the midnight shift leapfrogged ahead to San Carlos de Bariloche on a U.S. Air Force C-130, and of the thousands of flights I took in my career, that was one I'll never forget. We were strapped into the belly of the airplane on bench seats—not very comfortable to begin with—but suddenly we hit extreme turbulence. First there was a jolt. Then the plane dropped, losing hundreds of feet of altitude. Then another jolt, and up we went. The plane was bouncing hundreds of feet at a time, up and down, up and down. If we hadn't been secured to our seats, there would have been bodies bouncing all over the place. Instead, many of the agents turned green and began vomiting. I found out, fortunately, that I was not prone to motion sickness, and I was one of the few who was able to hold everything in. The turbulence seemed to last forever, and I'm sure every single one of us wondered at some point if we were going to make it out alive. The pilot did an amazing job of getting us through it, however, and we finally landed.

We were all eager to get to the hotel, and when we arrived it was like we had landed at Shangri-la. The Llao Llao Hotel was a magnificent chalet-style lakeside resort nestled at the foot of the Andes, complete with—you guessed it—a golf course.

On Monday, February 29, it was on to Santiago, Chile. Chile was struggling with one of the worst cases of inflation in South America, and Chilean president Jorge Alessandri Rodríguez's austerity measures to improve the economy were not universally liked. Support for Communism was growing, and while we saw mostly enthusiastic crowds along the route from the airport into the city, several union groups had put up banners supporting Fidel Castro to send a clear message during Eisenhower's visit.

We would face a similar conflict in Montevideo, Uruguay, two days later. After the typical arrival ceremony at Carrasco Airport, the presidential motorcade proceeded into the downtown area of the capital city, which is located in the southernmost tip of Uruguay. It was a beautiful sunny day, with the temperature in the low 70s, and as we drove along the palm-tree-lined bay, thousands waved handkerchiefs and cheered at the sight of President Eisenhower standing in the back of the Lincoln convertible 4-B. It was another typically exuberant reception—until we came upon the University of Montevideo.

A group of students was standing on the roof of the School of Architecture, where they had erected two huge banners: OUT WITH YANKEE IMPERIALISM IN LATIN AMERICA and LONG LIVE THE CUBAN REBELLION.

Army trucks and police vehicles had roared ahead of the motorcade, and by the time we passed in front of the university, the police were spraying high-pressure fire hoses at the students on the rooftop. It was by far the most negative demonstration we had encountered, but with the help of the Uruguayan police, the rest of the motorcade proceeded without incident.

After a twenty-one-hour stay in Montevideo—during which I was introduced to beef and cheese fondue—we headed back to Ramey Air Force Base, where the president would have a relaxing three days reviewing the overwhelmingly positive reaction to the South American trip and, of course, playing a few rounds of golf. For me, the trip to South America was yet another eye-opening experience that showed the impact the United States had on the political and economic situations of countries far from our shores and the enormous influence wielded by our president. President Eisenhower represented all the people of the U.S.A., and there was no greater ambassador. It was a testament to his deep and profound love of his country that he was working so hard during his final year in office—not for his personal benefit, but to build the foundation for a future that rested on trust and cooperation between nations. That foundation—along with President Eisenhower's stellar reputation—was about to come crashing down in a fiery blaze.

5

Spying on the Soviets

W hen we returned to Washington after the highly successful South American trip, President Eisenhower continued to have a full agenda, but the schedule was much more predictable. I was able to spend time with Gwen and Chris, eating meals at home and sleeping in my own bed—almost like I had a normal job, with the exception that I rotated shifts every two weeks.

At this point in Eisenhower's presidency, Americans were better off economically than they ever had been before, and the world was a far safer place than it was when Ike took office. President Eisenhower had had several successful meetings with Khrushchev, so that, while the Cold War still existed, U.S.-Soviet relations seemed to be heading in the direction of compromise and peaceful coexistence leading up to the Summit Conference with Khrushchev that was set for May 16, 1960, in Paris.

President Eisenhower had authorized development of a single-engine airplane capable of flying at ultrahigh altitudes and equipped with cameras that could capture incredibly clear images on the ground 70,000 feet below. These Top Secret U-2 surveillance planes were put into use around 1956 primarily to gather intelligence on Russia's military potential, specifically its short- and long-range missile capability. This was a Central Intelligence Agency project, and because Eisenhower knew it would be politically catastrophic if an American plane was found spying in Soviet airspace, he insisted Air Force pilots not be used. Any violation of Soviet airspace would be considered a direct provocation, and for this reason he personally authorized each and every flight. By 1960, however, Eisenhower was growing increasingly apprehensive about the riskiness of using the U-2 because any discovery of the project would undermine his standing with Khrushchev. He felt we had enough information at this point and wanted the missions ceased, especially in the weeks leading up to the Summit Conference in Paris. At the urging of the CIA, however, he reluctantly authorized one final flight over Russian airspace, stipulating that it not happen any later than May 1. An experienced pilot, Francis Gary Powers, was given the assignment, and was all set to take off from Peshawar, Pakistan, at the end of April, but due to weather delays the flight didn't occur until the deadline—Sunday, May 1.

President Eisenhower was spending the weekend at Camp David with family and friends when he received word that the U-2 had gone missing. The CIA had assured the president that if the worst possible scenario had happened—that the Russians had intercepted and shot down the plane— there would be no way the pilot could survive and the plane would be destroyed upon impact. As a last resort, the pilot was supposed to activate the plane's self-destruct mechanism and take a CIA-issued suicide pill before bailing out.

The next few days, President Eisenhower conducted business as usual, virtually ignoring the incident because his advisors were confident there would be no evidence indicating the United States was conducting aerial reconnaissance over the Soviet Union.

Meanwhile, however, a Top Secret statement was dispatched to a select group of officials: "Following is a cover plan to be implemented immediately. U-2 aircraft was on weather mission originating Adana, Turkey. Purpose was study of clear air turbulence. During flight in Southeast Turkey, pilot reported he had oxygen difficulties. This last word heard at 0700Z over emergency frequency. U-2 aircraft did not land Adana as planned, and it can only be assumed is now down. A search effort is under way in Lake Van area."

Normal procedures to search for a missing aircraft were initiated by the Adana base commander, and an initial press release was sent from Adana, with no official statement from the White House. The idea was to keep the president as far removed from the incident as possible.

On Thursday, May 5, four days after the plane had gone missing, the game changed. It turned out that the Russians had indeed shot down the plane; they knew it was a spy plane; and it had been flying deep inside the Soviet Union. There was no mention of the pilot.

Everyone assumed Powers was dead, and NASA immediately sent out a press release embellishing the cover story with flight path details and conjecture that if the pilot had lost oxygen, the plane likely would have continued on automatic pilot in a northeasterly direction, which could have put the plane in Soviet airspace. President Eisenhower was fully aware of the lies being spread, but in an effort to keep the issue at a distance, he had not yet made any public statement.

The president went to his home in Gettysburg for the weekend, and on Saturday morning I was on duty as he played a round of golf with his friend George Allen at the Gettysburg Country Club. Partway through the game, a senior staff member sped up in a golf cart and pulled the president aside. I couldn't hear what was said, but I saw the reaction.

Eisenhower flew into a state of rage. Curse words spewed from his mouth, his neck veins bulged, and he was clutching his golf club so hard I thought he was going to break it in half. Whatever information had been passed to him had clearly infuriated him.

It turned out that the initial information the Soviets had released about the downing of the U-2 was not the entire story. Not only did they have remnants of the plane, but they also had the pilot, and he was alive. Premier Khrushchev had just announced that they had Francis Gary Powers in custody, and they knew everything about him, including that he worked for the CIA.

The timing couldn't have been worse. Eisenhower knew that his greatest asset going into the Paris Summit was his reputation for being honest and trustworthy. That had been obliterated. Allen Dulles, the director of the CIA, offered to resign and to make a statement that an unnamed official had acted without the authority to do so, but President Eisenhower rejected that option.

"I'm not going to shift the blame to my underlings," he said. But he was not yet ready to take full responsibility, and thus agreed to go along with a plan to continue to hedge the truth. Publicly, officials admitted that for the past four years planes of this type—civilian planes—had been flying along the frontier of the free world because of the concern of a surprise attack by the Soviet Union. The State Department admitted knowing that a U-2 plane was missing, but there was no authorization for an intrusive flight into the Soviet Union. Perhaps, in an effort to obtain information concealed from behind the Iron Curtain, an unarmed U-2 did enter Soviet airspace, unauthorized to do so. The perpetuation of the cover-up would come back to haunt the president.

Khrushchev reacted by warning that Soviet rockets would shoot down any more spy planes that ventured over Soviet soil, and his government would take "appropriate countermeasures." Eisenhower was so distraught over the situation that he contemplated resignation. With the Paris Summit just a few days away, he decided that the only option he could live with was to come out with the truth, finally. He admitted that the administration had been involved in systematic espionage and had lied, publicly, about the U-2 flights. He later said, "Incidentally, if anyone should be punished, they should punish me first." President Eisenhower was not someone who looked to blame others—he would much rather accept responsibility himself. This incident, and the way it was handled, was a good lesson that covering up something and lying about it, rather than acknowledging the truth of the matter, will cause more trouble than admitting wrongdoing at the outset. Now, with the Paris Summit just days away, he would have to confront Khrushchev with the whole world watching.

TYPICALLY, BEFORE A major international trip, President Eisenhower would issue a farewell statement, but on the evening of Saturday, May 14, 1960, as we escorted him to Air Force One at Andrews Air Force Base, he bypassed the row of press microphones, offering only a slight wave and a smile. I was one of seven agents aboard Air Force One on the overnight flight to Paris, and while the president slept in his compartment, the other agents and I went over the detailed security plans that had been sent back from the advance team. We knew the president was deeply concerned about how the U-2 fiasco would affect the sessions, so we wanted to make damn sure everything from a security aspect went flawlessly.

Shortly after arriving in Paris on Sunday, the president met with the other Western leaders—Charles de Gaulle, Konrad Adenauer, and Harold Macmillan—to prepare for the summit with Khrushchev on Monday, and while he appeared calm and cool in public, in private he was clearly anxious about what would happen when he came face-to-face with the Soviet premier.

On Monday morning, May 16, we took the president to the Élysée Palace and escorted him up a wide marble staircase to a high-ceilinged room. The agents remained outside the door, so I did not witness what occurred inside. What happened, however, was that as soon as all the leaders were present, Premier Khrushchev flew into a tirade, lambasting President Eisenhower and ranting for forty minutes straight about the U-2 incident. The Soviet premier not only withdrew his invitation for Eisenhower to visit the Soviet Union—which was supposed to take place the next month—but he demanded Eisenhower promise not to conduct any more intelligence flights over the Soviet Union and insisted the president punish all those responsible for the May 1 U-2 flight. His voice got louder and louder as he hurled insult after insult at President Eisenhower while repeating threats of retaliation against the United States as well as any allies that provided bases. In a final affront, Khrushchev suggested the summit be postponed for another six or eight months until the United States had elected a new president.

When President Eisenhower was finally able to speak, he refused to accept any ultimatum by the Soviet leader, and there were some terse words between the two, while de Gaulle and Macmillan tried to ease the tension. The meeting lasted for three hours, but the main agenda for the summit—arms control—had barely been broached. When President Eisenhower emerged from the room, he was visibly shaken, and as he walked outside the palace, with General Goodpaster by his side, the president let forth a rant of his own, calling Khrushchev every swear word in the book. I had never seen him in such a state of outrage, and it was the first time I had ever heard him use profanity off the golf course.

The summit was over before it ever began, and President Eisenhower felt the weight of responsibility on his shoulders. Everyone had had such high expectations for fruitful negotiations, but the U-2 incident had changed everything, and now it seemed that instead of heading toward peace, the world faced a dangerously uncertain future. The opportunity for real conciliation between the West and the Soviets had been lost, and Eisenhower realized it would not be regained during his tenure.

The consequences of the U-2 cover-up and his personal sense of defeat were devastating to President Eisenhower. Indeed, in an interview after he left the White House, he admitted the biggest mistake he made during his presidency was "the lie we told about the U-2. I didn't realize how high a price we were going to pay for that lie."

6

The Asian Trip

Not long after Eisenhower returned to Washington from the failed summit, Khrushchev began turning up the heat in the Cold War. At a Kremlin news conference in early June, he mocked President Eisenhower, calling him "completely lacking in willpower" and "dangerous." But more serious than his verbal attacks against Ike were his chilling threats to retaliate against any air base that facilitated U.S. spy plane activity over the Soviet Union with an immediate nuclear attack.

All plans for President Eisenhower's visit to the Soviet Union in June had been scrapped, but a tour through Asia that had been scheduled in conjunction with that visit was still on the agenda, with stops planned in the Philippines, Taiwan, Japan, and South Korea. Khrushchev's latest vitriolic rhetoric, however, was riling up Communist sympathizers, especially in Japan, where large protests were being organized against Eisenhower's visit and the Japan-U.S. security treaty that had just been signed between Ike and Premier Nobusuke Kishi. Despite concerns for his safety, the president was adamant about visiting Japan, so a pre-advance team was sent to Tokyo to evaluate the situation. The purpose of a pre-advance team is to visit the proposed venues and to confer with the host officials regarding the possible visit. They decide if the visit is feasible and worthwhile from the White House point of view before sending an advance team to make the final arrangements.

On June 10, press secretary Jim Hagerty and appointments secretary Thomas Stephens flew to Tokyo, accompanied by Secret Service agents Floyd Boring and Jack Holtzhauer. U.S. ambassador Douglas MacArthur II was there to greet them, but as the group departed the airport a frenzied mob swarmed their car. Five thousand protestors, most of whom were students armed with bamboo sticks, shouted "Goddamn Eisenhower!" and "Yankee go home!" as they surrounded the vehicle. Police were quick to get to the area, but even though they clubbed the students with heavy truncheons, they couldn't gain control of the situation. The Americans were trapped in the limousine for more than an hour until a helicopter piloted by a U.S. Marine came to the rescue. As Japanese police and the two agents formed a protective shield around Hagerty, Stephens, and MacArthur to move them from the car to the helicopter, the mob pelted them with rocks. Finally, they were able to scramble into the chopper and it flew them to safety.

We got news of the incident almost immediately, and it obviously gave the Secret Service grave concern about President Eisenhower's trip and how we could protect him if a similar situation were to occur, because when you are in a foreign country, you are really at the mercy of the local law enforcement. The president insisted on continuing the trip despite the risks, so plans moved forward, and two days later we were headed to the Far East. As the rotation worked out I was on the day shift for this trip, so I would be right in the middle of the action.

I was assigned to one of the charter planes, along with members of the press. Although not as comfortable, it was much more relaxed on the press plane than on Air Force One, and it was on these long trips that the Secret Service agents and the press really got to know one another. Many of us were about the same age—in our late twenties or early thirties—and although our jobs had two entirely different missions, we all had a keen sense of how privileged we were to be traveling with the President of the United States on these historic adventures.

Air Force One flew to Clark Field in the Philippines, where the president changed to a smaller aircraft, the propeller-driven *Columbine III*, for the flight into Manila. Meanwhile, our plane flew straight to Manila to await his arrival.

It was mid-afternoon, and as soon as I stepped out of the aircraft, I felt like I was walking into a sauna. Dressed in my normal working attire of a suit and tie, I immediately started perspiring, and soon my eyes were stinging from the droplets of sweat that streamed down my forehead. By the time the president's plane landed, I was drenched with perspiration, and I had to continually blink my eyes to be able to focus in the bright sunlight. I thought Washington summers were hot, but this was extreme. My Norwegian, North Dakota–raised blood was unaccustomed to this tropical weather.

Once the president deplaned, there was the conventional arrival ceremony: host country president meets and greets President Eisenhower, pleasantries are exchanged with members of the reception committee, the honor guard is toured, and an open car is entered for the motorcade into the city. The entrance into Manila, however, was anything but typical.

Four million people lined the route—*four million!*—the largest crowd ever before assembled in the Philippines, and the most people we in the Secret Service had ever encountered. It was a wildly exuberant atmosphere that indicated how extremely grateful the Philippine people were to President Eisenhower and the United States for all that had been done for them. Everywhere you looked there were people waving, cheering, whooping, clapping. On top of buildings and hanging out windows, people tossed streamers and threw so much confetti it was as if we were in a cloud of swirling colored paper. At street level, they were fifty to one hundred deep on either side of us, packed in so tightly that they clogged the streets right up against the presidential vehicle so that we were forced to proceed at a crawl. The motorcycle police had started in a perfect diamond formation out front, but at times they were swallowed up by the crowd that kept pressing in, trying to get close to the American hero.

The only thing we could do was walk alongside the presidential vehicle as an additional barrier between the crushing horde and the president. People were pushing and reaching to try to touch President Eisenhower as we inched forward, and we had no choice but to forcefully shove them away. The adrenaline was on overload as we scanned the millions of faces surrounding the motorcade in front, behind, around, and above for anyone who looked out of place amid the enthusiasm. But the fact was, being encircled by such a tremendous mob, if someone had wanted to cause harm to the president, there was hardly anything we could do. We were at the mercy of the local law enforcement, and they were unable to control the situation. Through it all, President Eisenhower stood, beaming, in the open-top car, taking in all the glorious admiration and respect. He appeared to have no fear, yet through much of the motorcade he kept one hand firmly on the shoulder of Special Agent in Charge Jim Rowley, who crouched like a human shield directly in front of him.

The ten-mile drive from the airport to Malacañang Palace took well over an hour, but we finally got President Eisenhower safely into his suite. All of us looked like we had been through a war—drenched with dirt and sweat, our clothes ripped and soiled—and thankful that the motorcade was over.

Meanwhile, in Japan, an entirely different scenario was taking place. As a result of the helicopter rescue of the American dignitaries in Tokyo, the Japanese government had initiated stricter security measures ahead of President Eisenhower's visit, but rather than deterring the protestors, the police reinforcements incited violent riots. Tens of thousands of Communist-led demonstrators overwhelmed the security forces, broke through the exterior gates, and besieged the Parliament buildings. Clearly, the Japanese government could not guarantee President Eisenhower's safety in this volatile environment, and just days before he was to arrive in Tokyo, Premier Kishi withdrew the invitation. While the cancellation was a relief to the Secret Service, it required the entire schedule to be revised midway through the trip.

The next stop was Formosa (Taiwan), the Republic of China island nation located one hundred miles off the coast of Communist-controlled Mainland China. When we arrived in Taipei, the weather was as stifling as it had been in Manila, with 90-degree temperatures and unbearable humidity, and yet the people had come out in droves to welcome the American president to their fortress nation. Enormous crowds lined the wide thoroughfares of the parade route, while every balcony and open window in every building was filled with people enthusiastically cheering, waving, and throwing confetti as President Eisenhower and President Chiang Kai-shek rode together in an open car into the capital city. It was like we were traveling through a Chinese carnival with dancers positioned all along the route, some waving colorful Chinese dragons, while others wore traditional costumes singing with drums and flutes. Fortunately, the boulevards through Taipei were nice and wide, and the local authorities were able to keep the masses of cheering people well contained along the sidelines. It was just the way we liked it—friendly crowds with outstanding security by the host country, which allowed us to proceed swiftly and without incident to our destination.

The timetable had been revamped, and the next day we traveled to Seoul,

South Korea, for a one-night visit, two days ahead of the original schedule. The Secret Service had flown cars to Japan in anticipation of the presidential visit to Tokyo, but when that visit was canceled, the cars were hastily transported to Seoul. This turned out to be a wise decision.

The itinerary called for a motorcade from Yongsan Golf Club, where the president had arrived by helicopter, to Kyung Mu Dai, the presidential residence. When my shift arrived in Seoul on the charter plane, we were immediately transported to the palace in three U.S. Army automobiles to establish security for President Eisenhower's arrival. Upon arrival at the palace, we were advised to park the cars outside the palace gates and proceed inside. We had a short window of time to get everyone in place, and although the communications we had were very poor, they were good enough that we were able to track the movement of the president, and we did not envision any problems.

Because President Eisenhower had played a key role in ending the Korean War, the South Koreans viewed him as a hero, and it seemed the entire country had gathered in Seoul to get a glimpse of the revered American president. Upward of one million people were crammed in the open areas along the motorcade route, cheering and shoving in a giant swarm, desperate to see President Eisenhower.

The police were unable to control the mass of humanity, and over the radio we heard the sounds of chaos as the roaring crowd inundated the vehicles in the motorcade. The situation was becoming more perilous by the minute, and in a quick-thinking move, SAIC Rowley ordered the driver to make a detour and head straight for the American ambassador's residence, bypassing the palace altogether.

Suddenly we were scrambling to get out of the palace and back into our cars to join the presidential party at the new destination. In the short time we had been inside the palace, an enormous crowd had formed outside in anticipation of the president's arrival, and a mass of people was flowing through the gates onto the palace grounds. The three vehicles we'd left parked were now surrounded by the huge throng, and there was no way we could move them.

Our shift leader, Art Godfrey, a fearless World War II veteran who had earned both a Bronze and Silver Star, was not about to let anything stand in the way of our mission. "Come on!" he yelled. "We've got no choice but to walk."

Guided by the U.S. Army agents, we began to shove our way through the sea of people on foot. It felt like we were slogging through a stampede in the wrong direction, and in an effort to get around the crowd, we jumped over fences, walked through chicken-filled yards, and even traipsed through some private homes to reach the embassy residence.

Meanwhile, one of our agents, Ron Pontius, was trapped inside the palace grounds, still trying to get out. A pair of Korean police officers on horseback rescued him and brought him to join the rest of us. As for the cars, one was destroyed when the throng of people, unable to get around it, trampled over it. The weight of thousands of people literally compacted the car nearly to the ground. The other two were battered and dented, but were able to be salvaged later.

Seoul, Korea, was one more lesson in how any crowd, even a friendly one, can easily spiral out of control when you least expect it. Even with the most diligent and thorough advance planning, you can never anticipate every possible scenario, and the key is to remain flexible, always prepared to adjust according to the situation.

Seoul was the last stop on the journey, and I know without a doubt that everyone on the trip was eager to get home. We departed Seoul at 8:15 p.m., and after flying all night and crossing the International Date Line, it was just after noon the same day when we arrived in Honolulu. It was a long flight at the end of a sixteen-thousand-mile journey with a grueling schedule, and the press noted that President Eisenhower, understandably, appeared weary as he stepped out of Air Force One.

Hawaii had officially become the fiftieth state less than a year earlier, and 100,000 people had shown up at the Honolulu airport to bid a rousing aloha to the president. Everyone on the trip was exhausted, the press included, but there was the obligatory arrival ceremony, followed by a one-hour-and-ten-minute drive to the Kaneohe Marine Corps Air Station, where President Eisenhower intended to relax for the next several days. It was my first time to Hawaii, and while the scenery was simply breathtaking, all I wanted to do was sleep.

I fully expected the president would take it easy that afternoon, but two hours after arriving at Kaneohe, no kidding, he was on the golf course. At least there were no crowds, no screaming and cheering; just the sound of the ocean breeze blowing through the palm trees and the occasional curse word after a flubbed shot.

7

The 1960
Presidential Campaign

At the beginning of the year, President Eisenhower's approval rating had been as high as 77 percent, but by June, as a result of the U-2 incident and the increased East-West tensions, it had plummeted to 50 percent. The perceived loss of respect by the American people, combined with the growing threat of nuclear war, was devastating to the president. Then, in July 1960, things went from bad to worse.

Eighteen months earlier, thirty-six-year-old Fidel Castro had overthrown the longtime dictator of Cuba, and while the United States initially recognized the new Castro regime, Eisenhower subsequently severed diplomatic relations when Castro took over American-owned oil refineries that had been operating in Cuba for fifty years. In the ensuing months, Castro had become increasingly cozy with Soviet premier Nikita Khrushchev, and on July 9, Khrushchev declared Cuba—which lies just ninety miles off the coast of Florida—a Russian satellite, threatening to use Soviet missiles against the United States "in case of necessity."

Eisenhower responded publicly with a sharp warning that the United States would not tolerate the establishment of a regime dominated by international Communism in the Western Hemisphere. Behind the scenes, he had already authorized a Central Intelligence Agency plan to train a group of Cuban refugees to overthrow the Castro regime.

At this time, the 1960 presidential campaign was starting to get into full swing, and despite the president's decline in popularity, it was widely accepted that Vice President Richard M. Nixon would have no trouble becoming the Republican nominee. For the Democrats, a young senator from Massachusetts named John F. Kennedy was rising in the polls against the other major candidates, Senate majority leader Lyndon B. Johnson of Texas and Adlai Stevenson II, the party's nominee in the previous two elections. On July 14, 1960, at the Democratic National Convention in Los Angeles, Kennedy succeeded in receiving the party's nominee for president. His decision to add his chief rival, Lyndon Johnson, to the ticket as vice president came as a shock to many, but appeared to be a shrewd move to fortify the party and strengthen the Democratic national ticket in the South.

Eleven days later, President Eisenhower flew to Chicago to attend the Republican National Convention in support of Vice President Nixon. His arrival there was as grand a reception as we had seen all over the world, with showers of confetti raining down on the motorcade as he rode through the downtown streets in an open-top car. The outpouring of respect for President Eisenhower was so phenomenal that even in the diehard Democratic areas of Chicago, people were hanging out of windows, cheering. Not surprisingly, Nixon received the nomination, with Henry Cabot Lodge as his running mate.

In the weeks before and after the convention, President and Mrs. Eisenhower vacationed in Newport, Rhode Island, staying in the commandant's house at Fort Adams. It was a nice respite, not only for the president, but for the agents as well. Even though it was termed a "vacation," the president still conducted meetings with visiting dignitaries and government officials and had daily National Security Council briefings. But no matter the situation, we could pretty much bet on eighteen holes of golf at the Newport Country Club on an almost daily basis. The ninety-two-foot presidential yacht, *Barbara Anne*—named after President Eisenhower's first granddaughter— was sailed up from Washington, and while Eisenhower had rarely used the yacht previously, he delighted in using it almost every day as transportation between Fort Adams and his office at the Newport naval base. In order to protect the president on the water, the Secret Service had several small maneuverable jet boats that we used to provide a perimeter of security around the *Barbara Anne*. A group of Navy personnel drove the boats, while one or two agents would be aboard each one, responsible for keeping other watercraft a significant distance from the presidential yacht. Growing up in Wash burn, North Dakota, my only previous experience with water activities had been swimming in the Missouri River, and now here I was zipping along the rocky Rhode Island coastline dotted with extraordinary mansions.

Between the trips to Newport, the convention, and a trip out to Denver somewhere in the middle, we had been away from Washington for a full month. It was great to get back home to Gwen and Chris, but somehow my own apartment hardly felt like home anymore. Chris had changed from a toddler into a little boy with a growing vocabulary, and Gwen had, out of necessity, become much more independent. There was always an adjustment period, and it didn't seem to be getting easier. Being away from home was part of the job. If you didn't like it, there were plenty of guys who'd jump at the chance to take your place.

On the morning of September 29, we got word that Mrs. Eisenhower's mother, Mrs. Elvira Doud, had passed away at her home in Denver. She was eighty-two years old and had been ill for quite some time, but still, the news came with the sadness that death always brings.

A very private funeral was held at Mrs. Doud's gray-brick home at 750 Lafayette Street, with just family and close friends. I was standing outside the house, keeping an eye on the crowd that had gathered across the street, when Mrs. Eisenhower came outside.

"Agents?" she called out in a soft voice, her eyes damp with tears. "I know some of you spent time here over the years. We'd like those of you who protected my mother to please join us for the service."

It was, in the midst of her grief, a surprising but thoughtful gesture that showed the type of person Mrs. Eisenhower was, and I was touched to be included.

I nodded, walked toward her, and said, "I'd be honored, Mrs. Eisenhower."

"Thank you for all you did for her," she replied with a sad smile. "She appreciated all of you so much."

The service was brief but very personal to the family, and as I stood there with my head bowed, the memories of those many nights on duty, right here in this house, swept through my mind: eating those horrible sandwiches Mrs. Eisenhower's sister Mike made for the agents; spending nighttime hours reading President Eisenhower's paperback Western novels; and, of course, the unforgettable night we carried the nurse's dead body down the stairs and quietly slipped her into the coroner's car. It had been an unusual assignment my first year in the Secret Service, and I was honored to be standing there alongside the Eisenhower family as we mourned Mrs. Doud together.

On October 14, 1960, President Eisenhower officially became the oldest U.S. president when he turned seventy. It called for a grand celebration, and someone decided it would be a good idea to invite the general public to a party on the White House lawn. The gates were thrown open, and six thousand people flooded onto the South Grounds.

When President Eisenhower emerged from the South Portico, the crowd burst into a rousing rendition of "Happy Birthday," after which he walked along the temporary fence line that had been installed, shaking hands, pinching ears, and patting heads of youngsters, and graciously accepting small gifts while trading quips with the people in the crowd.

It was a short event, and agents were spaced around the crowd, but in 1960 there were no magnetometers, no snipers on the roof, no attack dogs. Looking back now, I shudder at the thought. But those were different times. We were still living in an age of innocence.

In the weeks leading up to the election, President Eisenhower did very little campaigning for Vice President Nixon—in large part because Mrs. Eisenhower and the president's physician intervened. They were so concerned about Ike's stress level that they convinced Nixon to dissuade the president from accompanying him. In the final week, however, the race had become so close that the Republicans had to pull out all the stops, especially in New York, where forty-five electoral votes were on the table, and Kennedy appeared to have the lead. It was time to bring in the GOP's biggest asset, the President of the United States.

A daylong swing through New York was set for November 2 that included two rallies in different cities, a ticker tape parade through Manhattan ending with a rally in Herald Square, and an evening rally at the New York

Coliseum. I was one of four agents assigned to do the advance, and as we had just a few days to get all the logistics and police reinforcements lined up for each location, we had no time to spare. Special Agent Stu Knight—who would later become director of the Secret Service—was in charge, and he assigned me the motorcade and Herald Square rally.

Nixon's campaign staff had devised the general plan, and it was up to us to implement it. The motorcade would begin in the Battery at the southern tip of Manhattan and end at Herald Square at Thirty-fourth Street and Broadway—a distance of more than four miles through the canyons of high-rise buildings in the most densely populated city in America, with the president and the vice president traveling together in an open-top car. The event was scheduled for noon, a time when people would naturally be emerging from their offices to go to lunch, and with many side streets blocked off by uniformed police officers, there would automatically be a massive crowd, making it look like the entire city of New York was Republican. I was not at all familiar with New York City, but having traveled around the world with President Eisenhower, I knew this would be a security nightmare.

Fortunately, a couple of agents from the New York City Secret Service Field Office were assigned to assist me. New York was their territory, but most important, they had a great relationship with the New York City Police Department and the city's Bureau of Special Services and Investigations (BOSSI). These guys knew the city inside and out—not only the names and locations of every medical facility and specialist in case of emergency but also where potential trouble spots were throughout the city and who might stir up problems. My biggest concern was how to corral overflow crowds on the sidewalks and streets to allow the police motorcycles and the vehicles in the motorcade plenty of space to move. Two weeks earlier, Senator Kennedy had campaigned here, drawing uncontrollable crowds estimated at well over a million, in a scene similar to what we'd seen in New Delhi and Manila. It was my responsibility to make sure that didn't happen during President Eisenhower's visit.

The weather was crisp and cool on Wednesday, November 2, a perfect day for a fall parade, and New York City was abuzz. The Nixon campaign people had released the motorcade route to the press a couple of days earlier, and the crowds had started gathering up and down Broadway. Our relationship with the NYPD had paid off, and the city's entire force was called in to assist with security. Preparations started at dawn, blocking off side streets, strategically posting officers along the parade route and speech sites, and readying mounted officers on horseback for additional crowd control.

At 11:55 a.m. President Eisenhower arrived at the 30th Street Heliport, right on schedule. We whisked him to the beginning of the parade route in lower Manhattan, where a string of cars filled with dignitaries was lined up and ready to go. Tens of thousands of people packed the area, turning Wall Street into a sea of people, with NIXON FOR PRESIDENT banners and WELCOME TO OUR COUNTRY'S FIRST TEAM signs bobbing overhead. The Republican committee had supplied tons of multicolored paper to the high-rise offices, and as soon as Nixon and Eisenhower emerged, a swirling blizzard of confetti poured down from above as the crowd erupted into cheers and applause.

When I saw the president and vice president climb into the back of Secret Service car 4-B—the black presidential convertible—I jogged to the front of the motorcade. The chief of the NYPD and SAIC Al Whitaker of the New York Field Office were in the pilot car out front, and as the advance agent for the motorcade, I would ride in the front passenger seat of the lead car—the car immediately in front of the presidential limousine—guiding the long string of cars behind us.

The portable radio crackled with the voice of the supervising agent in the follow-up car: "Providence departing."

Using Eisenhower's code name, it was the signal that the president was ready.

"That's it," I said. "Let's go." A team of NYPD motorcycle officers, lights flashing, pulled out ahead of us, and the motorcade was under way.

As we traveled up Broadway, hundreds of thousands of people were jammed on the sidewalks behind police barricades, while thousands more draped themselves out of windows, hurling bucketsful of confetti as we crept along at ten miles per hour. It felt like we were driving through Times Square on New Year's Eve, and Vice President Nixon was in his glory, standing up in the back of the car, his arms outstretched to the cheering throng, getting a taste of what it would feel like to be president after having spent eight long years in Eisenhower's shadow. Sitting a few feet behind him, Ike was perched

on the backseat, waving and smiling, mindful that this was Nixon's day to be in the limelight.

The sole purpose of this parade was for the candidate to be seen by as many people as possible, and from that standpoint, it was a roaring success. From where I was sitting, this entire situation—the president and the vice president riding together in a slow-moving open-top car, in broad daylight, surrounded by a million unscreened people—could hardly have been any more tense.

Fortunately, the NYPD did an outstanding job of crowd control, and while everyone was covered in confetti, we made it without incident to Herald Square. The president gave some glowing remarks about Nixon, took a few minor stabs at Kennedy's lack of experience, and then turned the stage over to Nixon. As Nixon finished his stump speech, we got Eisenhower back in the car and drove straight to the Waldorf-Astoria, where, once the president was safely in his suite, I finally breathed a sigh of relief.

ON ELECTION DAY, Tuesday, November 8, while President Eisenhower helicoptered to Gettysburg to vote, I was assigned to secure the suite at the Sheraton Park Hotel in Washington, where Ike intended to visit vice presidential candidate Henry Cabot Lodge before giving a speech to supporters in the Grand Ballroom. If Nixon and Lodge won the election, I was instructed to remain there to protect Mr. Lodge.

At some point well after midnight, Mr. Lodge came out of the suite and said, "Agent, you might as well go home. We have lost the election."

I couldn't just leave without authorization from my supervisor, so I stayed at my post outside the door until shortly after dawn, when I got the word that I could go home. Throughout the night, I imagined what it would be like to protect the newly elected president, John F. Kennedy. I didn't know much about him other than the fact that he was a forty-three-year-old senator from Massachusetts, and would be the first Catholic president of the United States. He seemed to have a vibrant, charming personality, and surely the mere age difference between Kennedy and Eisenhower would be an adjustment.

I thought back on the twelve months I'd been on the White House Detail—the privilege of traveling all over the world, witnessing historic

events—experiences most people would never have in an entire lifetime. And in that time, those of us who made up the small group of Secret Service agents that covered the president had developed into a tight-knit team, bonded by our shared experiences. When we were away from Washington, we worked together, ate together, and often slept together in shared hotel rooms. We trusted and relied on each other like brothers. As the hours passed and I thought ahead to the future, I looked forward to being assigned to the new president.

THE DAY AFTER the election, President Eisenhower headed straight to Augusta for some post-election golf. The mood on the plane was somber, and some of the secretaries were even crying as they came to terms with the reality of their personal situation. Many had expected that Nixon would win and they would continue at the White House, but now Kennedy would be bringing in his own people. They would all have to find new jobs.

Ike played eighteen holes that afternoon, and when he was finished, Special Agent in Charge Rowley called two other agents and me into his office. Rowley explained that he needed to reassign some of the agents in order to continue covering President Eisenhower, as well as President-elect Kennedy, until the Inauguration on January 20.

Rowley told the other two guys to pack their bags and catch a flight to Palm Beach, Florida, to join the President-elect Detail. Kennedy was staying at his father's residence there, and intended to stay through the holidays as he sorted out his administration. An uneasy feeling started to come over me as Rowley was talking, and I wondered why I wasn't included and going with them.

Finally, he turned to me and said, "Clint, Defense Secretary Tom Gates is here briefing the president and is returning to Washington shortly. I want you to fly back with him, then go to Secret Service headquarters and talk to Chief Baughman. The chief is expecting you."

My heart sank. *Why? Why aren't I going to Palm Beach? Have I done something wrong? Am I being fired?* I had a dozen questions, but I simply answered, "Yes, sir."

Like the secretaries on the plane down to Augusta, I was suddenly filled with a sense of foreboding.

PART TWO

With President Kennedy

John F. Kennedy's election in 1960 coincided with the transition to a new era in American history. There was a marked difference between the outgoing Republican president—a seventy-year-old grandfather and former general—and the incoming charismatic forty-three-year-old Democrat with the attractive wife, young daughter, and new baby expected before the Inauguration.

The challenges facing this new, relatively inexperienced president were daunting, however, and he would have to prove himself. In the wake of the U-2 spy plane incident, tensions with the Soviet Union were high, and there was growing fear of the spread of Communism in the Western Hemisphere as Cuba's revolutionary leader, Fidel Castro, aligned his regime with the Soviets. Many Americans believed war with the Soviet Union was inevitable. Additionally, racial tensions were mounting—especially throughout the South—as the civil rights movement was coming to the forefront.

Kennedy would note in his Inaugural Address, "Let the word go forth from this time and place, to friend and foe alike, that the torch has been passed to a new generation of Americans."

There was a confidence in John F. Kennedy, and his vision provided a sense of hope and promise.

8

On the First Lady Detail

"How old are you, Clint?" Chief Baughman asked.

"I'm twenty-eight, sir," I replied. I was sitting in the Treasury Department office of Secret Service Chief U. E. Baughman along with his deputy chief, an assistant chief, and two inspectors, and feeling very ill at ease.

They were asking me all kinds of questions about my background, my family status, my previous work experience—and I knew they had all this information in my file. It didn't make sense. I couldn't imagine what I might have done wrong, but it felt like I was being interrogated for an investigation and I was about to be fired. And then the questions got even stranger.

"Do you have experience riding horses? Know how to play tennis? Are you a good swimmer?"

Every so often, the men would confer in a corner of the room, whispering so I could not make out what was being said, and then return with another round of questions. Finally, Chief Baughman said, "Clint, we have made a decision. You are being assigned to Mrs. John F. Kennedy."

The First Lady's Detail? Why me? I thought. I was grateful I hadn't been fired, but to be on the First Lady's Detail felt like a demotion. While those of us with President Eisenhower were traveling around the world, always on the go, I had felt sorry for the guys assigned to Mrs. Eisenhower going to tea parties and canasta games. Now that was going to be me. I was devastated.

There would be just two of us on Mrs. Kennedy's Detail—Agent Jim

Jeffries and myself—responsible for her protection around the clock, and my new assignment was to begin immediately.

WHEN I FIRST met Mrs. Kennedy on November 11, 1960, in the living room of the Kennedys' Georgetown town house, it was clear that she was not looking forward to having a Secret Service agent around her at all times, and this was going to be an adjustment for all of us. She was nearly eight months pregnant, and over the next couple of weeks she didn't leave the house very often, except to take long, leisurely walks outside each day for exercise.

President-elect Kennedy had gone to Palm Beach, where his father had a residence, to focus on the transition and the selection of his cabinet and staff, and I didn't meet him until the day before Thanksgiving, when he returned to Georgetown.

Mrs. Kennedy introduced us, and he immediately reached out his hand and gave me a firm, vigorous handshake. It was a brief meeting, but even so, I got a sense of John F. Kennedy, and it was easy to see how he had been able to connect with voters. He was charming as hell, but I also saw a man who really cared about his family as well as the people around them.

I had the opportunity to check in with the agents who had been assigned to President-elect Kennedy and had been with him down in Palm Beach for the past two weeks, and the stories they told reaffirmed my initial impression. Unlike President Eisenhower, who had referred to most of us on his detail simply as "Agent," Kennedy had taken it upon himself to learn every agent's name. Harry Gibbs told the story of how he had suddenly been dispatched to Hyannis Port when Kennedy was elected and then flew with the detail immediately to Palm Beach. He didn't have time to pack any warmweather clothing, and as soon as he landed, he was directed to stand post at the left corner of the backyard, on the seawall.

"I was standing there in my wool suit and fedora, the sweat just pouring down my face," Harry said. "The president-elect had some reading material with him outside on the patio, and he kept looking over in my direction. Finally, he got up, walked over to me, and asked me what my name was. And then he asked me why I was wearing a wool suit when it was about eighty degrees outside!" Gibbs said with a laugh.

"I told him I'd just flown in from Washington and didn't have time to change. So he suggested I move to a different spot, under a tree, where I'd at least be in the shade."

I shook my head with a grin. Kennedy clearly meant well, but obviously he didn't understand that we had specific designated posts around the perimeter of the building for a reason. Moving to a different position because you were hot or cold or wet was not an option.

"Of course I told him I couldn't do that," Gibbs said, "and then he asked how many agents were on the post at that time, and turned and walked into the house.

"When he came back out, he had a stack of short-sleeved golf shirts in his arms, in all different colors. He put them down on the ground and said, 'Pass these out to the agents with my compliments. I think you'll do a better job of protecting me if you're not uncomfortable.'"

There was no doubt this administration was going to be entirely different from the last. Our job was to protect—we had no political allegiance—but from the very beginning, the courtesy and respect with which both Mr. and Mrs. Kennedy treated all of the agents set the groundwork for what would become one of the most memorable times in not only my life, but for my colleagues' lives as well. None of us realized it at the time, but we were being swept into Camelot.

AFTER HAVING THANKSGIVING dinner with his family in Georgetown, President Kennedy departed Washington on the *Caroline*, the Kennedy family's private plane, and headed back to Florida with plans to return a few weeks later when the baby was due. As it turned out, Mrs. Kennedy went into labor that night, and I ended up at the hospital pacing the floor like an expectant father, while President-elect Kennedy immediately flew back from Palm Beach.

At 12:22 a.m. on November 25, 1960, Mrs. Kennedy delivered a healthy, six-pound-three-ounce baby boy. Thankfully, both the baby and Mrs. Kennedy were doing well, and as the nurses brought the baby out to place him in an incubator, I got my first glimpse of John F. Kennedy Jr. Four hours later, President-elect Kennedy arrived and, having just flown to Florida and back

in less than ten hours, he was a bit disheveled but anxious to see his wife and the new baby. I was standing outside her room when he arrived.

The Kennedys' firstborn son was the first child ever to be born to a president-elect, and news of the surprise, premature birth spread quickly. Members of the press were bombarding the hospital with phone calls and swarming outside the maternity wing trying to get in, but keeping the press and other intruders at bay was one of our chief concerns and priorities—not only as a matter of personal security but also as a matter of privacy.

President-elect Kennedy was overjoyed with his newborn son, and over the course of the next several days I could see the genuine care and concern he had for his wife during his daily visits. He knew me by name at this point, and before entering Mrs. Kennedy's room, he'd stop for a moment to check with me about everything that had happened since his last visit. Had she slept? Had she eaten? Everything all right with the baby?

Mrs. Kennedy was very weak following the cesarean section, and at the recommendation of her doctors she and the baby remained in the hospital for nearly two weeks. Finally, on December 9, Mrs. Kennedy was well enough to be released, and the press was invited to take photographs. I tried to stay out of the way, but managed to be caught in the background of one picture, which fortunately didn't make it into the newspapers, but that the photographer printed out a copy for me to keep for posterity. At the time I was somewhat embarrassed, but looking back, I'm so thankful for all the photos I managed to collect in this manner.

Later that same day, after taking Mrs. Kennedy to the White House for a tour of the private family quarters with outgoing First Lady Mamie Eisenhower, we were off to Palm Beach, where the Kennedys would remain until after New Year's. Already, in just a month, my new assignment with the first lady had been far from what I had expected, and surprisingly, I realized that although I wasn't going to be on JFK's detail, it was clear to me that my role was important—I was responsible for protecting the people in his life that mattered most to him: his wife and his children.

9

Palm Beach

The home at 1095 North Ocean Boulevard in Palm Beach that would be known as the Winter White House was actually owned by the president's father, Ambassador Joseph Kennedy. The 8,500-square-foot Mediterranean-style house sat on two acres of well-manicured, palm-tree-lined lawns and gardens that contained a tennis court and a swimming pool with pumped-in salt water, all with a breathtaking view of the Atlantic Ocean. I had never seen such a luxurious private home before, but to the Kennedys, this was just another place for the family to gather: their warm-weather getaway.

Meanwhile, all of the agents on the White House Detail required accommodation as well, so one of the supervisors had negotiated good rates at a place in West Palm Beach, about twenty minutes away, called Woody's Motel. Woody's wasn't fancy, but it had a small swimming pool in the center of the U-shaped structure, the rooms were air-conditioned, and it fit our meager budgets. At that time, our per diem allowance was $12, out of which we had to pay for our room, meals, dry cleaning, laundry, and miscellaneous expenses. To save money, many of us shared rooms.

I would arrive at the ambassador's residence at around eight o'clock each morning to be there before Mrs. Kennedy arose, but because she was still quite weak, she spent most of the days resting—often sunbathing by the swimming pool—and rarely leaving the grounds, so I spent a good deal of time standing by in the command post. I had missed the camaraderie of being on the larger detail with the president—especially after two weeks on duty at Georgetown Hospital—so it was enjoyable for me to be back with the other agents in the central hive of activity.

One of the things I learned was that President-elect Kennedy had been receiving a lot of hate mail—much of it due to the fact that he was Catholic—and for that reason all letters and packages sent to the Kennedys were diverted to Washington for examination. The previous week, several letters had come to our attention—letters written by a man in New Hampshire in which he threatened to kill President-elect Kennedy by turning himself into a "human bomb." The man had sold all his possessions in New Hampshire and had gone missing, and now an intensive search was under way, but no one knew where or when he might show up.

The first Sunday after our arrival in Palm Beach, President-elect Kennedy had informed the supervising agent that he was planning to attend ten o'clock Mass at St. Edward's Roman Catholic Church, the parish church in Palm Beach, and that Mrs. Kennedy would not be going along. When the president-elect emerged from the house, however, Mrs. Kennedy and their three-year-old daughter, Caroline, walked out with him and, at his urging, walked with him to the front gate to wave to the small group of people that were waiting outside, hoping to catch a glimpse of the family. Mrs. Kennedy obliged, and the people were thrilled to see the president-elect's wife and daughter even for just a moment. The people waved and hollered out to President-elect Kennedy as he rode off in a white convertible with a Secret Service agent at the wheel and several others in a car following closely behind, while Mrs. Kennedy and Caroline retreated back to the house, behind the high walls that surrounded the property.

Four days later, Palm Beach police found the person behind the threatening letters—a seventy-three-year-old mentally ill man named Richard Pavlick, who was staying in a West Palm Beach motel. He was arrested when the cops found dynamite, detonating caps, and battery wiring in his car and still more bomb-making material in his motel room. It turned out that Pavlick had been sitting in his car down the street from the Kennedy residence the previous Sunday as President-elect Kennedy was leaving for church, and had planned to ram his car into the president's vehicle—setting off the bombs to kill them both. But when Mrs. Kennedy and Caroline came out with JFK, Pavlick couldn't do it—and he decided to wait for another opportunity when the president-elect was alone.

Knowing how close we had come to an assassination attempt even before Kennedy was inaugurated was a strong reminder that an attack could come anytime, anywhere. It wasn't just in motorcades or on official trips that you had to be cautious. Anytime we left the confines of a secured residence, there was the possibility that something could happen. And it was someone like Richard Pavlick that worried us most: someone acting alone, either mentally unstable or simply a delusional loner hoping to make a name for himself—or herself—by killing a president.

EVEN THOUGH THE homes in Palm Beach and West Palm Beach were decorated with lights and store windows were filled with Santa displays, being in that tropical climate didn't feel like Christmas to me. It was tough on all the agents being away from our families, but we made the best of it.

Shortly after New Year's, SAIC Jerry Behn came to me and said, "Clint, the president-elect and Mrs. Kennedy have decided they won't bring Caroline and John back to Washington for the Inauguration. They will be staying here with Miss Shaw, and we have decided to have you stay here in Palm Beach to supervise their security."

I hadn't seen this coming, and I felt like I'd been punched in the gut. While all the other agents were witnessing history, playing an important role in the transfer of power, I was relegated to the Kiddie Detail.

On Inauguration Day, I joined the children's nanny, Maud Shaw, and Caroline inside Ambassador Kennedy's residence to watch the live coverage on television. Caroline was more interested in finger painting than watching her father take the oath of office, so she didn't pay much attention, but I watched the ceremony from start to finish, all the while wishing I were there.

I could see U. E. Baughman, the outgoing chief of the Secret Service, seated just behind the president on one side, and SAIC Jim Rowley—who would soon become chief—on the other as President Kennedy made an impassioned plea for our nation's citizens to ask not what the country could do for them but what they could do for their country. As the president stepped away from the podium, the audience rose to its feet and burst into thunderous applause. The torch had been passed.

I STAYED IN Palm Beach for two more weeks while the children's rooms were being redecorated in the White House, and finally, on Saturday, February 4, 1961, we brought John and Caroline back to Washington on the *Caroline*. Three agents were assigned to the children full-time, and I returned to Mrs. Kennedy's detail with Agent Jeffries.

During her stay in the hospital, Mrs. Kennedy had informed me that she had rented a home in Middleburg, Virginia—an eighteenth-century colonial with a swimming pool and riding stables on four hundred acres of rolling hills in hunting country—which she intended for the family to use as a weekend getaway from Washington. The estate was called "Glen Ora" and the Kennedy family's use of it resulted in some major expenses on the part of the Secret Service as well as other government agencies: the Secret Service had to call in agents from around the country on a temporary basis to help maintain perimeter security, while the White House Police provided civilian-clothed personnel to man the checkpoints; assistance was required from the General Services Administration and the military services for guard booths placed strategically around the property; emergency fire suppression equipment had to be available when helicopters arrived and departed; communication equipment had to be installed for both the Secret Service and the president so that he would have ready access as if he were in the Oval Office; and finally, additional electrical lines had to be installed to provide adequate power and lighting for all these services.

Beginning in early February 1961, Mrs. Kennedy spent almost every weekend in Glen Ora with the children. Often, she would stretch the time from Thursday to Monday, depending on her obligations in Washington, while the president—who wasn't as enamored with the place—would fly in by helicopter on Saturday and leave Sunday after attending Mass at the Middleburg Community Center. It started off that I would drive the fifty miles back home each evening, but when the trips became a weekly occurrence and the weekends stretched into three or four days, I ended up renting a room in a private home nearby on a semipermanent basis.

As a matter of security, code names were used for all radio communication. Each group of people had names beginning with the same letter to make them easier to remember, and each location was given a code name as well. The White House was "Crown," Camp David was "Cactus," and Glen Ora became "Chateau."

The code names given to the Kennedys all began with the letter "L." JFK was "Lancer," Mrs. Kennedy was "Lace," Caroline was "Lyric," and John was "Lark."

Not every Secret Service agent had a code name—the shift agents didn't really need them—only the supervisors who would be using radios did, and they all began with the letter "D." When I started on Mrs. Kennedy's detail, they gave me the name "Dazzle." I don't know who came up with it or why, but it stuck, and I had it for the rest of my career.

The first weekend of April 1961 was Easter, and I had learned that, as with Christmas and New Year's, tradition was for the Kennedy family to spend Easter weekend in Palm Beach, so that's where we headed. With tensions rising in Laos and Cuba, President Kennedy spent much of the weekend meeting with advisors. News photographers were invited to the ambassador's residence for an update, and I was one of the agents on duty at the time. I stood off to the side of President Kennedy and Secretary of State Dean Rusk where they were seated on the patio and kept a watchful eye on the reporters as they asked questions and snapped a few photos.

The next morning I was dismayed to see that I figured prominently in the Associated Press wire photo that was sent to newspapers across the country. As a Secret Service agent, the whole idea is to remain as anonymous as possible, but there I was, standing with my arms folded, dressed in a loud, short-sleeved floral print shirt; and while my eyes were hidden behind dark sunglasses, there was no mistaking it was me. My mother was thrilled to see her boy "Clinton" in the *Bismarck Tribune* with the president, but I sure got a ribbing from the other agents about it.

President Kennedy found it amusing too. "You'll have to find a better disguise from now on, Clint," he teased. "Back to the suit and tie, I suppose."

The weekend of April 15 and 16 seemed like any other, with Mrs. Kennedy going to Middleburg on Friday and the president arriving by helicopter Saturday afternoon, accompanied by his sister Jean Kennedy Smith and her husband, Stephen Smith. The president seemed relaxed—even joining his wife at the Middleburg Hunt races—and while there were lots of phone calls from Washington, which he took privately, nothing in his demeanor gave hint to the disaster that was unfolding in Cuba and the heavy decisions he was forced to make.

Two years earlier, Fidel Castro's guerrilla fighters had taken over the Cuban government, overthrowing dictator Fulgencio Batista. Initial enthusiasm for Castro faded quickly, however, as Castro embraced Communism and aligned himself with the USSR, which led thousands of Cubans to flee to southern Florida. Tensions escalated between the U.S. government and Cuba to such a degree that in January 1961, just weeks before Kennedy's inauguration, President Eisenhower had severed diplomatic ties with Cuba and closed the U.S. Embassy in Havana.

Now, three months into John F. Kennedy's presidency, there were reports that low-flying aircraft had bombed Cuba's three major airports, and Fidel Castro was accusing the United States of being behind the attacks. In an emergency session of the United Nations Political Committee, U.S. ambassador Adlai Stevenson denied U.S. involvement and claimed that, "to the best of our knowledge," the B-26 planes "were Castro's own air force planes."

In fact, the raid was part of a CIA operation that had been hatched under Eisenhower, and to which President Kennedy—after wrestling with the moral and political decision—had given the green light. For months Cuban exiles had been secretly training under American supervision in Guatemala for a planned attack on Cuba, with the intention of overthrowing Castro and inserting a new government headed by politically active—and U.S.-friendly—Cuban exiles. To make the raid appear like an internal Cuban uprising, obsolete World War II B-26 bombers were painted to look like Cuban air force planes, but one had been shot down, and the evidence pointed to U.S. involvement.

Meanwhile, 1,400 American-trained Cuban exiles—known as Brigade 2506—had moved from Guatemala to Nicaragua and were headed for Cuba by boat. A second round of air strikes was planned to occur simultaneously with the brigade's landing on beaches in the *Bahía de Cochinos*—the Bay of

Pigs—but when the link to the United States was discovered after the first air assault, President Kennedy canceled the second round of strikes. So when the brigade landed on the beaches, Castro was ready for them with an army of twenty thousand, and with no further air strikes to assist the exiles on the ground, more than one hundred of the rebels were killed and the rest were captured.

On Monday morning, April 17, President and Mrs. Kennedy departed Glen Ora by helicopter and returned to the White House. I did not know it at the time, but President Kennedy was receiving reports throughout the day of the disaster that was unfolding as the ill-prepared Cuban rebels confronted Castro's army. President Kennedy, knowing he had sent all those brave men either to their deaths or to certain imprisonment, managed to hide his anguish behind a mask of diplomacy and composure as he kept to previously scheduled engagements, which included hosting the visiting prime minister of Greece, Konstantinos Karamanlis, and his wife at a luncheon and formal state dinner that evening.

Over the next couple of days, the botched Bay of Pigs invasion had reverberations that threatened to turn into a world war. Russia's Premier Khrushchev was pledging to provide Cuba with whatever military or economic support it needed to defend against what appeared to be a U.S. invasion. Still, President Kennedy vehemently denied involvement, and in a terse message to Khrushchev, he wrote, "I have previously stated, and I repeat now, that the United States intends no military intervention in Cuba."

On Thursday, April 20, President Kennedy used a speech at the American Society of Newspaper Editors to make a statement about the Cuba situation, discussing it in context of general U.S. policy. He again reiterated that he had not committed U.S. troops—and would not involve our military—because unilateral intervention would violate international obligations. For this reason, his administration was following a "policy of restraint" out of concern that any move against Cuba would likely incite Khrushchev to act against West Berlin. Not wanting to appear weak, however, he stated, with a tone of defiance, "Let the record show that our restraint is not inexhaustible. . . . I want it clearly understood that this government will not hesitate in meeting its primary obligations, which are to the security of our nation."

The following day, President Kennedy held a press conference to discuss a number of issues but declined to answer questions on Cuba, citing national security. This did not satisfy NBC News reporter Sander Vanocur, who pressed the president to provide more information. In what appeared to be an admission of involvement and indeed of failure, President Kennedy responded, "There's an old saying that victory has one hundred fathers and defeat is an orphan." Choosing his words carefully, he added, "I will say to you, Mr. Vanocur, that I have said as much as I feel can be usefully said by me in regard to the events of the past few days. Further statements, detailed discussions, are not to conceal responsibility because I'm the responsible officer of the government—and that is quite obvious—but merely because I do not believe that such a discussion would benefit us during the present difficult situation."

Without admitting the invasion was indeed a U.S.-backed operation, President Kennedy took full responsibility, and while he maintained his composure in public, privately you could see that this fiasco—the first major decision of his presidency—had shaken his confidence. On April 22, he invited President Eisenhower to join him at Camp David. The two met alone in one of the guest cabins for nearly an hour and a half, and when they emerged, they spoke briefly with a group of reporters and photographers. Neither the current nor former president revealed the nature of what was discussed, but when reporters asked Eisenhower whether he approved of President Kennedy's stand on Communist-oriented Cuba, Ike—undoubtedly remembering all too vividly a similarly difficult position he himself had been in a year earlier—replied, "I say I am all in favor of the United States supporting the man who has to carry the responsibility for our foreign affairs."

Clearly, the new, young president realized the former general had many more years of wisdom, and although he represented the opposing political party, was truly the one person in the world who could offer substantive advice and in whom Kennedy could confide. There was no further military escalation, but President Kennedy had to live with the knowledge that one hundred lives had been lost, and the surviving members of Brigade 2506 were suffering in captivity.

10

Traveling with the Kennedys: Europe

Around the time the Bay of Pigs disaster was unfolding, Mrs. Kennedy informed me that she was going to be joining President Kennedy on his first presidential trip to Europe, with stops in Paris, Vienna, and London. Additionally, Mrs. Kennedy had decided to tack on a personal vacation to Greece at the end of the official trip. This news came as somewhat of a surprise because Mrs. Eisenhower had rarely traveled internationally with Ike, and I assumed Mrs. Kennedy—especially with two young children—would not be traveling much either. I was extremely pleased when I was assigned to handle the advance—first in Paris and then, while she and the president went to Vienna, I would fly ahead to Athens to conduct the advance for her trip there.

Shortly before I departed for Paris, I got word that President Kennedy wanted to see me in the Oval Office. I had never been summoned to the Oval Office before; this was highly unusual. When I walked in, I was surprised to see not only the president but the attorney general—his brother Bobby—standing with him.

"Clint," President Kennedy said, "I understand you will be doing the advance for Mrs. Kennedy in Greece."

"Yes, Mr. President," I answered. "That's what I have been advised."

President Kennedy glanced at the attorney general and then looked back at me.

"The attorney general and I want to make one thing clear . . . and that is, whatever you do in Greece, do not let Mrs. Kennedy cross paths with Aristotle Onassis."

At the time, I had no idea why he would make such a request, but I simply answered, "Yes, sir, Mr. President."

A TEAM INCLUDING White House press secretary Pierre Salinger, presidential aide Ken O'Donnell, and Secret Service director Jim Rowley had flown to Paris for a two-day pre-survey trip, during which they decided the agenda, the accommodations, protocol, and general security. They made connections with our French counterparts, returned to Washington, laid out the framework, and then it was up to the advance teams to do all the work.

President Kennedy's main purposes for the visit were to get acquainted with President Charles de Gaulle; to promote greater unity within the Atlantic Alliance, the military partnership between the United States and Europe; and to seek common policies on disputes between the Soviet Union and the West. Meanwhile, Mrs. Kennedy and her social secretary, Tish Baldrige, had planned an elaborate schedule for her that overlapped with the president's only for official functions. My biggest concern was that I didn't speak a word of French, so I was fortunate that Tish, who spoke fluent French, would be with me on the advance. When we arrived in Paris along with the president's advance team, we had only about a week to coordinate the thousands of details that go into a state visit. Everyone had their roles—security, press, communications, transportation—and we all worked long days to make sure this important visit went off without a hitch. I don't think the general public has any idea what goes into planning a presidential visit, and it was on this trip—my first overseas advance—that I gained a tremendous amount of respect for the guys in the White House Army Signal Agency.

The WHASA team had gone over with the pre-survey group, and over the span of a few weeks they were tasked with preparing a complex telephone system that would serve the president, his staff, and the Secret Service while we were in Paris. Each of us would have a special telephone that was connected to all other extensions of the visiting party in Paris, but also connected directly to the White House switchboard in Washington. I had a room in the Quai d'Orsay, the headquarters of the Foreign Ministry, where

President and Mrs. Kennedy would be staying, while the majority of the entourage—including more than one hundred White House correspondents and photographers and the majority of the Secret Service agents—would stay in nearby hotels. At each of these hotels and at the Quai d'Orsay, WHASA set up switchboards operated by their personnel, and when someone called, the switchboard operator would answer, "Paris White House." Thinking back now, with the kinds of technology—or lack thereof—that we had back then, the work they accomplished was nothing less than brilliant.

As we conducted the advance, it became clear that the government of France wanted not only President Kennedy to be seen by as many people as possible but Mrs. Kennedy as well. Due in part to the pre-visit media campaign organized by Pierre Salinger, much was being made of Mrs. Kennedy's affection for the country and the fact that her father's ancestors—the Bouviers—hailed from France.

A grand motorcade procession was planned for President and Mrs. Kennedy's arrival, in which President Kennedy and President de Gaulle would ride together in an open-top limousine. The wives would follow in a car with a hardtop, under the assumption that the ladies wouldn't want to risk rain or wind messing up their hair.

Tish Baldrige and I were in a meeting when one of the French officials seemed to be distressed about something. I looked at Tish, questioning what was being said, and she interpreted for me.

"He says the people of France are just as eager to see Madame Kennedy as well as her husband. Hundreds of thousands of people will be lining the streets of Paris, and they will surely be disappointed if Mrs. Kennedy is not visible."

An idea suddenly struck me. "It would be ideal to have a bubbletop like our Secret Service car 4-B," I said to Tish.

Tish translated, and the French officials loved the idea so much that they decided to take a new Citroën sedan, cut off the metal top, and insert a Plexiglas roof in its place, thus giving Mrs. Kennedy maximum exposure as she traveled to various venues in Paris. I was impressed by their desire to do everything possible to make this a memorable visit, and even more impressed that, within days, they had created the Citroën bubbletop.

Meanwhile, back in Washington, an army of specialists in the State Department was also working long hours to prepare extensive briefings for the president, his staff, and the traveling press. When the president arrived in Paris, he would know specifics about the current condition of France's social, economic, political, and military situations, as well as the names and backgrounds of President de Gaulle's top advisors.

President and Mrs. Kennedy arrived in Paris on the morning of May 31, and the French put on an incredible spectacle that rivaled any state visit I had ever seen for President Eisenhower. There was a full military ceremony at the airport, followed by a motorcade through the streets of Paris that included more than one hundred police motorcycle escorts and another hundred Republican Horse Guards in full military regalia.

It was estimated that *two million* Parisians lined the streets. There were people hanging out windows and packed on balconies, and the wide boulevards of the city were filled with people holding welcome signs and cheering *"Vive le présidente Kennedy!"* But even more frequently you would hear voices in the crowd yelling *"Vive Jac-qui! Vive Jac-qui!"*

In the past, first ladies were seen but seldom, if ever, heard. Here in Paris, Mrs. Kennedy accompanied the president to the Hôtel de Ville—Paris's City Hall—helping to translate for her husband when he met with French officials, and at the spectacular white-tie dinner at Versailles, as she conversed in French with the notoriously surly President de Gaulle, there was no doubt she helped ease relations between the two men. At one point during the trip, President Kennedy appeared at a luncheon for four hundred journalists and said, "I do not think it altogether inappropriate to introduce myself. I am the man who accompanied Jacqueline Kennedy to Paris. And I have enjoyed it."

The two-country summit in Paris was reported as an enormous success, and representatives from both France and the United States stated publicly that after six in-depth meetings between Kennedy and de Gaulle, the relationship between our two countries was stronger than ever.

From Paris I went directly to Athens, Greece, while President and Mrs. Kennedy flew on to Vienna for a summit with Premier Khrushchev. I was not in Vienna, but by all accounts afterward, the meetings between Kennedy and Khrushchev were a disaster for President Kennedy. Coming just six weeks after the Bay of Pigs fiasco in Cuba as they did, the president needed to show that he was up to the task of leading America on the world stage. Just the opposite happened. Instead, Khrushchev took the opportunity to lecture President Kennedy on U.S. foreign policy and warned him about surrounding the Soviet Union with military bases.

By treaty we had free access from West Germany to West Berlin, deep inside East German territory. The Communists wanted to stop the exodus of East German people and skilled manpower passing freely into West Berlin and beyond into West Germany by signing a peace treaty with East Germany that would impinge on Western access to Berlin. Khrushchev threatened that our resistance could lead to war.

Indeed, after the failed summit, both sides made sudden and dramatic moves that had perilous implications. The U.S. Congress approved an additional $3.25 billion in defense spending, a tripling of the draft, a call-up of the reserves, and a strengthened civil defense program. The Soviets resumed above-ground nuclear tests and began building the Berlin Wall. The following year, they would begin installing nuclear missiles in Cuba.

It was a sober lesson for President Kennedy—that in a dangerous world, the perception of weak American leadership can embolden our enemies to take aggressive action. Khrushchev came away with the opinion that the new American president was weak and inexperienced, while President Kennedy, in an interview with James Reston of the *New York Times*, said the summit meeting had been "the roughest thing in my life."

Meanwhile, Mrs. Kennedy had become a star on the world stage, which made protecting her all the more challenging. Her trip to Greece had been highly publicized, and as soon as she arrived people would swarm around us, trying to get close to her. After touring the historic sites in Athens with intrusive crowds following her every step, she decided to spend the rest of her holiday in the seaside town of Kavouri. She stayed in a private villa, where we also had use of the owner, Markos Nomikos's, private yacht, the *Northwind*. It was on this trip that I began to realize being on the first lady's detail wasn't nearly as bad as I had envisioned it would be.

I never did figure out a good explanation for President Kennedy's request to keep Mrs. Kennedy away from Aristotle Onassis other than the fact that

Mr. Onassis had been in legal trouble with the United States, and perhaps the president was concerned about repercussions should the press have gotten photos of Onassis and Mrs. Kennedy together.

On that trip in 1961 however, Mrs. Kennedy did not cross paths with Aristotle Onassis.

11

Hyannis Port

Just as Ambassador Kennedy's residence in Palm Beach became the Winter White House, the Kennedy compound in Hyannis Port, Massachusetts, became the Summer White House. I had never been to Cape Cod before, but it didn't take long for me to fall in love with this New England beach haven, about seventy miles from Boston, where the extended Kennedy family spent their summers. The centerpiece for the family's gatherings was Ambassador Kennedy's home—a large, rambling, white-shingled house with a huge front porch that overlooked an expansive lawn that became the playing field for football games as well as the landing pad for the presidential helicopter. Behind the main house were three smaller homes in the same Cape Cod style, which belonged to JFK, Eunice Kennedy Shriver, and Robert Kennedy. There was always something going on—touch football, water-skiing, swimming, tennis, golf, sailing. I had never seen such a close family, or a family with so much energy and competitiveness. And there I was, right in the middle of it all.

We set up the Secret Service command post in a little guest cottage between Bobby's and the president's houses. From noon on Mondays to noon on Fridays, the president would be in Washington, while Mrs. Kennedy, John, and Caroline stayed in Hyannis Port.

At noon on Friday, the whole routine changed. For the next forty-eight hours, activity on the compound was at its maximum. Almost like clockwork, President Kennedy would arrive at Otis Air Force Base on Air Force One. From there he would transfer to an Army or Marine helicopter—military green with a white top, denoting it was a presidential chopper—and fly to Hyannis Port, landing in the front yard of Ambassador Kennedy's residence.

The helicopter arrival was a huge event for the children. The kids would all come running when they heard the distinctive sound of the rotors getting louder and louder overhead. As soon as the chopper touched down, the door would open and the president would bound down the steps. Caroline would be first in line, followed by all her cousins, running to meet him. President Kennedy would be laughing, a look of sheer joy on his face, as if the sight of the children and his beloved Hyannis Port made all the worries of his office disappear for one brief moment. We would have a golf cart waiting in the driveway, and he'd go straight for it, hop behind the wheel, and yell, "Anyone for ice cream?"

Ten or twelve kids would pile onto the cart, and the president would take off down the driveway, a huge grin on his face as he cut across the lawn behind Bobby's house in an effort to lose the Secret Service follow-up car. He'd end up at the tiny News Store, where he'd buy ice cream cones for all the children.

Lunchtime cruises were almost a daily event—either on the *Marlin*, Ambassador Kennedy's fifty-two-foot motor yacht, or the presidential yacht (previously the *Barbara Anne*), which Kennedy had renamed the *Honey Fitz* after his maternal grandfather, who had been given the nickname "Honey Fitz" because of his personal charm and charisma. We would create a security perimeter around the yacht consisting of one or two Coast Guard boats and two Navy jet boats, all operated by military personnel under the direction of the Secret Service agents on board. I always worked one of the speedy jet boats, and I have to say that some of my best and happiest memories are of those weekends in Hyannis Port.

Frequently, the president would sail the *Victura*, the twenty-five-foot Wianno Senior sailboat his parents gave him for his fifteenth birthday. He loved that boat. He could maneuver it with such grace and ease that it was almost like it was an extension of himself. We would surveil him and prevent anyone from venturing too close, but basically he was on his own, with no telephones, no advisors, nothing to interrupt an hour or so of respite from the enormous responsibility that comes with being President of the United States.

One day, the president and his good friend Chuck Spalding were sailing the *Victura* close to shore, just off the dock from the ambassador's residence. They were in the midst of a deep conversation and didn't realize they were coming upon some rocks. Suddenly, the boat stopped dead in the water as it got wedged between the rocks.

I was in a jet boat nearby, watching the scene unfold, fully expecting the president to get the boat moving again with ease, but the boat wasn't budging. President Kennedy dropped the mainsail to let the wind out of it, stood up, and turned toward me.

"Hey, Clint, can you give us a little help? We seem to be stuck."

"I'll be right there, Mr. President," I said as I jumped into the water.

We were so close to shore that the water was only up to my thighs, so I waded over to the stuck sailboat. I couldn't tell what the problem was, due to the glare on the water, so I took a deep breath and went under the boat. Sure enough, the hull was wedged in between two good-sized boulders.

"Looks like you're wedged in between two big rocks, Mr. President," I said. "Let me see if I can rock the boat to get it moving. You may want to sit down."

The president laughed and said, "Good idea. But I'm more concerned about the boat than Chuck and myself."

I placed my feet on top of one of the boulders and squatted with my back against the bottom of the hull. "Hang on, Mr. President," I said. "Here we go."

I began to rock up and down, and as the boat started to move I gave one big thrust upward with my body while simultaneously pushing down with my legs. As I did so, the *Victura* slid off the rocks, causing my feet to slip down each side of the rock on which I was standing. The rock was shaped somewhat like a cone, and that final thrust caused me to go straight down, with the cone-shaped rock crashing into my groin area.

I gritted my teeth to keep from yelling out in pain as the president immediately raised the sail and turned the tiller, allowing the boat to slowly glide away.

"Thanks, Clint!" the president called back to me, unaware of what had just occurred under the water.

"No problem, sir," I replied. "Glad I was able to help."

I walked gingerly through the water back to the jet boat, and as I climbed over the side I noticed blood running down my legs. I had almost crushed a very important part of my anatomy. Pained and bloody, I continued on for the rest of the day.

I didn't realize that Cecil Stoughton, one of the White House photographers, happened to catch the ordeal on film, and apparently word got back to the president that I had been injured. A few days later I received an 8-by-10 photo of the president and Chuck Spalding standing on the *Victura* as I waded through the water toward the stuck boat. The president had signed the photo with the inscription:

> *For Clint Hill*
> "*The Secret Service are prepared for all hazards*"
> *John F. Kennedy*

There was always some kind of activity going on, including those legendary football games on the lawn. Somebody would start rounding up players and picking teams, and I'd get a call at the command post from Bobby or Teddy.

"Clint, come on down here. We need another guy for our team."

They treated me just like one of them—almost like part of the family. I thoroughly enjoyed it—not just for the sport, but also because it gave me the opportunity to occasionally throw a good hard block across certain family members. It was all in good fun.

The typical routine was that President and Mrs. Kennedy would go to Newport, Rhode Island, after Labor Day to spend time with Mrs. Kennedy's mother, Janet, and stepfather, Hugh Auchincloss. The Auchinclosses had a large home with a dock overlooking Narragansett Bay, and the presidential yacht would be sailed from Hyannis for the family to use. The weather in the fall could be unpredictable, though, and fog was sometimes a problem.

So it was in late September 1961 when I was trying to fly from the Newport area to Washington to be at Gwen's side as she went into labor with our second child. Fog had blanketed the entire area, and hard as I tried, I could not get there before our son Corey Jonathan was born.

It might have appeared that President Kennedy was on vacation whenever he was in Hyannis Port, Newport, or Palm Beach, but in reality the responsibility of the job never leaves the occupant of the Office of the President. That summer of 1961, there were myriad serious international and domestic issues. First, the Soviets, together with the East Germans, had begun to tie a noose around West Berlin—tightening the borders and building a wall that divided Berlin. In response, the United States promptly called up some 150,000 reservists to active duty and sent 40,000 regular Army troops to Europe. Cuba remained a major concern, and the situation in Southeast Asia, including Laos, Cambodia, and Vietnam, was heating up. Domestically, attempted hijackings of commercial airliners necessitated the placing of armed federal personnel on board some flights as air marshals, while segregation problems continued throughout the South. There is no such thing as a presidential vacation.

12

Traveling with
the Kennedys:
South America and Mexico

In March 1961, a month before the Bay of Pigs fiasco, President Kennedy had initiated an ambitious program called the Alliance for Progress that would provide $20 billion in aid to promote economic development, social progress, and political freedom in Latin America. On December 15, 1961, he and Mrs. Kennedy set off on a whirlwind goodwill trip to South America.

The first stop was San Juan, Puerto Rico. A month earlier, President and Mrs. Kennedy had hosted Puerto Rican governor Luis Muñoz Marin at the White House with a historic performance by legendary cellist Pablo Casals, and the governor was happy to have the opportunity to reciprocate. Nearly a quarter of a million people lined the motorcade route chanting "Viva President Kennedy! Viva President Kennedy!"

This was just a one-night visit, and early the next morning we were off to Caracas, Venezuela. Everybody was a bit on edge as we headed to Caracas. In May 1958, then Vice President Richard Nixon and his wife, Pat, had taken a tour of Latin America, and when they arrived in Caracas, they were met by a high level of anti-American sentiment. Pro-Communist supporters spat at Nixon, and at one point during the motorcade through the city an angry mob surrounded the vice president's car and began throwing stones and bashing it with clubs. Secret Service agents used their bodies to shield the vice president, and eventually, with the help of Venezuelan security, Nixon's driver managed to speed away. The vice president and his wife were unharmed, but understandably terrified. Now, just three and a half years later, we had received intelligence that leftist contingents—most likely affiliated with Castro—were threatening Kennedy's visit with violent protests.

Our advance team and security officials in Venezuela assured us that they had assembled the most massive security forces ever in that country for such an occasion, but still, when you're going into that type of environment, it puts everyone on edge. One thing in our favor were erroneous newspaper reports that the U.S. Secret Service was bringing two "bulletproof limousines." In fact, we did not have any bulletproof cars at that time, but our philosophy was: let them believe what they want to believe. What we did have was "SS-100-X," a midnight blue Lincoln convertible that had been specially designed for presidential motorcades, but it was not armored. We did not correct the reporters.

When we arrived at Maiquetía International Airport in Caracas on December 17, 1961, there was a huge, very enthusiastic crowd, and no anti-American demonstrators in sight. Venezuelan president Rómulo Betancourt had ordered thirty thousand soldiers and five thousand police to stand six feet apart along the twenty-seven-mile motorcade route, which was undoubtedly a deterrent to would-be troublemakers, and which we in the Secret Service greatly appreciated. Hundreds of thousands of people lined the parade route cheering "Bienvenidos, Presidente Kennedy!" And just as often, "Jackie! Jackie!"

This tremendous outpouring for Mrs. Kennedy did not go unnoticed by the president. Mrs. Kennedy spoke fluent Spanish, and the president urged her to speak in the Venezuelan native tongue at every opportunity. In his main speech of the day, President Kennedy stood at a podium on an outdoor stage in front of thousands, pausing every minute or so to let the interpreter translate what he had said. When he finished, he said, "One of the Kennedys does not need an interpreter—my wife, who would like to say a few words."

The president beamed as Mrs. Kennedy spoke to the adoring crowd in fluent Spanish, without use of notes or need of an interpreter. When she ended her brief remarks with a cheery *"Hasta luego!"* the crowd broke into thunderous applause and cheers.

After a mere twenty-four hours in Venezuela, we flew on to Bogotá, Colombia, where President and Mrs. Kennedy received another tumultuous reception—more than half a million people lining the streets from the airport into the city, waving white handkerchiefs, cheering, many with tears in their eyes. As we made our way into the downtown area, people were standing on balconies and rooftops—anywhere they could to get a glimpse of President and Mrs. Kennedy—showering confetti on the motorcade in a show of extreme admiration and welcome. These were the biggest crowds we'd seen since President Kennedy had taken office, and it reminded me of the incredible receptions President Eisenhower had received in South Korea and India. President John F. Kennedy was a hero to these people—their hope for a brighter future—and in this predominantly Catholic country they were especially proud that the American president and his wife were also practicing Catholics.

Being that it was a Sunday when we arrived in Bogotá, arrangements had been made for President and Mrs. Kennedy to accompany Colombia's president, Alberto Lleras Camargo, and his wife to Mass in the private chapel in San Carlos Palace; then, after a glittering dinner reception, we returned to El Dorado Airport, and at 1:05 a.m. we were airborne and headed for Palm Beach. The entire trip had been just sixty-seven hours and thirty-five minutes, but in that brief amount of time President Kennedy had left an indelible imprint on the hearts and minds of the people of Puerto Rico, Venezuela, and Colombia—and in effect on all of Latin America. It was remarkable to see the enormous influence this new president had—and how beloved both he and Mrs. Kennedy had become around the world over less than a year in office.

The president's father, Ambassador Joseph P. Kennedy, was waiting on the tarmac waving when we arrived in Palm Beach. Because there had been a lot of scrutiny surrounding Joe Kennedy's influence over his son's election to the presidency, the ambassador rarely came to the White House, so the time President Kennedy spent with him in Palm Beach and Hyannis Port was precious. President Kennedy respected his father's opinion and advice and often used him as a sounding board.

As it turned out, this short visit to Palm Beach would be the last time

Ambassador Kennedy would be able to offer his advice and support to his son. Shortly after the president left, the ambassador had a stroke. President Kennedy was devastated. That Christmas was particularly difficult on the entire family, as they spent hours every day visiting the ambassador in the hospital and doing all they could to help him recover. Sadly, Ambassador Kennedy never fully recovered. The stroke rendered him speechless and confined him to a wheelchair for the rest of his life.

President Kennedy went on with the business of running the country, but having lost my own father, I could identify with the anguish and added sense of responsibility that now weighed on his shoulders without his father's guidance.

PRESIDENT KENNEDY HAD seen how his wife was revered in France and South America, and he realized she could be extraordinarily useful for diplomatic relations, so it was with his full support and encouragement that Mrs. Kennedy traveled fifteen thousand miles to fulfill one of her longtime dreams—to visit India and Pakistan. It was the first time an American first lady had visited either of these countries, and on February 16, 1962, I was on a plane with fourteen other Secret Service agents headed to New Delhi to advance this complex and historic trip. As the supervising agent, I became the intermediary between President Kennedy and Ambassador Kenneth Galbraith as the details were ironed out—a sort of tug-of-war between Galbraith's desire to have Mrs. Kennedy tour India for a month and the president's insistence that it be kept to a more reasonable week or ten days. The president prevailed, and finally Mrs. Kennedy arrived—along with her sister, Lee Radziwill—on March 12, 1962. It was a fascinating adventure—which I chronicled in much detail in *Mrs. Kennedy and Me*—during which a series of events led to my supervising agent, Jim Jeffries, being sent back to Washington and transferred off the First Lady's Detail. I was in Karachi, Pakistan, when I got three separate Top Secret messages—one from Secret Service Chief James Rowley, a second from Secretary of State Dean Rusk, and a third from the National Security Council on behalf of President Kennedy—all stating the same thing:

PROCEED FIRST AVAILABLE FLIGHT TO LAHORE, PAKISTAN.
UPON ARRIVAL OF MRS. KENNEDY IN LAHORE ON
MARCH 21 FROM NEW DELHI, YOU ARE TO ASSUME
COMMAND OF FIRST LADY'S PROTECTIVE DETAIL.

The good news was that I had just received a promotion. The bad news was that while we previously had two agents assigned to the first lady, now there was just one—me.

ONCE I BECAME the SAIC of Mrs. Kennedy's detail, I set up an office—well, it wasn't really an office, but a corner of the Map Room with a desk, a phone, a typewriter, and an ashtray that was usually filled by the end of the day. Located on the ground floor, directly across from the elevator that went to the residence, it was an ideal location from which, with the door open, I could see the comings and goings of everyone.

Presidents, like most people, have behavioral patterns that continue when they take office, and each president's routine is different. The Secret Service does not enter the private residence unless there is an emergency, but we were aware that President Kennedy normally arose between 7:30 and 8:00 a.m., would eat breakfast while being visited by Caroline and John, and then be off to the Oval Office. It was common knowledge that President Kennedy suffered from chronic back pain, and the form of exercise that helped ease the pain most was swimming. On weekdays when he was at the White House, it was an almost daily routine for him to take a twenty-to-thirty-minute swim in the heated White House pool just before lunchtime. The pool was situated next to the colonnade between the West Wing and the main White House structure, so it was an easy stop between the two. When I saw President Kennedy enter the elevator in his robe or wrapped in a beach towel, I knew it was lunchtime. He would eat lunch upstairs, and normally Mrs. Kennedy would join him. Everyone knew this was personal time for the two of them and they were not to be interrupted.

The president would return to the Oval Office in the mid-afternoon to conduct whatever business needed to be done, and then, at the end of the business day, he would take another swim in the pool, don the robe or towel, and proceed to the family quarters for dinner. In order to accommodate the president's habit of dropping his suits poolside and returning to the residence in a robe or towel, doors were cut into the adjoining exercise room and flower shop so he didn't have to walk outside the building.

Shortly before Ambassador Kennedy had his stroke, he commissioned an artist to paint a mural around the pool as a gift for the president. When the mural was finished in June 1962, it transformed the swimming pool area. What had been stark cement walls were now painted from floor to ceiling on three sides with a colorful scene of sailboats in brilliant turquoise Caribbean waters, while a mirrored fourth wall reflected the entire mural, making the room look twice as large. The president loved it.

Now THAT I was the Special Agent in Charge of Mrs. Kennedy's protection, whenever she traveled with the president on Air Force One, I would also be on the presidential aircraft instead of being relegated to the backup plane or the press plane. On June 29, 1962, I was on Air Force One with the president and Mrs. Kennedy, headed for Mexico City. It was an important trip for the president as part of the Alliance for Progress program he had initiated, and since Mrs. Kennedy had so enjoyed the previous trips to South America, she was eager to join him.

The motorcade from the airport in Mexico City to Los Pinos, the official residence of President Adolfo López Mateos, was just nine miles, but it was by far one of the most difficult motorcades any of us Secret Service agents had ever encountered. It was a clear day, and as was typical in a parade situation in which the whole idea was for the two presidents to be seen by the people along the motorcade route, President Kennedy and President López rode in an open-top car—a Mercedes provided by the Mexican government. Jerry Behn, the Special Agent in Charge, was in the front passenger seat along with a Mexican government driver, while the follow-up car, which had been flown in from the United States, held a mix of both our agents and Mexican security agents. Behind the security car, I sat in the front seat of another open-top convertible, with Mrs. Kennedy and Mrs. López in the backseat. As we started along the route from the airport, I could hardly believe the size of the crowd. The city streets were packed with people, thirty or forty deep on either side, while the tall buildings seemed to be bursting with people hanging out every window and crammed onto each balcony. The decibel level of the joyous reception was nearly deafening as the mass of people cheered, whistled, clapped, and shouted, "Bienvenido Presidente Kennedy!"

Paper and petals began showering down on us as people threw flowers and confetti from the high-rise buildings. It started slowly and was kind of festive until, as we got into the downtown area, the paper was swirling around us like a blizzard. You couldn't see a damn thing, and as people surged toward the vehicles, the pace of the motorcade slowed to a crawl. It was the largest, most boisterous and colorful reception President and Mrs. Kennedy had ever received—an estimated crowd of *two million*. Two million people packed into a nine-mile stretch of road. Clearly the people of Mexico loved President and Mrs. Kennedy. The atmosphere was overwhelmingly positive, but the blinding confetti combined with the slow pace of the motorcade was nerve-racking. A shot or a hand grenade could come from anywhere. It was like we were trapped in a snow globe.

My senses were on overload as I sat on the edge of my seat, poised to jump out and grab Mrs. Kennedy should anything go awry. I looked back to check on her every few minutes, and she seemed oblivious to any danger. She was chatting in Spanish with Mrs. López and clearly enjoying the outpouring of admiration from the Mexican citizens. To make matters more complicated, one thing we hadn't anticipated was the fact that Mexico City lies more than 7,300 feet above sea level. All of the agents were in top-notch physical condition, but those who jogged alongside the president's vehicle found themselves out of breath, due to the lower oxygen level at that higher elevation. Fortunately, someone had placed an oxygen tank in the follow-up car so that the agents could drop back and take a few puffs of air before returning to their positions.

It took us nearly an hour and a half to cover the nine-mile drive, and while both the president and Mrs. Kennedy were thoroughly enjoying the party-like atmosphere, for the agents it was a security nightmare.

Our third and final day in Mexico City was a Sunday. President and Mrs. Kennedy were scheduled to attend Mass at the Basilica of Guadalupe, and since President López and his wife didn't accompany them, we used our own vehicles, the midnight-blue presidential limousine, SS-100-X, and the Secret Service follow-up car. Once again, large crowds were expected along the route from the U.S. Embassy to the basilica, and after the confetti storm two days earlier, it was decided that even though it was a beautiful sunny day, it would be a good idea to use the Plexiglas bubbletop on SS-100-X.

The crowds were nowhere near as dense as they had been for our arrival, but still there were people stacked ten deep at points along the streets, waving flags and shouting "Bienvenido Presidente Kennedy! Viva Jackie!" It was a much more comfortable situation because we were using our own vehicle, with the president's normal driver, Special Agent Bill Greer, at the wheel, and Special Agent in Charge Jerry Behn in the right front passenger seat. I ended up jogging alongside the left rear of the presidential limousine, no more than a couple of yards behind where Mrs. Kennedy was seated, for much of the route. By the time we reached the church, not only was I finding it somewhat difficult to catch my breath due to the elevation, my suit coat was soaked with sweat, and the soles of my shoes had taken such a beating that I'd need a new pair as soon as we returned to Washington.

On the four-hour flight back to Washington, President and Mrs. Kennedy were clearly elated by the tremendous reception they had received, and newspapers were touting their arrival as the largest turnout *ever* for a foreign leader. Politically, the trip couldn't have been more successful. Once again, Mrs. Kennedy's command of the Spanish language was a tremendous asset to her husband, as she conversed easily with their hosts and made a few public speeches, which endeared her—and the president—to the Mexican people.

From the communications center aboard Air Force One, President Kennedy radioed back to the Mexican president, "We shall always remember the warmth and affection that you and your people have shown us. The conversations we have held shall provide firm basis for continued effective cooperation. I came to meet a president and statesman. I have left you as a friend. Viva Mexico."

MEANWHILE, MRS. KENNEDY had made plans to spend a few weeks on the Amalfi Coast in Italy with Caroline, and had decided that she didn't need any additional staff except for her personal assistant, Providencia "Provi" Paredes, and me, so I was in charge of all the logistics. The president wouldn't be accompanying his wife on this holiday, and before we left he made it clear that he was counting on me to protect Mrs. Kennedy's image as well as her physical safety.

"I don't want to see photos of her at luncheons with eight different wines in full view or jet-set types lolling around in bikinis," he told me. "Do what you can to remind her to be aware of that. And above all, no nightclub pictures."

I wrote in detail about the three weeks we spent in Ravello, Italy, in *Mrs. Kennedy and Me*, and although there were some run-ins with the infamous Italian paparazzi and a surreptitious visit to a nightclub in Positano—oh, and yes that crazy night in Capri with Princess Irene Galitzine—we managed to avoid any nightclub pictures in the press.

Ever since I received the Top Secret telegrams in Pakistan that put me in charge of the First Lady's Detail, I had been the sole agent protecting Mrs. Kennedy. Although I received the temporary assistance of Agent Paul Rundle when needed, I realized that I desperately needed someone to work with me full-time. During the trip to Italy, I observed how well Paul Landis, one of the agents on the Children's Detail, interacted with Mrs. Kennedy and Caroline, and I asked him to be my assistant. He readily accepted, and then we brought in another young agent from Florida named Tommy Wells to fill the open spot on John and Caroline's protective detail. The transition took place at the beginning of October 1962—two weeks before President Kennedy would face his biggest challenge yet.

13

The Cuban Missile Crisis

T he morning of October 16, 1962, National Security Advisor McGeorge Bundy showed up at the White House and was taken upstairs to meet with President Kennedy in his bedroom. This was highly unusual.

It wasn't until later that I learned the reason for Bundy's early morning visit: a U-2 spy plane had taken aerial photographs of Cuban military bases, which showed nuclear missiles installed on launchpads, and there was evidence the intermediate-range missiles were being brought to Cuba on Soviet ships. Premier Khrushchev had just turned up the heat in the Cold War, ninety miles from the coast of Florida, and the ramifications were terrifying.

Upon learning of the missile sites, President Kennedy immediately organized a high-level, confidential group of advisors that consisted of the regular National Security Council members as well as several other men whom he believed could add valuable insight into the decision-making process—including his brother, Attorney General Robert Kennedy. Designated the Executive Committee of the National Security Council, the group came to be known simply as "ExComm." Not wanting to incite fear in the American public, nor let the Soviets know we were aware of the missiles in Cuba, it was decided that the president should maintain his schedule as if everything were normal. He would continue to make public appearances, travel, and attend social functions, while the ExComm met in the Cabinet Room of the White House. The president would attend the meetings and be briefed in between his previously scheduled events.

The Secret Service had well-established plans to protect the president, his family, and key members of the government in the event of an emergency or a major catastrophe. Whether we would go to the bomb shelter on site at the White House or relocate to an undisclosed site outside the metropolitan area would be determined by the threat and our location at the time.

During the next few days the situation was very tense. The president continued to try to maintain his previously scheduled trips and appointments to make everything appear normal, while quietly popping into and out of the Cabinet Room where the ExComm was secretly meeting.

On Saturday, October 20, I was in Middleburg with Mrs. Kennedy and the children when Mrs. Kennedy came to me and said, "Mr. Hill, the president just called and he is on his way back from Chicago. He wants the children and me to return to the White House. Will you arrange for a helicopter?"

Additional photos and analysis had concluded that the Soviets were readying fighter jets and bombers and assembling cruise missile launchers. Additionally, there was evidence that SS-5 missiles were being assembled, which were capable of reaching anywhere in the continental United States. President Kennedy decided it was time to alert the American public that we were facing a chilling crisis, and he had to make a final decision on military options.

I was at the White House when, on the evening of Monday, October 22, President Kennedy addressed the nation from the Oval Office and somberly laid out the indisputable evidence that had been gathered over the past six days. In the seventeen-minute address, he gave Khrushchev an ultimatum to "halt and eliminate this clandestine, reckless, and provocative threat to world peace and to stable relations between our two nations," or the United States would, justifiably, take military action.

Looking directly into the cameras, the president stated, "I have directed the Armed Forces to prepare for any eventualities; and I trust that in the interest of both the Cuban people and the Soviet technicians at the sites, the hazards to all concerned in continuing this threat will be recognized."

He outlined the immediate steps the United States was taking, including a strict "quarantine"—essentially a blockade—on all ships containing cargoes of offensive weapons, as well as a request for an emergency meeting of the Security Council of the United Nations.

In closing, he said, "My fellow citizens, let no one doubt that this is a difficult and dangerous effort on which we have set out . . . but the greatest danger of all would be to do nothing. The path we have chosen for the present is full of hazards, as all paths are—but it is the one most consistent with our character and courage as a nation and our commitments around the world. The cost of freedom is always high—and Americans have always paid it. And one path we shall never choose is the path of surrender or submission.

"Our goal is not the victory of might but the vindication of right—not peace at the expense of freedom but both peace and freedom, here in this hemisphere and, we hope, around the world. God willing, that goal will be achieved."

THE EXCOMM WAS meeting daily, sometimes twice a day, and the president was in and out of the Situation Room for immediate updates. At the same time, the Secret Service was on heightened alert for whatever might happen. We were braced for an evacuation of key personnel by helicopter and knew exactly who would go in which helicopters. We all knew that in the event a nuclear attack was imminent, there would be people scrambling to get aboard the helicopters. If people who were not authorized tried to get on, as an absolute last resort, we would have no choice but to shoot them. It was a sickening thought, but this was the reality of the situation we faced.

On the following Friday, October 26, word came that Khrushchev had agreed to keep his ships out of the quarantine zone for forty-eight hours. That morning, Mrs. Kennedy decided to take Caroline and John to Glen Ora, and advised me that the president would be joining them the following day.

As it turned out, the president did not come to Glen Ora on Saturday, and I was about as tense as I'd ever been. All of the agents were on high alert, fully expecting that at any moment the word would come for us to evacuate immediately. You didn't want to think about what might happen, but you had to go over every possible scenario in your mind to be prepared. It was excruciating. The worst part for all the agents was that we could not discuss the situation with our own families, and if something happened—if there were a nuclear attack—we would go with the president and his family to an underground facility, and our families would most likely perish. It was truly unthinkable.

On Sunday morning, President Kennedy arrived in Glen Ora, and when I saw him step out of the helicopter smiling broadly, I knew everything was going to be all right. Khrushchev had agreed to dismantle the missiles in Cuba, and the Russian ships carrying nuclear materials had turned around. President Kennedy had redeemed himself after the Bay of Pigs disaster and was in high spirits. But most important, he had won Khrushchev's respect, and the two of them had averted nuclear war.

ONE IMPORTANT PIECE of the Cuban Missile Crisis was the quiet negotiations for the release of the Bay of Pigs prisoners. President Kennedy had vowed that the United States would not invade the island of Cuba, and in return Fidel Castro had agreed to release the 1,113 men who had been held captive in Cuba since the failed invasion twenty months earlier, for the ransom of $53 million in food and medical supplies.

On December 29, 1962, we flew to the Orange Bowl in Miami so that President and Mrs. Kennedy could publicly honor all the Bay of Pigs survivors who had just been freed. Forty thousand people filled the Orange Bowl stadium to welcome home the brave freedom fighters, all of whom were dressed in their khaki uniforms—many of them missing arms and/or legs. The ceremony was fraught with emotion as President Kennedy was presented with the brigade's war-torn flag, which had flown during the three-day battle at the Bay of Pigs.

As he graciously accepted the flag, President Kennedy stepped up to the microphone and boldly proclaimed, "I can assure you that this flag will be returned to this brigade in a free Havana."

The stadium erupted into a thunderous roar.

Then Mrs. Kennedy stepped to the microphone and spoke, without notes, in fluent Spanish. There was barely a dry eye in the arena as she concluded her brief remarks, and again the audience roared with applause. At the conclusion of the program, President and Mrs. Kennedy got into a white convertible, and as the car slowly drove out of the stadium, they stood and waved to the exuberant crowd. Finally, the president could put the failed invasion behind him and move forward with a renewed sense of purpose as he entered the third year of his presidency.

14

1963: Great Expectations

Being physically fit was something that was important to President Kennedy, and shortly after he was elected he published an article in *Sports Illustrated* titled "The Soft American," in which he noted how the television set and the use of cars to travel everywhere, along with a myriad of other modern conveniences, had resulted in a generation of people who were not used to strenuous physical activity. He realized there would be many disadvantages to the country if our population became obese.

In January 1963, after coming upon a 1908 executive order in which President Theodore Roosevelt set forth rules for Marine officers to be able to complete a fifty-mile hike in less than twenty hours, President Kennedy sent a memo to Marine Corps Commandant David Shoup suggesting that a similar fifty-mile challenge would be a good test for present-day officers. When President Kennedy announced that he would put his White House staff to the fifty-mile test as well, it kick-started a national fitness campaign that eventually developed into the President's Council on Physical Fitness.

In late February 1963, we were in Palm Beach for the weekend. I had returned to my room at Woody's Motel on the evening of Friday, February 22, when Mrs. Kennedy called me with a special request.

She informed me that the president's brother-in-law, Prince Stash Radziwill, and Chuck Spalding were taking on the challenge of the fifty-mile hike by walking on the newly completed Sunshine Parkway—a north-south highway running from Miami to Fort Pierce along the east side of Florida that was not yet fully operational. Because the president and Mrs. Kennedy would be going out to visit the two men periodically, she surmised, there would have to be an agent advancing the situation.

"The president and I would like you to be the one to go with them," she said. "They're starting tonight at midnight."

It was one of those things that, at the time, I had no idea what I was getting into, but when the first lady made a request on behalf of the president, it wasn't in my nature to question it. So I got dressed in some casual clothes, put on the only shoes I had with me—my Florsheim dress shoes—and contacted the Army sergeant who was assigned to me to drive Mrs. Kennedy. I told him I needed him, the station wagon—which was fitted with radio equipment so I could stay in touch with the Palm Beach base and the Secret Service command post—and a big cooler with ice.

It turned out that Prince Radziwill and Chuck Spalding had been practicing for this hike for months, and a wager of $1,000 was involved. The president had bet his buddies that they were not in good enough shape to do what Americans were doing all across the country. It was quite an adventure, which I detailed in *Mrs. Kennedy and Me*, and fortunately, professional photographer Mark Shaw, who had been with *Life* magazine, came along to photograph the hike for posterity. We finished the hike in about twenty hours, and a few weeks later, Mark gave each of us a leather-bound photo album filled with photos from "That Palm Beach 50."

One of my favorites is a photo taken when President Kennedy paid us a visit just as Chuck and Stash had decided to lie down for a short break, and the president was ribbing me for allowing them to rest.

Another special memory is when we returned to Palm Beach and President Kennedy invited me to join them for a celebratory drink of champagne, and presented me with a medallion—handmade out of purple construction paper attached to a ribbon of yellow crepe paper.

"For Dazzle. February 23, 1963. The Order of the Pace Maker, He whom the Secret Service will follow into the Battle of the Sunshine Highway. Signed John F. Kennedy."

I still have that simple paper medal. It is one of my most treasured possessions.

• • •

SHORTLY BEFORE THE fifty-mile-hike adventure, Mrs. Kennedy had confided in me that she was pregnant. She wanted to keep it private for as long as possible, but finally, on April 15, after celebrating Easter in Palm Beach, a public announcement was made that the president and his wife were expecting their third child, due in late August. This would be only the second baby born to a sitting U.S. president—the last time was in 1893, when Grover Cleveland's wife had a baby girl—and the public's excitement was enormous. Because Mrs. Kennedy had previously had two miscarriages and had delivered a stillborn baby, she informed me that she wouldn't be accompanying the president on any more trips until the baby was born, and would be curtailing her social and athletic activities.

Meanwhile, President Kennedy was dealing with a number of issues that all seemed to be coming to a head at the same time. Communist forces in Laos and Vietnam were gaining ground, while Haiti's dictator president François Duvalier had declared martial law and was threatening to overthrow the neighboring Dominican Republic. President Kennedy was committed to helping those nations defend themselves from the spread of Communism.

In our own country, civil rights leaders were growing impatient with President Kennedy's slow response to their movement and were taking matters into their own hands by organizing protests against segregation in the South. Nowhere was the tension greater than in Birmingham, Alabama, where Rev. Martin Luther King Jr. had organized a series of marches. The entire nation was horrified when television film crews captured images of firefighters using fire hoses to blast the peaceful protestors—most of whom were teenagers—and send them into lines of police with German shepherd attack dogs. President Kennedy sent U.S. Army units trained in riot control to the area, which infuriated Alabama's segregationist governor, George Wallace, who accused the president of overstepping his authority.

In the midst of the turmoil throughout the world, there was one thing that had captivated the attention of all Americans—something President Kennedy had strived to make a priority—and that was the race to space. When the Soviets launched the satellite Sputnik in 1957, it was seen as a major victory in the Cold War, to which President Eisenhower responded by creating the National Aeronautics and Space Administration (NASA) and the development of Project Mercury. Shortly after President Kennedy took office, he convinced Congress to dramatically increase funding to NASA, with the intention that "this nation should commit itself to achieving the goal, before the decade is out, of landing a man on the moon and returning him safely to earth." Many had scoffed at the notion that this was achievable, but less than a year later, on February 20, 1962, John Glenn Jr. became the first American to orbit earth. Within the following year, astronauts Scott Carpenter and Walter Schirra Jr. had also orbited the earth, and on May 16, 1963, astronaut Gordon Cooper splashed into the Pacific Ocean, having just orbited our planet more times than any human being yet. It was a shining moment amid the hatred and violence that seemed to be everywhere you turned, and five days later Major Cooper was honored with a parade down Pennsylvania Avenue and a ceremony in the White House Rose Garden. On the portico, in the back of the crowd, Paul Landis and I stood close to Mrs. Kennedy, who was watching the ceremony with two-year-old John in her arms, trying to avoid the attention of the press.

Speaking off-the-cuff, President Kennedy paid tribute to the distinguished group of astronauts who had participated in Project Mercury, noting that they had, "in this rather settled society, demonstrated that there are great frontiers still to be crossed, and in flying through space have carried with them the wishes, the prayers, the hopes, and the pride of 180 million of their fellow countrymen."

His remarks were brief but sincere, and at the last moment he broke into a smile, adding, "You have given the United States a great day, and a great lift!" His vision for putting a man on the moon was moving forward, and with all the turmoil in the world, this was indeed a welcome positive accomplishment.

MAY 29, 1963, was President Kennedy's forty-sixth birthday—and it is one of those days that has remained vivid in my memory. At the end of the workday, at around 5:45, President Kennedy walked down to the Navy Mess, where a small group of his staff and Mrs. Kennedy were waiting with a cake. When the president walked in, we yelled, "Surprise!" and as soon as somebody handed him a glass of champagne, we all started singing "Happy Birthday."

He broke into a big smile and played along like he really was surprised, as he was presented with an array of gag gifts. There was a miniature rocking chair, boxing gloves to deal with Congress, "Debate Rules" supposedly from Richard M. Nixon. But he got the biggest kick when Mrs. Kennedy gave him her present—a basket of dead grass.

"Mr. President," she deadpanned, "on behalf of the White House Historical Society, it is with great honor and with the utmost respect that I present to you genuine antique grass from the antique rose garden."

The president loved it.

That evening, Mrs. Kennedy had planned an intimate cruise for twenty-four guests aboard the presidential yacht, the USS *Sequoia*. None of President Kennedy's political advisors had been invited—the guest list included only family members and his closest friends—and while we had Secret Service agents on a couple of security boats, there were just three agents aboard the *Sequoia*—Floyd Boring and Ron Pontius from the president's detail, and myself.

It was a dreary, rainy evening, making the open-air top deck unusable, so everybody was crammed inside the main and aft salons. There were plenty of toasts, and after birthday cake at the dining table, the president opened presents—more gag gifts that had everyone laughing with delight and amusement. The champagne flowed, people danced, and as the evening wore on the party got louder and livelier. I had never seen the president and Mrs. Kennedy having so much fun—and while no one wanted the night to end, the captain finally docked the *Sequoia* around 1:20 in the morning signaling it was time for everyone to go home.

What a privilege it was for me to have been there, to witness the joy and laughter on that wild and raucous night. It was such a special evening, one that everyone aboard would remember forever—none of us capable of imagining that President Kennedy's forty-sixth birthday would be his last.

15

Triumph and Tragedy

On June 22, 1963, President Kennedy departed on an ambitious ten-day trip to Europe that included stops in Germany, England, Ireland, and Italy. Mrs. Kennedy, now in the sixth month of her pregnancy, had settled in for the rest of the summer in Hyannis Port, so Paul Landis and I had a relatively easy schedule, while the agents protecting President Kennedy faced enormous and exuberant crowds rivaling those we had seen during President Eisenhower's foreign tours three years earlier.

My colleagues would later regale me with stories of near chaos. From the moment President Kennedy landed in Germany, he was treated like royalty. Hundreds of thousands of Germans lined the motorcade route—cheering, screaming, and waving—as President Kennedy rode from Wahn Airport to Cologne with Chancellor Konrad Adenauer. As a matter of protocol, the two leaders rode in the Germans' car—an open-top Mercedes limousine—while our Secret Service agents rode on the running boards of the follow-up car. A diamond-shaped formation of white-uniformed German motorcycle police led the way through country roads and into the city, but at times the crowds were so large, and the people so eager to get close to the handsome American president, that not even the motorcycles could keep them back. The agents ended up jogging alongside the Mercedes most of the way, fending people off. People were everywhere—hanging out open windows, standing on ledges and balconies—anywhere they could stand to get a fleeting view. There was no way to check every building or every rooftop. You had no idea who was in the crowd, and if someone had really wanted to take out either

President Kennedy or Chancellor Adenauer, there was little the agents could do but react. For the agents, many of whom were new to the detail and had not seen anything like this before, it was harrowing. And then, hours later, the afternoon-shift agents experienced the same thing as Adenauer and President Kennedy drove to Bonn.

After two days of meetings in Bonn, Adenauer and Kennedy flew to Berlin, where Kennedy would make one of the most memorable and powerful speeches of his presidency.

In mid-August 1961, less than seven months into JFK's presidency, the government of East Germany, in coalition with Soviet premier Khrushchev, had erected a concrete-block wall topped with razor-sharp wire, complete with sentry towers and minefields around it, to halt the exodus of people leaving Communist-controlled East Germany for the West. President Kennedy was deeply disturbed by the photographs he'd seen and stories he had heard of people being killed as they tried to climb over the wall to freedom, and one of the primary reasons for this trip was for him to see the situation for himself.

Agent Win Lawson had done the advance for the Berlin trip.

"It was incredible," he told me. "There were hundreds of thousands of people along the motorcade route—thirty-eight miles—from Tegel Airport into the city. The German police were out in force; they'd erected barriers and there were dozens of motorcycle police, yet that didn't stop the people from breaking through the police lines to swarm the presidential car."

They had flown our presidential limousine, the midnight-blue SS-100-X, to Berlin, and Lawson said President Kennedy, along with Adenauer and Berlin mayor Willy Brandt, stood nearly the entire way, waving to the crowds.

"At times it sounded like thunder," Lawson said. "The crowds were enormous. At one point, two women ran toward the car—narrowly missed being run over by one of the motorcycles—and President Kennedy leaned over to shake their hands as the car was still moving.

"Jerry Blaine was riding on the rear step of 100-X, so he jumped off, while Boring and Sulliman ran up from the follow-up car. It took all three of them to pry the shrieking ladies away and repel them into the crowd."

Lawson recalled how moving it was as President Kennedy stood atop the viewing platform at Checkpoint Charlie and peered over the wall.

"On the other side, hundreds of Communist police stood on guard with submachine guns," he said. "And behind them, there were at least a thousand people who had come out just to see President Kennedy, and they stood there waving scarves and handkerchiefs with tears in their eyes.

"He stayed for four minutes—and let me tell you, those were the longest four minutes of my life!" Win said. "And then we went to the huge square in front of City Hall, and you can't even imagine the crowd, Clint. The people were packed in there tighter than sardines. They were on rooftops, on balconies, dangling out of windows, and when the president yelled out '*Ich bin ein Berliner*'—I am a Berliner—the place erupted."

Win Lawson was not one to exaggerate or be emotional, but the scene evidently had made an impact on him. Press secretary Pierre Salinger told reporters, "This is the greatest reception the president has received anywhere in the world."

Agent Jerry Blaine recalled that the crowds in Ireland and Italy were just as enormous. "By the end of the trip I had holes in my shoes, and all my suits were soiled and ripped beyond repair," he said, shaking his head. "We were living on pure adrenaline. It was almost overwhelming. But to see the immense admiration for President Kennedy—you couldn't help but be proud to be American."

In Rome, the crowds had welcomed President Kennedy with genuine affection as throngs filled the streets to cheer and wave as the motorcade passed. At the Vatican, President Kennedy had a private audience with the newly inaugurated Pope Paul VI, becoming only the third sitting American president to have an official visit with a pope—but for this Catholic president it was an especially meaningful visit on both sides.

ONCE PRESIDENT KENNEDY returned from Europe, he began the usual summer schedule in which he arrived at Hyannis Port on Friday afternoons, and left Monday mornings.

On Wednesday, August 7, 1963, Mrs. Kennedy suddenly went into early labor and was helicoptered to Otis Air Force Base hospital. President Kennedy was notified and was on his way from Washington, while I paced the floor just as I had done when John was born two and a half years earlier.

Shortly before one o'clock in the afternoon, while the president was still airborne, Dr. John Walsh came out of the surgery room and informed me that Mrs. Kennedy had delivered a baby boy, and she was fine, but the baby weighed just four pounds, ten and a half ounces, and was having difficulty breathing.

President Kennedy arrived about forty minutes later, and as soon as he learned the critical situation of his baby's health, he came to me and said, "Clint, find the base chaplain. We need to baptize the baby right away."

The child was baptized Patrick Bouvier Kennedy—"Patrick" after President Kennedy's paternal grandfather, and "Bouvier" for Mrs. Kennedy's father.

It was determined that Patrick had a condition known as hyaline membrane disease—a common affliction in premature babies caused by incomplete lung development—and he needed to be moved to Children's Hospital in Boston, where they had the equipment and expertise to help him.

President Kennedy helicoptered to Hyannis Port for a quick visit with John and Caroline and returned an hour later to check on Mrs. Kennedy. He was the President of the United States, but in these hours he was simply a husband and a father, concerned for the well-being of his family more than anything else. When he emerged from Mrs. Kennedy's room, he had a faraway look in his eyes.

"Clint, I'm going to Boston to be with Patrick. I know you'll make sure Mrs. Kennedy is well taken care of. Just make sure I'm kept informed."

Protecting Mrs. Kennedy was my job, but in the past three years I had spent more time with her, the president, and their children than I had with my own family. I cared about them not as the president and the first lady but as people, and to witness their anguish over the uncertainty of their newborn son's life was heartbreaking.

The next day, August 8, President Kennedy flew back and forth between Boston and Otis Air Force Base and Hyannis Port, while Mrs. Kennedy continued to sleep for most of the day. I had not left Otis since we arrived on the morning of August 7, and had taken over one of the bedrooms in the hospital suite so I could at least try to get some sleep.

At 4:15 a.m. on Friday, August 9, Jerry Behn, the Special Agent in Charge of the White House Detail, phoned from Boston and told me that Patrick had died. My heart ached for Mrs. Kennedy and for the president. It was a devastating loss.

President Kennedy flew in from Boston later that morning, and I was there to greet him as he entered the hospital wing. We had managed to keep the members of the press outside the hospital building itself, but when the president arrived, they lined up like vultures, capturing his every move. I knew they were just doing their jobs—and many of them were friends of mine—but it sickened me that they couldn't leave the president alone during this time of personal grief.

The president looked like he had been to hell and back, with swollen eyes and sorrow etched all over his face. As I escorted him to Mrs. Kennedy's room, I didn't know what to say. What do you say to anyone who has lost a child? So I simply looked at him, my own eyes melting with sadness, and said, "My condolences, Mr. President."

He looked at me and replied softly, "Thank you, Clint."

I turned the knob and opened the door to Mrs. Kennedy's room, and as soon as he walked in, I quietly closed it to give them the privacy they needed. Standing outside the room, I could hear their muffled sobs as they grieved over the loss of their son.

SAIC Jerry Behn would tell me later of the heart-wrenching scene he and the other agents had witnessed in Boston. The doctors had called the president in the middle of the night, knowing death was imminent. They had released Patrick from the lines and tubes, and President Kennedy was able to hold his son in his arms for the first and last time.

The funeral services for Patrick Bouvier Kennedy were held on Saturday, August 10, in Boston, but Mrs. Kennedy was still so weak from the cesarean operation that she was unable to fly to Boston. Paul Landis and I stayed with her while the agents on the President's Detail accompanied President Kennedy to the somber private funeral Mass delivered by Cardinal Cushing, and then to Brookline Cemetery, where they watched—most struggling to blink back tears—as President Kennedy's shoulders heaved up and down at the sight of the tiny white coffin being placed in the ground of the Kennedy family plot.

On each of the next two days, President Kennedy brought John and Caroline to the hospital to visit their mother, and while they tried to boost her spirits, the death of baby Patrick was immensely difficult for the entire family.

Mrs. Kennedy remained in the hospital for a week, but the president had to return to Washington to deal with the nation's business. The world does not stop for the death of a president's son.

CARDS AND FLOWERS and gifts poured into the White House and the Kennedy residence in Hyannis Port as people all over the world grieved with President and Mrs. Kennedy over the death of baby Patrick. Meanwhile, all of the agents noticed that something had changed in their relationship. I first observed it in the hospital suite at Otis Air Force Base, but it became publicly visible when Mrs. Kennedy was released from the hospital a week after she gave birth. With press photographers snapping away, President and Mrs. Kennedy emerged from the hospital suite hand in hand. There was a tenderness, a closeness between them that had deepened as a result of the tragedy, and suddenly they seemed much more willing to show their affection for each other in public.

Mrs. Kennedy and the children stayed in Hyannis Port for the rest of the summer, but when the president came on the weekends I noticed that he seemed to be taking great pains to be supportive to Mrs. Kennedy, while also spending more time with the children. He would go swimming with John and Caroline in the ocean, watching with delight as they jumped to him from the deck of the *Honey Fitz*; he began taking Caroline to Sunday church services regularly; and when he had to return to Washington, he would bring Caroline and John with him on the short helicopter ride from the Kennedy compound to Otis Air Force Base.

Meanwhile, Mrs. Kennedy was having a much more difficult time getting back to a normal routine. As the weeks went by, she seemed to be spiraling further into depression. One day, at the end of August or the beginning of September, she told me that her sister, Lee, had been trying to convince her to take a trip for a change of scenery. Aristotle Onassis had offered them the use of his private yacht for a relaxing cruise around the Mediterranean, and President Kennedy agreed it would be an ideal way for Mrs. Kennedy to get away and avoid the press.

As we began to make the plans for the trip, members of the president's staff were expressing concern about how this would appear to the public—that Aristotle Onassis, who had some long-standing legal issues with the United States government, as well as a reputation for being a womanizer and opportunist, was providing his personal yacht for use by the president's wife. President Kennedy was aware of the political ramifications, but he was so concerned about Mrs. Kennedy that he insisted she should go.

On October 1, Mrs. Kennedy; her personal assistant, Provi; Paul Landis; and I flew to Athens, where we boarded the *Christina*. I wrote in detail about the trip—including some interesting encounters with Aristotle Onassis himself—in *Mrs. Kennedy and Me*, but the end result was that the trip did indeed help Mrs. Kennedy immensely, and on the way back to Washington two weeks later she informed me that she had decided she was going to make an effort to help her husband as much as she could in the upcoming 1964 presidential campaign. A trip to Texas in November was already in the planning stages, and she intended to go with him.

THE PRIOR YEAR, when Mrs. Kennedy found out they would not be able to renew the lease at Glen Ora in Middleburg, she and President Kennedy had purchased some land in the area, near Atoka, Virginia, and had a home built to their specifications. It was a sprawling ranch-style house that was very secluded, with beautiful views of the acres and acres of rolling hills that surrounded it. On Saturday, October 26, 1963, President and Mrs. Kennedy spent their first night in their new home together, and two weeks later they returned with the children and their friends Ben and Tony Bradlee.

It was a crisp fall weekend in November, perfect weather to enjoy the outdoors. Young John played army in the woods with nanny Maud Shaw as the Army nurse, while Caroline rode her pony. The president and the Bradlees sat outside on a stone wall at the edge of the patio overlooking the property as Mrs. Kennedy and friend Paul Fout demonstrated their equestrian skills, riding and jumping fences and other barriers. Everyone was relaxed and enjoying themselves.

At one point, after all the riding, everyone was at the side of the house watching the children play, when Mrs. Kennedy walked over to them leading Caroline's pony. The president was seated on the grass, his back propped up by the house, not paying much attention, when Mrs. Kennedy let go of the lead. The president apparently had some food in his pocket or his hand, and the pony stepped right up and began nuzzling him. The president was squirming with laughter as the horse nuzzled his neck. It was one of the funniest scenes I ever witnessed around a president, and it was all caught on film.

I remember how nice it was to see the family laughing and enjoying simple times together again.

16

The Trip to Texas

I arrived at the White House around eight o'clock on the morning of Thursday, November 21, with my bags packed for the short trip to Texas. We would be gone for only two nights, but an intense schedule was planned that included stops in San Antonio, Houston, and Fort Worth on the first day; on to Dallas and Austin the next, with an overnight at Vice President Johnson's ranch outside Austin; and returning to Washington late Saturday afternoon, November 23. There would be motorcades, speech sites, and fund-raisers, and the fact that Mrs. Kennedy was going with the president on this trip added a whole different dimension to the preparations and the logistics. Although she had traveled with her husband on several official foreign trips, this would be the first domestic political trip President and Mrs. Kennedy had taken together since JFK became president. To make things even more complicated, since Texas was LBJ's home state, Vice President and Mrs. Johnson would be traveling with the Kennedys as well.

Advance teams had been sent to each city about ten days earlier to coordinate the political and security logistics—a relatively short amount of time, considering the countless details that needed to be arranged—and on the final schedule, everything was planned to the minute. President Kennedy had just returned late Monday night from a three-day trip to Florida that was centered around a visit to Cape Canaveral—where he saw a test launch of a Polaris missile and got an exceptionally encouraging briefing on the space program—but the trip also was politically motivated. With the 1964 presidential election only a year away, the president's staff had set up the trips to Florida and Texas to get a feel for Kennedy's popularity in each of those key southern states. Monday, November 18, was nonstop activity, with multiple motorcades and speeches in Tampa and Miami. The venues were overflowing with supporters, and although there were pockets of protestors challenging the administration's stance on Cuba and civil rights at various points along the motorcade routes, the crowds were larger and more enthusiastic than anyone had expected. By all accounts it had been an enormously successful trip.

Meanwhile, I had been with Mrs. Kennedy for another long weekend at the new home in Atoka. When we returned to the White House on Wednesday, I checked in with my supervisors to get a better handle on what to expect for the trip to Texas.

Before we got into that, Assistant Special Agent in Charge Floyd Boring informed me of something that had happened in Florida.

"We had a long motorcade in Tampa," Floyd said, "and it was decided that we should keep two guys on the back of the car for the entire route— just for added precaution."

That wasn't anything uncommon. SS-100-X had steps and handholds built onto the back specifically for that purpose. The idea was to have agents as close to the president as possible in that type of situation. If there was a sudden problem, our training was to "cover and evacuate."

"So," Floyd continued, "we had Chuck Zboril and Don Lawton on the back of the car the entire way. But partway through the motorcade, in an area where the crowds had thinned, the president requested we remove the agents from the back of the car."

That surprised me. I had never heard the president question procedural recommendations by his Secret Service detail. "What was the reason?"

"He said now that we're heading into the campaign, he doesn't want it to look like we're crowding him. And the word is, from now on, you don't get on the back of the car unless the situation absolutely warrants it."

"Understood," I said.

The conversation replayed in my mind as I was sitting in my office in the Map Room, going over the schedule one more time, when President Kennedy came out of the elevator directly across the hall. Seeing me through the doorway, he called out cheerfully, "Good morning, Clint."

"Good morning, Mr. President," I said as I snuffed out my cigarette in the ashtray.

Walking toward me, he said, "Clint, just so you know, John will be riding with us to Andrews."

"Yes, sir. I figured that might be the case. I'll make sure Agent Foster is aware."

Agent Bob Foster was one of three agents on the children's Secret Service detail—the Kiddie Detail, as we called it—and it had almost become routine for the president to bring John, who would turn three on November 25, on the short flights between the White House and Andrews Air Force Base whenever possible.

At exactly 10:50 a.m. we lifted off from the White House grounds, landing six minutes later at Andrews, where pilot Colonel Jim Swindal had the presidential aircraft with tail number 26000, ready to go, engines running. As soon as the chopper landed on the tarmac alongside the presidential plane, young John's whole demeanor changed. He had been told he wasn't going with Mummy and Daddy on the big plane today, and now it was time to say good-bye. There were lots of tears, and while you could see that President Kennedy hated to leave his son like this, we all knew he couldn't come with us.

Agent Bob Foster slid into the seat next to John and was trying to calm him down when the president, standing in the doorway of the helicopter, took one last look at his inconsolable son and said, "Take care of John for me, won't you, Mr. Foster?"

"Yes, sir, Mr. President," Foster replied. "I'll be glad to do that."

As the last one off the helicopter, I took a quick look around to make sure nobody had left anything. Poor John was still sobbing. I felt so sorry for him.

"Bye-bye, John," I said. "You have fun with Mr. Foster, now, okay? We'll be back in a few days."

That's one memory that still chokes me up, every time.

• • •

IT WAS 1:30 local time when we landed at San Antonio Airport. Hundreds of people were packed onto the rooftop of the airport terminal, screaming and cheering, and when President and Mrs. Kennedy emerged from the rear door of the aircraft, the crowd went wild. At the bottom of the stairs, Vice President and Mrs. Johnson and Texas governor John Connally and his wife were lined up to greet them in a formal receiving line. There was a standard protocol we followed so that arrivals like this were almost always the same. On this particular trip, the Connallys were the official hosts, so they would be traveling with President and Mrs. Kennedy, riding in the presidential limousine and on Air Force One throughout Texas.

The presidential car, SS-100-X, and the Secret Service follow-up car, which we called "Halfback," had been flown to San Antonio by cargo plane and were lined up ready to go, with the other vehicles that would carry the vice president, other dignitaries, and the press staggered in procession behind.

Unlike the motorcades in foreign countries, for which we had to negotiate and compromise with the host country's security forces, when we were in a parade-type situation in the United States, the Agent in Charge always rode in the right front passenger seat of the presidential vehicle, while the rest of the agents in the motorcade rode in Halfback. Like SS-100-X, the follow-up car had been modified with some special features. It could hold nine people in seats and had running boards along both sides, which, when you were standing on them, provided an elevated vantage point to observe the crowds. The running boards also served as launching platforms to get off of and onto the vehicle. Handholds attached to the edge of the windshield frame aided in our movement back onto the car. Behind the front seat, built into the divider, was a cabinet that held additional weapons.

It was a cloudless, sunny day—perfect weather for a political parade— and as we drove from the airport through San Antonio to our destination at Brooks Air Force Base, it seemed that half the city had come out to see President and Mrs. Kennedy. In fact, a presidential visit was such a rare occasion that the local schools had declared the day a holiday so the students could have the opportunity to see their president in person.

At Brooks Air Force Base, eleven thousand people had been waiting in the hot sun for a couple of hours before President Kennedy arrived. He made a brief speech, and when the audience erupted into a standing ovation, the president grabbed Mrs. Kennedy by the hand and headed straight for the crowd. The people went wild, pushing and screaming as the president and first lady intermingled with them, while we, the agents, stayed as close as possible. We finally got everyone back into their respective vehicles for the motorcade to Kelly Air Force Base, and then it was on to the next city.

It was a thirty-five-minute flight to Houston, and when we landed, we did the whole routine all over again. There was a welcome reception at the airport, and a large, boisterous crowd pushing against the rope line.

President and Mrs. Kennedy waved to the enthusiastic crowd, and when a group behind the fence line beckoned them to come closer, sure enough, President Kennedy strode toward them, with Mrs. Kennedy following behind. A bunch of people were waving KENNEDY IN 64 placards, and as the president got close the crowd roared. Ladies were shrieking at the sight of President Kennedy, while others yelled out "Jackie! Jackie!"

There hadn't been time to securely transport SS-100-X and the follow-up car, so they had been sent on to Dallas, to be used the following day. In Houston, the local Lincoln Mercury dealer had loaned us cars, so there were no running boards or handholds like we had on our customized Secret Service cars. Using a standard Mercury convertible as the follow-up car, I sat on top of the car frame with my legs straddling the door, one inside and one out. When the crowds were bigger and I thought I might have to jump off quickly, I would move to a sidesaddle position. It was very awkward and uncomfortable, but the only other option was to run alongside the presidential vehicle the entire way.

A huge crowd was waiting at the entrance of the Rice Hotel, so we had to push through to get the president and Mrs. Kennedy into the elevator and up to the suite that had been arranged for them to rest and relax in for a few hours before the evening's activities. I waited outside the suite with ASAIC Roy Kellerman as various people came and went. At 8:40 the president and Mrs. Kennedy came out of the suite, both of them having showered and changed into evening attire. They made a brief appearance at a reception being held by the League of United Latin American Citizens (LULAC) at the hotel, and then we were back in the cars and off to the Coliseum for a dinner honoring Congressman Albert Thomas. Another grand entrance, a speech by the president, and then back into the cars headed for Houston International Airport.

At 10:15 Air Force One took off from Houston, finally headed to the last stop of the day—Fort Worth—where we would be spending the night. Vice President and Mrs. Johnson had arrived a few minutes before and were waiting at the bottom of the airplane steps to welcome the Kennedys and the Connallys to Carswell Air Force Base after the fifty-minute flight.

It was dark and drizzling, an hour before midnight, and yet thousands of people were standing there in the rain—mothers and fathers with children, students, and senior citizens—all waiting to see President and Mrs. Kennedy. It was almost beyond my comprehension why people would go to these lengths, especially at such a late hour, just for a brief glimpse of their president and first lady, but I suppose I had become somewhat jaded. I was around them all the time, and to me they were just regular people. But for these folks, this was a once-in-a-lifetime chance to be able to say that they had seen President John F. Kennedy the night he came to Fort Worth, Texas.

It was 11:50 when we pulled up to the Hotel Texas, but you could hardly see the entrance because of the mass of humanity standing outside. The Fort Worth police had set up some temporary barricades to try to corral the people, but it was obvious they hadn't expected this number. There had to be close to four thousand people outside, and when President and Mrs. Kennedy emerged from the car, the crowd erupted with excitement. People were pushing and tugging each other to get into a better position, and although at first President Kennedy dove into shake a few hands, I think he quickly realized this crowd was one snap away from becoming a stampede, so he allowed us to move him and Mrs. Kennedy inside the hotel as quickly as possible.

We had to push through yet another large crowd inside the lobby, but finally we got them up to the eighth floor, away from the screams and hollers and hands to Suite 850, where they would spend what would turn out to be their last night together.

● ● ●

WITH THE PRESIDENT's midnight shift in place, I was finally off duty. It had been a long day for everybody. It was nearly 1:00 a.m. local time, but by my body clock it was 2:00 a.m. I hadn't eaten in over thirteen hours, and except for the short airplane rides between cities I'd been on my feet the entire time.

After checking into my room, which was immediately next door to President and Mrs. Kennedy's suite on the eighth floor, I went down to the lobby to see if I could locate something to eat, but the hotel restaurant was long since closed, and back in 1963 there was no such thing as a twenty-four-hour fast-food joint. Paul Landis and a few of the other agents who had come in on the press plane were in the lobby with some of the press corps, and everybody had the same idea. We were all famished.

Word was that the Fort Worth Press Club was nearby, and there might be something to eat there. Merriman Smith from United Press International (UPI) grabbed me by the arm. "Come on along, Clint," he said. "We'll get you fed."

So we all walked over to the Press Club, only to find that the local newsies had cleaned out the buffet, and nothing was left. The bar was still open, so everybody decided we might as well at least have a drink. I ordered a scotch and water, which didn't do anything to quell my hunger pangs, but at least it helped me wind down after running on pure adrenaline for the better part of the day.

Someone said there was another place nearby where the kitchen might still be open, so after one drink, I bought some cigarettes and walked over there with a few of the other guys. Once again, no food; all they were serving was some kind of fruit drink, which tasted horrible, so I went back to my hotel room and—after arranging for a wake-up call from the White House switchboard—promptly fell sound asleep.

17

Dallas

The morning of November 22, I got the wake-up call at six o'clock sharp. The sun had not yet risen and it was raining lightly, but outside hundreds of people were already gathering in the parking lot across the street. The president planned to make a few remarks—a last-minute addition to the schedule prior to the Chamber of Commerce breakfast—and a stage was already being erected for that purpose. By the time I had finished my breakfast, there were thousands packed into the square. Just like the night before at Carswell, there were people of all ages—including families with young children—standing in the drizzling rain for hours just so they could see President Kennedy for a few precious minutes.

While the president spoke to the cheering crowd in the parking lot, and then proceeded inside to the hotel ballroom for the Chamber of Commerce breakfast, I waited outside the presidential suite for Mrs. Kennedy to get ready. She had indicated to me that she would not attend the breakfast with the president, but at 9:10 I got an urgent call from Agent Bill Duncan.

"Clint, I'm down here at the breakfast with the president. He wants you to bring Mrs. Kennedy down, *right now*."

"Mrs. Kennedy isn't intending on going to the breakfast," I said.

"The president just told me to tell you to get her down here *now*," Duncan replied. "Everyone is waiting for her."

I went into the suite and informed Mrs. Kennedy of the situation, urging her to hurry. Fortunately she was already dressed, but she hadn't finished her makeup. Seven minutes later, she emerged wearing a pink hat that matched the two-piece pink suit she had chosen to wear to Dallas, and a pair of wrist-length white gloves. No one would ever guess she hadn't planned to attend the breakfast function.

Inside the Grand Ballroom, the 2,500 guests were visibly restless, wondering why Mrs. Kennedy hadn't yet appeared. The event was now more than half an hour late getting started. Paul Landis and I escorted Mrs. Kennedy through the kitchen, as we'd been instructed, and then I opened the door leading to the rear of the ballroom so the master of ceremonies could see Mrs. Kennedy behind me.

Clearly elated to see her, the MC leaned into the microphone and enthusiastically declared, "And now the event I know all of you have been waiting for!"

The sight of Mrs. Kennedy brought the entire room to a standing ovation.

As I led her to her seat on the dais between her husband and Vice President Johnson, I glanced at the president. He seemed relieved that she was finally here, and after allowing the applause to continue for a little while longer, he stepped up to the podium.

"Two years ago, I introduced myself in Paris by saying that I was the man who had accompanied Mrs. Kennedy to Paris. I am getting somewhat that same sensation as I travel around Texas."

The audience burst into laughter. They loved him. Then he added, glancing at Mrs. Kennedy, "Nobody wonders what Lyndon and I wear."

Mrs. Kennedy blushed as the audience howled with laughter. It was so typical of President Kennedy—to speak off-the-cuff, using humor to connect with the crowd—and from that moment on, Mrs. Kennedy's tardiness would be forgotten, and all anyone would remember was the inimitable charisma of John F. Kennedy.

AT 10:40 A.M. we left the Hotel Texas and motorcaded to Carswell Air Force Base, where Air Force One, the vice president's plane, and the backup plane were ready to go. It was a short, fifteen-minute flight to Love Field in Dallas—we had barely reached flying altitude before we began the descent—but this was all about politics. Our destination in Dallas was the Trade Mart, where 2,600 people had paid to have lunch with President and Mrs. Kennedy and to hear him speak. It would have been much quicker to drive directly from Fort Worth to the Trade Mart in Dallas. Instead we drove from the Hotel Texas in Fort Worth to Carswell Air Force Base, boarded Air Force One, flew to Love Field, then drove through downtown Dallas toward the speech site. All of this to get a photo of President and Mrs. Kennedy coming off Air Force One in Dallas and to have a motorcade for maximum exposure.

It would be nearly fifty years before I could recount the details of what happened in Dallas—not because I was sworn to secrecy or because I had anything to hide. The reason is simple: the memories were just too damn painful. To this day, every moment is still vivid in my mind.

There was a large crowd waiting behind a chain-link fence as Air Force One pulled up to its arrival point at Love Field. I checked my watch and noted the arrival time in the little black datebook I always carried: 11:40 a.m. Central Standard Time.

President and Mrs. Kennedy exited the plane through the rear doors, and as they walked down the stairs the crowd went wild. Flags waving, people applauding, and calling out—it was another exuberant welcome in yet another Texas city. As soon as they had gone through the receiving line, the president headed straight for the crowd behind the fence, with Mrs. Kennedy following closely behind. The two of them moved along the fence line shaking hands for about five minutes, much to the great delight of the people who had come to greet them, while the other agents and I formed an envelope of security around them, constantly scanning the crowd for signs of trouble.

Finally, they took their places in the presidential limousine—SS-100-X. Mrs. Kennedy sat in the left rear seat, the president in the right rear. After they were seated, Governor and Mrs. Connally folded down the jump seats, with Mrs. Connally directly in front of Mrs. Kennedy and the governor in front of President Kennedy.

Earlier in the morning it had been raining lightly, but the drizzle had stopped, the clouds were dissipating, and it was clearing up to be a beautiful sunny afternoon. The agents in Dallas had been monitoring the weather, and as soon as the rain stopped, the decision had been made to leave the top off the presidential limousine. Those were standard orders from the president and his staff. The whole idea of this trip to Texas was for the president to be seen by as many people as possible.

At 11:55 a.m. we departed Love Field and headed for the Trade Mart. There were people lining the streets from the moment we left the airport, but as we neared the center of town, the crowds got bigger and bigger. People were yelling and clapping, waving banners and signs. It was a repeat of the day before—large, exuberant, friendly crowds. At various points, the crowds became so large—ten- and twenty-people deep on each side—that the motorcycles had to drop back, and the pace of the motorcade slowed. At these points Agent Bill Greer, the driver of the presidential car, would steer the car closer to the crowd on the left in order to keep more distance between the crowd and the president on the right. But this put Mrs. Kennedy right next to the people—causing them to shriek with delight and reach out to try to touch her. Between the noise of the motorcycles and the people, you could hardly hear yourself think. I didn't like being so far behind Mrs. Kennedy in this situation, so I made a sudden decision and jumped off Halfback, ran to catch up to 100-X, and leaped onto the rear step of the car. I knew the president didn't want us on the back of the car, but I had a job to do.

I crouched on the step, in an effort to be less conspicuous, yet still be in proximity should anything happen. Several times I moved back and forth between the follow-up car and the rear step of SS-100-X, depending on the moment-by-moment situation. I constantly scanned the crowd. People were everywhere—yelling, cheering, clapping. There were people on rooftops and balconies and fire escapes. People hanging out of windows. Windows were open all along the route. It was a tremendous reception from the people of Dallas—no different from any of the other motorcades I'd worked with both President Kennedy and President Eisenhower.

At times, both sides of the street were jammed with people so thick that the motorcade could barely make its way through, but at the end of Main Street we turned right onto Houston, and suddenly the number of spectators diminished considerably. The street was wide open, with just a smattering of people here and there on the sidewalk and the open grassy areas on the other side of the street. We had just entered Dealey Plaza.

I looked back at Halfback, let go of the handhold, jumped off SS-100-X onto the pavement, and, in one fluid motion, jumped back to my position on the left running board of the follow-up car as the cars continued at a steady pace.

Immediately in front of us as we traveled down Houston Street was the seven-story Texas School Book Depository. Some windows were open in the building, but there was no indication of anything unusual. We had seen people hanging out of open windows all along the route.

We were headed for the Stemmons Freeway, which would take us to the Trade Mart, and in order to get to the on-ramp, we had to turn left from Houston onto Elm Street. This was an unusually sharp turn, which required the drivers of these heavy, oversized vehicles weighted down with people to slow down considerably. Bill Greer was mindful of President Kennedy's chronic back pain, and turning too quickly on a sharp turn was something he always tried to avoid.

As the cars straightened out and began to return to the normal parade pace of about ten miles per hour, I was now standing on the left running board of the follow-up car, in the forward position. It was noticeably calmer in this area compared to the enveloping crowds back on Main Street. There were a few people on the triple overpass directly in front of us and a few dozen people on the grassy slope to the right, including a family with small children. I turned my attention to the left, scanning the sparse crowd closest to my side of the car.

Suddenly, there was a loud explosive noise, like a firecracker, that came from behind. Instinctively, I turned toward the noise, which seemed to have come from an elevated position, from the right rear, and as my eyes moved across the president's car, I saw President Kennedy grab at his throat and lurch to his left. I realized the explosive noise had been a gunshot.

I jumped off the running board, hit the pavement, and ran. My sole intention was to get onto SS-100-X and place myself between the shooter and the president and Mrs. Kennedy. My adrenaline was flowing, as the car kept moving forward and I raced with all my might to catch up.

While I was running, there was a second shot. I didn't hear it—perhaps because I was so focused on catching up to the car, or because the sounds of the motorcycles on either side of me drowned out the sound—but I am convinced, from all the evidence I've seen, read, and studied, that this second shot was the one that hit Governor Connally.

Mrs. Kennedy had turned toward the president at the sound of the first shot and was leaning toward him as he fell slightly to his left, the back brace strapped around his midsection keeping him upright. I thrust myself forward, reaching for the handhold, my eyes now focused on President and Mrs. Kennedy. Her head was nearly touching his.

I was nearly there, running as fast as I could. And then came a third shot. I heard it and felt it. The impact was like the sound of something hard hitting something hollow—like the sound of a melon shattering onto cement. In the same instant, an eruption of blood, brain matter, and bone fragments exploded from the president's head, showering over Mrs. Kennedy, the car, and me.

My legs were still moving as I desperately reached for the handhold on the presidential vehicle. I assumed more shots were coming, and I had to get up on top of that car.

Just as I grabbed the handhold, Bill Greer stepped on the gas, and the car lurched forward. I slipped, but I wasn't about to let go. I was gripping with all my strength, propelling my legs forward, my feet hitting the pavement as I held on, trying to keep up with the rapidly accelerating car. Somehow—I honestly don't know how—I lunged and pulled my body onto the car, and my foot found the step. In that same instant, Mrs. Kennedy rose up out of her seat and started climbing onto the trunk.

The car was really beginning to pick up speed, and I feared she was going to go flying off the back of the car or, God forbid, be shot by the next round. Her eyes were filled with terror as she reached out and grabbed a piece of the president's head that had flown onto the trunk. I realized she didn't even know I was there. She was in complete shock. Her husband's head had just exploded inches from her face.

I thrust myself onto the trunk, grabbed her arm, and pushed her back into the seat.

When I did this, the president's body fell to the left onto her lap.

"My God! They have shot his head off!" Mrs. Kennedy screamed.

Blood was everywhere. The floor was covered in blood and brain tissue and skull fragments. The president's head was in Mrs. Kennedy's lap, his eyes fixed, and a gaping hole in the back of his skull.

"Get us to a hospital! Get us to a hospital!" I screamed at Bill Greer.

Gripping the left doorframe with my left hand, I wedged myself between the left and right sides of the vehicle, on top of the rear seat, trying to keep my body as high as possible to shield the car's occupants from whatever shots might still be coming as we raced down Stemmons Freeway.

The time between the moment I heard the first shot and the impact of the fatal third shot was less than six seconds. Six seconds that changed the course of history. Six seconds I would relive more than anyone can imagine.

Not a day would go by, for the rest of my life, that something wouldn't remind me of President Kennedy and that day in Dallas. One gunman. Three shots. Six seconds.

It was 12:34 when we screeched to a stop at the emergency area of Parkland Memorial Hospital. Four minutes since the horror began. I jumped off the trunk just as Agent Win Lawson, the Dallas advance agent, raced inside to get two gurneys, and the agents from the follow-up car rushed to the president's car.

Dave Powers and Ken O'Donnell—President Kennedy's closest aides—had been riding as passengers in the follow-up car, and when they saw the condition of their longtime friend, they burst into sobs.

In order to get the president out, we first had to move Governor Connally, who had also been shot. Mrs. Kennedy was still in a state of shock, clutching the president's lifeless body, his bloody head still in her lap. She wouldn't let go.

"Mrs. Kennedy, please let us help the president," I said.

On the other side of the car, Paul Landis urged her too. "Please, Mrs. Kennedy."

"Please, Mrs. Kennedy, please let us get him into the hospital," I pleaded once more. Yet still she didn't move.

Knowing her as well as I did, I finally realized that she knew. She knew he was dead. She wouldn't let go because she didn't want anyone else to see him like this.

I took off my suit coat and placed it over his head and upper torso, and as I looked into her sad, hollow eyes, she finally let him go.

INSIDE TRAUMA ROOM No. 1 the doctors were doing everything they could to try to save President Kennedy. Meanwhile Governor Connally was moved from Trauma Room No. 2 to an operating room for immediate surgery.

Agent Kellerman asked me to get a line open to the White House to let our SAIC, Jerry Behn, know what had happened. Normally Behn would be on the trip, but as fate would have it, he had decided to take a few days off— his first vacation in years—before the heavy travel of the campaign began.

I was speaking to Behn when the operator cut in.

"Mr. Hill," he said. "The attorney general wants to talk to you."

"Yes, Mr. Attorney General," I said. "This is Clint."

"What is going on down there?" Robert Kennedy asked.

"Both the president and the governor have been shot . . ." I began. "We are in the emergency room at Parkland Hospital in Dallas."

And then the president's brother asked me something that haunts me still.

"Well, how bad is it?"

I did not have the courage to tell Robert Kennedy that his brother was dead. So I simply said, "It's as bad as it can get."

WE HAD NO idea who was behind the assassination. Was it one person? A conspiracy? Were they after the vice president or others as well?

What we did know was the sooner we got out of Dallas, onto Air Force One, and back to the White House, the better. But Vice President Johnson wouldn't leave on the presidential plane without Mrs. Kennedy, and Mrs. Kennedy wasn't leaving without the body of the president.

Then there was another problem. The Dallas County medical examiner had arrived and informed us that we could not remove the president's body from the hospital until an autopsy had been performed. Texas state law required that, in the case of a homicide, the victim's body could not be released until an autopsy was performed in the jurisdiction in which the homicide was committed. It could be hours or perhaps a day or more before the procedure would be complete. This was completely unacceptable to us.

After a much heated discussion, Roy Kellerman, Ken O'Donnell, and Dave Powers convinced the authorities that since this involved the President of the United States, we should be able to take his body back to the nation's capital for an autopsy.

Finally, the Texas authorities conceded—with one stipulation. We could take the president's body and return to Washington, as long as there was a medical professional who stayed with the body and would return to Dallas to testify.

"We have the right man for the job," I volunteered. "Admiral George Burkley, the president's physician." The discussion was over. Mrs. Kennedy insisted on riding in the back of the hearse with Admiral Burkley, so I climbed in right behind her. Scrunched together, sitting on our knees, still in our bloodstained clothes, we didn't say a word on the drive back to Love Field. What could one say? The world had stopped. And there I was, in the back of a hearse with Admiral Burkley, Mrs. Kennedy, and the body of President John F. Kennedy.

VICE PRESIDENT LYNDON Johnson had been secretly rushed back to Love Field shortly before President Kennedy's death was publicly announced and was waiting aboard the presidential aircraft for Mrs. Kennedy. The crew of Air Force One had removed some seats in the rear of the aircraft to make room for the casket, and now we had to get the casket up the steps and into the back of the plane.

Paul stayed with Mrs. Kennedy while I helped my fellow agents lift the casket out of the hearse. Silently, and with as much dignity as possible, we heaved the heavy bronze casket up the narrow steps of the portable staircase, only to discover that it was too wide to go through the door.

We were all emotionally shattered, and the frustration of the moment was nearly unbearable. We had been trained to think of every possible scenario, to plan every detail down to the minute, but none of us had ever envisioned this. The only solution was to break off the handles in order to get the casket through the door.

Once the casket was in place, Mrs. Kennedy walked up the stairs and sat in the seat next to the casket. For all intents and purposes, Lyndon Johnson was now the president, so the agents on the 4:00–midnight shift were protecting him, but soon we got word that Johnson needed to be officially sworn in by a federal judge before we took off.

Calls were made, and soon thereafter federal judge Sarah Hughes arrived and boarded Air Force One.

Before the swearing-in ceremony began, I was notified that Mrs. Kennedy wanted to see me in the presidential cabin. I walked through the aircraft, past Vice President Johnson and his staff, and into the compartment.

"Yes, Mrs. Kennedy, what can I do for you?"

Still in her pink suit, encrusted with blood, she walked toward me and grasped my hands. "What's going to happen to you now, Mr. Hill?"

I clenched my jaw and swallowed hard. *How could she be thinking about me?* "I'll be okay, Mrs. Kennedy," I said. "I'll be okay."

Minutes later, I stood in the doorway of the presidential suite behind agents Roy Kellerman and Lem Johns and watched as Lyndon B. Johnson took the oath of office with his left hand on President Kennedy's Catholic prayer book, to become the thirty-sixth president of the United States. White House photographer Cecil Stoughton captured the historic moment, and whenever I see that iconic photo, a crushing sadness washes over me, just as it did that Friday afternoon in Dallas.

At 2:47 p.m. Central Standard Time, Air Force One departed Love Field in Dallas, headed back to Washington with a new president.

It was dark when we arrived at Andrews Air Force Base at 5:58 p.m. Eastern Standard Time. As soon as the plane came to a stop, the front steps were put in place, and a hydraulic lift was raised to the rear door of the plane to facilitate the removal of the casket. Seconds later, Attorney General Robert Kennedy came bursting down the aisle toward Mrs. Kennedy. No one was closer to President Kennedy than his brother Bobby, and it was heart-wrenching to witness the reunion of the brother and the widow of the president.

It had been decided on the way back to Washington that the autopsy would take place at Bethesda Naval Hospital, and as soon as we were on our way, President Johnson emerged from Air Force One with his wife, Lady Bird.

America was in a state of shock over what had transpired just a few hours earlier, but it was important to know that a peaceful and orderly transition had been made and that our new president was firmly in charge. And so, standing before the blinding lights of the television crews, with Mrs. Johnson by his side, Lyndon Baines Johnson made his first remarks as President of the United States to the American people.

"This is a sad time for all people," he began. "We have suffered a loss that cannot be weighed." His slow, deliberate Southern drawl was markedly different from the crisp Boston accent to which the American people had become accustomed.

"For me, it is a deep, personal tragedy," Johnson continued. "I know that the world shares the sorrow that Mrs. Kennedy and her family will bear. I will do my best. That is all I can do. I ask for your help—and God's."

THE AUTOPSY WENT on through the night, and it wasn't until 4:24 a.m. that we returned to the White House.

A military honor guard was waiting at the North Portico to carry the casket into the White House to the East Room, where it was placed on a catafalque identical to one used for Abraham Lincoln in 1865. And then the honor guard was posted around the casket to keep vigil during the period of repose.

My good pal Paul Rundle had come to the White House to be there when we arrived.

"Clint, is there anything I can do?" he asked.

I shook my head. No, there was nothing anyone could do. Our president was dead.

When Mrs. Kennedy finally went up to the second-floor living quarters,

I went to my office in the Map Room and scrawled some notes about my recollections of the horror I had witnessed. It was hardly necessary, for every detail was seared into my soul.

At 6:00 a.m., I left the White House and drove the seven miles to my home in Arlington. The boys were still asleep, but Gwen was in the kitchen when I walked in the front door. When I saw the look on her face, I realized how bad I must have appeared. Unshaven and still wearing the same clothes I'd had on for the past twenty-four hours, my white shirt and pants still caked with President Kennedy's blood.

She wanted to know the details of what had happened, but I couldn't talk. I knew that if the words came out of my mouth, if I spoke about what I had been through, my emotions would get the best of me. I couldn't allow that to happen.

There was no time to grieve, no time to rest. I had to get myself cleaned up and back to the White House.

18

The Funeral

The agents who had been on President Kennedy's detail were now, suddenly, protecting President Johnson and his family. Agents were being flown in from field offices all over the country in preparation for the state funeral, and most of the men were working double shifts. Still, Paul Landis and I were the only agents with Mrs. Kennedy.

There was a private Mass for the Kennedy family and close friends in the East Room at 10:00 a.m. on Saturday, November 23, after which I accompanied Mrs. Kennedy to the Oval Office to make note of President Kennedy's personal items that she wanted to bring with her—his rocking chair, the glass-encased coconut shell from his PT-109 rescue, family photos, the whale's tooth scrimshaw she had given him as a gift the previous Christmas. That afternoon we drove to Arlington National Cemetery to choose the burial site.

Meanwhile, in Dallas, a man named Lee Harvey Oswald had been arrested and charged with the assassination of President Kennedy. On the sixth floor of the Texas School Book Depository, where Oswald worked, detectives found boxes stacked into a sniper's nest near the window; three spent cartridges on the floor below the window; and a gun believed to be the murder weapon—a 6.5mm rifle stashed in a corner near the freight elevator, also on the sixth floor. Oswald had fled the building immediately after the assassination, killed a police officer named J. D. Tippit, and was found hiding in a movie theater.

I would analyze the assassination from every angle for the rest of my life, but at the time I couldn't dwell on who had killed President Kennedy; I had to focus on protecting Mrs. Kennedy and on the countless arrangements that had to be made for the state funeral.

SUNDAY, NOVEMBER 24, was the day the president's body would be taken to the Capitol to lie in state. That morning, SAIC Jerry Behn summoned me to his office in the East Wing. He knew I was struggling to hold it together—we all were—but he wanted to thank me, and try to lift my spirits. While I was there, I got an urgent message to return to the mansion. Mrs. Kennedy and her brother-in-law Robert Kennedy wanted to view the president's body one final time.

I raced to the hallway outside the East Room, where General Godfrey McHugh was waiting with Mrs. Kennedy and the attorney general. After requesting the honor guard to turn around and move back from the casket, General McHugh carefully folded back the flag, and together we raised the lid of the casket. When I saw President Kennedy lying there, confined in that narrow casket with his eyes closed so peacefully, just like he was sleeping, it was all I could do to keep from breaking down. McHugh and I slowly moved back from the casket as Mrs. Kennedy and the president's brother walked over to view the man they loved.

Weeping, Mrs. Kennedy turned to me and asked if I would bring her a pair of scissors. I quickly found some in the drawer of the usher's office across the hall, and after placing them in her hands, I turned away to give her some privacy. Standing a few feet behind Mrs. Kennedy, I heard the sound of the scissors, beneath the painful cries, as she presumably clipped a few locks of her husband's hair.

Robert Kennedy gently closed the lid of the casket, grabbed Mrs. Kennedy's hand, and together they walked out of the East Room. General McHugh and I checked the casket to make sure it was securely closed, and out of habit I looked at my watch to take note of the time—12:46 p.m. I had seen President Kennedy for the last time; the casket would never be opened again.

It was shortly after this that I got word that Lee Harvey Oswald had been shot and killed in Dallas while being transferred from one location to another. Press photographers and reporters were covering the transfer of the suspect closely, and when the unpredictable shooting was shown on live television, witnessed by millions of Americans who had been glued to their TVs for the past two days, the entire nation was left in a state of utter shock.

In sharp contrast to the chaos that was unfolding in Dallas, the White House was a somber scene as President Kennedy's casket was placed on an artillery carriage and led by a team of gray horses in a solemn procession to the U.S. Capitol. Directly behind the caisson, Mrs. Kennedy rode with the children, the attorney general, and President and Mrs. Johnson in a Cadillac that was now being used as the presidential limousine.

We headed out the Northeast Gate of the White House, the procession moving slowly, at the pace of the marching horses, and as we turned onto Pennsylvania Avenue, thousands of people stood—ten and fifteen deep—on both sides of the wide street. From my position in the motorcade, I had a clear view of the tearful, anguished faces lining the route. It was unlike any other motorcade I had ever been in. There were no cheers or hollers, no clapping hands or waving banners; 300,000 people, dead silent. The only sounds you could hear—sounds that would remain forever in my memory—were the clip-clop of the horses' hooves and the repetitive cadence of the military corps' muffled drums all the way to the Capitol.

For twenty-two hours, President Kennedy's flag-draped casket stayed in the Rotunda. A tidal wave of people had come from suburbs and neighboring states, queuing for hours on into the night, just to have a few seconds to pay their respects to their beloved president. At one point, the line was ten people wide, stretching for three miles, and by the time the doors finally closed on Monday morning, a quarter of a million people had filed past the casket.

Mrs. Kennedy was heavily involved in the funeral plans, and while there was a certain protocol in place for state funerals for a deceased president—it had been assumed that either Truman or Eisenhower would be next—there were certain things Mrs. Kennedy added to make it personal. One of the things she was insisting on was to walk behind the caisson from the White House to St. Matthew's, where the funeral Mass would take place, and then on to Arlington National Cemetery. With heads of state from countries all over the world planning to participate, we knew that if Mrs. Kennedy walked, they too would feel compelled to walk. The President of the United

States had just been assassinated in broad daylight, and to have every major world leader walking slowly through the streets of Washington, D.C. was going to be a security nightmare. I tried to talk Mrs. Kennedy out of it, and ultimately she agreed to compromise by walking just one segment of the procession—from the White House to St. Matthew's. Agent Landis and I would be right alongside her, but I knew it would be the longest mile I had ever walked.

MONDAY, NOVEMBER 25, was the day of President Kennedy's funeral. It was also John F. Kennedy Jr.'s third birthday.

That morning, Paul Landis and I accompanied Mrs. Kennedy and the president's two brothers, Bobby and Teddy, in the Chrysler limousine back to the Capitol, and after a brief ceremony the casket was carried back down the Capitol steps and placed on the caisson for the procession back to the White House.

The car pulled into the Northeast Gate, and up ahead we could see the entourage of dignitaries and world leaders assembled on the steps of the North Portico. It was an extraordinary gathering: France's President Charles de Gaulle, Ethiopia's Emperor Haile Selassie, Belgium's King Baudouin, Ireland's President Eamon de Valera, Britain's Duke of Edinburgh, Germany's President Heinrich Lübke, Berlin's Mayor Willy Brandt, Norway's Crown Prince Harald, Greece's Queen Frederika—just to name a few. And of course, the new U.S. president, Lyndon Baines Johnson, and his wife, Lady Bird.

A company of U.S. Marines led the procession out the Northwest Gate, followed by nine pipers from the Scottish Black Watch, who—marching in their red tartan kilts and white spats, their bagpipes echoing a poignant wail that seemed to be synchronized with the clip-clop of the horses pulling the caisson carrying President Kennedy's body—were there at Mrs. Kennedy's insistence because her husband had so enjoyed their performance on the White House lawn just two weeks earlier. The presidential flag came next, followed by Black Jack, the riderless horse, and then the mass of walkers.

The details of the day are etched in my mind forever, as I wrote about them in *Five Days in November.*

With her face shrouded by a black veil, Mrs. Kennedy led the procession to St. Matthew's, flanked by the president's brothers, Bobby and Ted, while Paul Landis and I walked solemnly alongside them. Camera crews filmed every step so that people around the world could watch via satellite broadcast. The three U.S. television networks had ceased regular programming to run the funeral uninterrupted, and 95 percent of Americans were watching.

For all the scripted pageantry, planned out minute by minute, the one moment that the world would remember was entirely spontaneous. At the conclusion of the Requiem Mass at St. Matthew's, Mrs. Kennedy walked hand in hand with Caroline and John, and then stood on the outside steps watching as the casket was brought out and placed back on the caisson. I was standing just behind and to the right of them. When the military simultaneously saluted their fallen commander in chief, I saw Mrs. Kennedy lean down to John and whisper in his ear. With the world's eyes on him, young John Fitzgerald Kennedy Jr., three years old on that day, thrust his tiny shoulders back, raised his right hand taut to his brow, and rendered a perfect salute to his father.

Shortly thereafter, I was helping Mrs. Kennedy into the backseat of the limousine—in which she would ride to Arlington National Cemetery for the burial—when former presidents Harry S. Truman and Dwight D. Eisenhower approached the car. Having just witnessed that poignant salute, they were both having difficulty controlling their emotions. Profound sorrow was etched in every line of their faces as they expressed their sympathies to Mrs. Kennedy. It was not the proper order of things, that these two men should be here at the funeral of their much younger successor, and for me to see the utter despair in General Eisenhower's eyes—a man I revered as one of the world's great leaders—was heart-wrenching.

And so it was that amid this remarkable gathering of the world's most powerful men and women, it was the spontaneous salute by the innocent boy to his dead father that captured our hearts.

19

The Year After

With President Kennedy laid to rest, President Johnson now had the difficult task of pulling the country together. On Wednesday, November 27, Thanksgiving Eve, he addressed the nation in a joint session of Congress. After several minutes of standing ovation, the Congress members sat, and President Johnson began.

"All I have, I would have given gladly not to be standing here today. The greatest leader of our time has been struck down by the foulest deed of our time. Today, John Fitzgerald Kennedy lives on in the immortal words and work that he left behind. He lives on in the minds and memories of mankind. He lives on in the hearts of his countrymen. No words are sad enough to express our sense of loss. No words are strong enough to express our determination to continue the forward thrust of America that he began."

Again the room erupted into applause. The president continued with a stirring speech reminding the people of President Kennedy's dreams—conquering the vastness of space; developing partnerships with other like-minded nations around the world; education for all children; care for the elderly; and, above all, equal rights for Americans no matter their race or color. President Johnson urged the lawmakers before him that the most fitting tribute to President Kennedy would be to continue what he had begun.

Knowing he had a limited amount of time to capitalize on this period of grief, President Johnson set the wheels in motion. No one but the president himself could have envisioned that over the course of the next year he would get more legislation passed in such a short time frame than any other president had in the history of the United States.

NORMALLY, WHEN A new president takes office, he moves into the White House immediately following the Inauguration. But this was no normal transition. President Johnson did not want it to appear that he was forcing Mrs. Kennedy and the children out of their home, so he told them to take their time as she decided where she wanted to live. I had assumed that I would stay with Mrs. Kennedy and the children until she left the White House, but beyond that, I didn't have any idea what the Secret Service would do with me.

Several days after the funeral, Secret Service Chief Jim Rowley called me into his office.

"Clint," he said, "President Johnson has requested the Secret Service provide protection for Mrs. Kennedy and the children for at least one more year. We have agreed to do so."

"I'm glad to hear that, Mr. Rowley," I said. "I think it's a good decision."

Rowley explained that Mrs. Kennedy had been informed that she could keep the agents currently working with her and the children or choose a new team. Whatever she wanted.

A lump filled my throat as Rowley was talking. To be assigned to a former first lady would be a career ender. But I couldn't imagine leaving her. Not now. Fortunately, it wasn't my choice. I would go wherever Rowley assigned me.

"Mrs. Kennedy didn't hesitate," Rowley said. "She wants Bob Foster, Lynn Meredith, and Tom Wells to stay with the children."

I nodded. That would be best for the children, to maintain consistency.

"And for herself," Rowley continued, "she said there was no choice to be made at all. She wants Paul Landis and Clint Hill."

I would be the Special Agent in Charge of the small five-man team of agents that would be known as KPD—Kennedy Protective Detail. I was officially no longer on the White House Detail.

• • •

Ten days after the assassination, Chief Rowley informed me that I was going to be given a commendation for my actions in Dallas—the Treasury Department's highest award for bravery. Agent Rufus Youngblood, who had jumped on top of Vice President Johnson immediately upon hearing the gunshots in Dealey Plaza, was also being honored in a separate ceremony.

I did not want an award, nor did I believe I deserved one, but I agreed to show up. Gwen brought Chris and Corey for the brief ceremony in the Treasury Building on December 3, standing by as Secretary Douglas Dillon handed me the citation and a medal. Mrs. Kennedy had come, along with her sister, Lee, and President Kennedy's sisters Jean Smith and Pat Lawford, and it meant a lot to me that they were there—far more than the medal itself. It was the first and only time Mrs. Kennedy met my wife and my sons.

Shortly after we returned to Washington from Dallas, Undersecretary of State Averell Harriman, who had been a close friend to both President and Mrs. Kennedy, offered his home in Georgetown at 3038 N Street as a temporary residence for Mrs. Kennedy and the children until they found a permanent home. She accepted the generous offer, and on December 6 they moved out of the White House. That same day, I packed up my files and moved everything out of my little office in the Map Room.

After many tearful good-byes to the White House staff, Mrs. Kennedy, Miss Shaw, Caroline, and John got into the limousine at the South Portico, and we drove away from the White House together for the last time. No one said anything as we headed to Georgetown. Everything had changed, and none of us knew what the future held. Our hearts were heavy, and we were all just so terribly sad.

Christmas of 1963 was exceptionally difficult. Excruciating. We flew to Palm Beach as we had for the three previous years, and while Ambassador Kennedy and much of the rest of the family were there, there was no *Honey Fitz* to take out for a lunchtime cruise, no laughter around the swimming pool, and just the small group of agents on the Kennedy Protective Detail.

In hindsight, there is no doubt I was suffering from what is now known as post-traumatic stress disorder, or PTSD. I'm sure Mrs. Kennedy, along with everyone else in the presidential limousine and in the follow-up car— the other Secret Service agents, Governor and Mrs. Connally, Dave Powers, and Ken O'Donnell—were all suffering the same mental distress I was. But none of us talked about it—certainly not with each other. There was no counseling. We each just went on with our lives the best we could.

AFTER THE HOLIDAYS, we returned to Washington. Mrs. Kennedy bought a house across the street from the Harrimans', at 3017 N Street—a large brick colonial that had lots of room and two beautiful magnolia trees out front—and at first it seemed ideal. The private backyard was paved and had a big tree in the center, and John would ride his little tricycle around and around. But almost immediately, the crowds started to come. People would stand on the sidewalk with cameras, trying to peer in the windows, and as soon as we walked out the front door, they'd snap photos, one right after the other. It really got bad when a tour company started bringing buses by the house. The buses would squeeze down the narrow street and stop, allowing the people to get out and take pictures. We tried to have the operation ceased, but the city allowed the buses to carry on.

Mrs. Kennedy and the children started spending more and more time away from Washington. They went skiing in Stowe, Vermont; she took a trip to Antigua in the Caribbean, and a lot of trips to New York City, where we stayed at the Carlyle Hotel. We were all trying to keep busy, planning the next trip, making arrangements. But everywhere we turned, there was something to remind us of what had happened. You couldn't look at a newspaper; you couldn't watch television.

The nation was obsessed with the assassination and finding out what had really happened. Even though the Dallas police were confident that Lee Harvey Oswald was the assassin—they had plenty of evidence against him—when Jack Ruby killed Oswald on November 24, it sparked a flurry of distrust and conspiracy theories. There were questions regarding Cuban or Russian involvement because of Oswald's connections to both; suspicions that the CIA or the Mafia had been behind it; and speculation that there had been more than one shooter.

President Johnson took swift action, and on November 29, 1963, one week after the assassination, he created the President's Commission on the Assassination of President Kennedy and appointed Chief Justice Earl Warren the chairman. The commission consisted of two U.S. senators—Richard Russell, a Democrat from Georgia, and John Cooper, a Republican from Kentucky; two U.S. congressmen—Hale Boggs, a Democrat from Louisiana, and Gerald Ford, a Republican from Michigan; the former director of the CIA, Allen Dulles; and John J. McCloy, former president of the World Bank. The commission was supported by a staff that included J. Lee Rankin as general counsel, a number of assistants counsel, and other staff members. All of the men were highly respected, and Johnson purposely chose the politically diverse group to avoid any appearance of bias. The goal was simply to seek the truth and to report the findings and conclusion to President Johnson, the American people, and to the world.

When I returned to the White House on the morning of November 23, I had gone to my office and written down everything I could remember about what had happened. Whenever there was any kind of incident, we were always required to write a report. I knew even before the Warren Commission, as it came to be known, was organized that the loss of the president—still as unimaginable as it was—would require an intensive investigation, and I knew that the sooner I recorded my recollections, the more accurate they would be.

On November 29, Chief Rowley requested all of us who had been in Dallas to provide him with a typewritten, signed statement of what we had witnessed. None of us talked to each other. We all wrote exactly what we had seen and heard and remembered.

I wrote the report from my notes, typing five and a half pages, single-spaced, ending at the time we arrived at the White House at 4:24 a.m. when the casket was placed in the East Room. At the bottom, I signed my name, Clinton J. Hill, and beneath it typed: Special Agent, U.S. Secret Service.

In the following months, the Warren Commission began conducting personal interviews, and I was summoned to appear before the commission on March 9, 1964. I knew it was something that needed to be done, but I was not looking forward to talking about what had happened. I hadn't discussed the assassination with anyone—not Gwen, not the other agents, not Mrs. Kennedy. Speaking to the Warren Commission would be the first time.

Assistant counsel Arlen Specter asked the majority of the questions, while members of the commission listened, took notes, and interjected when they required more information. Specter began with questions about my age, education, previous employment, and entry into the Secret Service. Then he went straight to the trip to Texas.

"Did you have any special duty assigned to you at that time?" he asked.

"Yes, sir. I was responsible for the protection of Mrs. Kennedy."

"And, in a general way, what does that sort of assignment involve?"

"I tried to remain as close to her at all times as possible, and in this particular trip that meant being with the president, because all of their doings on this trip were together rather than separate. I would go over her schedule to make sure she knows what she is expected to do; discuss it with her; remain in her general area all the time; protect her from any danger."

Specter then asked me to describe what the president and Mrs. Kennedy did upon their arrival in Dallas. I didn't get very far before Specter interrupted and began asking specific questions, one right after the other. As soon as I'd answer, he'd fire off the next round. "What size was the crowd? What time did the motorcade depart? How many cars in the motorcade? What speed were you going?"

Finally, he asked me to describe what happened when we turned onto Elm Street.

I took a deep breath. "Well, as we came out of the curve and began to straighten up, I was viewing the people scattered throughout the entire park. And I heard a noise from my right rear, which to me seemed to be a firecracker. I immediately looked to my right and, in so doing, my eyes had to cross the presidential limousine, and I saw President Kennedy grab at himself and lurch forward and to the left."

It was the first time I'd said these words out loud. It was awful. I could see it all happening right before my eyes. *Oh God. Something is wrong. I have to get there. Someone is shooting at the president.*

I must have paused as the images and thoughts swirled in my head, because Mr. Specter said, "Why don't you just proceed, in narrative form, to tell us."

Before I could answer, Representative Boggs interjected, "This was the first shot?"

"This is the first sound that I heard. Yes, sir," I said. "I jumped from the car, realizing that something was wrong, ran to the presidential limousine. Just about as I reached it, there was another sound, which was different than the first sound. I think I described it in my statement as though someone was shooting a revolver into a hard object—it seemed to have some type of an echo."

That sound. Oh, that awful sound.

"I put my right foot, I believe it was, on the left rear step of the automobile, and I had ahold of the handgrip with my hand, when the car lurched forward. I lost my footing and I had to run about three or four more steps before I could get back up in the car."

And then Mrs. Kennedy . . . oh God, what is she doing?

"Between the time I originally grabbed the handhold and until I was up on the car, Mrs. Kennedy—the second noise that I heard had . . ."

I closed my eyes, hoping the image would go away, but I kept talking anyway.

". . . had removed a portion of the president's head. And he had slumped noticeably to his left. Mrs. Kennedy had jumped up from the seat and was, it appeared to me, reaching for something coming off the right rear bumper of the car, the right rear tail, when she noticed that I was trying to climb on the car. She turned toward me, and I grabbed her and put her back in the seat, crawled up on top of the backseat and lay there."

In fact, even though there was a still photo and two separate amateur films taken of Mrs. Kennedy climbing onto the trunk just as I had described, I would later read that she told the commission she had no recollection of doing that. None whatsoever. She was in shock. Who wouldn't be?

No one expected there to be gunfire. Hearing the sudden loud noise and in the same instant seeing her husband's body jerk forward as his hands raised to his throat, Mrs. Kennedy instinctively turned toward him. Trying to determine what was wrong, she leaned toward him, placed her hands on his left arm, and turned to look into his face, so close that her head was nearly touching his. Another loud crack, and suddenly, blood, brain, and bone fragments exploded out of her husband's head, before her very eyes. A few inches to the left, and it would have been her head instead of his.

Mr. Specter continued with his questions, and I answered each one as best as I could, all the while trying to maintain my composure. Finally, it was over; there were no more questions, and I was able to go home.

MAY 29, 1964, would have been President Kennedy's forty-seventh birthday. That morning I accompanied Mrs. Kennedy, John, Caroline, and Robert Kennedy and his wife, Ethel, to Mass at St. Matthew's Roman Catholic cathedral, and then we went to Arlington.

In the six months since President Kennedy was buried at Arlington National Cemetery, more than three million visitors had passed by his grave, turning it into the number one tourist destination in Washington, surpassing the White House and the Lincoln Memorial. A permanent gravestone was still being designed, so in the meantime all that marked the final resting place of the thirty-fifth president was the eternal flame, centered on a twenty-by-thirty-foot square of grass, surrounded by a low white picket fence.

I had requested the cemetery officials rope off the area for the short time we would be there, to give the family some privacy from the gawkers, but there was no way to keep the public away completely. Sniffles and sobs emanated from the bystanders as the widow, dressed completely in black, and her young children, in matching ivory coats, walked solemnly toward the grave and then knelt to pray.

On June 12, 1964, Paul Landis handed in his resignation. He had given himself six months to see if he felt better, but being with Mrs. Kennedy and the children every day was too difficult. I was disappointed he was leaving; we had been through so much together that we were like brothers. It would be hard to find someone else with whom I could work so seamlessly under these fragile circumstances.

It was around the time Paul left that Mrs. Kennedy decided to move to New York City. The tour buses had not stopped, and she just didn't feel comfortable in Washington's political bubble without her husband. She had always loved New York, and she hoped that amid the crowds she might be able to come and go without anyone noticing.

I was with her as she searched for a suitable place, and she finally settled on a large apartment that occupied the entire fifteenth floor at 1040 Fifth

Avenue. It was close to the Metropolitan Museum of Art, just a few blocks from Stephen and Jean Kennedy Smith's residence, and within walking distance of the Carlyle Hotel. Once she moved, I too relocated to New York, where I lived in a small room at the Carlyle. It didn't make sense to uproot Gwen and the boys because Mrs. Kennedy was frequently traveling—and besides, there was no way we could afford to live in the vicinity. The move was difficult for everybody—Mrs. Kennedy, Caroline, John, the agents, and the staff. Everything was different. Routines changed; the familiar surroundings of Washington were exchanged for the hustling, unfamiliar streets of New York; temporary agents came and went as needed to fill the shifts. There was a trip to Italy, a rental house on Long Island, and occasional trips to Boston, where plans were begun for the John F. Kennedy Presidential Library—always something in the works to keep our minds distracted and focused on the future rather than the past. It was the only way we managed to get up each day.

THE 1964 DEMOCRATIC National Convention was being held in Atlantic City at the end of August, and a tribute to President Kennedy was planned for the last night of the convention. I was not involved in the politics, but it was clear that President Johnson and his staff were concerned about the effect Robert Kennedy might have on the nomination proceedings. Even though President Johnson was very popular, the political power of the brother of the assassinated president couldn't be underestimated.

Mrs. Kennedy was reticent about being involved in the convention, but she felt obliged to do something, and in the end she agreed to attend a reception for all the delegates who had supported her husband in 1960. We departed almost immediately after the reception was over, flying on the *Caroline*, the Kennedy family's private plane, to Newport, and then continuing on to Mrs. Kennedy's mother's Hammersmith Farm residence by car.

That evening, when Robert Kennedy stepped to the podium on the stage at the Democratic National Convention to introduce *A Thousand Days*, the film honoring his brother, the huge auditorium erupted into a roaring ovation. Kennedy, who was now a candidate for the U.S. Senate from New York, tried to begin his speech seven times, but he no more than opened his mouth and the roar swelled even louder. The applause went on for seventeen minutes.

ON SEPTEMBER 24, 1964, the Warren Commission presented its 888-page report to President Johnson. The exhaustive investigation included testimony and questioning from more than five hundred witnesses, the details of which would be published in twenty-six volumes. When the documents were released to the public several days later, the highlights were revealed in bold headlines: "Report Blames Oswald Alone in Death of JFK."

The Warren Commission jointly and unanimously concluded that Lee Harvey Oswald was the lone shooter, and the shots that killed President Kennedy and wounded Governor Connally were fired from the sixth-floor window at the southeast corner of the Texas School Book Depository. This conclusion was based on many facts, including: the Mannlicher-Carcano 6.5mm Italian rifle from which the shots were fired was owned by and in the possession of Oswald. Oswald carried this rifle into the Book Depository building on the morning of November 22, 1963. Oswald, at the time of the assassination, was present at the window from which the shots were fired. Additionally, based on testimony from experts and their analysis of films of the assassination, the commission concluded that a rifleman of Lee Harvey Oswald's capabilities could have fired the shots from the rifle used in the assassination within the elapsed time of the shooting. In addition, seven months earlier, Oswald had attempted to kill Major General Edwin A. Walker in Dallas, thereby demonstrating his disposition to take a human life.

When it came to the motive for the assassination, the commission admitted it could not make any definitive determination, but clues could be found in Oswald's family history; his lack of education; his deep-rooted resentment of authority; his inability to enter into meaningful relationships with people; and his avowed commitment to Marxism and Communism, along with an overtly expressed antagonism toward the United States. The twenty-four-year-old man had failed at nearly everything he had ever attempted throughout his short life, yet he yearned to "be somebody"—someone who would be remembered in history.

Regarding the killing of Oswald by Jack Ruby on November 24, 1963, the commission blamed lapses by the Dallas Police Department, yet found no evidence that Oswald or Ruby was part of any conspiracy, domestic or foreign.

As I read through the newspaper accounts, there was some comfort in knowing they had determined that Oswald had acted alone. I was glad to know that speculations of conspiracies were unfounded. But most important to me were the commission's statements regarding the Secret Service.

The commission recognized the various challenges faced by the Secret Service in performing its duties and boldly stated that "consistent with their high responsibilities, presidents can never be protected from every potential threat. The Secret Service's difficulty in meeting its protective responsibility varies with the activities and the nature of the occupant of the Office of President and his willingness to conform to plans for his safety."

In large part, the commission praised the Secret Service, and the particular agents on the trip, for well-conceived advance preparations that were ably executed according to standard operating procedures. But, clearly, improvements needed to be made.

The Protective Research Section was found to be inadequate in that it lacked sufficient trained personnel, and the current system of index-card tracking needed to be updated with "mechanical and technical assistance." When it came to threat suspects, there was insufficient liaison and coordination of information between the Secret Service and other federal agencies. The FBI had been tracking Lee Harvey Oswald because of his relations with the Soviet Union and affinity for Communism, but because he had never made a specific threat against, or shown any interest in, the president, the FBI had no reason to share his identity with the Secret Service. We didn't know he existed, let alone that he worked at the Texas School Book Depository, which happened to be directly on the route of the presidential motorcade in Dallas. And, while it was not a matter of practice to investigate and check every building along a motorcade route, this was something that needed to be changed.

There was the issue of the presidential vehicle itself, which was neither bulletproof nor bullet resistant, and the fact that the access to the president by the agent riding in the right front seat of the car was interfered with by a metal bar some fifteen inches above the back of the front seat, as well as by passengers in the jump seats.

It was noted that the Secret Service did not have sufficient personnel or adequate facilities at the time of the assassination and would need increased resources—resources that Congress would have to approve—to achieve what was being recommended. "Within these limitations," the report stated, "the Commission finds that the agents most immediately responsible for the president's safety reacted promptly at the time the shots were fired from the Texas School Book Depository Building." Specifically, the report stated, "at the time of the shots in Dallas, Agent Clinton J. Hill leaped to the president's rescue as quickly as humanly possible."

I was satisfied with the commission's conclusion that Oswald acted alone, and to this day, I believe that to be the case—there has never been any factual evidence to prove otherwise. The one conclusion with which I disagree is the "Magic Bullet Theory"—the notion that the first shot which passed through President Kennedy's neck then entered Governor Connally's body. Governor and Mrs. Connally and I were all of the same opinion—having been up-close witnesses—that the governor's wounds were caused by the second shot, the one that did not hit President Kennedy.

But almost immediately there were cries of foul play and accusations of a cover-up. There were indeed discrepancies in the investigation, but the majority of them were due to inconsistent recollections that came out in the chaos of the minutes and hours following the tragedy. No two people will react to a tragedy of such magnitude in the same way, or remember the events exactly the same. Just as Mrs. Kennedy had no recollection of climbing onto the trunk of the car, in spite of the undeniable photographic evidence. But despite the lack of concrete evidence of a conspiracy, people did not want to believe that one person—an insignificant loner—could have the power to take the life of our beloved president.

For those of us on the White House Detail, the report didn't change anything. President Kennedy was dead. We had failed. I had failed. And I would have to live with that for the rest of my life.

NOT LONG AFTER the release of the Warren Report, I was notified that immediately following the presidential election in November I would be transferred to a new assignment. I was not given any indication where I might be sent, but I assumed it would be a field office somewhere far from Washington, where I'd return to doing investigations.

I didn't have much interaction with the agents on the White House Detail anymore, but I would read in the newspaper that President Johnson was traveling here and there as the campaign heated up, and I knew the guys had their hands full. One day, I got word that President Johnson was coming to New York City and wanted to stop by 1040 Fifth Avenue to pay his respects to Mrs. Kennedy.

Shortly before the president was due to arrive, Robert Kennedy showed up at the apartment. Mrs. Kennedy had requested that he be there during the president's visit. It was well known that President Johnson and Robert Kennedy did not care for each other—to put it mildly—and I wondered if the president had any inkling the attorney general would be there when he arrived.

I was waiting in front of the building to greet the president and his entourage when the unmarked black cars pulled up. The agents in the follow-up car got out and moved into position, and then Agent Rufus Youngblood stepped out of the right front seat of the president's limousine to open the rear door for the passenger in the backseat.

It was a crisp fall evening, with a slight breeze, and as President Johnson stepped out of the car he straightened his suit coat and smoothed back his hair. He was an imposing man, standing about six feet four inches tall, and as he approached I extended my hand and said, "Hello, Mr. President, I'm Agent Clint Hill."

He looked at me with a bit of a squint, and then moved his right hand into his rear pocket, pulled out a handkerchief, and blew his nose. No handshake occurred. It all happened in front of the agents on the White House Detail, and I will never forget the embarrassment I felt. It was humiliating.

Clenching my jaw, I escorted the president up to Mrs. Kennedy's apartment and then waited with Rufus Youngblood outside the door of the apartment. The president stayed for twenty-five minutes, and then the door opened and out he came, accompanied by Mrs. Kennedy and the attorney general.

"Bobby and I will escort you to your car, Mr. President," Mrs. Kennedy said. So down we went, the two Kennedys, the president, Agent Youngblood, and me, crammed into the elevator. I followed closely behind Mrs. Kennedy as the three of them walked outside and stood under the awning at the front of 1040 Fifth Avenue. President Johnson had a great big smile on his face as he grasped Mrs. Kennedy's hands and said good-bye, while Robert Kennedy's thoughts seemed to be elsewhere. White House photographer Cecil Stoughton happened to snap a photograph, which he sent to me the next day. The look on my face says it all.

On my last day in New York, Mrs. Kennedy threw a surprise farewell party for me in her office. There weren't many people there—just her small staff and the other agents. They tried to make it upbeat, and we shared memories of the fun times we had had together. Mrs. Kennedy brought out a large cardboard poster with a cutout picture of an anonymous Secret Service agent wearing sunglasses, and above the agent in big letters it said: MUDDY GAP WYOMING WELCOMES ITS NEWEST CITIZEN. It was a gag gift typical of Mrs. Kennedy's humor, insinuating I was being sent to some remote town out in the middle of nowhere, and everyone had signed their names.

Then she handed me a black three-ring binder that she had titled: "The Travels of Clinton J. Hill."

The plastic sleeves inside were filled with photos that chronicled our four years together—a priceless memento of the good days. A reminder that there had been good days before that one dreadful day.

As it turned out, I would not be going to a remote field office. I was being sent back to the White House Detail to protect President Lyndon B. Johnson.

PART THREE

With President Johnson

From the moment he took office on November 22, 1963, President Johnson was a man on a mission, determined to use his powerful position to create a better life for all Americans, in all aspects of their lives, and by the end of 1965 his administration would pass more transformative legislation than most presidents achieve in their entire terms. His vision for a Great Society and his War on Poverty were not just rhetoric; he proved that strong leadership, combined with knowledge of the political system, could indeed effect change. Things we now take for granted—Medicare, federally funded public education, laws that protect our water, air, and environment, as well as the historic Civil Rights Acts that banned discrimination—were all passed through Congress in LBJ's first two years as president.

Despite this long list of notable accomplishments on domestic issues, it would be the U.S. involvement in Vietnam that would become his overriding concern, and which would become synonymous with his presidency.

Clinton, mother Jennie, sister Janice, father Chris, Christmas 1942. *Clint Hill personal collection.*

Agents Frank Bales and Clint Hill stand post as President Eisenhower exits a Gettysburg church with a member of the clergy. 1959. *Dwight D. Eisenhower Presidential Library*

President Eisenhower enjoying a golf outing with Arnold Palmer.
AP Photo/Paul Vathis

Huge crowds greet President Eisenhower in Karachi, Pakistan, as he rides with President Ayub Khan in the slow-moving presidential horse-drawn carriage. Dec. 1959.
AP Photo

Crowds were so thick upon our evening arrival in New Delhi, India, that at times Prime Minister Nehru exited the car and beat the crowds with a swagger stick. Dec. 1959.
AP Photo

SAIC Jim Rowley scans the surging crowd as President Eisenhower waves from the open-top car in New Delhi, India. Dec. 1959. *Getty/SLADE Paul*

President Eisenhower with controversial dictator Generalissimo Franco in Secret Service car 4-B. Madrid, Spain. Dec. 1959. *Dwight D. Eisenhower Presidential Library*

President Eisenhower, Press Secretary Jim Hagerty, Mrs. Eisenhower, and me in Newport, Rhode Island.
Dwight D. Eisenhower Presidential Library/Jerry Taylor

President Eisenhower
with his hand on SAIC
Jim Rowley's shoulder
as the crowd engulfs the
motorcade in Manila,
Philippines. Jerry Behn
(left) and other agents
form a barrier. *AP Photo*

President Eisenhower rides in the back of an open convertible in San Diego as I work the motorcade route. *Clint Hill personal collection*

President Eisenhower and Vice President Nixon—then a presidential candidate—ride together in an open-top car through the streets of Manhattan during the 1960 campaign. *AP Photo*

I keep a watchful eye on the press as President Kennedy meets with Secretary of State Dean Rusk in Palm Beach. April 1961. *AP Photo*

Nicole Alphand (wife of the French ambassador) interprets for Mrs. de Gaulle and President Kennedy as Mrs. Kennedy charms President de Gaulle using her fluency in French during the trip to Paris. 1961. *John F. Kennedy Presidential Library & Museum/Boston*

Crowds and the press swarm around President and Mrs. Kennedy in Hyannis Port with me (behind photographer), and agents Bill Payne and John Campion. Aug. 1961. *AP Photo*

Keeping a watchful eye as President and Mrs. Kennedy exit St. Francis Xavier Church in Hyannis Port. *John F. Kennedy Presidential Library & Museum/Boston*

President Kennedy sought advice from former President Eisenhower at Camp David after the Bay of Pigs fiasco in April 1961. *John F. Kennedy Presidential Library & Museum/Boston*

President Kennedy signed this photo after learning I was injured while helping him and Chuck Spalding out of the rocks on the sailboat *Victura*. July 1962. *Clint Hill personal collection*

I had difficulty breathing at Mexico City's high elevation as I jogged alongside SS-100-X. July 1, 1962.
John F. Kennedy Presidential Library & Museum/Boston

Massive amounts of confetti created a security nightmare as President Kennedy rode with President Adolfo López of Mexico through Mexico City. Two million people lined the motorcade route. June 30, 1962. *John F. Kennedy Presidential Library & Museum/Boston*

President Kennedy jokingly chides me for allowing his friends to rest during the 50-mile hike. Standing left to right: Corpsman Tom Mills, JFK, Dr. Max Jacobson, and me. Chuck Spalding and Prince Radziwill on ground. © *2011 Mark Shaw/mptvimages.com*

JFK presents me with a paper medal, "To Dazzle," after the 50-mile hike. Behind left to right: Lee Radziwill, Dr. Jacobson, other friends, and Prince Radziwill. *Clint Hill personal collection*

We often wore tuxedos to blend in. Agent Jim Johnson, Mrs. Kennedy, JFK, and me, leaving a formal event. *John F. Kennedy Presidential Library & Museum/Boston*

My favorite photo of President John F. Kennedy. Happy at the helm of *Manitou*. 1962. *John F. Kennedy Presidential Library & Museum/Boston*

Surprise party for President Kennedy in the White House Navy Mess on his 46th birthday. JFK, Muggsy O'Leary, me, Mrs. Kennedy, Nancy Tuckerman, and other staff members. *John F. Kennedy Presidential Library & Museum/Boston*

President Kennedy opening birthday presents aboard the USS *Sequoia*. Left to right: the back of Lem Billings, Ethel Kennedy, JFK, Paul "Red" Fay, Mrs. Kennedy, and Mrs. David Niven. *John F. Kennedy Presidential Library & Museum/Boston*

President Kennedy rode in open-top cars throughout Europe, attracting massive crowds wherever he went, with only a handful of agents available to protect him. Cork, Ireland. *John F. Kennedy Presidential Library & Museum/Boston*

President Kennedy treasured time with his children. Here with Caroline, summer 1963. *John F. Kennedy Presidential Library & Museum/Boston*

I keep an eye on the press as President Kennedy, Caroline, and John exit the Otis AFB hospital after visiting Mrs. Kennedy two days after the death of baby Patrick. Aug 11, 1963. *US Air Force Photo*

President Kennedy enjoying time with his children his last weekend at Atoka. Nov. 10, 1963. *John F. Kennedy Presidential Library & Museum/Boston*

JFK squirms with laughter as a pony nuzzles him, with Tony Bradlee at Atoka. Nov. 10, 1963. *John F. Kennedy Presidential Library & Museum/Boston*

President Kennedy laughs with John as they enter Arlington National Cemetery Nov. 11, 1963. Generals Ted Clifton and Godfrey McHugh (rear). *AP Photo*

President and Mrs. Kennedy prepare to depart Carswell Air Force Base for Love Field, Dallas. Me in sunglasses, Agent Ned Hall on right. Nov. 22, 1963. *University of Texas at Arlington Library Special Collections*

Turning onto Main St., Dallas, I crouched on the rear bumper to be closer to Mrs. Kennedy. Agents Jack Ready and Paul Landis scan the crowds from the follow-up car. *Darrell Heikes, photographer, Dallas Times Herald Collection/The Sixth Floor Museum at Dealey Plaza.*

Expecting more shots were coming, I wedged myself up on the rear seat to protect the stricken president, Governor Connally, and their wives as we raced to Parkland Hospital. *AP Photo*

Trying to control my emotions as former Presidents Truman and Eisenhower pay condolences to Mrs. Kennedy (in car) outside St. Matthew's Cathedral with the flag-draped coffin in the foreground. Margaret Truman, Ted Kennedy, and Robert Kennedy also in photo. *John F. Kennedy Presidential Library & Museum/Boston*

Escorting Mrs. Kennedy with John, Caroline, and Robert Kennedy to visit JFK's burial site on what would have been his 47th birthday. May 29, 1964. *Lee Lockwood/Getty/LIFE Images Collection*

President Johnson bids goodbye to Jacqueline Kennedy (with Robert Kennedy) at her 1040 Fifth Avenue residence as I look on. Oct. 1964. *LBJ Library photo*

my own sons. In many ways, I was a stranger to them. It was the same for all the agents on the White House Detail. When the president and first lady traveled, it was our job to be with them. There weren't enough of us to be able to get time off for special occasions or family events. I had been gone for every holiday, birthday, and anniversary over the past four years. Now, President and Mrs. Johnson were going to be spending Thanksgiving at their ranch in Texas, so that's where the agents would be too.

THE JOB OF the President of the United States is around-the-clock, seven days a week, 365 days a year. Even when they are on "vacation," they are never away from the phone or the latest domestic or international crisis. But every president needs a place where they can try to find some relaxation, a retreat away from the White House. President Eisenhower had his estate in Gettysburg; President Kennedy had Hyannis Port and Palm Beach. For President Johnson, there was no better place on earth than his beloved ranch in the Texas Hill Country.

On November 19, 1964, I flew with my shift from Andrews Air Force Base to Bergstrom Air Force Base in Austin, Texas. The agents had negotiated a good rate at the Commodore Perry Hotel, and from there it was an hour-and-a-half drive to the ranch, with not much in between. The drive back and forth added close to three hours to your eight-hour shift, making for long days, but at that time there was nowhere else to stay.

The landscape reminded me of the gently rolling hills around Washburn, North Dakota, where I spent my childhood—lots of wide-open spaces, dotted with pecan and oak trees instead of North Dakota cottonwood and elm, and every once in a while there'd be a white farmhouse set back a ways from the highway, with a few horses, cattle, or sheep in the yard.

The LBJ Ranch was an actual working cattle ranch. Johnson had about four hundred head of Hereford cattle, and the property was close to 2,700 acres. I would learn that there was nothing President Johnson loved more than driving around looking at his land and checking on his prized cows, and within a few short days I saw damn near every inch of the place.

The Texas White House was a large but unpretentious two-story white clapboard house with covered front porches on both the ground

20

The LBJ Ranch

On November 22, 1963, President and Mrs. Kennedy were supposed to have spent the night at the LBJ Ranch in Stonewall, Texas. One year later, nearly to the day, that's exactly where I was headed, now as an agent on President Johnson's Secret Service detail.

It was hard to believe that a year had passed, and somehow the world had kept turning, life had gone on. It had been a rough year, to say the least. My entire focus had been on Mrs. Kennedy, Caroline, and John, making sure they had everything they needed. While I knew they were in capable hands with the new Agent in Charge, it was going to be strange not to be in daily contact.

With my new assignment, I received a pay grade promotion—from GS-12 at $10,605 to GS-13 at $12,075 annually—but the new job was actually a demotion in title and responsibility, as I went from being the Special Agent in Charge of the Kennedy Protective Detail, supervising my own small team of agents, to being a member of one of the three shifts on the President's Detail. I knew that ultimately it was in my own best interest to leave New York City and return to the White House, but it wasn't an easy transition.

I had been given a week off before starting my new assignment, which I spent at home with Gwen and the boys. Because I had been gone more than 90 percent of the time over the previous four years, it was always somewhat strained when I got to spend more than a day or two at home. My family had their own routine without me, and it was an adjustment for all of us. It wasn't an ideal situation for a strong marriage, and sadly, I felt like I hardly knew and second floors. The main floor consisted of several living and sitting rooms; an office, which had room for the president's desk and three other desks for staff and secretaries; a big kitchen and dining room; several bathrooms; and two large bedrooms—one for President Johnson and one for Mrs. Johnson. Upstairs were six additional bedrooms and five bathrooms, accessible by the main staircase, as well as a steep, narrow back staircase off the dining room.

Inside, the house was relaxed and informal, filled with comfortable furnishings and family photos, nothing fancy or ostentatious. Outside, an expansive front lawn shaded by a beautiful live oak tree had a commanding view of the Pedernales River, which snaked through the property. Off to one side of the house was a large, kidney-shaped swimming pool, which was frequently used by the president, his family, and guests. Around the back of the house was a carport that held a variety of vehicles that the president had collected—and which he insisted on driving himself whenever he was on the ranch—then beyond the carport was an airport hangar adjacent to a runway that could accommodate small private aircraft, as well as serving as a helicopter landing pad.

I couldn't help but think what Mrs. Kennedy would have thought of the ranch, had she and President Kennedy come here. It had been the one part of the Texas trip that she wasn't really looking forward to, but I think she would have found it charming in its own way. Tolerable, at least, for one night.

As it turned out, I almost didn't get to stay more than one night myself.

Shortly after arriving, I was standing post outside the main house when I heard President Johnson call out to Rufus Youngblood, the Agent in Charge. Rufus responded immediately, and while I couldn't hear what was being said, I saw President Johnson pointing at me and talking sternly to Rufus. I couldn't imagine what I might have done wrong, but obviously the president was not happy about something.

After our shift was over, Rufus pulled me aside and explained what had transpired. "Clint, listen, I know you may have overheard some things, and I wanted to set your mind at ease . . . You see, President Johnson saw you today for the first time, and he recognized you."

"What do you mean he recognized me?"

"He knew that you were new on the shift, and that . . . uh . . . that you had been with the Kennedys."

"So?" I asked. *What did that have to do with anything? Lots of the guys had been with the Kennedys.*

"Well," Ruf began, "the one thing President Johnson demands from everybody around him is loyalty. He questioned your loyalty because you were so close to the Kennedy family."

I shook my head in bewilderment. "Well, Ruf, you know me. I'm here to do the job."

"I'm gonna talk to him," Rufus said. "Look, Clint, I know—we all know—that you would do the same thing again . . ." His voice trailed off. He looked down. He didn't want to mention it.

I looked directly into Rufus's eyes and said, "If he doesn't want me here, then I won't be here."

"Let me work this out, Clint. We all want you here."

I knew the decision wasn't up to me, or to Rufus Youngblood. It was President Johnson's call, and I was convinced this would be my first and last day on the detail.

The next day, before I went on shift, Rufus called me into the command post. He and his assistant, Lem Johns, had gone to the president to plead my case.

"We told him you were not political, that you were the consummate professional. That you had no allegiance to the Kennedys, but only to the United States Secret Service and our mission."

I turned my gaze away from Rufus and looked down at the ground. I was sure what the response would be. President Johnson did things on his terms. He wasn't about to let the Secret Service tell him who was going to be on his detail.

"Clint, the president wants you to stay."

I was surprised that President Johnson had agreed to allow me to stay on his detail, but I also knew that all it would take was one minor mistake and I'd be transferred to a field office far from Washington, D.C. I wasn't about to let that happen.

• • •

THE TRANSITION FROM Jacqueline Kennedy to Lyndon Baines Johnson was like sailing on a magnificent yacht along the Amalfi Coast on a cloudless summer day, and suddenly being tossed overboard into an aluminum trough filled with ice-cold water. There were not two more opposite people on the planet. Mrs. Kennedy was soft-spoken, refined, and empathetic, while President Johnson could be crude, demanding, boisterous, and intolerant.

I quickly learned that when President Johnson was at the ranch, there was no set schedule: his activities were completely unpredictable and often spur-of-the-moment. He believed surprise was the best form of defense against anyone who might try to harm him, and that included not informing his Secret Service agents of impending activity. We had to continually be on our toes, ready for movement by foot or car. President Johnson would be in the house and suddenly decide to take a drive. He'd stride out the back door, dressed in his tan gabardine ranch trousers and matching pocketed jacket, a Western-style hat, and boots, headed for the carport, usually with several of his guests in tow. Rarely did he give advance warning to the agents, so as soon as one of us saw what was going on, we'd radio the command post and race for the Secret Service follow-up cars.

President Johnson refused to allow an agent to drive him around on his own ranch, and most times forbade any of us from being in the same car with him. He'd jump into the driver's seat of his white Lincoln convertible, with the top down, barely waiting for his passengers to sit before he stepped on the gas, kicking up a plume of dust as he sped away. The agents on duty would scramble into a couple of other cars, fast on his trail.

It was often the same situation if he wanted to fly somewhere. Our first notification would be seeing him come out of the house and head straight for the helicopter pad or the JetStar parked at the end of the runway behind the residence. The word would go out on the radios, and simultaneously the aircraft crew would come running out of their standby trailer to try to beat him to the appropriate aircraft. Thinking back on it now, it makes me laugh, but at the time it was extremely stressful, and not conducive to our preferred security methods.

Lady Bird Johnson, on the other hand, was always thoughtful and considerate of those of us who worked in various capacities around the president. A petite woman, Mrs. Johnson was active and energetic, and she always seemed to have a smile on her face. Her given name was Claudia, but apparently when she was an infant a nurse commented that she was "as pretty as a ladybird," and the nickname stuck. The president simply called her "Bird."

Because President Johnson had such a domineering personality, Mrs. Johnson might have seemed demure to some, but in reality she was quietly forceful, and very intelligent. She had graduated with honors from the University of Texas with degrees in both journalism and history, and having been married to Lyndon Johnson for over thirty years, she understood his personality, and how hurtful he could be, better than anyone.

One day during that first trip to the ranch, I was on duty when President Johnson stalked over to one of the other agents and began berating him for something that hadn't gone exactly as the president had wanted. Johnson towered over the other man, and as his voice got louder, he moved in closer until his face was scarcely an inch from the agent's. For the next ten minutes, Johnson exploded with curse words and accusations, haranguing, scolding, and degrading the poor man until he nearly crumbled.

Finally, it stopped just as suddenly as it had begun, and as the president stormed off, the agent became physically ill, vomiting into the grass. Mrs. Johnson had witnessed the scene from a distance, and as soon as her husband was out of sight, she brought a towel to the agent, gave him a hug, and said, "Oh, Bobby, Lyndon didn't mean it. He thinks so highly of you. Please forgive him—you do a wonderful job."

I had just witnessed "the Johnson treatment." Over the next four years, I would see the same situation played out with senators, congressmen, even the vice president, and nearly every agent on the detail, myself included. No one was immune.

THE JOHNSONS HAD two daughters, Lynda and Luci, and the minute their father became president, their lives changed dramatically. At the time, the children of vice presidents did not have Secret Service protection, but within hours of President Kennedy's assassination, the girls each had agents assigned to them. Lynda was nineteen years old and a student at the University of Texas in Austin, while Luci was living at home with her parents in Washington attending the National Cathedral School for Girls. The Johnsons were a close family, and the girls often joined their parents at the White House and were always at the ranch for holidays.

As the first anniversary of the assassination approached, you couldn't pick up a newspaper or turn on the radio or television that week without hearing endless recaps and analyses. President Johnson had called for Sunday, November 22, 1964, to be a day of "national rededication" to the ideals of President Kennedy, but a presidential declaration was hardly needed. All across the United States, and all over the world, people were paying tribute to President Kennedy at memorial Masses and somber ceremonies of remembrance. More than thirty thousand people entered the gates of Arlington National Cemetery to personally pay tribute at President Kennedy's gravesite, among them Bobby Kennedy and Eunice Kennedy Shriver. Meanwhile, Mrs. Kennedy had taken John and Caroline to her leased home in Glen Cove, Long Island, to spend the day privately with her children and her sister, who had flown in from London.

President and Mrs. Johnson attended a memorial service in Austin, accompanied by Texas governor John Connally—who had fully recovered from his injuries—and his wife, Nellie. It was torture for me to be back in Texas on that day one year later. Everything was a reminder—the cloudless blue sky, the Texas twang of the locals, the sound of an airplane flying overhead—and in an instant the horrific images flashed into my mind, haunting me, taunting me, as they did almost every night in my sleep. A year had passed, but the nightmares endured, along with the emptiness and feelings of failure; my heart was as heavy as ever. The only way I knew how to deal with it was to focus on my job—checking and rechecking every detail so that nothing was ever left to chance, being the first one to volunteer for undesirable assignments, and all the while trying to prove to President Johnson that I was worthy of his trust and confidence.

THE LBJ RANCH was the place where President Johnson went to unwind, to relax from the stresses of the office, and he loved his ranch so much, and was so proud of it, that he wanted to share it with everyone. Visitors were constantly coming and going—friends, family, select members of the press, cabinet members, staff, and even heads of state from all over the world.

When the visitors arrived, which was usually by fixed wing aircraft or helicopter, they invariably were given a tour of the ranch with LBJ as the tour guide, driving his Lincoln convertible or an old fire truck he kept on the premises. It didn't matter the status of the guest—everyone was treated pretty much the same and given the tour whether they wanted it or not. The agents had another convertible and a station wagon we used as follow-up cars on the ranch, which took a real beating driving at high rates of speed trying to keep up with the president on the rutted dirt roads. The president would take off, never in the same direction twice, suddenly careening across a pasture when he spotted one of his prize bulls.

"Just look at the size of the balls on that bull!" he'd exclaim with delight. It didn't matter who was in the car—if there were women present or not— and I often wondered if he was truly reveling with pride, or if he merely loved to see the shocked look on his guests' faces. While we were stopped, he'd pick up the radio and holler, "Need a little help up here, boys!"

That was the signal that it was refreshment time. In the morning it was Fresca; in the afternoon, Scotch. Cutty Sark and soda. There was more than one occasion when I mixed the president a drink myself—and learned the hard way that you always, *always* used a fresh bottle of soda, because he could tell the difference—but we tried as often as possible to have an Air Force steward with us for just that reason. Our job was to protect the man, not be his bartender, but if you refused, you were guaranteed a reassignment off the detail the very next day.

President Johnson had his own radio system and frequency, which he used to continuously stay in touch with the ranch foreman, other employees, and friends who owned nearby ranches. We monitored the frequency in an attempt to stay abreast of the situation, but you could never predict where he would go or what he'd do next. The Hill Country of Texas was his backyard playground, and while he knew every inch of it, along with everyone who lived there, we did not. There were a number of ranches the president visited frequently, and sometimes we would get to a neighboring ranch by car only to find out he had changed his mind and wanted to go to a different ranch in the opposite direction, by helicopter. We'd have to hightail it to the new destination to get there before the helicopter arrived. He was constantly changing his plans at the last minute, which resulted in enormous, and frustrating, logistics problems.

The various ranches were separated with barbed wire fencing and gates across the dirt roads to control the livestock, and whenever we'd come upon a closed gate, it was expected that one of the agents would jump out and open the gate to allow the cars to proceed, and then close it after all the vehicles had passed.

Along with the herds of cattle, the ranch was heavily populated with white-tailed deer, and one of the president's favorite activities was to take his guests deer hunting. If the president were taking someone hunting, he wanted to make sure they were successful, so he'd have the ranch hands, specifically foreman Dale Malechek, keep him informed of where the deer were located. He also knew, having lived there for years, where the deer were likely to be at any time of the day. This was one activity that got him up and out early in the morning, and he got a real kick out of seeing his guests shoot their own deer.

I had grown up deer hunting as well, so this was nothing new to me, but in my home state of North Dakota we did things a little differently. We didn't drive around in cars seeking the deer. We traipsed through woods or lay in a deer stand up in a tree waiting for the deer to come within range. LBJ's method was a considerably different approach to the sport.

There were all kinds of creatures that roamed the ranch—armadillos, wild turkeys, skunks, foxes, raccoons—but by far the ones that were the biggest source of anxiety were the peacocks. The guys had warned me about the peacocks, but I really couldn't believe that such beautiful birds could be as much of a nuisance as they said they were. I was wrong.

Someone had given President Johnson a few peacocks, and now there were at least a dozen of the large birds wandering freely around the ranch. They seemed to particularly like the area along the river near the main house, and I must say they were a magnificent sight when they spread their iridescent tail feathers into an enormous fan. Despite their size, they built nests high up in the trees, and at night, camouflaged by the leaves and branches of the lush live oaks, this created some terrifying moments for those of us on the midnight shift rotating posts around the house. If you happened to walk too close to one of the nesting trees, you'd suddenly see the giant bird flapping its wings as it wailed a blood-curdling screech that echoed across the lawn. And as if that wasn't enough to scare the living daylights out of you, the next thing you'd hear was the booming voice of the president, yelling through his open bedroom window, irate as hell that he'd been woken up in the middle of the night.

"Will you shut those damn birds up!"

Much as we would have liked to shut them up for good with one clean shot, we resorted to tossing small rocks at them. The idea was to scare them, not necessarily injure, and sometimes it worked, sometimes it didn't.

The Johnsons also owned a home on Granite Shoals Lake, which was about an hour's drive from the ranch, but just fifteen or twenty minutes by helicopter. It wasn't unusual for the president to be entertaining guests and suddenly decide it was a great day to be out on the lake, and invariably he wanted to fly. There wasn't much room in the U.S. Army Huey, so one agent would climb aboard with the president and his entourage, while the remainder of the shift would speed away in vehicles, attempting to get there in time to meet the chopper. Half the time, though, the president would change his mind midflight and decide to make a stop at a friend's ranch in the opposite direction. We'd have to scramble to figure out how to get from where we were to the new destination and race to get there before the president landed.

The president had a motorboat he liked to drive around the lake, so the Navy bought some high-speed Donzis to keep up with President Johnson on the lake in Texas. The first time I went out there, I was surprised to see a familiar face handling the boats. My old friend Jim Bartlett—the U.S. Navy man who had taught me how to water-ski in Hyannis Port and had voluntarily moved my family to our new apartment the week after the assassination—was now in charge of the boats here in Texas. It was great to see him, and whenever we were out on the boats, it brought back memories of the good times we had had at the Cape.

On Thursday, November 26, I left the Commodore Perry Hotel in Austin and drove with my shift out to the LBJ Ranch as usual, not even thinking about the fact that it was Thanksgiving Day. President and Mrs. Johnson spent the day visiting friends—flying by helicopter to the Moursund Ranch for a late lunch, and then on to the Wesley West Ranch, where they spent the afternoon hunting and riding—before returning to the LBJ Ranch to entertain a houseful of guests for a late Thanksgiving dinner. Usually we were able to get something to eat from a restaurant in Stonewall, near the LBJ Ranch, but on this day, no such luck. Everything was closed. It was a bleak and miserable day without food, but at least we learned a lesson that we had to be self-sustaining on holidays at the ranch.

On November 29, President Johnson returned to Washington, and my first trip to the LBJ Ranch was over. It had been an interesting and enlightening introduction to my new boss.

I WAS RELIEVED to be back in Washington, able to sleep in my own bed and to have a ten-minute commute, at least for the next three weeks. This was also my first opportunity to observe how President Johnson operated in the White House—which, not surprisingly, was vastly different from either Eisenhower or Kennedy.

President Johnson spent most mornings making and receiving telephone calls from the second-floor residence. Various staff members would arrive at the White House for a meeting, only to be summoned upstairs to the president's bedroom, where he was likely still in his pajamas. Unless there was a morning function at which his presence was required, he usually didn't go to the Oval Office until at least 11:00 a.m. Another major difference I noticed in this president's routine was his eating habits. It was almost always breakfast in bed, or at least in the bedroom; lunch was a maybe because he sometimes just kept on going; and dinner was usually very late. Often he would work late into the evening and then eat. By late, I mean sometime around ten o'clock or later. Knowing this was not conducive to good health, Mrs. Johnson tried her best to get him on a regular schedule, to no avail.

Unlike his predecessors, LBJ did not have a regular exercise routine. No afternoon golf like President Eisenhower or daily swims like President Kennedy. When he was at the ranch, he did use the outdoor swimming pool rather frequently, but it was more to cool off and relax than to exercise. And while he might not have been particularly active physically, his mind was in constant motion—listening, absorbing, thinking, plotting, planning, directing—from the moment he awoke to the moment he fell asleep. His workdays were long, and it wasn't unusual for him to call a senator or congressman at eleven o'clock in the evening—irrespective of any time zone difference, so that it might be two or three hours later on the recipient's end—after which he'd be so wound up, he'd call for one of the Navy medical corpsmen to give him a "rub"—his term for a massage.

PRESIDENT AND MRS. Johnson planned to spend Christmas and New Year's at the ranch, but with the end of the year fast approaching, there was still plenty of unfinished national business. No problem. LBJ simply moved his office from the banks of the Potomac to the banks of the Pedernales, bringing his cabinet along with him.

Three days before Christmas, Secretary of Defense Robert McNamara and all the members of the Joint Chiefs flew to the ranch to finalize the 1965 defense budget and to discuss urgent matters concerning the escalating war in Vietnam. President Johnson held court in his living room as his secretarial staff took notes and kept the coffee cups filled. It was a beautiful sunny day—warm for December—so after lunch, President Johnson suggested they continue their discussion outside. He called for someone to bring out some chairs, while the Joint Chiefs gathered up their briefcases and file folders.

LBJ, dressed in his ranch clothes, slumped down comfortably into one of the webbed folding chairs like this was a perfectly normal setting to decide critical issues affecting the American people and the world, while Chairman General Earle Wheeler; U.S. Army General Harold Johnson, Chief of Naval Operations Admiral David McDonald, and General Curtis LeMay—all in full military dress—looked decidedly out of place, huddled around the splintered picnic table in the flimsy chairs, holding down stacks of classified information so the pages didn't scatter in the breeze.

By Christmas Eve, the official guests had come and gone, leaving just the family, a few staff members, and the Secret Service. Then on Christmas Day, the press descended on the ranch to photograph the first family and to follow them to church services in Fredericksburg. After the photos at the house were finished, President Johnson walked out the back door with Mrs. Johnson, Luci, and Lynda.

"Goin' to church, boys!" he hollered as he plunked down into the driver's seat of his white Lincoln convertible. Now, the road to Fredericksburg was a well-traveled highway, and our preference, and strong recommendation to the president, was for an agent to drive him and his family in one of our cars, with a Secret Service follow-up car trailing behind, but the president would have none of it.

"That is ridiculous," he said. "I'm driving my own damn car to church, and you boys can follow me."

During the course of the next four years, I would spend countless weeks at the LBJ Ranch, including every Thanksgiving and Christmas, and no matter how much turmoil the world might be in, President Johnson always insisted on driving himself to church.

21

Inauguration 1965

Having won the 1964 election against Republican candidate Barry Goldwater with 61.1 percent of the popular vote, Lyndon Johnson finally felt validated. He hadn't just inherited the presidency; now he had earned it. It was the largest popular referendum since 1820, and in fact no president since Johnson has won with a larger majority. Not only had he nurtured America through the dark aftermath of the assassination of JFK, but he had moved forward like a steam train, passing numerous bills to protect the environment and improve everyday life for all Americans, most notably using his unrivaled knowledge of the democratic system and powers of persuasion to pass the sweeping Civil Rights Act of 1964. And now he had four more years ahead of him to make even bigger changes.

Although Lyndon Johnson was the third president I had served, this would be my first time participating in a Presidential Inauguration and I felt privileged to be a part of it. Coming on the heels of the assassination, however, the 1965 Inauguration was the single biggest security challenge the Secret Service had ever faced, and planning had been under way for months. The two-mile stretch between the Capitol and the White House was checked and rechecked multiple times, with every building on Constitution and Pennsylvania Avenues inspected and every window along the route ordered to be closed. Manhole covers were sealed, agents would be flying in helicopters overhead, and for the first time a three-sided barrier of bulletproof glass was installed around the podium where Johnson and his vice president, Hubert Humphrey, would take their oaths.

There was an inch of snow on the ground the morning of January 20, under cloudy skies with temperatures in the 30s, but despite the frigid air, 1.2 million people had come to witness the historic event—the largest crowd ever for an Inauguration.

At 12:03 p.m. President Lyndon Baines Johnson stood in front of the podium on the East Portico of the Capitol, with Mrs. Johnson close by his side, and solemnly swore to faithfully execute the office of the President of the United States, and, to the best of his abilities, to preserve, protect, and defend the Constitution of the United States. *So help me, God.*

The audience in the Capitol plaza rose to its feet, clapping in the cold, and as I scanned the crowd, I couldn't help but think what a starkly different scene it was from the last time I had heard Lyndon Johnson utter those same words, in the sweltering cabin of Air Force One, with Mrs. Kennedy still in a state of shock, still covered in her husband's blood, standing nobly by his side. *So help me, God.*

After a twenty-two-minute Inaugural Address, there was a luncheon in the Capitol, followed by the Inaugural Parade. Four years earlier, President and Mrs. Kennedy had ridden the entire length of the parade in an open-top car as a million spectators waved and cheered. Now, for the first time in America's history, the president was relegated to riding in an enclosed vehicle, and although it may be hard to believe, the car in which President Johnson rode through the streets of Washington, D.C., on January 20, 1965, was the same car in which his predecessor had been assassinated.

After being transported from Dallas back to Washington in a C-130, guarded continuously by Secret Service agents, SS-100-X had been scrupulously inspected for evidence and then sent back to the Hess & Eisenhardt facility in Cincinnati to be refurbished. Because the Secret Service had a lack of vehicles, and because it would have taken two or three years to design and build a brand-new car—at a much higher cost—the decision was made to take what we had and improve it. A nonremovable roof made of bulletproof glass was installed, along with titanium plating in the trunk and around the backseat area; the floor was reconstructed of steel to withstand a grenade attack; and all the windows were replaced with thick bulletproof glass. The additional weight required a new and more powerful engine, and an additional air-conditioning unit was installed to compensate for the greenhouse effect of all the thick glass. Finally, at President Johnson's request, the exterior paint color was changed from midnight-blue to black. The refurbished car had been put back into use in May 1964, but because I had been with Mrs. Kennedy up until November, this Inaugural Parade was the first time I had worked a motorcade with the car since that day in Dallas.

The sun had broken through the clouds as the procession began shortly after two o'clock in the afternoon, with a phalanx of police motorcycles leading the way from the Capitol down Pennsylvania Avenue. President Johnson waved and smiled at the cheering crowd from behind the bulletproof window in the rear seat of the shiny black Lincoln limousine.

Overshadowing the president, however, was the intimidating entourage of Secret Service agents—some armed with assault rifles—strategically positioned like a small militia around and behind the presidential vehicle. Agent Bill Greer was driving, with Special Agent in Charge Rufus Youngblood in the front passenger seat, while six agents conspicuously surrounded the car. Two agents stood like hawks on the platform on the back, two others walked in line with the front bumper, another agent walked on the right rear side next to President Johnson, and then there was me. By sheer coincidence or cruel irony, I had been assigned to the left rear of the car, next to the first lady.

I walked the entire two-mile route alongside the car—which at least kept the blood flowing, because it was cold—and while I wore a glove on my left hand for warmth, I kept my right hand—my shooting hand—gloveless in case I suddenly needed to grab for my gun.

Shortly after the parade began, there was a lull, slowing the car almost to a complete stop, and the president spotted several band majorettes from Southwest Texas State College, his alma mater. I could hardly believe my eyes when the president opened the rear door, got out, and strode over to the young ladies to shake their hands.

We could have a foolproof security plan, but when the president himself chose to disregard it, all bets were off. Several of us rushed to surround him, urging him to get back into the car. Fortunately, he did as we asked and remained in the car for the rest of the parade.

That evening, the president and Mrs. Johnson attended all five of the Inaugural Balls. At each one LBJ made a short speech of gratitude, had a first dance with Lady Bird—who glowed adoringly at her husband all night long—and then proceeded to waltz around the room in the arms of numerous other women.

The Inauguration on January 20, 1965, was LBJ's moment to shine, and he bathed in every drop of the glory. I don't think he could have possibly fathomed what the future had in store for him, and how he would be tested like few presidents had ever been tested before.

22

The Civil Rights President

Four days after the Inauguration, Special Agent in Charge Rufus Youngblood informed me I was being promoted to shift supervisor, with the formal title Assistant to the Special Agent in Charge (ATSAIC). Although my pay would stay the same, it was confirmation that I was doing my job well and was a respected member of the detail. I welcomed the additional responsibility.

While I had been with Mrs. Kennedy in New York for most of the previous year, the major political issues confronting President Johnson had been of little consequence to me because they had no effect on Mrs. Kennedy's safety. Now that I was back at the White House on the president's protective detail, however, tensions over civil rights and U.S. involvement in Vietnam were gradually escalating, and in turn, threats to the president himself had increased exponentially.

Despite being a Southerner, President Johnson was a proponent of civil rights, and in the months immediately following President Kennedy's assassination, he had made the passage of a meaningful Civil Rights Act his primary priority. His passion stemmed from a heart-to-heart conversation he had had with one of his domestic employees, Gene Williams, a black man who had served as Johnson's driver for many years. In the four years I spent on Johnson's protective detail, I heard the president tell the story many times.

Back when LBJ was a senator, he'd fly back to Texas for the summer, and Gene Williams would drive the Johnsons' car from Washington to Texas, accompanied by his wife, Helen, who was the family's cook. One year, LBJ asked Williams to bring the family dog along with him, and when Williams balked, Johnson asked him what the problem was about bringing the dog in the car.

Williams responded, "A Negro has enough trouble getting through the South without a damn dog."

When LBJ queried him to elaborate, Williams replied, "We drive all day, but when we want to go to the bathroom just like you all do, we have to go out a side road and our women have to get behind a tree, because we can't go into a filling station like you do. We get hungry and we've got to eat just like you do, but we have to go across the tracks to a grocery store and get some cheese and crackers because we can't go into a café. Or if some hamburger stand would take a chance on being insulted, we have to go around to the back and wait till everybody else is served to get something to eat. We drive hard all day long, and it comes to ten or eleven o'clock and Helen and I want to go to sleep. We can't go into a motel or a hotel. We have to drive across the tracks and find some boarding house way down there where they'll take us in for the night, because we're not allowed in the hotels or motels. But you're not allowed in any place, even across the tracks, if you've got a damn dog with you."

Every time Johnson told the story, it nearly brought tears to his eyes. It was heartfelt. With twenty-eight years in Washington politics—having first been elected to Congress in 1937, and subsequently to the Senate in 1948—President Johnson was not only adept at navigating bills through both the House and the Senate, he also knew each and every congressman and senator on a personal basis. These personal relationships, built over nearly three decades, combined with his unmatched powers of persuasion, are what ultimately helped him pass the Civil Rights Act of 1964, just seven months after becoming president.

Despite the broad reach of the Civil Rights Act, however—which prohibited discrimination on the basis of race, religion, sex, or national origin, and required equal access to public places, as well as the right to vote—some individual states continued to make it almost impossible for minorities to register to vote. Two major civil rights groups—the Southern Christian Leadership Council (SCLC) and the Student Nonviolent Coordinating Committee (SNCC, known as "Snick")—had developed campaigns to register black voters, but their efforts were increasingly being shut down by horrific violence. President Johnson understood that without unrestricted access to the ballot, blacks and other minorities had no political power whatsoever. He had developed a good relationship with Martin Luther King Jr., and he urged King to find "the worst condition" of black folks being denied the right to vote in Alabama, Mississippi, Louisiana, or South Carolina, and to "get it on the radio, get it on television, get it in the pulpits." LBJ was convinced that if people all across America saw the injustice, they wouldn't tolerate the unfairness, and that would drive the momentum to get Congress to act with legislation.

The "worst place" Dr. King found was Selma, Alabama, where less than one percent of eligible black voters were registered. King and the leaders of SCLC and SNCC organized a fifty-mile protest march from Selma to Montgomery, the state capital, despite a warning from Alabama's governor, George Wallace, that such a march was unlawful.

President Johnson had a bank of three television sets in the Oval Office so he could monitor all three television networks at the same time, and on Sunday, March 7, he watched in horror—along with the rest of America—as Alabama state troopers, under the orders of Governor Wallace, fired tear gas into the crowd of six hundred black protestors and brutally attacked them with billy clubs as they walked across the Edmund Pettus Bridge in Selma.

Just as LBJ had predicted, the incident sparked outrage. In cities all across the country, blacks and whites walked together in protest over the events in Selma, demanding federal guarantees of the right to vote and the right to assemble peacefully. Police reinforcements were required to handle demonstrations in New York City, Boston, Chicago, Cleveland, Los Angeles, and Detroit.

In Selma, people poured in from all over the country—rabbis, nuns, priests, and sympathizers of all ages—to march with Martin Luther King on Tuesday, March 9. Once again the state troopers forced the marchers back, but this time it ended without violence. Later that night, however, a white group beat and murdered civil rights activist James Reeb, a minister from Boston, who had come to Selma to march.

Meanwhile, we were closely monitoring a group of about one thousand protestors who were marching on the north sidewalk outside the White

House fence, carrying picket signs and singing "We Shall Overcome." Pennsylvania Avenue at that time was open to traffic, and there were safety concerns as the picketers started spilling into the street, in front of cars and buses.

The National Park Service conducted public tours through the White House every morning except Sundays, Mondays, and holidays, and in 1965 all you had to do to get on one of the "come one, come all" tours was stand in line. No identification was required, and there were no magnetometers; the uniformed White House police simply did visual checks on people as they entered. On Thursday, March 11, at shortly after eleven in the morning, a group of a dozen young people, blacks and whites, walked in with the regular flow of tourists, but when they reached the East Hall, they sat down in a circle on the floor and demanded to meet with President Johnson.

The chief of the White House Police, Major Ralph Stover, calmly informed the students that they could not see the president without an appointment and that by sitting there they were in violation of the law. The students had no intention of moving, however, and they responded by locking arms and chanting, "We shall not be moved."

The Secret Service has the right to forcibly remove anyone from the White House at any time for any reason, but if we hauled these kids out kicking and screaming, the press would have a field day, and President Johnson did not want that being the front-page story. So we let them stay, under close guard, as the president went ahead with his agenda, and all other visitors were rerouted around the hallway where the sit-in was happening. We thought they'd get hungry and leave at some point, but at four o'clock the protestors still had not budged.

Upstairs, the president was consulting with his aides, trying to figure out how best to handle the situation. A reception was scheduled for later that evening, and the hallway needed to be used. Finally, the president summoned Rufus Youngblood and told him, "This damn thing has gone on long enough. Get 'em outta here."

All at once, a group of agents and uniformed officers surrounded the students and we physically removed them from the White House, taking them out the rear door, where there were several police vehicles waiting to whisk them away. The story made front-page news, but fortunately there was no violence and the reception went on as planned.

Meanwhile, we in the Secret Service were reevaluating our security procedures in light of the sit-in. Nothing like this had ever happened at the White House, but there was no doubt others would attempt to do the same thing. It was a tricky situation, because we didn't feel it warranted discontinuation of the White House tours to the public, but it did require an immediate increase in security, including additional officers and agents posted throughout the White House, as well as undercover detectives and Secret Service agents posing as tourists.

On Pennsylvania Avenue, the picketers continued around the clock, their chanting and singing clearly audible inside the White House, where President Johnson was working every angle to find a solution—meeting with civil rights leaders, legal and political advisors, and lawmakers. The entire country was on the verge of exploding in violence, and as I watched the various groups coming and going from the White House, I was impressed by the fact that President Johnson was meeting with people on all sides of the issue in an effort to find a solution.

The biggest adversary of the Selma-to-Montgomery marchers was Governor George Wallace, who reluctantly agreed to meet with President Johnson on Saturday, March 13, at the White House. Johnson and Wallace met for about three hours, after which they appeared in the West Wing Lobby for a hastily arranged press conference. Standing more than half a foot taller than Wallace, Johnson towered over the beleaguered-looking governor, and with the power of the White House behind him, the president vowed to use federal troops, if necessary, to ensure that "the offense of last Sunday cannot and will not be repeated."

It was a masterfully orchestrated event by Johnson, with the Alabama governor standing next to him as if in unity, when the reality was that Wallace had just been bulldozed, and he looked like he was still trying to figure out what had just hit him.

Two days later, on Monday, March 15, just eight days after what came to be known as Bloody Sunday, President Johnson addressed a joint session of Congress. In an eloquent forty-five-minute speech, broadcast live on television, Lyndon Johnson spoke from the heart as he implored the country's lawmakers to pass his Voting Rights bill without delay.

"I speak tonight for the dignity of man and the destiny of democracy," he began. "At times history and fate meet at a single time in a single place to shape a turning point in man's unending search for freedom. So it was at Lexington and Concord. So it was a century ago at Appomattox. So it was last week in Selma, Alabama."

Speaking with clarity and conviction, the president announced that he would be sending to Congress a law designed to eliminate illegal barriers to the right to vote, and he urged the members of the House and the Senate to pass the bill as quickly as possible.

"We have already waited one hundred years and more, and the time for waiting is gone," he said. "What happened in Selma is part of a far larger movement which reaches into every section and State of America. It is the effort of American Negroes to secure for themselves the full blessings of American life. Their cause must be our cause too. Because it's not just Negroes, but really it's all of us, who must overcome the rippling legacy of bigotry and injustice."

He looked around at the lawmakers seated before him, and then he turned directly to everyone watching on television and, with utter conviction, declared, "And we shall overcome."

With that phrase—the lyrics of the anthem that had become the movement's theme song—he was making a promise to black Americans that their fight had become his fight, and come hell or high water, he was going to get that bill passed.

It would take a lot of arm-twisting, negotiating, and compromising, but Lyndon Johnson knew how to play the game better than anyone else, and on August 6, 1965, he signed the Voting Rights Act of 1965 with numerous civil rights leaders by his side.

23

A President's Burdens

Vietnam did not begin with President Johnson; it was an inherited situation that developed during the Eisenhower administration in 1954, when the United States joined with seven other nations to form the Southeast Asia Treaty Organization (SEATO). The intention of the treaty was to combat the spread of Communism—much like NATO in Europe—and each treaty member agreed to resist armed aggression against any member nation. When North Vietnam began a large-scale military campaign against South Vietnam in the late 1950s, President Eisenhower began sending American military "advisors" to assist the South Vietnamese in protecting their freedom. President Kennedy continued to honor SEATO, gradually adding more support, and by the time of his assassination, we had more than fifteen thousand American troops in Vietnam. Kennedy's key advisors—Secretary of State Dean Rusk, Secretary of Defense Robert McNamara, National Security Advisor McGeorge Bundy, and the Joint Chiefs of Staff—had all remained in their positions when Johnson became president, and their unanimous recommendation was that the United States had no choice but to stay the course in South Vietnam.

By early 1965, however, the North Vietnamese had stepped up their military aggression to the point that the United States had to make a decision to either withdraw completely or escalate our military involvement. So at the same time President Johnson was sending troops to Selma, Alabama, to protect the civil rights protestors, he also authorized a substantial increase of American soldiers in Vietnam, including ground force combat troops. About four hundred Americans had already been killed in the conflict, and this new move sparked a wave of antiwar demonstrations. The president realized he needed to convince the American people that our continued involvement in this war on the other side of the world was critical, so a speech was scheduled for the evening of April 7 at Johns Hopkins University in Baltimore, Maryland.

The day before the speech, we got word that another six Americans had been killed in the past twenty-four hours, including a four-man helicopter crew that had been shot down by Vietcong ground fire. This news wasn't going to make the president's speech any easier. He remained at the White House all day, constantly on the telephone or in meetings, fine-tuning the language of the speech until just before seven in the evening, when he left with his special assistant, Jack Valenti, to make a brief appearance at the Smithsonian Museum of History and Technology for the ribbon-cutting ceremony for a new science and engineering exhibit. He stayed for less than half an hour, and then got back into the presidential limousine for the short drive back to the White House.

It had been raining on and off all day, but there was a steady drizzle now, and as the car proceeded down Constitution Avenue, the president spotted four reporters—three men and one woman—walking in the rain without umbrellas.

President Johnson told the driver to slow down, and as the car came alongside the group, he rolled down the rear window, stuck his head out, and said, "You walkin' or ridin'?"

Sid Davis, Charlie Mohr, Bill Evenson, and Muriel Dobbin—all reporters in the White House press corps who had been at the Smithsonian covering the president's remarks—looked at each other in wonderment. Was the President of the United States offering them a ride?

Thirty-five-year-old Sid Davis, a whip-smart reporter from Westinghouse Broadcasting who had been in the motorcade when President Kennedy was assassinated, didn't hesitate.

"We'll take a ride, Mr. President," he said.

"Come on in, then," Johnson said. "Jack, make some room."

Jack Valenti moved to one of the jump seats, while the four reporters climbed into the car, squeezing into the rear compartment with Johnson and Valenti.

"When's my next appointment, Jack?" the president asked Valenti.

"Your next appointment's been waiting, sir," Valenti said.

"I've got time to buy these folks a Scotch and soda," the president said with a wink.

When we arrived at the White House, the president brought the group upstairs to the family quarters, calling for the stewards to bring everyone a Scotch and soda. He gathered them in the Yellow Sitting Room, and as the drinks were served, President Johnson began talking about the War on Poverty and the need for the Elementary and Secondary Education Act that he'd just passed through Congress.

"Something has got to be done," he said. "Nowadays, a poor kid can't even get a job pumping gas if they don't know how to read or write." He went on to tell the reporters that one in five Americans lived below the poverty level of $3,000 a year, and this sweeping education reform would help level the playing field so that every American child had access to quality education.

The reporters sat there, drinking their Scotch, listening intently, surely still a bit stunned that the president had invited them upstairs, on a whim, like it was the most natural thing in the world. And then Charlie Mohr, the seasoned and tenacious reporter from the *New York Times*, jumped in and asked the president about U.S. policy in Vietnam.

The president stood up from his seat and said, "Come with me."

He led the reporters out of the Yellow Room, down the center hall, and to the elevator. They took the elevator to the ground floor and emerged just across from where my office used to be, then walked out the mansion past the flower room and the swimming pool, down the colonnade, and into the Oval Office. He flipped on the light and then walked behind the desk and said, "Hey, you guys haven't eaten, have you?"

In fact they hadn't.

The president squatted down next to his desk and picked up an enormous wooden box.

Dropping the box on his desk—it must have weighed twenty-five pounds—he said, "I got these Israeli figs. A gift from the prime minister of Israel."

The box was covered in cellophane, which the president tried ripping off with his fingers, but that was futile. Without batting an eye, LBJ reached into his trouser pocket, whipped out a tiny pocketknife, and began slicing through the yellow cellophane. Strips of cellophane were flying everywhere as he slashed the wrapper to shreds. The reporters exchanged glances. It was astonishing. *The President of the United States carries a pocketknife?*

Once the cellophane was removed, the president opened the box and held it out to the reporters. "Here y'all. Have some dinner."

Then he turned to Jack Valenti and said, "Jack, bring me the Hopkins speech."

Valenti scurried down the hall to another office and returned with a stack of typewritten pages.

"We're still working on it, Mr. President," he said as he handed it to Johnson.

The president looked at the reporters and said, "This is the speech I'm going to make tomorrow night at Johns Hopkins University outlining our policy towards Vietnam. Now, I'm gonna read it to you, but you cannot reveal anything until we release it tomorrow."

So there they were, the reporters, bedraggled from walking in the rain, sitting in the Oval Office, eating Israeli figs from a box as Lyndon Johnson tested out this very important speech on them. He explained the commitment our nation had made more than a decade earlier to help South Vietnam defend its independence and the moral obligation we had to carry out that promise, building to the thrust of the speech—a one-billion-dollar aid package to Southeast Asia, and a bombing halt if Ho Chi Minh would agree to peace talks.

When he finished reading, he turned to the reporters and asked, "What's the lead?"

Sid Davis, the radio man, said, "I'd lead with the bombing halt."

Muriel Dobbin and Charlie Mohr, both print reporters, said, "No, no. The billion-dollar development aid."

Turning to Valenti, President Johnson said, "Print people like numbers."

Then he turned back to the reporters, his brow furrowed, and looked earnestly into the eyes of each one, turning from one to the next.

"What does Ho Chi Minh want? Roads? Dams? Bridges? A cheaper and more effective means of growing rice? Hell, if I only knew what he wants, we could find a compromise to peace. All he's got to do is meet with me."

The president truly believed that if he could just get a face-to-face meeting with the leader of the Vietcong, if he could figure out what the man needed, and what we could provide, he could sway him, manipulate him, just as he did to get things passed through Congress.

By this time the reporters had been in the White House for well over an hour, but Johnson had one more thing he wanted to share. "Come on with me," he said. "I want to show y'all something."

Back to the mansion and upstairs they went, down the hall to the Lincoln Bedroom. The centerpiece of the large room was the bed itself, which, with its intricately carved mahogany headboard that stood against the wall like the back of a throne, had been witness to a century of presidential burdens.

"Sit down on the bed," President Johnson said to the reporters.

"Oh no, Mr. President," they said. "We can't sit on that bed."

The president insisted. "No, I want you to sit on the bed. Everybody else does. We have visitors who come here and sleep on the bed."

Muriel Dobbin, the spunky, red-haired, Scottish-born reporter for the *Baltimore Sun*, and the only female of the group, piped up and said, "All right, Mr. President, I'll sit on the bed."

The fellows followed her lead, and once they were seated, the president explained why he'd brought them up there. In a somber voice, he said, "I come down here virtually every morning about two o'clock, and I sit on that bed. I pick up the phone and I call the Situation Room, and I say, 'How many of my boys are out there?'"

The only light in the room was coming from the hallway, so it was difficult to see the president's expression, but the desperation in his voice was unmistakable.

"I may stay here through the night, and I keep calling to find out how many of my boys didn't come back today."

The reporters sat there, speechless. This was a side of Lyndon Johnson none of them had ever seen before.

He walked over to a portrait of Abraham Lincoln and said, "You know, doing what is right is easy. The problem is knowing what is right." He looked up at the president who had weathered the burdens of the Civil War and said, "I sure hope I have better generals than he did."

With that, he led the four reporters back downstairs, out to the North Portico, and bid them good night.

It was still raining slightly, and as they walked down the driveway the reporters were silent, barely able to believe what they'd just experienced. Each of them was already writing the story in their heads. As they approached the Northwest Gate, finally Sid Davis could hold it in no longer. He turned to Muriel Dobbin and blurted out, "Can you believe what just happened? We've got one hell of a story!"

At that moment, just as they were about to leave the White House grounds, they heard the sound of someone running toward them. They turned, and there was Jack Valenti, breathless, a look of anxiety on his face.

"Now listen, you guys," he said as he caught up to them. "Everything, and I mean *everything*, you heard in there is strictly off the record. You got that?"

Reluctantly, the reporters agreed. And each of them kept their word.

It was only recently that Sid Davis shared this story with me, and the profound impact it had on him as a young reporter. He would go on to have an impressive career, eventually becoming Vice President and Washington Bureau Chief of NBC News. But on that rainy evening, he was able to see the president as a man, a man who carried unimaginable burdens on his shoulders.

"He was the loneliest man in the world that night," Davis said.

In the coming years, I too would witness President Johnson's lonely burden, many times over. But on that night in April 1965, Lyndon Johnson still had hope for peace; he still believed he could bring an end to the Vietnam War.

WE HAD LEARNED that twenty thousand college students from around the country were planning a demonstration against U.S. policy in South Vietnam in front of the White House on Saturday, April 17. Being that it was Easter weekend, President and Mrs. Johnson were at the LBJ Ranch, but there were indications protestors would show up there too, so we had agents working double shifts to ensure we had adequate protection.

Secretary of Defense McNamara and his wife were houseguests for the weekend, and as was typical, President Johnson wanted to show his guests around the area.

"We're goin' on a ride, boys!" he hollered toward the command post as he jumped into his white convertible with the secretary of defense in the front passenger seat and their wives in the back, and sped away. The on-duty agents scrambled into the station wagon and took off after him, with no idea where he was going.

The president roared off down the gravel road. Minutes later, he stopped in front of the small house where he was born. LBJ was immensely proud of his humble beginnings, and every visitor to the ranch invariably got a look at "the birthplace," where on August 27, 1908, Lyndon Baines Johnson came into the world and spent the first five years of his life. After a quick eight-minute stop the president had the car in gear, speeding off toward the neighboring Scharnhorst Ranch.

The president's car was equipped with a two-way radio system, which he used constantly while he was driving. White House Communications Agency (WHCA) personnel ran the system from the communications trailer near the main house, and they would connect him with whomever he wanted to speak. It was an unsecured radio transmission that could be heard by anyone on that frequency, and while we could monitor all the communications, so too could anyone else in the area.

The president would pick up the radio receiver, hold it to his mouth, press the button, and say, "Base, this is Volunteer. Get me Dale Malechek."

He'd give the ranch foreman instructions about clearing brush or tending to the cattle. Click. The next minute it was, "Base, this is Volunteer. Get me Marvin Watson."

On this particular occasion, once WHCA got Chief of Staff Watson on the line, the president gave instructions to postpone invitations to the prime ministers of Pakistan and India. Not necessarily something you'd want anyone else to intercept.

With one hand holding the radio and the other hand intermittently guiding the steering wheel or pointing to objects of interest along the way, the president was tour guide, master of his ranch, and commander in chief, all while speeding down the road at sixty miles an hour. In the follow-up car behind him, we just did the best we could to keep up, constantly trying to anticipate his next move.

After an hour-long tour of the Scharnhorst Ranch, the president got on the highway and drove straight to Johnson City, nearly twenty miles away. As we passed cars going the opposite direction, you could see the brake lights go on as the drivers inevitably did a double take, wondering if that was really the President of the United States and the secretary of defense driving down the highway in an open-top car, like they were on a joyride.

From there it was on to his boyhood home, where he'd lived from the time he was five years old until he graduated high school. The house was being reconstructed as a historic site, and the president loved to walk through the house, sharing remembrances of his childhood with his guests—the outhouse in the backyard, the small bedroom where he'd shared a bed with his brother, Sam. I think he felt that if people saw where he'd come from, they'd understand why he stood for the things he did. He hadn't grown up privileged, yet he'd made the most of what God had given him, and here he was, the leader of the free world.

The tour went on for four and a half hours, with the group finally returning to the LBJ Ranch for lunch. Fortunately, we had not run into any protestors, but the day wasn't over yet, and we had no idea what the president had in mind for the afternoon's activities.

Around 2:30 p.m., the president and his entourage—which now included two of his secretaries and Marvin Watson, along with the McNamaras and Mrs. Johnson—emerged from the house and headed toward the helicopter pad.

"Goin' for a chopper ride, boys!" the president called out.

With no indication of where he was going, but having been through this routine many times before, we put agents in two separate vehicles and headed toward the Haywood Ranch, where the president kept his boats. On the way there, the agents in the helicopter radioed that the chopper was headed to the Davis Ranch, not the Haywood. A flurry of curse words spewed from the agents in the car as we changed course and hightailed it to the Davis Ranch to get there before the chopper landed.

Thinking back now, it sounds like a comedy skit of the Keystone Kops variety, with agents radioing back and forth trying to figure out what the president was going to do next, and when we got it wrong, swiftly finding the best place to turn around or take a shortcut to beat the chopper, but at the time it was frustrating as hell.

Once we got to the Davis Ranch, the president and his guests got out of the helicopter and were met by the president's good friend Judge Albert W. Moursund.

The president had obviously called Moursund, who was waiting there with a vehicle to take everyone on a tour of his ranch. Now, by this time, the McNamaras had seen the LBJ Ranch, the Scharnhorst Ranch, the Lewis Ranch, and now the Davis Ranch. They're all in the Texas Hill Country, and to be honest, every damn ranch looked the same. But no one would dare say that out loud to the president.

After an hour of driving around the Davis Ranch, the entourage was back in the helicopter. We had an inkling the lake at Haywood Ranch would be the next stop, and we sent a car ahead so the agents could prepare the boats. Sure enough, fifteen minutes later the chopper arrived, and the guests split up into two motorboats. President Johnson got behind the wheel of the small motorboat and, for the next hour, sped up and down the lake with Secretary McNamara and the president's secretary, Vicki McCammon, water-skiing behind, while we raced alongside in security boats.

At around six o'clock, the president and his guests returned to the beach house for drinks and snacks. It had been a beautiful day, the weather was still warm, and everyone was having a wonderful time. Meanwhile, all the agents had been running around trying to keep up with them since eight in the morning, with no time or place to get any food. Shortly before eight o'clock, the president informed us they were taking the helicopter to the Wesley West Ranch for dinner. So a couple of agents stayed with the president, and the rest of us jumped into our vehicles and drove ahead to the West Ranch. It was probably as much a surprise to Mr. and Mrs. West as it was to us, but that was the way President Johnson operated. A last-minute phone call, a question of "What's for dinner?" and then a quick helicopter ride to the friend's ranch to enjoy a hastily prepared meal. This seemed to be a standing arrangement between Johnson and his friends. Oftentimes the friends received a last-minute invitation to dine at the LBJ Ranch. Somehow it always worked out because, I suppose, Lyndon Johnson was like this long before he was president, and his friends adapted and were willing to make a quick adjustment in plans.

Finally, we all returned to the ranch at ten o'clock that evening. The president had a rub and went to bed, and those of us who had been on duty since eight in the morning drove back to Austin for the night.

Two AND A half weeks later, another crisis erupted. On April 24, President Johnson got word that a civil uprising in the Dominican Republic was under way in an attempt to overthrow the pro-American dictator. The situation escalated quickly, with rumors circulating that Fidel Castro was behind the rebellion, and by April 28, the country was out of control. With 1,500 American citizens in the country, and worried that the Dominican Republic could turn into another Cuba, beginning a "domino effect" of Communism in the Western Hemisphere, President Johnson authorized American troops to descend on the Dominican Republic, which shares the island of Hispaniola with Haiti.

He knew that sending thousands more American soldiers into yet another foreign conflict was not going to be popular, but in a televised speech with daughter Luci by his side, President Johnson explained that more U.S. troops were needed to help return order to the country, to distribute food and medical supplies, and to safely evacuate U.S. citizens and other refugees.

"I want you to know that it is not a light or easy matter to send our American boys to another country, but I do not think the American people expect their president to hesitate or to vacillate in the face of danger just because the decision is hard, when life is in peril," he said.

Six months after the high of winning the election in a huge landslide, President Johnson was now dealing with three major crises—racial divisiveness, Vietnam, and now the Dominican Republic—all of which were on the verge of exploding.

• • •

IN THE FALL of 1965 President Johnson began suffering from fairly severe abdominal pain. The medical staff had determined that he needed to have gallbladder surgery, and while the surgery was scheduled for Friday, October 8, no announcement had yet been made to the press. The president was concerned about how his operation would be perceived by the American public and whether it should be announced prior to the procedure, or if he should simply wait until it was over and he was on the mend. He needed advice, and there was only one person who could tell him the best way to handle it.

Shortly before 9:00 a.m. on Tuesday, October 5, ASAIC Lem Johns had a driver pull up to the South Portico of the White House in an unmarked Oldsmobile sedan. The door of the White House opened, and out came photographer Yoichi Okamoto, accompanied by Jack Valenti and President Johnson. Okie slipped into the front seat with Lem Johns and the driver as Valenti and the president ducked into the rear. With another unmarked sedan filled with agents following closely behind, the Oldsmobile proceeded out the Southeast Gate and headed to Anacostia Naval Station.

It was a strictly off-the-record movement—no motorcycle escorts, no police presence, and absolutely no press.

At Anacostia, we boarded an unmarked helicopter and flew to Andrews Air Force Base. Agents had secured an area of the base for the helicopter to land near two airplane hangars, and when the president departed the helicopter, we led him between the two hangars to where a JetStar was parked, obscured from view.

Inside the JetStar, General Eisenhower was awaiting President Johnson's arrival. The purpose of the meeting for LBJ was twofold: to discuss myriad international issues and ask for advice on how to handle his upcoming surgery with the press.

When it came to the president's hospitalization, Eisenhower said, without hesitation, "Be absolutely frank. That is the key. Put out the absolute truth, and that will be the best thing you can do." He also recommended the doctors issue periodic bulletins to ease the concerns of the American public and to give the press something concrete so they didn't find the need to speculate.

The secretive meeting lasted just twenty-four minutes, and then we whisked President Johnson back to the White House before anyone knew he had been gone. That afternoon, a press conference was held to announce the president's upcoming surgery.

The surgery was successful, and after two weeks of recuperation in the hospital, the president could hardly wait to be released. He returned to the White House for one day, and then on October 23 we were off to the LBJ Ranch, where we would spend fifty-seven of the sixty-eight days left in the year.

The airstrip at the ranch might as well have been a runway at National Airport, there were so many flights coming and going. Aides, military advisors, cabinet members, secretaries, congressmen, senators, the press—if they wanted to meet with the president or the president wanted to meet with them, they had to come to Texas. The days were consistently unpredictable, with rarely a dull moment. The anniversary of the assassination came and went, and while that day, along with Thanksgiving and Christmas, was an exceptionally difficult one for me—it always would be—at least when I was working, my mind was occupied.

The day after Christmas happened to be a Sunday, and as usual the president and Mrs. Johnson drove to Johnson City in the white convertible to attend the eleven o'clock service at the First Baptist Church. There were a few members of the press there, and at the conclusion of the service, the president posed for photos with members of the congregation and the tourists who had gathered. After a few minutes, he turned to Mrs. Johnson and said, "Bird, let's go on over to the boyhood home and say hello."

Restorations had recently been completed so that his boyhood home, which was just a few blocks away from the church, was now open to the public. So President and Mrs. Johnson got back into the convertible, with our team of six agents following closely behind in Secret Service vehicles.

The president drove slowly down Avenue F, and after crossing Main Street, just as he turned the corner, I heard a loud explosive noise. It sounded like a firecracker.

Oh God. Across the street, a teenage boy was walking across the front yard of a home with a .30-30 rifle in his hands.

I jumped out of the car and ran toward the boy with my arms outstretched and waving above my head, yelling, "Put the gun down! Put the gun down!"

The boy turned as white as a starched shirt as he dropped the gun at his feet.

Meanwhile, the other agents, with guns drawn, raced to surround the president's car as it moved out of sight.

"What are you doing, son?" I asked the boy.

He was so distraught he could barely speak. "I'm uh, I was, uh, I was going hunting."

"Did you just shoot that gun?" I asked. The sound seemed to have come from a different direction, but here was the boy standing there with the gun.

"No, sir," he said. "I was just heading to my truck. I had no idea the president would be driving by. I guess I picked the wrong time to go hunting."

As it turned out, the noise had indeed come from another direction—where a young girl had set off a firecracker. The teenage boy was from San Antonio and happened to be visiting his grandparents, who had known the Johnsons for nearly thirty years. It turned out to be a series of unfortunate coincidences; as the boy said, he had picked the wrong time to go hunting. President Johnson was completely unfazed by the incident and carried on with his day as if nothing unusual had happened.

Each president deals with the stress of the office in his own way. Lyndon Johnson found relaxation at the LBJ Ranch, and in 1965 alone he spent more than 110 days there—nearly a third of the year. For the press and many of the agents, the long stretches of time at the LBJ Ranch were really miserable. For me, the Texas Hill Country reminded me of the simplicity of my childhood, and in retrospect I've come to realize that, as frustrating as President Johnson's unpredictability was, I thrived on the constant activity. The workdays were so long and exhausting—both mentally and physically—that by the time I fell into bed, sleep came easily. The busier I was, the fewer the nightmares. As it turned out, being on the Johnson detail kept me sane.

24

Traveling with LBJ: Honolulu and Mexico City

The Warren Commission made a number of recommendations for changes within the Secret Service, many of which required additional funding and authorization by Congress. When LBJ took office, however, one of his major directives was that his White House budget and the number of staff in his administration never exceed that of President Kennedy's, and thus, despite the Warren Commission's findings that the Secret Service had inadequate personnel, outdated equipment, and insufficient resources to adequately protect the president and his family, President Johnson was reluctant to increase the agency's budget.

Fortunately, Secretary of the Treasury Douglas Dillon refused to allow politics to override our mission, however, and in early 1965 he boldly appeared before Congress asking for $4 million more than President Johnson had appropriated. At that time we had 130,000 open threat cases, and we were still using a manual index card filing system. When the president traveled anywhere, sorting through the potential threats in a given area was slow, tedious, and most likely incomplete. The chances that we would miss a potential assassin, even if we had him on file, were huge. The money Dillon was requesting would be used to purchase an automated database, hire 183 new agents, and procure two new armored vehicles—a presidential limousine and a Secret Service follow-up car—built to Secret Service specifications. Before Congress even began deliberating, however, President Johnson stepped in and flat-out rejected the request for the two new vehicles, which together had a price tag of $522,000, saying he would not use nor condone the use of the cars for his protection. It made no sense to those of us whose responsibility it was to protect the man, but he was the president; we were not.

In the end, we did not get the cars, but Congress approved the other requests, and in November of 1965—two years after the assassination—the Secret Service was authorized to hire new agents. At the same time, the agency underwent a complete reorganization.

James J. Rowley's title was changed from chief to director, giving him equal rank to that of FBI director J. Edgar Hoover, and the organization was divided into four divisions—administration, investigations, intelligence, and protective services—each of which would be headed by an assistant director. SAIC Rufus Youngblood was promoted to assistant director of protective services, and would oversee not only the White House Detail but also the protection of the vice president and his family, former presidents Truman and Eisenhower and their wives, as well as the Kennedy Protective Detail, which protected Mrs. Kennedy, John, and Caroline.

ASAIC Lem Johns became the Special Agent in Charge of the White House Detail, and in January 1966 I was promoted from shift leader to Assistant Special Agent in Charge. My new position came with a slight increase in pay, much more responsibility and decision-making authority, and more direct contact with the president.

Shortly after my promotion, Assistant Director Youngblood summoned me to his office for a confidential briefing.

"Clint," he said, "President Johnson has just confirmed plans to meet General Westmoreland in Hawaii for a summit with Prime Minister Nguyen Cao Ky and Chief of State Nguyen Van Thieu. I don't have all the details yet, but I need you to get to Honolulu as soon as possible to lead the advance. The trip will be announced Friday, and the president leaves Saturday."

This was a Tuesday. I had less than four days to get to Hawaii and make security arrangements for a critical meeting between the President of the United States, his military advisors, and the leaders of the South Vietnamese government.

The purpose of the trip was a firsthand exchange of views between those who actually lived in Vietnam and those who were working on the Vietnamese problem in Washington. There were significant risks to having the heads of both the American and South Vietnamese governments together in one place, and it was an especially dangerous trip for the Vietnamese officials whose government was susceptible to a coup. There was a lot at stake, but everyone on the advance team had been handpicked, and all had experience with international events, so I was confident we could get the job done, even with such limited time.

When President Johnson arrived at Honolulu International Airport on the evening of Saturday, February 5, about five thousand people were there to greet him. And while the majority of the crowd was supportive, there were plenty of antiwar demonstrators chanting and holding up signs like MURDERER GO HOME! and STOP JOHNSON'S WAR!

Undaunted by the protestors, the president headed straight for the fence—much to our dismay—and reached into the crowd to shake a few hands before getting into the car and heading to the Royal Hawaiian Hotel.

The next morning, arrangements had been made to take the president to church services at St. Augustine Church, accompanied by some staff and the governor of Hawaii, John Burns, and a number of senators and congressmen. All went well until we were driving back to the hotel and President Johnson spotted a Dairy Queen.

"Pull over here!" he called out. "Let's get some ice cream."

Traffic was already a mess, and now we were about to make matters worse. The motorcade came to a stop, and much to the surprise and delight of the tourists and locals lining the street, the president got out of the car and walked up to the Dairy Queen stand as the agents sprang into action around him. He bought four ice cream cones, shook hands with some of the people, and got back into the car, grinning like a kid who had just pulled a fast one on his parents. Not the usual Sunday outing for a president attending an international conference.

When the Vietnamese delegation arrived that evening, President Johnson met the party planeside with the typical arrival ceremonies, and in his remarks he addressed those who were pressuring him to retreat from our involvement in the Vietnam conflict.

"Were we to follow their course, how many nations might fall before the aggressor?" he implored. "Where would our treaties be respected, our word honored, our commitment believed?" He argued that in the early years after

World War II, the United States stood firm in Europe to protect freedom, and now, like then, "Our stand must be as firm as ever. If we allow the Communists to win in Vietnam, it will be easier and more appetizing for them to take over other countries in other parts of the world."

The summit lasted for three days, resulting in the Declaration of Honolulu, in which the Republic of Vietnam and the United States of America declared their common commitment to defend against Communist aggression. The discussions included further increases in the number of U.S. troops, which was now over 200,000, in addition to an investment in broad social programs with the belief that progress in agriculture, education, health, and democracy building was essential to winning the war.

Hope prevailed, but both sides knew the end of the war was nowhere in sight.

IN EARLY APRIL 1966 it was announced that Mrs. Johnson and Secretary of State Dean Rusk would be traveling to Mexico City to unveil a statue of Abraham Lincoln that had been commissioned as a gift from the United States to Mexico. Shortly after the official announcement, Lem Johns informed me that they wanted me to handle the advance. It turned out that there was more to the trip than was being presented to the press. In fact, President Johnson would be going on the trip as well. It would be his first overnight visit to a foreign country since taking office nearly two and a half years earlier, but he didn't want anyone to know about it until the last possible minute.

"You know the president," Lem said. "He believes the element of surprise is the best security plan there is."

President Johnson's decision to send thousands of American troops to the Dominican Republic was not popular with some factions in Mexico, and there was a concern that opposition groups would stage large and potentially violent protests if they had enough lead time before the president's visit. There was a lot riding on this trip to begin with, but setting up the appropriate security arrangements for the President of the United States in a foreign country without letting on that he was actually going to be there would be a real challenge.

Our advance team included Bill Moyers from the White House press office, Jack Valenti on the political side, a representative from WHCA to handle communications, and a USAF military aide. We were all given explicit instructions to not even allude to the fact that President Johnson would be accompanying Mrs. Johnson until the last possible minute.

Our team flew down to Mexico City about a week prior to the Johnsons' arrival, set up a base at the U.S. Embassy, and got straight to work on the arrangements for the clandestine presidential visit. In meetings with officials of the Mexican government, we discussed only Mrs. Johnson's attendance at and participation in the unveiling and dedication of the statue, with no mention of the president, but in the course of the discussions it became apparent to me that the Mexican officials were aware President Johnson was coming. Still, neither side acknowledged it, continuing on with the ruse that everything being planned was strictly for the first lady.

Forty-five hours before the scheduled arrival time, the White House made the announcement that President Johnson had decided "on the spur of the moment" to accompany Mrs. Johnson to Mexico City, along with their daughters, Luci and Lynda. This somewhat quiet visit by the first lady was now turning into a full-fledged official visit, which required a completely different protocol. It was a huge relief to be able to deal openly with my Mexican counterparts, but now we had very limited time to get all the details in place. My biggest concern was the ten-mile motorcade from the Mexico City Airport to Los Pinos, the presidential palace.

I had arranged to have the armored presidential limousine flown in on a C-130, but now the Mexican officials were insisting that President Johnson ride with Mexican president Gustavo Díaz Ordaz in *their* convertible presidential limousine—with the top down.

Two vivid memories collided in my mind: the enormous crowds that turned out for President and Mrs. Kennedy's visit to Mexico City four years earlier—two million people along the motorcade route, storms of confetti so thick that by the end the open-top convertible was filled to the brim with the stuff—and the image of President Kennedy's head exploding in Dallas. There was no way we could allow President Johnson to ride through the streets of Mexico City in an open-top car. No way.

Our ambassador to Mexico, Tony Freeman, spoke with Mexico's foreign minister, hoping to find a solution that would appease both sides, but none of the options he returned with were acceptable to us. Ambassador Freeman explained that the president of Mexico never rode in an enclosed vehicle in these types of motorcades—it was culturally important for him to be seen by the people. So, basically, we had three choices: one, the president and Mrs. Johnson ride in our limousine, and President Díaz Ordaz rides in his open limo; two, both presidents ride in the open limo; or three, we cancel the visit.

None of us wanted our president to ride in an open car, but the whole purpose of this trip was to show our alliance with the Mexican people, and if Johnson didn't ride in the same car as the Mexican president, it would appear that there was a rift between the two leaders. Moyers and Valenti decided the only thing to do was to lay out the situation to President Johnson and let him decide.

President Johnson wasn't too pleased that our advance team couldn't work this out, and he told Valenti, "I really don't care what kind of car I ride in. Hell, I'll ride a burro if that's the only way to get to the city. Whatever you and Moyers and Ambassador Freeman decide, that's okay with me."

I was adamant that President Johnson ride in a closed vehicle, but Valenti and Moyers argued that that would be a diplomatic disaster. In the end, President Johnson and his staff decided that he would ride with President Díaz Ordaz in the Mexican presidential limousine, with the top down. The two first ladies, Mrs. Johnson and Mrs. Díaz Ordaz, would ride in a closed car a short distance behind the presidential vehicle, followed by an additional closed car carrying Lynda and Luci. The decision was out of my hands, but the responsibility to keep everyone safe was entirely on my shoulders.

Unbeknownst to me, Valenti had called FBI director J. Edgar Hoover to get his perspective on the matter. Our intelligence agents were already working with the FBI and the CIA, but the next thing I knew, Marvin Watson, President Johnson's chief of staff, sent me a Top Secret message informing me that the FBI was sending fifty agents to bolster our protective forces, and I should arrange to use them in the best way possible.

We also had more than six thousand Mexican police working with us, and their efforts were critically important. Not only did they provide crowd control, but they were responsible for securing every building along the route, as well as providing snipers in strategic locations. As a means of additional pre-caution, the Mexican government took care of hundreds of known dissidents in their own way, by rounding them up and jailing them during LBJ's visit, while potential troublemakers were kept under surveillance. Still, my biggest concern was, and always would be, the lone wolf who just hadn't popped up on anybody's radar. The Secret Service agents were the last line of defense, and the key would be to keep agents close to the president at all times.

At 5:30 p.m. on Thursday, April 14, just before dusk, Air Force One 26000 made its grand arrival at Benito Juárez International Airport. This was not scheduled as a state visit, but you wouldn't know it from all the cere-monial trappings that had been arranged—all supposedly in less than forty-five hours. Thirty-foot-tall paintings of both President Díaz Ordaz and President Johnson had been placed on top of the terminal, while thousands of spectators were on hand at the airport, standing on rooftops, balconies, and special viewing stands. There was a full arrival ceremony complete with twenty-one-gun salute, a reception committee, and an exchange of remarks by both presidents.

At 6:38 p.m., with the sun falling low on the horizon, the motorcade got under way with the two presidents standing in the rear of the Mexican government's Lincoln convertible, waving to the crowd. We had run the ten-mile route and planned for it to take about forty-five minutes at a standard motorcade speed of twelve to fifteen miles per hour. What we had not antici-pated was the enormous crowds the Mexican government had turned out. In an effort to give President Johnson a welcome rivaling that given President and Mrs. Kennedy back in 1961, the government had bused in people from outlying areas, and nearly half the city's population of six million was right here along the parade route. Everywhere you looked, people were hanging out of windows, standing on rooftops and balconies, and spilling into the street. Red, blue, yellow, and orange confetti swirled from above like a color-ful winter snowstorm, while mariachi bands stationed along the route sere-naded the crowd with the festive sounds of trumpets and strummed guitars. The crowds were so large that even with thousands of Mexican police stra-tegically positioned, the throng of people could not be contained. Time after time, the cars in the motorcade were forced to stop when a portion of the crowd surged through police lines and swarmed them. Our agents and the

Mexican security police surrounded the presidential vehicle in an effort to form a barrier between the people and the presidents, alternating between jogging and walking, depending on the speed of the motorcade.

Once again the high altitude caused problems for some of the agents who had just landed with the president, but I was impressed with their determination to keep up.

President Johnson was thrilled with the exuberance of the crowd, and as people clamored to touch him, he'd lean out of the car, trying to shake hands and touch as many people as he could, while at the same time we were forcibly pushing people away. My adrenaline was on overload as I scanned the sea of humanity, knowing the presidents were sitting ducks if anyone was out there with a high-powered rifle, intent on taking down a president and willing to risk his own life.

Darkness fell, and we trudged on for what seemed like an eternity, finally arriving at Los Pinos at 9:07 p.m. It had taken us two and a half hours to go ten miles. All of the agents had traveled by foot the entire way, and by the end not only were we completely exhausted, we looked like a band of vagrants—our hands and faces slathered with sweat and grime, our suits ripped and soiled beyond repair.

The Mexican authorities estimated the crowd at somewhere between two and three million—the largest ever to view a motorcade in Mexico City. It was a politician's dream scenario—President Johnson remarked that it was "the most wonderful reception" of his life—and a Secret Service agent's living nightmare.

25

Traveling with LBJ: Down Under

During my annual physical examination in 1966, the doctors at Bethesda Naval Hospital discovered I had a double hernia, and they recommended surgery as soon as possible. I was concerned about missing some interesting presidential activity, but the upcoming schedule was not very travel intensive, so I scheduled the surgery for June 7. A few days before I went into the hospital, Director Rowley called me into his office.

"Clint," he said, "in my most recent discussion with the president, he specifically inquired about you."

Oh no, I thought. *President Johnson still doesn't think I'm capable?*

"Yes, sir. In what way?"

"He commented on your work ethic and dedication to the job, and he asked about your pay grade in comparison to some of the other agents. When I gave him the information, he told me we needed to raise your grade."

Was I hearing this correctly? "The president thinks I deserve an increase in pay?" I asked.

"That's right," Rowley said. "I agree wholeheartedly, and I've just initiated the paperwork to increase you to a GS-15. The president is extremely pleased with your performance."

I was astounded. The president's confidence in me was an indication that he considered me trustworthy and loyal to the Office of the President. Considering that a year and a half earlier he had requested that I be removed from the detail, this was a major accomplishment.

It wasn't long before I was back in the regular routine, but during my absence the problems facing the president, and the world, seemed to have escalated. Civil rights activist James Meredith had been shot and wounded while marching in Mississippi. Race riots had broken out in Cleveland, and Martin Luther King had been assaulted with rocks in Chicago. The Vietnam situation had intensified, and on June 29 the United States began to bomb Hanoi and Haiphong. The president of Argentina had been deposed by a coup, and the prime minister of South Africa had been assassinated. There had been a sniper shooting at the University of Texas that left thirteen dead and thirty-one wounded. In Chicago, a mass murderer had brutally killed eight student nurses, and, in an upscale Chicago suburb, the daughter of U.S. Senate candidate Charles Percy had been murdered in her bedroom. Everywhere you turned there was violence and killing.

AUGUST IN WASHINGTON, D.C., is typically very quiet, with most of Capitol Hill on vacation, but in 1966 a big event kept a lot of people in town—the wedding of the president's daughter. On Saturday, August 6, seven hundred guests attended the wedding ceremony of Luci Baines Johnson and Patrick J. Nugent at the magnificent Basilica of the Immaculate Conception—the national Roman Catholic Church—in northeast Washington, D.C., and the reception afterward at the White House, while 55 million people tuned in to watch the event on live television. It was a wonderful, happy occasion for the Johnson family, but for the Secret Service, one of our main concerns was that the ever-present antiwar picketers would spoil the day, so we had hundreds of policemen posted around the White House. The demonstrators persisted throughout the day and into the evening. The guests were largely oblivious to what was happening just outside on Pennsylvania Avenue, but every so often, when the band stopped playing, you could hear the protestors chanting, "Hey, hey, LBJ, how many kids have you killed today?"

AT THE END of September, Philippine president Ferdinand Marcos invited President Johnson to meet in Manila with the leaders of six other nations allied in the anti-Communist military effort in South Vietnam to try to find a resolution to the growing conflict. By this time, we had around 300,000 Americans in Vietnam, and more than five thousand of our boys had been killed, as well as thousands more from the allied nations. Johnson readily accepted the invitation and expanded the trip to include stops in New Zealand, Australia, Thailand, Malaysia, Korea, and American Samoa. There was much speculation that President Johnson would also use this trip to make a stop in South Vietnam to visit the troops, but the White House consistently denied that was going to happen. In fact, a surprise visit to South Vietnam was in the plans from the beginning; the key was keeping it from being leaked to the press.

Not only was it an ambitious itinerary with tremendous logistical challenges, but it was also Johnson's first trip outside North America as president, and the first time a sitting president would visit Australia, New Zealand, Malaysia, and American Samoa. With just a few weeks of lead time, advance teams were hastily organized and sent to the various locations.

On October 17, there was a grand send-off ceremony at Dulles International Airport in Washington for the president and first lady. Now that I was one of the Assistant Special Agents in Charge of the White House Detail, I had the privilege of flying on Air Force One with the president during each leg of this long journey. There was limited space on the presidential aircraft, and typically seats were reserved for just six to eight agents, with the majority of the detail traveling in the backup plane or the press plane.

We landed at Honolulu International Airport to a large crowd and the typical arrival ceremonies, Hawaiian-style—with hip-swaying hula dancers, ukulele music, and stacks of floral leis presented to President and Mrs. Johnson to wear around their necks.

Our armored presidential vehicle, SS-100-X, had been sent by cargo plane, and as we motorcaded into downtown Honolulu, the streets were lined with schoolchildren and people holding up signs that read ALOHA MR. PRESIDENT! and WELCOME TO THE 50TH STATE! Hundreds of thousands of people waved and cheered—it was an exuberant, happy crowd—and at least a dozen times along the way, President Johnson ordered the driver to stop the car so he could get out and shake hands.

President Johnson was clearly elated with the wonderful reception in Honolulu, but as we prepared to head Down Under, we received some concerning information from the Australian Security Service. Apparently, several anonymous calls had been made to newspapers in Adelaide and Sydney saying an attempt would be made on President Johnson's life when he visited Australia. One caller told a reporter that he planned to take a rifle with a telescopic sight to Sydney. The man said his nineteen-year-old son had recently been killed in Vietnam and chillingly added, "I'm going to blow Johnson's head off."

Australia had nearly five thousand troops in Vietnam, and while the majority of Australians supported the war effort, many were opposed to the policy of sending draftees and held President Johnson personally responsible.

You couldn't cancel a trip because of random threats, however, and there was never any discussion of doing so. Whenever the president left the White House or the security of the LBJ Ranch—whether it was driving to church in Johnson City, Texas, or traveling in a grand motorcade through downtown Sydney, Australia—there was always the concern that a lone gunman might be in the crowd. The best we could do was investigate with the information we had, remain vigilant at all times, and hope that the president himself wouldn't take any unnecessary risks.

WE DEPARTED HONOLULU early on the morning of October 18, had a brief refueling stop in Pago Pago, American Samoa, crossed the International Date Line, and headed to Wellington, New Zealand.

It was drizzling rain, but still there was a good-sized crowd of about three thousand at the airport for the arrival ceremony. Speaking briefly, President Johnson endeared himself to the people of New Zealand when he referred to the last time he was there, twenty-four years earlier in 1942, as a lieutenant commander in the U.S. Navy serving alongside New Zealanders during the dark days of World War II. In all of his speeches on this trip he would compare that war to the current situation in Vietnam—how the world might have been a different place if the "snowball of aggression" had been stopped in the 1930s. It was our obligation to keep our word, and, as a larger nation, to support the people of a smaller nation like South Vietnam "to keep the momentum from gathering." But the task ahead would not be easy, he said, "because the securing of peace is not done by miracles," and there should be no expectations that "a rabbit would be pulled out of a hat" on this trip.

People of all ages had come out to welcome the president, and while there were a couple of placards protesting the war as we proceeded along the motorcade route from the airport to Government House—the official residence of the governor-general—the response was overwhelmingly warm and friendly. It had already been a long day, and our body clocks had not adjusted to the seventeen-hour time difference, but still there was a formal dinner reception, and by the time we got President Johnson tucked into his suite, it was after 10:30 in the evening.

Morning seemed to come much too quickly, and the next day's activities began early, with motorcades to the National War Monument and Parliament House. It was a crisp, sunny day, and because schools had declared it a holiday in honor of President Johnson's visit, it seemed the entire city had turned out to line the streets of Wellington. Riding in SS-100-X, the president used the car's microphone to connect with the people.

"Thank you for coming!" his voice boomed from the speakers. "Good morning! Glad to see you!"

The people loved it. "Welcome! Good on ya, Yank!" they yelled back.

With all this adoration surrounding him, the president couldn't contain himself inside the vehicle. At one point, there was a particularly large and boisterous group, including dozens of children dressed in their school uniforms waving and cheering. The car stopped—at the president's request—and without warning, Johnson opened the door, got out, and went straight into the crowd, beaming with delight as he shook as many hands as he could. The people went wild—clapping, cheering, so thrilled to see this American president, larger than life, right here in front of them.

We finally got him back into the car, but the next thing we knew, he was instructing Marvin Watson, his chief of staff, to get the advance man in the lead car to radio back and let them know which were the best spots—with the biggest crowds—so he could get out and greet the people, with maximum exposure. He invited the CBS pool cameraman into the car so he could film what the crowd looked like from the president's perspective. Johnson was simultaneously directing traffic, telling the driver where to stop, and connecting with the crowd via the car's loudspeaker system—he had taken charge of the whole damn motorcade. Needless to say, this put all the agents on edge, and we had to have guys running alongside the vehicle to make sure the president was covered anytime he decided to stop and jump out of the car.

Every so often we'd see signs proclaiming OUT OF VIETNAM and STOP UNLIMITED KILLING IN ASIA, but the overwhelming majority of the crowds were friendly and enthusiastic, holding up signs like LBJ FOREVER and SUPPORT U.S. POLICY IN VIETNAM.

The twenty-four-hour stay in Wellington was not just pomp and circumstance, though. President Johnson had substantive talks with the prime minister as well as the leader of the opposition party, and upon delivery of his speech in Parliament House the governing body applauded with two standing ovations. President Johnson was thrilled with the tremendous reception he had received, and as soon as he boarded Air Force One, he retired to his cabin and slept for the entire two-hour flight to our next stop—Canberra. Meanwhile, with reports of threats and demonstrations in Australia continuing to file in, our team of agents spent the time reviewing strategies for protecting the president and first lady in a potentially hostile environment—a task made all the more difficult with a president who haphazardly ignored prearranged security plans and was willing to expose himself to large, unchecked crowds in order to bask in the shower of adoration.

It had been drizzling in Canberra, but just as Air Force One touched down at Fairbairn Royal Australian Air Force Base shortly after six in the evening the rain stopped, and rays of sunlight burst through disappearing thunderhead clouds.

Prime Minister Harold Holt and his wife were waiting to greet President and Mrs. Johnson, and after the usual arrival ceremonies, President Johnson stepped up to the podium and made a few remarks to the press and the crowd at the airport.

"I came to Australia in 1942 on a mission of war," he said. "And now tonight, more than twenty-four years later, I return on a mission of hope. I cannot say that miracles will occur at Manila. I carry no magic wands. The hard work of securing the peace is never done by miracles."

The schedule called for everyone to move immediately to their assigned vehicles for the motorcade into downtown Canberra, but the cheering crowd along the fence beckoned. Unable to resist the human contact, President Johnson dove into the crowd, shaking hands, kissing babies, and handing out presidential pens as the press stumbled all over themselves trying to get photos.

What the hell is he doing? Running for prime minister of Australia? I thought. *If anyone needs a magic wand, it's us. If he keeps this up, it'll be a damn miracle to get him home alive.*

Finally, after he'd gone up and down the fence line, the president got into the car with Prime Minister Holt, and the motorcade got under way. There were tremendous crowds along the route, and once again the president halted the motorcade no fewer than six times to jump out and greet the people. Fortunately, there were no threatening incidents, and we eventually got President and Mrs. Johnson to Prime Minister Holt's residence for a nine o'clock private dinner.

Meanwhile, our advance team at the Canberra Rex Hotel—where the president would be staying overnight—warned us that a large crowd of anti-war demonstrators had gathered at the hotel's entrance and was waiting for the president's arrival. They were all riled up, shouting profanities and even hurling things at the American visitors who passed through the doors.

It was eleven o'clock by the time President Johnson departed the Holt residence, and we informed him that we were going to bring him to the back entrance of the hotel to avoid any confrontation. I was riding in the front seat of the follow-up car, and as we were driving along, I realized I could no longer see the president sitting in the car ahead. He had crouched down in the backseat, and as soon as we arrived at the hotel we surrounded him and scurried up to his suite without anyone observing his arrival. It was quite different from the welcoming reception he had received only hours earlier, and it was the only time I ever saw a president duck down in the rear seat of a car to avoid being seen.

EARLIER IN THE day, Youngblood informed me that President Johnson was considering an intensive campaign trip when he returned to the United

States to support Democratic candidates in the upcoming 1966 midterm election. He wanted to visit a number of cities in a variety of states before Election Day, November 8, and an advance team headed up by Special Assistant to the President Sherwin Markman was being formed to preview potential stops.

"The trip is extremely confidential," Youngblood said. "They need an agent to go with them, and the president and I decided you would be the best person for the job."

"Yes, sir," I said.

"The plan is that the president will make this trip a day or two after we get back, so we need you to make arrangements to fly back to Washington as soon as possible to join the advance group."

I was disappointed that I wasn't going to be able to participate in the rest of the president's trip to the South Pacific and Asia, but at the same time the fact that I was being given the responsibility for this important advance was an indication that my abilities were being recognized and appreciated.

The following day, I remained in Canberra to finish making my departure arrangements while the rest of the detail accompanied President Johnson to Melbourne. Being that this was the first time a sitting American president had ever visited Australia, President Johnson's every move was big news. Despite the protestors at the hotel and other small pockets of demonstrators during the motorcades, the overwhelming majority of Australians seemed almost starstruck by LBJ. They loved him.

The president's arrival and motorcade through Melbourne was covered live on television, so I was able to watch everything in real time from my hotel room. It felt strange to be watching the events unfold when I would normally be right in the middle of the action, and I found myself filled with anxiety. The crowds were enormous—newscasters estimated at least half a million people and perhaps as many as a million. It was a frantic mob scene of children, teens, and adults screaming and shrieking. American and Australian flags fluttered from hands in every direction. The absolute hysteria reminded me of the Beatles' arrival in New York City back in 1964. As the motorcade drove slowly through Melbourne's downtown area, the presidential vehicle was forced to come to a complete stop as it became enveloped in a swarm of people. My stomach was in knots as I anticipated what was about to happen, and sure enough, the president took the opportunity to open the back door and step onto the side running board, and, clutching the side of the vehicle, he hurled himself up so that he was standing above the crowd. The people went absolutely crazy—shrieking and cheering, clamoring to get close enough to touch him. As he stood there, fully exposed, his ego overwhelmed by the adoring crowds, the agents were desperately trying to push people back from the car and create space so the motorcade could proceed.

Finally, a path was cleared, and as the car began moving again President Johnson got back inside. I could see agents Lem Johns, Rufus Youngblood, Bob Heyn, and Jerry Kivett walking alongside the slow-moving limousine, the tenseness of the situation written all over their sweat-drenched faces. When the cars were able to move faster, Johns and Youngblood rode on the back of the limousine, clinging to the handholds.

Then, suddenly, out of nowhere, something came hurling at the vehicle, splattering all over the windshield and the agents. On the black-and-white television, it looked like they were covered in blood.

In fact, someone had launched several balloons filled with red and green paint. The agents struggled to carry on, the paint stinging their eyes and dripping down their faces. It was horrifying to watch this unfold, and I felt helpless sitting there in my hotel room. *What if this had happened when the president was standing outside the car? What if it had been acid instead of paint?*

The Australian police quickly caught the perpetrators, and eventually the agents were taken to a nearby hospital, where the paint was washed out of their eyes. Although the damage was serious, fortunately no one was permanently injured. The president and the agents returned to Canberra that night, and I got a full accounting of the horrific incident. Surprisingly, President Johnson didn't seem bothered at all, even joking about it. Meanwhile, SS-100-X was sent to a paint shop, and by the next morning it looked as good as new.

The itinerary for Saturday, October 22, included a side trip to Sydney, with a return back to Canberra that evening, and while SS-100-X was flown ahead on a cargo plane, Prime Minister and Mrs. Holt joined President and Mrs. Johnson on Saturday aboard Air Force One for the short twenty-five-minute flight. I had arranged a commercial flight from Sydney to Honolulu and then on to Washington, so I flew with the presidential party on Air Force One to Sydney. My flight didn't depart until late in the evening, so I intended to work with the detail throughout the president's Sydney visit. After the paint-bomb incident in Melbourne, everyone was on high alert, and no one could predict what awaited us in Sydney.

Watching Lyndon Johnson and Harold Holt interact, it was clear that the two had formed a genuine and sincere friendship. Their goals were aligned, and while they both faced increasing criticism for the Vietnam situation, they firmly believed that the strong alliance of SEATO would ultimately lead to peace in the region. In contrast to Mexico City, Prime Minister Holt did not object to riding with President Johnson in our armored car, so after the normal arrival ceremonies the two leaders got into the back of SS-100-X, while their wives rode behind in a separate car.

The crowds along the motorcade route were tremendous—more than one and a quarter million people had come out to welcome President Johnson to Australia's largest city. It was like a carnival, with balloons, people throwing confetti and streamers made from rolls of toilet paper from open windows above us, and thousands upon thousands of miniature American and Australian flags held up by screaming men, women, and children. The other agents and I started off on the running boards of the follow-up car, but almost immediately upon leaving the airport there was a loud group of antiwar demonstrators, so we jumped off and began jogging alongside the presidential vehicle. The vast majority of the crowd was enthusiastic and positive—many waving signs that said ALL THE WAY WITH LBJ—and although the president was inside the armored car, we knew that he might not stay there.

Sure enough, as the crowds grew from three deep to ten deep, the car suddenly stopped, and out came the president, walking beyond the police line and reaching out to shake hands with the people. He'd stop for a couple of minutes and then get back in the car, and three minutes later he'd be out again. Mobs of people were surging toward the car, and as we jogged along, pushing people back, we were getting reports that the *real* crowds didn't begin for several more miles.

We turned a corner, and there were hundreds of children waving and calling out to the president, so of course the car stopped. He stood on the running board reaching out to shake hands, grinning and shaking his head with glee at the response, and then, suddenly, he hauled himself up to the roof of the car and sat on the roof so the people could see him better. I could hardly believe my eyes.

Lem and Rufus and I made eye contact with one another, all thinking the same thing: *What in God's name is he doing? What the hell use is an armored car if the man sits on top of it like a target for anyone who wants to shoot him?*

Talking into the microphone of the loudspeaker system, the president thanked everyone and said how much he loved Sydney and the people of Australia as the crowd pressed in around the car. The agents were spread around, frantically scanning the throngs above, around, and behind us, hoping to God there wasn't someone in the crowd with a rifle. Truth be told, if there had been, there wasn't a damn thing we could have done. The first shot is free. After that, all you can do is react.

Youngblood finally convinced the president to get back in the car—by this time we were thirty-five minutes behind schedule, and as we drove slowly into the city the crowds got larger and larger. Suddenly a group of demonstrators holding antiwar signs began hurling eggs and black balloons at the car as they booed and yelled profanities. The Australian police surrounded them as we kept moving forward in a storm of toilet paper, ticker tape, and confetti.

The anti-Vietnam protestors seemed to be multiplying, and up ahead there appeared to be some kind of commotion. A bunch of young men and women were attempting to interrupt the motorcade by lying down in the street, and the police were struggling to remove them by grabbing their hands and feet.

The mounted police unit rode in to help us secure the motorcade, but it was absolute mayhem. Somehow we trudged through the demonstrators, but then we had another problem. There was so much paper in the air that the radiator and every intake vent of the presidential vehicle had become clogged, and the air-conditioning had stopped functioning.

People were screaming and cheering, throwing confetti, while we were on our radios trying to figure out what to do. We ended up moving the president into a regular sedan, but as soon as the motorcade got under way again, we got word of a bomb threat. The situation seemed to be unraveling, completely out of control. The only thing to do was divert from the planned route. We took off down a side street and headed away from the screaming throngs, finally arriving at our destination, the Art Gallery of New South Wales.

The president and Mrs. Johnson had a tour of the art museum—cut short because we were so far behind schedule—and then everyone piled back into the cars for a short drive to Circular Quay West to board a yacht for a cruise in Sydney Harbor.

After the intensity of the past couple of hours, it was a relief to be aboard the yacht and away from the clamorous masses of people. A band played "Anchors Away" as we departed on the *Captain Philip*, with two police boats providing escort. It was a glorious, sunny day, and the harbor was filled with hundreds of sailboats and motorboats, all jockeying to get a view of President Johnson, who stood on the deck with Mrs. Johnson, waving at the crowds on the water. We passed the Sydney Opera House—still under construction and at that time a somewhat controversial addition to Sydney's skyline—and sailed under the Sydney Harbor Bridge as the other boats frenzied around us. The local newspapers reported that in the history of Sydney Harbor there had never been as many boats as there were that day. It was a truly spectacular sight that I would remember for the rest of my life.

WHEN I ARRIVED back in Washington, I was able to stop at home for just a few hours—barely enough time to say hello to my family, drop off my dirty laundry, and repack—before reporting to Andrews Air Force Base, where I boarded an unmarked Lockheed JetStar along with the five other members of the survey team. This fact-finding mission was so secret that even the Air Force crew was wearing civilian clothes.

We flew all the way to the West Coast and started working our way back east checking possible venues, making stop after stop in city after city. The president and his staff did not want the press to find out about this possible political campaign trip, and everything was extremely hush-hush—so much so that when we arrived in Minot, North Dakota, where my mother was living at the time, I couldn't call or see her. It was discouraging because she was getting up in age and I hadn't seen her for quite some time, but I just couldn't take the chance that word would get out.

We had just a few more stops to make when suddenly, as we landed on an airstrip in New Hampshire, our plane developed mechanical problems. We notified the base Air Force unit at Andrews, and they secured another unmarked JetStar and flew it with mechanics and parts to our location. We took off in the new plane while the mechanics worked on the disabled jet, and finished our mission.

Our recommendation to the president was twenty-five speeches in twenty-two cities, covering seventeen states over a two-day period—an enormous undertaking, but we believed it to be doable. The report was forwarded to President Johnson's chief of staff, Marvin Watson, in Manila, Philippines.

Many had suspected that President Johnson might stop in South Vietnam since he was in the region for the summit, but the rumors were consistently and adamantly denied. In fact, even most of the president's staff believed the printed schedules—which did not include a stop in Vietnam—were firm.

The morning after the Manila summit ended, President Johnson traveled by helicopter to two other locations in the Philippines—scheduled visits that included short motorcades with President Ferdinand Marcos, with the press corps in tow. During this time, pilot Jim Cross surreptitiously transferred Air Force One from Manila International Airport to Sangley Point Air Base across Manila Bay.

Upon the return to Manila, the helicopter delivered President Johnson and all those aboard to Sangley, where they got on Air Force One. Meanwhile, the traveling press corps was taken to a hangar at the airport, the doors were locked and guarded by Secret Service agents, and everyone was told that they would soon be departing for Cam Ranh Bay in South Vietnam. All outside communications were banned until the trip was over.

President Johnson spent two hours and twenty-three minutes on the ground in Cam Ranh Bay talking with the troops, pinning Purple Hearts on the injured, and awarding the Distinguished Service Medal to General Westmoreland. It was the first time a U.S. president had visited South Vietnam and the closest an American president had been to a battlefield since Abraham Lincoln during the Civil War, and by all accounts it was an extremely emotional experience for the commander in chief. Everyone returned to Manila, and the trip continued on as planned to Bangkok, Thailand; Kuala Lumpur, Malaysia; and Seoul, South Korea. The trip had been a great success politically—President Johnson's appearances resulted in enormous crowds that were overwhelmingly positive in every city, while his participation at the Manila summit strengthened U.S. ties with the other nations that were resolved to defend South Vietnam and to continue working toward a peaceful resolution.

By the time President Johnson arrived back in Washington on November 2, however, he was thoroughly exhausted. Additionally, a medical evaluation had determined that he needed surgery to remove a growth from his vocal cords as well as an operation to repair a problem with the incision in his abdomen from his gallbladder surgery. The doctors urged President Johnson to get as much rest as possible before the surgery. Thus, the twenty-two-city, seventeen-state political campaign trip was shelved. All the work our advance team did was for naught, and on Friday, November 4, we were off to the LBJ Ranch so the president could rest up before the operation.

Ten days later we returned to Washington, and the president had his surgery at Bethesda Naval Hospital. Everything went smoothly, and three days after that President Johnson was released from the hospital. Rather than returning to the White House, we left Bethesda Naval Hospital by helicopter, flew directly to Andrews Air Force Base, boarded Air Force One, and flew back to Texas so the president could fully recuperate in the comfort of his home at the ranch. This meant that once again I would be in Texas on the anniversary of the assassination.

Three years had now passed since that dreadful day, and while it had drifted into the past for many people, including the media, my recollections and feelings of responsibility were as vivid as if it had happened yesterday. President Johnson remembered the anniversary with a telegram to Ambassador and Mrs. Joseph P. Kennedy and a handwritten letter to Jacqueline Kennedy but then it was ranch activity as usual, riding around inspecting the various ranches, spotting deer, and looking at sheep and cattle.

Between the lengthy foreign trips and the countless weeks at the LBJ Ranch, the agents on the White House Detail had been away from our wives and children for about 90 percent of the past year. I don't know what prompted it—perhaps Mrs. Johnson felt sorry for our wives, knowing they were home alone while we were working at the ranch on Thanksgiving—but out of the blue, President and Mrs. Johnson invited the wives of the senior agents on the White House Detail to be guests at the LBJ Ranch for the first weekend of December.

When I told Gwen about the invitation, she was beyond excited. She had never met President Eisenhower or President Kennedy, and had only met Mrs. Kennedy very briefly the day I received the commendation after the assassination. This was a big deal—not only for her but for all the wives. Finally, they were getting a perk.

AFTER THANKSGIVING, MRS. Johnson had returned to Washington for several days, so it worked out that on Friday, December 2, the Secret Service wives flew back to Texas with her on the presidential jet. The plane landed at Bergstrom Air Force Base, and from there they all boarded a helicopter that flew them directly to the ranch. Now, having been on the White House Detail for eight years by this time, I couldn't count the number of times I had flown on the presidential aircraft or ridden in helicopters, and it was the same for the other senior agents. But for our wives—most of whom had rarely flown much at all—to be able to fly with the first lady in the presidential aircraft, and then fly by helicopter to the LBJ Ranch, well, you can imagine it was quite a thrill.

It was shortly after five o'clock in the evening when the chopper landed at the ranch, and the president walked out to the airstrip to meet them. He put on the charm as he was introduced to Gwen and the others—Peggy Youngblood, Nita Johns, Loretta Taylor, Betty Godfrey, Donna Duncan, Ann Kivett, Mary Taylor, Heather McKinney, Barb Pontius, Pat Johnsen, and Beverly Olsson—grasping hands and kissing cheeks like they were old friends, and the ladies loved it.

As soon as the introductions were completed, he looked up at the sky and said, "I'm going out to look at my deer while there's still light enough." And then, turning to his guests, he smiled and added, "Anyone who wants to can come along."

The ladies, all in their traveling clothes—skirts or dresses and high heels—looked at each other without knowing quite how to answer this strange invitation immediately upon arrival.

Mrs. Johnson piped up and said, "Lyndon, perhaps our guests would like to settle into their rooms first."

"Oh, we can show them to their rooms later, Bird. Come on, y'all, let me show you my fine deer."

It was so typical of LBJ. No matter who his guests were, the first thing he wanted to do was drive around and give them a tour of the ranch. He never gave a thought that perhaps someone might need to use the facilities after traveling halfway across the country, and no one ever dared speak up.

Everyone split up into the various cars, with President Johnson at the wheel of the station wagon leading the way, using the two-way radio system so each carful of wives could hear him, and the ranch tour began. He gave a running commentary, describing the countryside, the deer, the turkeys, armadillos, cattle, and Barbados sheep that were on the property. Driving from one ranch to another, it was the grand tour, with the leader of the free world as guide in chief.

One obligatory stop on the tour was always the birthplace—the simple house where Lyndon Johnson had been born—and as everyone walked around the house, the President of the United States explained in graphic detail how, without any indoor plumbing, he had used a chamber pot as a young boy.

Each of the twelve couples was assigned accommodations nearby: some stayed in guesthouses on the Lewis Ranch, some at the Haywood Ranch, some in a guest trailer house, and some—including Gwen and me—in Johnson City in apartments owned by President and Mrs. Johnson.

On Saturday, President and Mrs. Johnson had a preplanned day trip to Del Rio and Ciudad Acuña, Mexico, to celebrate our nations' joint venture in the Amistad Dam. So while those of us on the White House Detail flew to Mexico, local agent Clarence Knetsch was in charge of entertaining the wives for the day. The president had given Clarence instructions to take them on the normal routine—a tour inside the ranch house, which they had seen the night before, as well as the president's boyhood home in Johnson City.

Meanwhile, it was another typical workday for us—jogging in a motorcade through Ciudad Acuña, fending off surging crowds in a blizzard of confetti, trying to keep President Johnson safe as he and President Díaz Ordaz stood waving from an open-top car.

That evening, the agents and wives all went for dinner at the Stonewall Café in Stonewall, where the main course happened to be venison—another first for most of the wives. The gals were really enjoying the opportunity to see and experience the ranch where we spent so much time, but without witnessing the protective activities like our trip to Mexico that day, they could not fathom the emotional and physical strain of our jobs.

The highlight of the weekend was dinner with the president and Mrs. Johnson at the ranch house. White House photographer Yoichi Okamoto was on hand to capture the festivities, and the president and Mrs. Johnson made time to pose for photos with each of the couples before sitting down to dinner in the dining room. We had assigned seats, and while I was at President Johnson's table, Gwen was seated at Mrs. Johnson's table. Throughout the evening, President Johnson held court, telling story after story about crazy things that had happened with the various agents, sending the room into fits of laughter.

It was a really special occasion—not just for our wives, but for the agents too—because for the first time we were not just agents, we were the president's guests. And while it wouldn't make up for years of missing birthdays, anniversaries, and holidays, the weekend the Secret Service wives got to spend at the LBJ Ranch went a long way toward holding together many a fragile marriage.

26

1967

For the third year in a row, we spent Christmas and New Year's at the LBJ Ranch, finally returning to Washington on January 2, 1967. The previous year we had spent more time at the ranch in Texas than anywhere else, including the White House.

On January 27, there was a devastating tragedy at Cape Kennedy. During a test launch for an upcoming two-week space mission, a spontaneous fire engulfed the Apollo 1 module, killing the three astronauts aboard. The horrific deaths of Virgil "Gus" Grissom, Roger Chaffee, and Ed White—all national heroes—threw the nation into mourning. The funerals for the three men would take place four days later, with Vice President Humphrey and Mrs. Johnson attending White's burial at the U.S. Military Academy at West Point, while President Johnson would attend the two separate services for Grissom and Chaffee at Arlington National Cemetery.

I hadn't been back to the cemetery in nearly three years—since the day I accompanied Mrs. Kennedy, John, and Caroline to pray at President Kennedy's gravesite on what would have been his forty-seventh birthday—and now here I was accompanying President Johnson to two burials, with full military honors, on the same day. I knew in advance what the plans were, but I was unprepared for the emotional impact. Every sight and every sound brought back memories of the day we buried President Kennedy: the clip-clop of the horses' hooves; the sharp cracks of the twenty-one-gun salute; the roaring flyover of jets in the missing man formation; the silence as the honor guard lifted the flag-draped casket from the caisson; and the soft sobs of the tearful widow as she was handed the carefully folded American flag before a mournful bugler ended the ceremony with taps. Clenching my jaw, I tried desperately to suppress the feelings that kept welling to the surface, but when President Johnson leaned over and shook the white-gloved hand of Chaffee's eight-year-old daughter, and then the tiny five-year-old hand of his son, I had to turn away.

IN THE THREE years since President Kennedy had been laid to rest in Arlington Cemetery, his gravesite had drawn more than sixteen million visitors. Every weekday, three thousand people per hour would come to pay their respects, and on weekends that number doubled. In 1965 it was decided that a larger site should be built to accommodate the flow of people, and Mrs. Kennedy worked with an architect to design a suitable memorial. The original gravesite had remained open to the public during construction, and the new site was due to be completed in the summer of 1967. We had recently returned to Washington from a trip to the LBJ Ranch in early March of 1967 when I was informed that President Kennedy's body was going to be moved from its original gravesite to the new location. Mrs. Kennedy would be coming from New York City for a private reburial ceremony, and she had invited President Johnson and Secretary McNamara to attend. All of this was to be carried out in the highest secrecy, and very few people were aware it was taking place.

Shortly after midnight on March 15, a small group of men set up floodlights around the gravesite, and with the use of a crane moved President Kennedy's casket about ten yards downhill from its original location to its new resting place in the new stone and marble memorial. At the same time, the bodies of the two infant Kennedy children—Patrick Bouvier and their unnamed stillborn daughter, who had been brought from Massachusetts to be buried next to their father—were also moved to the new location.

At 6:50 a.m., we departed the White House with President Johnson in a strictly off-the-record movement and motored to Arlington National Cemetery. It had been raining throughout the night, and although it was now after dawn, there was no hint of sunlight. As we pulled up to the site, I saw Mrs. Kennedy huddled under an umbrella with her brother-in-law Bobby and his wife, Ethel. Teddy, Pat, Eunice, and Jean were there too, each with their spouses, as well as Secretary McNamara. As President Johnson walked toward them, I hung back, remaining on the fringes of the burial site so as not to be noticed. This was a time for family and invited guests, and I was neither.

Cardinal Cushing, who had conducted President Kennedy's funeral Mass, had flown in from Boston to officiate, and a small Army band had been brought in, surely at Mrs. Kennedy's request. A ceiling of dark clouds hung overhead as a steady rain poured from the heavens, enveloping all of us in sadness and grief that had yet to be eased by time. It was a simple twenty-minute ceremony, during which the band played just a few selections, including "Navy Hymn" and "The Boys of Wexford," and the aging cardinal blessed the new grave.

"Be at peace, dear Jack," he said with his lilting Irish accent, "with your tiny infants by your side, until we all meet again above this hill and beyond the stars. May the Good Lord grant you eternal rest and let perpetual light shine upon you and yours."

As the somber ceremony concluded, Mrs. Kennedy leaned over to place a simple bouquet of lilies on the new grave, and as she stood up her head turned in my direction. Not wanting to feel like I was intruding, I looked down at the rain-soaked ground and turned away.

An hour later, I was on Air Force One with the president, headed for a long day of politicking in Tennessee. It wasn't until we were airborne and it had been confirmed that Mrs. Kennedy was on her flight back to New York that the press was informed of what had occurred that morning at Arlington Cemetery.

IN 1963, PRESIDENT Kennedy had requested funds for a state-of-the-art, $188.5 million aircraft carrier, and after the assassination President Johnson decided the carrier would be named after our slain president. Three and a half years later, the carrier was completed, and it was time to christen it. On May 27, two days before what would have been John F. Kennedy's fiftieth birthday, I flew with President Johnson to Newport News, Virginia, where the carrier was docked.

I accompanied President Johnson to a reception prior to the christening—Mrs. Kennedy was there with nine-year-old Caroline, six-year-old John, President Kennedy's mother, Rose, Bobby, Teddy, their wives, Cardinal Cushing, many Navy admirals, and assorted distinguished guests—and I tried my best to stay out of the way. When it was time for the ceremony, everyone walked out to a special platform that had been built under the enormous bow of the great ship and sat in their designated seats. After President Johnson spoke about President Kennedy and the meaning of this great ship named in his honor, Mrs. Kennedy, Caroline, and John stepped up to the bow. Someone handed Caroline a bottle of champagne, and after two sirens sounded she struck the bow of the ship with the bottle. The bottle remained intact, so she swung it back and struck the bow again, this time with all her might. There was a loud crack as the bottle broke open, spraying champagne all over her. She smiled shyly as someone handed her a towel to wipe her face and her clothes, and her mother leaned in to congratulate her on a job well done.

In June 1967, war erupted in the Middle East between Israel and its Arab neighbors. What became known as the Six Day War not only resulted in the controversial expansion of Israel's borders but also created sudden and immediate tension within the already fragile U.S.-Soviet relationship.

Soviet premier Aleksei Kosygin requested a special session of the United Nations General Assembly to demand Israel's withdrawal from Arab territories, and announced he would travel to New York for the session. This created an opportunity for President Johnson to meet with Kosygin, and the president immediately suggested a meeting at the White House or at Camp David, where security would present no problem. Kosygin was agreeable to the meeting, but not wanting to be an official guest of the U.S. government, which would undermine his relations with the Arabs and North Vietnam's Ho Chi Minh, he suggested they meet at the U.N., which was international territory. But a meeting in New York City created all kinds of security issues, not to mention that it would likely draw thousands of angry protestors on both sides. After going back and forth with various ideas, someone pulled out a map and a ruler, drew a line between Washington and New York City, and found that the midpoint was Glassboro, New Jersey, home of Glassboro State Teachers College.

On June 22, at 5:00 p.m., the two sides agreed to meet at Glassboro College the following day at eleven in the morning. An advance team was hurriedly called to action and departed Washington a few hours later, with less than fifteen hours to secure the location for this historic summit between the leaders of the world's two superpowers.

The president had some specific requirements for the meeting place: there needed to be enough room to accommodate a meeting of several dozen representatives from both countries, but at the same time have several small, informal rooms where private meetings between President Johnson and Premier Kosygin could take place; he wanted carpeted floors wherever possible to eliminate noise from staffers walking around; and there needed to be a suitable place for a luncheon that included an elegant meal.

The lead advance man was Sherwin Markman, one of President Johnson's assistants, and upon arriving at the college around midnight, he immediately met with the college president, Dr. Thomas Robinson, to determine the meeting location. After reviewing several of the college's buildings, Markman determined that the most appropriate option was Robinson's large Victorian home, called "Hollybush." The residence had a large living room, a big kitchen with a formal dining room, and an office on the main floor that was ideal for private meetings. There were some changes that would need to be made to the house, however, in order to provide the security and comfort necessary for such a high-level meeting, and there was no time to waste. Dr. and Mrs. Robinson consented to their residence being used, but they had no comprehension of what was about to happen to their beloved hundred-year-old home.

In the wee hours of June 23, Secret Service agents and White House Communications Agency engineers streamed into the house with massive amounts of tools and equipment. The first problem was that the home had no air-conditioning. It was a muggy night, and the forecast called for a hot, humid day ahead. Unfortunately, the home's antiquated wiring system couldn't support even small window air-conditioning units, so the power company was called in to deliver and install a transformer, while electricians rewired the entire house. By morning, air-conditioning units had been installed in every room.

That was only the beginning. Much of the Robinsons' furniture needed to be removed to make room for conference-style tables and chairs; heavy drapes were hung over the windows to ensure privacy; separate telephone lines were installed for the Soviet and American delegations, and the kitchen was completely ripped apart so that professional, heavy-duty appliances could be installed. Unbelievably, by the time we arrived with the president shortly before eleven o'clock, the old stone house had been transformed to fit all the necessary requirements for an international summit.

There was an army of press waiting outside, and when the Soviet entourage arrived, President Johnson and Premier Kosygin posed for photos before entering the house. The most pressing issues were, of course, the Middle East situation and the Vietnam conflict, but it just so happened that the day before, President Johnson had become a grandfather, with the birth of his daughter Luci's son, Patrick Lyndon Nugent. President Johnson had yet to see the baby, but he and Kosygin found common ground in the fact that they both had grandchildren, and that they shared a responsibility to not only avoid nuclear disaster but to make the world a safer place for future generations.

When it was time for lunch, the two leaders walked into the floral-wallpapered dining room, and with the Russian interpreter between them, President Johnson asked Kosygin what he would like to drink.

"I'll have whatever you're having," Kosygin said.

President Johnson broke into a sly smile and retorted, "I'm having what you're having . . . vodka."

Kosygin had presented the president with a special bottle of vodka, so the bottle was opened, two glasses were poured, and, grinning at each other, the American president and the Soviet premier quickly downed the vodka shots, Russian-style.

By the time the meeting was wrapping up, both Johnson and Kosygin agreed that the discussions had been fruitful, and perhaps it would be beneficial to schedule another meeting before Kosygin returned to Moscow. President Johnson was scheduled for a Democratic fund-raiser in Los Angeles that evening and Kosygin had to return to New York, so they decided to return to Glassboro on Sunday, two days later, much to the surprise of the press, the Glassboro community, and most especially to Dr. and Mrs. Robinson.

Air Force One was standing by at Philadelphia International Airport, and at 5:45 p.m. we were wheels up, headed for Los Angeles. During the five-hour flight, I managed to grab a bite to eat and catch some sleep before changing into my tuxedo for the formal event. We landed at Los Angeles International Airport at around 7:45 p.m. local time, transferred to a helicopter, and flew to the Century Plaza Hotel in downtown L.A., where nearly a thousand guests had paid $1,000 per couple to attend the black-tie Democratic Party fund-raiser.

Meanwhile, outside the front entrance of the hotel, ten thousand anti–Vietnam War protestors were clashing with police. It was a damn mess, but fortunately the advance team arranged for us to bring President Johnson in through a rear basement door, and he got inside without being noticed. The event was set up in an enormous ballroom that had been transformed into a glittering nightclub with a large dance floor surrounded by dozens of tables, and somehow I had drawn the short straw and was designated to walk in with President Johnson as he was introduced to the star-studded Hollywood crowd. Standing outside the door, we heard the master of ceremonies, comedian Jack Benny, announce, "Ladies and gentlemen, please rise for our honored guest, President Lyndon Baines Johnson!"

The room erupted with applause as the orchestra played ruffles and flourishes and "Hail to the Chief," and President Johnson strode into the room. A spotlight focused on him as he walked across the dance floor, and there I was, awkwardly walking a few steps behind, trying rather unsuccessfully to remain unobtrusive.

The night wore on as President Johnson mingled with the guests over dinner of beef filet. Wine and champagne flowed, and then, following dinner, there was entertainment by Fred Ames and Diana Ross and the Supremes.

The president was eager to meet his newborn grandson, so it was decided that we would fly directly from L.A. to Texas to visit Luci and the baby in the hospital in Austin before returning to Glassboro on Sunday. We departed L.A. just before midnight local time, and by the time we got to the LBJ Ranch, it was 4:30 a.m. Central Time—6:30 a.m. by our body clocks—and I realized we had been on the go for a full twenty-four hours. It was days like these that I was amazed by President Johnson's stamina and his ability to transition so easily from high-level international talks at which the world's fate hung in the balance to schmoozing and politicking with movie stars and entertainers, while still managing to make time to be with his family.

Of course LBJ also realized his daughter Luci had just given him a priceless photo opportunity, so the press was alerted, and a photo was circulated of President Johnson with his newborn grandson.

We returned to Glassboro on Sunday, where by now the tiny college town had become the focus of the world's attention, with nearly a thousand reporters and photographers staked out around Hollybush. Johnson and Kosygin met for five more hours, and by the end of the meetings both men acknowledged that although they failed to resolve any major differences, the one thing they agreed was to avoid the risk of nuclear war so that their grandchildren might live in a world of peace.

Just as the conference was ending, someone on President Johnson's staff learned that Premier Kosygin had scheduled a televised press conference at 8:00 p.m. at the United Nations. President Johnson had not planned to make any additional statements to the press, but in light of what Kosygin was doing, he decided that the American people should hear from their own president first. While we were en route back to Washington aboard Air Force One, arrangements were being made to have the TV networks set up at the White House. Normally we would land at Andrews Air Force Base and helicopter back to the White House, but it was already late, and pilot Colonel Jim Cross informed the president that the only way we could make it before eight o'clock was to land at National Airport in downtown Washington. The problem was that Federal Aviation Administration regulations prohibited such a large aircraft from landing there because the runway was considered too short.

President Johnson wouldn't be deterred. He asked Colonel Cross if he could land safely on National's runway, and Cross replied with great confidence that he could.

"Then do it," the president ordered.

The control tower at National gave Cross clearance to land—only because he was piloting Air Force One. I'm pretty sure I wasn't the only one holding my breath as the plane slid to a stop—very close to the end of the runway—at 7:31 p.m.

The presidential helicopter was standing by; it took off four minutes later and landed on the South Grounds at 7:40, and the president appeared live on television at 7:43 p.m.—seventeen minutes before Kosygin.

On December 9, 1967, President and Mrs. Johnson's older daughter, twenty-three-year-old Lynda, married Marine Corps Captain Charles S. Robb in the East Room of the White House. It was a beautiful ceremony amid the festive Christmas decorations, but there was also a bittersweet poignancy to the event, because it had been announced that Captain Robb would begin a tour of duty in Vietnam just a few months later. For President Johnson, having his son-in-law in the combat zone would make his efforts to find a peaceful ending to the conflict all the more urgent.

It was around this time that I was informed I was being promoted to Special Agent in Charge of President Johnson's protective detail. After initially wanting me kicked off of his detail, it turned out President Johnson had come to the conclusion that I really was a professional, and he trusted me with his life. From this point on, I would be the last line of defense for the President of the United States.

Just a few weeks into my new assignment, I was faced with my first big challenge. On the morning of December 17, 1967, we received word that fifty-nine-year-old Prime Minister Harold Holt of Australia had gone missing while swimming in rough surf off the Australian coast. Despite an exhaustive search, no trace could be found of his body, but a helicopter crew sighted a huge shark in the area where he had been swimming. This was an enormous shock, and as soon as I heard, I was sure President Johnson would be going to Australia to attend any services held on behalf of the prime minister. I had witnessed the sincere friendship that had formed between the two leaders over the past couple of years, and I knew President

Johnson would want to pay his respects to the Holt family and also to the people of Australia.

Any large gathering of world leaders is always an extremely difficult and tense situation for the Secret Service, but funerals are particularly challenging because of the short notice to prepare, and this one would test us like nothing else had before. It would end up being one of the most extraordinary, and arduous, trips of my career.

The first problem we encountered was that the premier presidential aircraft, USAF 26000, was undergoing a required biannual maintenance check and was unavailable for the trip. We would have to use the backup plane—USAF 86970—which didn't have a bed for the president, and had a much lower fuel capacity, requiring us to make more frequent refueling stops. President Johnson was of course furious that 26000 couldn't be ready in time, and in order to appease him, the maintenance team basically rebuilt the interior of the backup plane in forty-eight hours—including installing an extra-long bed—to make it amenable to the president for the long-haul flight.

We departed the White House at 11:47 on the morning of Tuesday, December 19, flew by helicopter to Andrews Air Force Base, and boarded the newly revamped plane, which became Air Force One as soon as President Johnson stepped aboard. The presidential aircraft crew was well accustomed to President Johnson's habits by this time, and they had stocked the plane with the president's favorite foods and drinks—plenty of Texas-style chili with saltine crackers, vanilla ice cream for dessert, and Fresca. LBJ loved his chili, and it was his favorite thing to have aboard Air Force One. To this day, I still enjoy a good bowl of chili, and it always reminds me of my days with LBJ.

Our first refueling stop was Travis Air Force Base, in California, and while we had not planned on deplaning, shortly before landing the president was informed that a group of wounded servicemen had been brought in that morning from Vietnam to the base hospital.

"Well, then, I'm going to go and see those boys," he said.

Everyone at the hospital was taken by surprise when the President of the United States suddenly walked in. He took the time to speak with the wounded men—all of whom were so very young—and hand out gold pens with his signature on them.

"Now you write me and let me know how you get along," he said as he thanked them for their service to our country. "You fellows have done a good job in Vietnam. I am proud of you."

Six hours later, we landed at Hickam Air Force Base, in Hawaii, at 6:05 p.m. local time, in driving rain. The governor of Hawaii and several thousand people were waiting in the downpour to greet the president, so while the jet was being refueled we deplaned, and President Johnson made a few remarks under an umbrella. The press that was accompanying us on the press plane were unprepared for rain, and with just one umbrella among them, they got completely soaked while taking notes of President Johnson's short eulogy for his friend Prime Minister Holt. The agents who rode on the press plane later informed me that everyone had stripped off their clothes and had them hung around the aircraft, hoping they'd dry out before we reached Australia.

There wasn't much rest to be had on the next leg of the trip, as we encountered heavy turbulence for much of the flight to our next refueling stop. It was midnight local time when we reached Pago Pago, American Samoa, but despite the late hour a large crowd had gathered to see and pay their respects to President Johnson. It was a hot and humid night, and there were about a thousand people, most in native dress—the men bare-chested, holding torches high above their heads. The flames danced against the pitch-black night sky, creating a mesmerizing backdrop to the melodic sounds of a children's choir singing the national anthem, and while it was a sight to behold, the muggy, tropical air was almost unbearable for those of us dressed in traditional business suits.

By the time we reboarded the air-conditioned cabin of Air Force One, everyone was dripping with perspiration, including President Johnson, who remarked that he just wasn't meant for these tropical climates.

We took off from Pago Pago shortly before one o'clock in the morning and crossed the International Date Line, and when we landed at Fairbairn Air Force Base near Canberra, Australia, six and a half hours later, at 4:34 a.m. on December 21, we had been traveling for more than twenty-five hours.

We motorcaded directly to the Canberra Rex Hotel, and even though it was still before dawn, there was no time to rest. We had a full day ahead, and I barely had time to take a refreshing shower and shave before it was time to get back to work.

When a president attends a state funeral or memorial service, it's an opportunity for him to meet and confer with other world leaders who are all there at the same time, and this was definitely going to be the case here in Australia. The memorial service was scheduled for the next day in Melbourne, but many heads of state were gathering in Canberra first, and it was a whirlwind of activity as Johnson had one meeting after another with representatives from Australia, New Zealand, South Korea, Thailand, Malaysia, Laos, Indonesia, Singapore, the Republic of China (Taiwan), the Philippines, and South Vietnam. There were press photographers and people coming and going—it was the usual madhouse situation. The one thing that was different was that President Johnson had been meeting privately with Colonel Jim Cross, his military aide and pilot, at various times during the day. Normally, they conferred by phone. I had the feeling something was up.

THE NEXT MORNING, Friday, December 22, everyone was up early to fly to Melbourne for the memorial services. President Johnson was clearly weary from the long journey, and the personal sense of loss he felt for his good friend Prime Minister Holt was written all over his face as he consoled Mrs. Holt and the rest of the family privately at Government House before the memorial service at St. Paul's Cathedral.

As we escorted President Johnson to the second-row pew, I took note of the remarkable gathering of dignitaries and heads of state who had come to pay their respects, which included a poised young man who took the place of honor in the first pew, immediately in front of President Johnson—twenty-year-old Charles, Prince of Wales, the heir to the British throne.

At the conclusion of the services, we motorcaded straight to the airport and were airborne from Melbourne at 2:30 in the afternoon. The assumption of most people on board, as well as those on the press and backup planes, was that we were headed back to Washington, following the same route by which we had come. Only a handful of us knew that we were not going home just yet, but even those of us on the inside didn't know exactly what President Johnson had up his sleeve.

When we left Washington, the Secret Service, WHCA, and other military units were aware that there was a distinct possibility this trip would be extended and might include a stop at the Vatican for a meeting with Pope

Paul VI. We were not sure of our exact route, or where or when additional stops might be made—only that we would be back by Christmas.

Shortly before the funeral service, Rufus Youngblood had pulled me aside.

"Clint, Valenti just told me, and I confirmed with Colonel Cross, that the president has decided to go to Korat. When we take off from Melbourne, we're heading west to Darwin to refuel. All details are top secret."

"Korat? The air force base?" I asked.

The Royal Thai Air Force Base in Korat, Thailand, was the largest frontline facility of the U.S. Air Force for bombing missions into Vietnam.

"Yes," Youngblood said. "Apparently the president wanted to go straight to Cam Ranh Bay, but that would mean we'd be landing in Vietnam at midnight. Obviously not a good idea."

"So what's the plan?"

"We'll land at Korat at around ten o'clock tonight. From what I understand, the pilots of the other aircraft aren't even being told where they're going until they're off the ground. We'll overnight in Korat and fly to Cam Ranh Bay early tomorrow morning. The press are going to be mad as hell, but we're going to prevent them from filing or making any phone calls until our next stop—wherever that is. I don't think the president has even decided where the hell he's going next."

"Any confirmation on the Vatican?"

"No. As far as I know, any meeting with the pope is still unconfirmed too."

I shook my head. "So we've got no advance teams? Nobody on the ground ahead of us?"

"That's right," Youngblood said. "Our security plan is the element of surprise."

"It's a goddamn nightmare, is what it is," I said. "One leak and we're all dead."

We had recently learned that the Vietcong now possessed long-range weapons, and there were no bases in Vietnam that were invulnerable. If word got out that President Johnson was going to be in Cam Ranh Bay tomorrow, there was no question he'd be a target.

The only people President Johnson had taken into his confidence about his intentions were Jack Valenti and Colonel Jim Cross, and he had sworn them to secrecy. Valenti had strong Vatican contacts and was apparently trying to arrange a meeting with Pope Paul VI to enlist his help to secure peace in Vietnam, while Cross had assembled a mini air fleet that included several giant cargo planes carrying staff, telecommunications, helicopters, and cars. The pilots of all the aircraft, including the backup plane and the Pan Am press charter, were only given the flight details of where they were headed next well after takeoff. Meanwhile, those of us charged with protecting the president were also left to guess what his next moves might be.

It was a little after 10:00 p.m. when we landed at Korat. Using U.S. Air Force vehicles, we took the president to a trailer house that had quickly been arranged for his use. He was inside for just a few minutes before he came out and said he wanted to go to the mess hall where the pilots gathered. Some flights had just returned from a bombing mission over Vietnam, and he wanted to see and talk with the pilots.

By this point, word had spread around the base that President Johnson had dropped in for an unannounced visit, but still, when he walked into the officers club, the men could hardly contain their surprise. The president made a few remarks and then spent about forty-five minutes with the pilots, asking pointed questions about the situation on the ground in Vietnam. It was almost as if he didn't trust what his advisors had been telling him for the past four years, and this was his chance to get the straight story from the men on the front lines. Finally, at midnight, he decided it was time to get some rest, and we escorted him back to his trailer.

Meanwhile, a bed in an adjoining trailer had been made available for me, and I gladly took advantage while the midnight shift stood post. I stripped down to my shorts and slung the rest of my clothes across the end of the bed so they'd be easily accessible for whatever time we ended up departing. As soon as my head hit the pillow, I was out. This was the only time I would have the use of a bed on this trip, and at this point I had no idea what President Johnson had planned beyond Cam Ranh Bay—and truth be told, I don't think even the president himself had figured it out just yet.

Five hours later, at 5:00 a.m., on Saturday, December 23, I was awakened by one of the midnight-shift agents.

"Clint, the president is up. Rostow and Bundy just went into his trailer."

Walt Rostow, the national security advisor, and William Bundy, the Assistant Secretary of State for East Asian and Pacific Affairs; the president must have summoned them.

"Do you have any idea why?" I asked.

"He told them to get going and find a way to get him into Karachi without the press finding out prior to arrival."

Karachi? "He's going to see Ayub Khan," I said as I jumped out of bed. "Goddamn it! I wish he'd realize we are on his side."

If we were headed to Karachi after Vietnam, and then possibly to the Vatican, my guess was we would continue flying west, all the way around the world. Who else was he going to visit on the way back to Washington? Charles de Gaulle? Queen Elizabeth? Here I was, the Agent in Charge of protecting the President of the United States, headed into a combat zone, and I had no idea what the man was going to do next.

God help me.

I quickly ran a razor up and down my face before throwing on the clothes I'd worn the day before, and managed to be outside the president's door when he emerged from his trailer, dressed in his tan gabardine ranch clothes.

The entire base—about two thousand servicemen—had gathered in a hangar where two jets were undergoing maintenance. The men were packed in there, standing room only, with dozens perched on horizontal beams and ladders dangling from the aircraft cockpits, and they all came to attention as President Johnson strode up to a podium on a stage that had been erected at one end. I followed and stood behind him as first he decorated a group of pilots with Silver Stars and the Distinguished Flying Cross, and then made a few remarks to the men about the importance of their service and the good job they were doing.

It was still dark when we took off from Korat at 5:53 a.m., escorted by two fighter jets, one on each wingtip. A team of agents on another aircraft had taken off a few minutes earlier, and would arrive mere minutes ahead of us to secure the landing zone.

IT WAS ABOUT 8:30 as we began our descent to Cam Ranh Bay, and looking out the window, if you didn't know any better, you might think we were headed to a tropical island vacation spot. Beautiful white sand beaches wound like ribbons along a rugged coast dense with palm trees, sandwiched between the land and the brilliant turquoise waters of the China Sea sparkling in the morning sun. But then the giant U.S. military base came into view—a sprawling city of barracks and hangars, buzzing with military vehicles—and the pristine coastline turned into a string of piers crowded with supply ships and destroyers. One hundred ninety miles northeast of Saigon, Cam Ranh Bay was the largest base the United States had ever built from the ground up in any foreign country, its pair of two-mile-long runways the largest in the world.

We touched down gently, and as soon as Air Force One came to a stop a portable stairway was rushed to the door at the front of the plane. White House photographer Yoichi Okamoto was first out the door, racing down the steps to get in position to begin shooting. I stood immediately behind President Johnson, and as he descended I stayed inches behind him, quickly taking note of the situation on the ground and where our agents were positioned.

Waiting at the bottom of the ramp to greet the president were Nguyen Cao Ky, now South Vietnam's vice president; U.S. ambassador Ellsworth Bunker; and General William Westmoreland, and as they all smiled and shook hands the advance agent pulled me aside.

"See that aircraft sitting at the end of the runway over there?" he said, pointing into the distance. "In the event of incoming missiles, you get yourself, the president, and Westmoreland on board. The pilot has instructions to take off immediately and get you the hell out of here. They've got their engines running, ready to go."

I gave a slight nod in acknowledgment, my jaw clenching at the unfathomable but all too real possibility.

I moved out of the way just long enough for a few photographs to be snapped and then urged the president to get into the backseat of the Air Force sedan that was prepositioned nearby, while I took my place in the right front passenger seat.

After a brief meeting with the senior unit commanders, we took the president to a hospital, where he walked down the rows of identical beds filled with injured young men. General Westmoreland walked alongside him, telling stories of the bravery of the men as President Johnson pinned

Purple Hearts onto the chests of their hospital pajamas, looked into their eyes, and told them how proud he and the rest of America were of the job they were doing to defeat the North Vietnamese.

We drove to another part of the base, where 2,500 servicemen were assembled along the runway and a makeshift stage had been erected. President Johnson and General Westmoreland led a group of dignitaries up to the stage as "Hail to the Chief" blared over the loudspeaker and 2,500 hands went to foreheads in a unanimous salute to their commander in chief. Standing next to General Westmoreland, President Johnson brought his hand to his heart as an honor guard presented the colors. The president was dressed in his khaki ranch clothes with a short-sleeved camp-style shirt—he'd removed the zippered jacked in the sweltering heat of the hospital and handed it to me to carry—and was hatless, so that when the hot tropical breeze kicked up, the long strands of hair lying across the top of his head blew straight up in a rather un-presidential look that many newspapers would run on their front pages the following day.

After a brief introduction, President Johnson and General Westmoreland stepped down from the stage and climbed into the back of an open-top Army jeep that was waiting nearby. Standing up out of where the roof would be, they each grabbed the roll bar, and just as the jeep started to pull away I stepped onto the rear platform directly behind them. *In the event of incoming missiles* . . .

It looked like a sea of camouflage-green helmets as we passed by in our one-vehicle parade, the president solemnly acknowledging the saluting men he referred to as "my boys" while I stared straight ahead, my ears on high alert for any sudden, unusual sound.

After reviewing the troops, President Johnson returned to the stage, holding his hand to his heart as the national anthems of both the United States and South Vietnam were played, and then proceeded to take the opportunity to present a number of medals and awards to enlisted men and officers. Finally, he approached the microphone to express his appreciation to everyone at Cam Ranh Bay.

"The enemy cannot win now in Vietnam," he said with unabashed confidence. "I bring you the assurance of what you have fought to achieve." The Communist enemy, he said, "can harass, he can terrorize, he can inflict casualties while taking far greater losses himself. But he cannot win. You—each of you—has seen to that."

After wishing all the men a merry Christmas, the president whispered something to General Westmoreland. I had an uneasy feeling as the general stepped up to the microphone.

"The president would like you to approach the stage," Westmoreland said.

Oh God.

"Men, fall out!"

They were hesitant at first, but then President Johnson threw his hands up in the air, beckoning them to come forward. He marched down the steps as the men ran toward him, clamoring for prime position to get a handshake from the President of the United States. I stayed as close as possible to him, constantly scanning the crowd of servicemen and the skies above as the president shook hand after hand.

"Where ya from, son?" he asked, over and over.

"Racine, Wisconsin!" "Mobile, Alabama, sir!" "Trenton, New Jersey!"

As they called out their beloved hometowns and states, a look of jubilance spread across their faces. You could just see the letters they'd be writing home that night, telling their loved ones how the President of the United States shook their hand and when he asked "Where ya from?" they'd been so proud to tell him. It broke my heart to see these young men, so far from their families, knowing I'd be back home by Christmas, while a good percentage of them would return mangled by war, or worse still, in a flag-draped casket.

Finally, after nearly two hours on the ground, we returned to Air Force One without incident. It was a relief to be airborne once again, but I knew still more challenges lay ahead. Up next, the unknown in Karachi.

An Air Force C-141 transport cargo plane carrying advance agents had taken off shortly before Air Force One and would arrive ahead of us to secure the airport. There wouldn't be much time in between, and all I could do was trust that the agents could get everything in place before we touched down.

We landed in Karachi at two o'clock, and after confirming with the agents on the ground, I followed President Johnson out of the plane and into a nearby building at the airport where President Ayub Khan was waiting. They greeted each other with a warm hug and then sat talking like two old friends. I remained close, and at one point President Johnson summoned me, requesting some refreshments.

I contacted the Air Force stewards, who promptly brought a variety of beverages and snacks from Air Force One. The meeting lasted over an hour as the plane got refueled, and then we were airborne again, headed for Rome.

Top Secret messages had been flying back and forth between the White House Situation Room and embassies all over Europe, trying to arrange the logistics for President Johnson's last-minute request for a meeting with Italy's president, Giuseppe Saragat, and an audience with the pope. You don't just pop in on the pope. But that's exactly what President Johnson wanted to do.

Meanwhile, the dozens of members of the press traveling on the press plane were almost at their wits' end. Word had gotten back to the president that they felt like they were being held captive. Like the rest of us, they hadn't slept or showered, and they felt like they were prisoners on an aircraft with no idea where they were going or when they would return home. They weren't buying the line that all the details were being ironed out as we went along, but that was God's honest truth. The only person who really knew what was happening was the president himself, and he was keeping everything close to the vest. The president had no pity on the press pool.

"Here I am desperately seeking peace, and they're bitching about their comfort," he fumed.

There were security concerns about landing at Rome's Fiumicino Airport due to a large, active anti-American community in the area that would love nothing better than to embarrass President Johnson, and while the smaller Ciampino Airport was less accessible and much easier to control, there we faced a lack of equipment and ground personnel, and a runway barely capable of handling Air Force One. Of the two options, Ciampino won.

The next problem was the transportation from the airport to visit President Saragat, who happened to be staying at one of his official residences, Castel Porziano, some fifteen miles outside central Rome. With more advance notice about the president's plans than the rest of us, Colonel Jim Cross had had the foresight to have two Huey helicopters transported to Spain in an Air Force transport plane so they'd be nearby if the visit to the pope and Saragat became a reality. As soon as the visit was a go, the helicopters were sent to Rome, but once they arrived, they had to be reassembled. Because everything was so last-minute, the helicopters weren't ready when we arrived at Ciampino at 8:30 in the evening local time.

The schedule was already tight—with just fifteen minutes allowed for the Saragat visit—and now, here we were on the ground with no way to get the president safely to the Italian president's residence. The U.S. Navy had some helicopters in the area, but they were much smaller, older, and far less comfortable than the Hueys. We had no choice. We needed them to make the airlift from Ciampino. Space was extremely limited, so it was decided that Rufus Youngblood would go with President Johnson in my place. I watched as the old Navy helicopters slowly lifted off from Ciampino for Porziana. Radio communications were limited, and I waited and listened intently for word indicating a successful arrival. Finally, it came through. By this time, the Army unit reported they had their helicopters ready to go, so we sent them to Porziana and used them to take the president from there to the Vatican.

The landing at the Vatican was just as tense, however, because of the lack of space for such an operation, the fact that the pilots had never landed there before, and that it was to be done in secret, at night. In fact, it was the first time anyone had ever paid a visit to the pope via helicopter. It was a tribute to pilots Peter Rice and Bill Carlson's expertise that everything went smoothly, and on schedule.

After spending almost two hours at the Vatican, the presidential party was back at Ciampino, and at 11:05 p.m. we were finally headed back to the United States, with just one stop left for refueling at Lajes Air Force Base in the Azores, Portugal.

President Johnson was in a great mood, feeling extremely pleased with the way the trip had turned out. He wandered through the plane talking about what he felt was a productive and worthwhile meeting with Pope Paul VI. Apparently there was a gift exchange during the meeting as well— the pope gave President Johnson a fifteenth-century painting, while the president's offering was an eight-inch bronze bust of himself.

Everyone was relieved when President Johnson finally retired to his cabin, and all of us could try to get some sleep.

Meanwhile, Colonel Cross had contacted the commanding officer at Lajes and requested he keep the Base Post Exchange (PX) open so the personnel traveling on Air Force One could buy some Christmas gifts, since it was now Christmas Eve, and because of this whirlwind trip no one had had any time to shop. Unfortunately, the members of the press were taking a different route through Shannon, Ireland, so they would end up arriving home on Christmas Eve not only exhausted, irritated, and in desperate need of a shower but also empty-handed.

It was 1:35 in the morning local time when we landed, but the Air Force One passengers were ready to shop, and off they went to the PX. The president was still sound asleep in his cabin, so I told the other agents to go ahead and join everyone else while I remained with the aircraft.

I was standing at the foot of the ramp of Air Force One when all of a sudden President Johnson appeared in the doorway in his pajamas.

"Clint!" he called out. "Where the hell is everybody?"

"They've all gone to the PX to do some Christmas shopping while we refuel," I explained. "It's Christmas Eve, Mr. President."

"Well, I need to do some shopping too," he said. "Let's go!"

He reached into the coat closet near the door and pulled out a trench coat, put it on over his pajamas, and trotted down the stairs. I grabbed an Air Force car and driver, and off to the base exchange we went.

As we walked through the store, the president greeted everyone with a big smile and a "Merry Christmas!" while peering into their shopping carts to inspect their purchases. He went straight for the baby department, picking out a few toys and clothes for his grandson, and then some bracelets and other items for Mrs. Johnson and his daughters. You'd think Santa Claus himself had just walked in from all the double takes we got. The press would have loved it and fought over the photos. For me, the image in my mind still makes me chuckle. Only Lyndon Johnson. And that's how I happened to go shopping in the Azores in the middle of the night on Christmas Eve with the President of the United States in his pajamas.

• • •

AT 4:30 A.M. on December 24, 1967, we landed at Andrews Air Force Base. We had been gone for one hundred twelve hours and twenty minutes—over four and a half days; flown 28,210 miles; and spent nearly sixty hours of that time in the air. I flew back on Marine One with the president to the White House, and let me tell you, that was a wonderful sight to see. I was exhausted, enormously relieved to be delivering the president back home safely after such a chaotic and harried adventure, and eager to crawl into my own bed. But it was Christmas Eve, and the president wanted to go to Mass with his daughter Luci and her husband, Patrick. So I accompanied President Johnson to the seven o'clock Mass at St. Dominic's Catholic Church in southwest Washington; we got back to the White House at 7:35, and then, finally, I was able to go home.

It was the first time in eight years that I'd been home for Christmas with my family. My son Chris was now eleven years old, and Corey was six, and as we opened presents on Christmas morning, I realized the last Christmas I'd been home was 1959, when Chris was just three years old, before Corey was born—and it was impossible for them to understand why all I wanted to do was sleep.

As 1967 came to an end, no one could have imagined what the next year would bring and how our country would be brought to its knees over and over again, and there I was, once again, smack-dab in the middle of some of our nation's most traumatic moments.

27

1968

The crises began almost as soon as the calendar turned.

"I report to you that our country is challenged at home and abroad," President Johnson said in his opening State of the Union remarks to Congress on January 17, 1968. There was still no end in sight to the war in Vietnam, and in this election year he knew there was much he had to prove. Despite the fact that Americans were more prosperous than ever before, with higher paychecks and more families owning their own homes, "there is in the land," he noted, "a certain restlessness, a questioning."

Four days later, the North Vietnamese Army launched a withering rocket and mortar attack on Khe Sanh, a strategic Marine outpost just fourteen miles south of the Demilitarized Zone between North and South Vietnam, and three days after that, one of our critical intelligence-gathering ships, the USS *Pueblo*, was seized by the North Koreans—the first time in more than one hundred years that an American naval vessel had been captured at sea. Then, in the predawn hours of January 31, during what was supposed to have been a multiday cease-fire in honor of Tet—the most important Vietnamese holiday, marking the Lunar New Year—the North Vietnamese conducted a coordinated surprise attack against military and civilian command and control centers in cities throughout South Vietnam, including a bold and blistering raid on the U.S. Embassy in Saigon. The numbers were staggering: over two hundred Americans dead, and nearly a thousand wounded, with more than two thousand civilian men, women, and children killed in Saigon alone. Yet General Westmoreland's optimistic report back to Washington was that the Tet Offensive had been an "all-or-nothing, go-for-broke" proposition, in which the North Vietnamese had failed to take and hold any major installations and had suffered far greater losses than the allies.

Despite the sheer numbers of people killed, what had a far bigger impact on the public were the photographs and film footage by American journalists that made their way onto the front pages of newspapers and the television screens in every American living room. One photo, taken by Associated Press photographer Eddie Adams, showed the horrific image of a young North Vietnamese man, terror written all over his face, his hands tied behind his back, as South Vietnam's national police chief fired a bullet, point-blank, into his head on a Saigon street, while children stood nearby.

By the beginning of 1968, more than 11,000 Americans had been killed in Vietnam. United States troop strength had been building gradually since 1960, and although we now had nearly 500,000 members of the U.S. military in Vietnam, with the latest increase in attacks, General Westmoreland had requested reinforcements of 10,500 more men.

Ever since we returned from the around-the-world trip after Prime Minister Holt's funeral, I had noticed that President Johnson was looking more and more haggard. Large bags under his eyes were becoming more pronounced, and although he was still packing far more into any given day than most, the strain of the job was becoming physically evident.

When I made mention of this to a member of the staff and to the White House physician, they both told me that the president was barely sleeping. He was phoning the Situation Room at all hours of the night to determine the situation in Vietnam and the status of the seized ship, the USS *Pueblo*, and its crew. Every call to the Situation Room was logged, and sure enough, when I checked the logbook, nearly every night, calls from the president's bedroom came in just before he retired, usually around midnight or one o'clock, and then there'd be another call at two, three, or four. The international crises were consuming him.

On Saturday, February 17, when I reported to the White House, I was informed that the president intended to make a surprise visit to some of the troops headed into combat. That afternoon, we flew to Fort Bragg, North

Carolina, to Pope Army Airfield, where a brigade of paratroopers from the 82nd Airborne Division was getting ready to board a C-141 transport jet. I stood on one side of the doorway of the aircraft as President Johnson, on the other side, shook hands with each soldier as they boarded the plane. Equipped for combat, they carried field packs, canteens, sheath knives, and M-16 automatic rifles. It had to be frightening for these young men—many of them barely out of high school—to be sent off to a combat zone on the opposite side of the world, and for the president, I could see it was ripping him apart.

When all the men were on board, an officer gave the pilot the command to start the engines.

"Wait a minute," President Johnson said. And then he turned to walk up the steps into the aircraft. *Uh oh,* I thought. *What does he have in mind?*

I followed him as he walked down the center aisle between the rows of helmeted troops, each lost in their own thoughts. President Johnson interrupted the silence.

"I hate to ask you men to go," he said. "I wish I did not have to send you into battle in a far-off country." His brow furrowed, and I knew he was speaking sincerely from the heart.

"Do your duty, as I know you will. I pray all of you will be back."

When he said that, my own emotions almost got the best of me. For I knew, as he did, that within hours of being on the ground in Vietnam, a significant number of these young men would suffer life-altering injuries or be killed in action.

After stopping at a nearby hospital to visit a group of wounded soldiers, we got back on Air Force One for a five-hour-and-twenty-minute flight to El Toro Marine Air Station in Southern California. It was 8:41 in the evening when we touched down, and after a brief speech to the troops and civilian personnel who had gathered to greet him, President Johnson repeated the scene from earlier in the day, this time shaking the hands of the U.S. Marines boarding military transport planes headed straight to Vietnam. After watching the planes take off, we boarded helicopters and flew to the USS *Constellation*, an aircraft carrier stationed off the coast of California, where we would spend the night. The president held a press briefing aboard the aircraft carrier shortly before ten o'clock, and by the time he retired to his suite, it was well after eleven—2:00 a.m. by our East Coast body clocks. It was no wonder he looked fatigued.

The following morning President Johnson was up early, and made the request to have breakfast with a representative group of sailors on the ship. He asked each of them to stand up and give their name, rank, and hometown, and then started asking questions. "How is the morale on the ship?" he asked. "Is it higher at some times than others?"

The boys were hesitant at first, but then one piped up and said, "Yes, sir. It depends on the amount of mail we get from home, and what we read in the newspapers."

"What do you mean, what you read in the newspapers?" President Johnson asked.

The young man said, "We read about the hippies and the flower children and all these people who are against the war. I don't understand why we have to go to war and these peaceniks get away from the draft by rebelling and having demonstrations. It doesn't seem right."

The president nodded in understanding. "Son, there are dissenters in every war. But I am so proud of you boys, and the entire nation is proud of you. Nobody wants to go to war, and nobody wants to die. But people must, and I'm proud of the way you boys have met your responsibility. You are fighting for the right to allow people to dissent."

He paused, and then looked around the table, taking a moment to look into each man's eyes. "If you make it—and that's what we want and pray for every day," he said, "and if you don't, then the good Lord knows that you went down swinging and fighting hard for your country. It's boys like you that makes America a free country."

In the newspapers the next day, President Johnson's visits to the troops made the front page, but the brief articles were overshadowed by the headlines: "U.S. Air Base Under Heavy Rocket Fire; Reds Shell 30 Cities in New Viet Offensive."

FEBRUARY 29, 1968, marked the last day of Robert McNamara's tenure as secretary of defense. Having been appointed in 1961 by President Kennedy,

McNamara had served seven years in the post, longer than any other defense secretary, and as he departed the office—to be replaced by Clark Clifford—President Johnson was to present him with the Distinguished Service Medal in a noontime ceremony at the Pentagon.

February had been unseasonably dry, but that morning the rain started early, and was pummeling down as we departed the White House in a small motorcade and drove directly into the Pentagon garage. Secretary McNamara was there to greet the president, and he led us to a bank of elevators.

Several members of the president's staff had come along, so we all piled into one large elevator—thirteen of us, in elevator number 13—including one other agent and myself. An Army master sergeant assigned to operate the elevator pushed the button to take us to the appropriate floor, the doors closed, and the elevator began to ascend. The president was bantering with Secretary McNamara when all of a sudden the elevator stopped, but the doors didn't open as they automatically would when we reached the intended floor.

Looking perplexed, the sergeant pushed a couple of buttons, but the doors remained closed, and the elevator wasn't budging. Secretary McNamara took over, pushing button after button on the control panel, but still, nothing. We were stuck.

The sergeant got on the emergency phone and notified the operator of our problem, but there wasn't much room to move, and with so many people in there it was quickly becoming hot and stuffy. We hadn't built any extra time into the schedule, and as I looked at my watch I realized we were already late for the beginning of the ceremony.

Drops of perspiration were forming on President Johnson's forehead, and he was clearly becoming irritated.

"What's wrong with this thing?" he said with a scowl.

"Don't ask me," McNamara quipped. "I don't work here anymore."

The president was not amused, and as the air got stuffier, I too was becoming concerned. We attempted to pry the doors open from the inside, and got maybe an inch or so. One of the president's assistants, Harry McPherson, was quite tall, and he managed to move a ceiling plate a few inches to create a small opening, but then the electricity cut off. Now we were in the dark.

The elevator had a capacity of fifteen, and we had just thirteen people, so weight should not have been a problem, but as the minutes ticked by, the situation was getting more and more tense, and I knew President Johnson's patience was nearing its breaking point.

"Let me have your radio," I said to the advance agent who was in the elevator with us. Other than the telephone inside the elevator, it was our only means of communication. I notified the agents posted outside the elevator of our predicament and requested they go to each floor and pry open the doors to try to locate us. It wasn't long before they found us between floors. The distance from the elevator to the next floor of the building, however, was too high for anyone to climb, so a chair had to be lowered into the elevator. President Johnson stepped onto the seat of the chair, and with two people up above grabbing his arms and two in the elevator lifting from below, we finally got him out, and the rest of us followed. Needless to say, he was not in the best of moods as we walked to the ceremony site—fifteen minutes late—and the situation just seemed to go from bad to worse.

The Air Force flyby had been canceled because of the weather. As President Johnson stepped up to the podium, a staff member juggled an umbrella over his head trying to keep him dry, but as the president began to speak, the sound system malfunctioned, making his voice inaudible to the two thousand attendees standing miserably in the rain. Everyone, including me, was soaked and chilled to the bone. It was a complete and utter disaster, and while I'm sure President Johnson found someone to blame, luckily this time it wasn't me.

Problems seemed to be mounting for President Johnson on all fronts. The war in Vietnam was going badly, there had been no resolution to the *Pueblo* seizure, a copper strike was looming, and the New Hampshire presidential primary was coming up on March 12. As sitting president, it was assumed Johnson would have no difficulty winning the Democratic primary, but with criticism of the war mounting and President Johnson's popularity declining with each news broadcast, others in the Democratic Party saw a potential opening. Senator Eugene McCarthy, a Democrat from Minnesota, decided to challenge President Johnson in the primaries with a fervent antiwar campaign.

Johnson prevailed in the New Hampshire primary, but his percentage margin of victory was in the single digits. He appeared vulnerable. The president, his family, friends, and staff, were all very upset. Four days later, Senator Robert Kennedy announced his candidacy for president—something he had repeatedly said he would not do—stating, "I am convinced that this country is on a perilous course."

On that same day, March 16, 1968, U.S. soldiers claimed a big victory after an assault on the Vietcong in the seaside village of My Lai. In reality, the soldiers had killed an entire village of men, women, and children in what later became known as the My Lai Massacre. The horrific details of the incident did not become public knowledge, however, for over a year.

On March 31, President Johnson scheduled a nationally televised address to the American people to announce an immediate de-escalation of attacks on North Vietnam as the first step in moving "toward peace through negotiations."

He had been working on the speech with his staff for days, and a final version had been distributed to the press shortly before he appeared on the air. I had gone home, and when the broadcast started I was sitting alone in my basement, where I had a small black-and-white television next to my desk. I was listening but not really watching the television screen as the president came to the end of his remarks. There was a pause, and then I heard President Johnson utter some words I never thought I would hear him say.

"I shall not seek, and I will not accept, the nomination of my party for another term as your president."

I was absolutely stunned. Did I hear him correctly? There had not been any indication I was aware of that he was going to do this. No indication whatsoever. The newscasters, all of them as shocked as I was, confirmed it: Johnson had taken himself out of the 1968 presidential election. Then, I thought, *Is this just a ploy on his part to gain sympathy and gather momentum for a presidential draft?* Was it being done simply to encourage the North Vietnamese to come to the bargaining table? How would this affect his activity and exposure over the next few months? How would it affect our security for the president? These and a million other questions ran through my mind. I didn't have time to dwell on it because we were flying to Chicago early the next morning, where President Johnson was scheduled to speak to the National Association of Broadcasters.

The entire nation was shocked by President Johnson's announcement, and that was all anyone was talking about. When I saw LBJ the next morning, however, he did not bring up the subject, and neither did I. It wasn't my job to advise or offer my opinion on his political decisions—my only focus, as it always had been, was ensuring his personal safety.

In his speech to the National Association of Broadcasters, President Johnson made some points that I thought were very significant, and still do.

"Men and women of the airways fully—as much as men and women of public service—have a public trust, and if liberty is to survive and to succeed, that solemn trust must be faithfully kept. I do not want—and I don't think you want—to wake up some morning and find America changed because we slept when we should have been awake, because we remained silent when we should have spoken up, because we went along with what was popular and fashionable and 'in' rather than what was necessary and what was right.

"Certainly, it is more dramatic to show policemen and rioters locked in combat than to show men trying to cooperate with one another. The face of hatred and of bigotry comes through much more clearly—no matter what its color. The face of tolerance, I seem to find, is rarely newsworthy."

Indeed, President Johnson's remarks are perhaps even more relevant in 2016 than they were in 1968, in this era of twenty-four-hour news cycles in which the news media's repetitive broadcasting of "dramatic" incidents often provokes and incites violence. And yet at that time, President Johnson could have had no idea what was about to unfold.

SENATOR ROBERT F. Kennedy had sent a wire requesting a meeting with President Johnson, and the meeting was set for ten o'clock Wednesday morning, April 3, at the White House. This would be the first meeting between the two since Robert Kennedy announced his candidacy, and Kennedy had asked to bring his brother's former speechwriter, Ted Sorensen, along. They wanted to keep the meeting quiet—no press—so to facilitate their movements within the White House complex, I arranged for them to park on the South Grounds, and then I met them at the South Portico.

"Hello, Clint," Robert Kennedy said solemnly when he saw me.

"Good morning, Senator," I said. "I'll escort you to the Cabinet Room. The president is expecting you."

The meeting lasted about an hour and a half, and while I didn't know what was said, when they came out of the Cabinet Room, none of them appeared happy.

Kennedy and Sorensen were silent as I escorted them out through the Rose Garden to the area near the South Portico. When we arrived at their car, Senator Kennedy simply said, "Thanks, Clint."

"My pleasure, Senator," I replied. And with that, they exited the White House grounds.

Now that President Johnson had taken himself out of contention for the presidency, I realized that Robert F. Kennedy had a very good chance of becoming the next President of the United States. The first thought that entered my mind was—*all those kids!* Bobby and his wife, Ethel, had ten children, and we'd be responsible for protecting all of them. The election was still a long way off, though, and I'd seen enough politics to know anything could happen.

My immediate concern was preparing for a busy travel schedule beginning the next day with a trip to New York City for the ordination of Terence Cooke as archbishop of New York, followed by a Democratic congressional fund-raising dinner back in Washington that evening, an overnight flight to March Air Force Base, in California, so President Johnson could confer with General Eisenhower, and then on to Hawaii for meetings about Vietnam and the still unresolved USS *Pueblo* situation. There were still a great many details to iron out.

Thursday, April 4, began quietly, with the president making phone calls from his bedroom all morning, which gave me time to work on the logistics for the complex travel schedule ahead. When we departed for New York City at noon, I at least felt like I had a handle on the itinerary.

Everything went smoothly at the ordination at St. Patrick's Cathedral, and at 3:20 we were in the helicopter at Sheep Meadow in Central Park, ready to take off for Kennedy International Airport, where Air Force One was standing by to take us back to Washington, when the president decided that since he was in New York, he might like to have a meeting with Ambassador Arthur Goldberg at the United Nations. All plans were tossed out the window as we hastily arranged security for the spur-of-the-moment U.N. visit, which required an impromptu motorcade through the streets of one of the busiest cities in the world. It was 6:30 p.m. by the time we finally got back to the White House.

I was standing by in W-16, the Secret Service ready room on the ground floor directly below the Oval Office, waiting for President Johnson to give word that he was ready to leave for the fund-raising dinner, when a call came in from the Intelligence Office. One floor above, all hell was breaking loose. The press office had direct wire tickers from the Associated Press (AP) and United Press International (UPI) that ran twenty-four hours a day, and at 7:24 p.m., Tom Johnson, a young White House press aide who would go on to run the *Los Angeles Times* and CNN, happened to be standing near the tickers when the bells started ringing like crazy. It wasn't unusual for bells to sound when there was a bulletin, but this type of nonstop ringing was reserved for news of the highest urgency—a FLASH. Tom Johnson read the FLASH, ripped the copy from the ticker, and raced down the hall to the small office where the president's secretaries, Juanita Roberts and Marie Fehmer, the official gatekeepers to the Oval Office, were still typing memos and correspondence.

"I have an urgent message for the president," he said. The look on Tom's face must have conveyed the seriousness of the situation, because, in a very unusual move, Marie waved him into the president's office without question.

Johnson burst into the Oval Office, interrupting a meeting between President Johnson, former governor of Georgia Carl Sanders, and Robert Woodruff, the chairman of Coca-Cola. Handing the strip of wire paper to the president, Tom Johnson said, "Mr. President, Dr. King has been shot."

President Johnson read the ticker tape, handed it to the other two men, and immediately got on the phone to FBI director J. Edgar Hoover.

Serious and methodical, President Johnson made one phone call after another, assembling those at the highest level of government in his office, asking questions and making decisions. Someone flipped on the televisions—the bank of TV sets along one wall of the Oval Office LBJ had had installed so he could watch all three networks simultaneously—as staff members scurried in and out, bringing new information and responding to the president's requests.

First it was decided to cancel the president's participation at the dinner, then to postpone the trip to California and Hawaii. At 8:20 p.m. press secretary George Christian got word from Hoover's office that Dr. Martin Luther King Jr. had died.

There was concern that outrage over King's death would trigger violence, and President Johnson realized, as the leader of the country, it was important for him to speak to the nation about the tragedy as soon as possible. People were already beginning to gather outside the Washington offices of King's Southern Christian Leadership Conference on Fourteenth Street, and while they were solemn and peaceful, that could change in an instant.

At nine o'clock, barely half an hour after Reverend King's death, the press set up lights and cameras outside the West Wing, and President Johnson addressed the nation.

"America is shocked and saddened by the brutal slaying tonight of Dr. Martin Luther King," he began. "I ask every citizen to reject the blind violence that has struck Dr. King, who lived by nonviolence. I pray that his family can find comfort in the memory of all he tried to do for the land he loved so well. I have just conveyed the sympathy of Mrs. Johnson and myself to his widow, Mrs. King. I know that every American of goodwill joins me in mourning the death of this outstanding leader and in praying for peace and understanding throughout this land. We can achieve nothing by lawlessness and divisiveness among the American people. It is only by joining together and only by working together that we can continue to move toward equality and fulfillment of all our people. I hope that all Americans tonight will search their hearts as they ponder this most tragic incident."

Meanwhile, the crowd on Fourteenth Street was growing larger, and the rage was intensifying. We started getting reports of storefront windows being broken and looting taking place, and of police on the street being stoned by angry mobs. Officers around the nation's capital were preparing for the worst—donning riot helmets, gas masks, and carrying tear gas canisters and billy clubs.

Shortly before eleven o'clock, two vehicles were torched at a Chevrolet dealership, and then more fires were set off in Columbia Heights, and now throngs of people were moving south on Fourteenth Street toward the White House.

We in the Secret Service were monitoring the situation closely, not only out of concern for President Johnson's safety but also how the spreading violence might affect our other protectees, who were scattered around the country. Plans for Dr. King's funeral in Atlanta were already under way, and a memorial service was scheduled for the following day at Washington National Cathedral. We had grave concerns about President Johnson attending either one, but he was adamant that he needed to be at the memorial service here in Washington.

It was after midnight when I finally went home to get some rest, but many staff members remained in the White House overnight.

When I became SAIC, a dedicated phone line with direct access to the White House had been installed in my home. Sometime around two or three o'clock in the morning the White House phone on the nightstand beside my bed rang, waking me out of a deep sleep. I reached for the receiver, put it to my ear, and groggily answered, "Clint Hill."

"Clint!" It was President Johnson. He had never called me at home before. "You know we're going to the memorial service for Dr. King at the National Cathedral tomorrow."

"Yes, sir."

"Now, listen," he said. "I want to make sure you have the car get me as close to the door as they possibly can. And I want you to be right next to me the whole time."

"Yes, sir. Everything will be taken care of."

"I want you to be as close to me as white on rice!"

"Don't worry, Mr. President," I reiterated. "I will stay as close as possible to you at all times."

"All right, then; see you in the morning," he said as the line went dead.

I tried to get back to sleep, but my mind was restless. It was obvious the president was deeply concerned for his own safety, and frankly, so was I.

WHEN I ARRIVED at the White House at 6:30 a.m., the city of Washington was smoldering from the overnight fires, and there were already signs that more violence and civil unrest were on the way. President Johnson had called for an urgent meeting with congressional leaders as well as black community leaders in the White House immediately before the memorial service, and then shortly before noon we proceeded by motorcade to National Cathedral.

We had secured the three-and-a-half-mile route with the help of D.C. Metropolitan Police, and had agents positioned in and around the church. The most precarious points were the moments moving President Johnson out of, and then back into, the limousine. I rode in the right front seat, and as soon as we pulled up to the front of the cathedral I got out and quickly scanned the surroundings to make sure the other agents were in position. I opened the rear door, and as President Johnson emerged from the backseat I was on high alert, my adrenaline flowing, ready to push him back into the car at the merest sign of anything unusual. We moved quickly into the church, and I remained, as promised, always within arm's reach.

Thousands of mourners packed the gothic basilica where the previous Sunday Rev. Martin Luther King had preached his last sermon, and after the solemn one-hour service it was time to get back into the car. The detail agents moved in a diamond formation as we filed out of the church with several members of the clergy, while I continued to stay directly behind the president until he was safely back in the armored limousine. We got back to the White House without incident, but by this time rioting was spreading throughout Washington, as well as other cities across America.

One of the individuals fanning the flame of violence was Stokely Carmichael, a member of the Student *Nonviolent* Coordinating Committee. At a news conference, his voice was calm and calculated as he warned "white America" what to expect.

"When white America killed Dr. King, she declared war on us," he said. "There will be no crying; there will be no funerals. The rebellions that have been occurring around the cities of this country is just light stuff to what is about to happen."

He promised retaliation and warned that "the execution of those deaths will not be in the courtroom—they are going to be in the streets of the United States of America. There no longer needs to be intellectual discussion." Later, he stood in front of a large crowd and urged every black man to "go home and get your guns."

The response was immediate, and within hours hundreds of stores in downtown Washington had been looted and set on fire. With the situation quickly spiraling out of control, President Johnson federalized the D.C. National Guard, called in additional military units to support the 2,800 officers of the Metropolitan Police Department, and brought troops from the 82nd Airborne Division to Andrews Air Force Base to stand by in case they were needed.

Shortly after one o'clock, the president appeared on live television and radio appealing for peace. From the Fish Room, he once again expressed his shock and sorrow at the loss of Dr. King, and designated Sunday, April 7, as a day of national mourning.

"My heart went out to his people—especially the young Americans who, I know, must wonder if they are to be denied a fullness of life because of the color of their skin." He said he remained convinced that the dream of Martin Luther King had not died with him, and he was consulting with Negro leaders to ensure the dream lived on.

"Men who are white, men who are black," he said, "must and will join together now as never in the past to let all the forces of division know that America shall not be ruled by the bullet but only by the ballot of free and just men."

Washington's mayor declared a thirteen-hour curfew within the District from 5:30 p.m. to 6:30 a.m. as five thousand soldiers poured into the streets with bayonets and battle gear. This sudden and overwhelming show of force prompted stores and offices to close, and by three o'clock in the afternoon there was citywide gridlock as panicked commuters tried to get out of the downtown area. Fires were consuming entire blocks of Fourteenth Street, Seventh Street, and H Street, but as firefighters attempted to douse the flames, they were being pelted by rock-throwing protestors.

In less than twenty-four hours our nation's capital had turned into a war zone, and similar scenes were playing out in Chicago, Boston, Memphis, Nashville, and Detroit. So many military personnel were brought to D.C. that we were housing some of them in the hallways of the Executive Office Building, adjacent to the White House.

As civil rights leaders and emergency management advisors flowed into and out of the West Wing, I remained in the Secret Service command center at the White House to keep abreast of the situation. Washington Field Office agents were spread out across the city, feeding information back to us and the Intelligence Division.

Every hour there was some new, more disturbing development, and as darkness fell, I realized there was no way I could leave the White House. I called Gwen and told her to monitor the news and stay inside with the boys. Hopefully I'd be home by Saturday.

FOR THE NEXT two days, violence raged across America. The air was heavy with smoke, and the smell of tear gas was prevalent as military units patrolled the streets. Fearful storeowners kept shops and restaurants closed; the Cherry Blossom Festival was canceled; and the opening game of major league baseball, which was to have been held in Washington, was postponed. The troop level was over eleven thousand in the District, while six thousand National Guardsmen had been mobilized in Baltimore and another five thousand federal troops sent to Chicago, where nine people had been killed as a result of the rioting. If I wasn't right in the middle of it, I never would have believed this was happening in the United States of America.

The morning of Sunday, April 7, newspaper headlines screamed the dire situation across the country:

NEGRO RIOTERS RAVAGE CITIES

11,600 TROOPS PATROL D.C.

"CRISIS" WRACKS BALTIMORE

With the rioting still not under control, President Johnson had canceled his trip to Hawaii, but the issues in Vietnam couldn't be set aside, so General Westmoreland flew to Washington instead, and spent much of Sunday morning briefing the president. Johnson had not left the White House since attending the memorial service the day after King's assassination—largely on our advice—but having declared this the official day of mourning, he decided he wanted to go to church with his daughter Luci and her husband, Pat Nugent. With very little notice, we quickly scrambled an advance crew of agents to secure St. Dominic's Catholic Church prior to his arrival. Not only was it a day of mourning for King but it was also Palm Sunday, so the church was packed.

We got the president situated in a pew near the front, which is where he always liked to be, but throughout the service I was concerned about people crowding him when it was time to leave. When the last hymn was over, I whispered, "Let's move now, Mr. President."

In a moving show of respect and understanding, the entire congregation remained seated as the president, Luci, and Pat walked down the aisle and out of the church. Nothing was said, but you could feel the empathy from the people as they looked at the president with warm smiles and nods of solemn encouragement.

On the way back to the White House, President Johnson told me he wanted to take advantage of General Westmoreland's helicopter departure that afternoon to view the damage from the riots. He wanted to see for himself exactly which sections of the city were affected, and the extent of the destruction. So after a press conference at the White House, we flew to Andrews Air Force Base, dropped off General Westmoreland and his aides, and then took off for an aerial tour.

As we flew three hundred feet above Washington, in the restricted area known as P-56, I could hardly believe what I was seeing. President Johnson had his face pressed to the window, and as we circled around the city he simply shook his head with despair. It looked like we were flying over a war zone.

Spattered throughout the city, whole blocks had been burned to the ground. Charred remains of stores and offices still smoldered, the smoke wafting from the rubble like a filthy cigarette that had been tossed carelessly on the ground beneath the gleaming white monuments of our nation's capital in indignant disrespect. It was utterly demoralizing. What was happening to our country?

Forty miles northeast, the city of Baltimore was also having serious arson and looting problems. The governor of Maryland, Spiro Agnew, had activated the Maryland National Guard in support of the Baltimore police, but it was not enough to quell the violence, and he requested federal troops.

Meanwhile, Martin Luther King's funeral was scheduled for Tuesday, April 9, in Atlanta. President Johnson wanted to go—he felt he needed to be there. FBI director Hoover urged him not to attend, and when President Johnson sought advice from Rufus Youngblood, Lem Johns, and me, we all told him the same thing. The situation was too volatile, emotions were still raw, and the crowd mentality that was sweeping through the black community made for extremely unpredictable circumstances. Finally, realizing that the country could not withstand an attempted assassination of the president at this time, Johnson heeded our advice.

"All right, fine," he conceded. "Humphrey can go."

Vice President Humphrey was now running for president. We in the Secret Service didn't like this idea either, but the agents on the VP Detail flew into action, and, working with local law enforcement and the FBI, managed to get Humphrey in and out with no incidents.

With the intervention of military troops, order was finally restored, but the devastation was extensive. In Washington, D.C., alone, more than 1,200 buildings had been destroyed. Hundreds of businesses had no choice but to close, resulting in the loss of thousands of jobs—all in mainly black areas. For President Johnson, after his relentless support of Martin Luther King and the passage of the Civil Rights Act and the Voting Rights Act, seeing the black community torching their own livelihoods and sending portions of cities into economic devastation from which they would not recover for decades was almost more than he could fathom.

He responded by working harder than ever. The trip to Hawaii was rescheduled for the following week—a whirlwind trip that included talks with President Park Chung-hee of South Korea over the still unresolved *Pueblo* situation, a meeting with former president General Eisenhower, and then a few days at the LBJ Ranch to recuperate. The weeks and days ahead were filled with nonstop activity: Democratic Party fund-raisers; dropping by a party honoring the speaker of the House of Representatives for ten minutes; on to a party given by a leading congressman and his wife and staying for thirty minutes; returning to the White House for dinner with Mrs. Johnson, often not until 9:30 p.m. or later, taking and making phone calls all the while. The middle-of-the-night phone calls from the president to the Situation Room continued as well, so that the president was often getting just two or three hours of sleep a night. It was not a sustainable regimen, and those closest to the president were deeply concerned about his health and well-being.

OCCASIONALLY PRESIDENT AND Mrs. Johnson entertained on the *Sequoia*, the presidential yacht on which Mrs. Kennedy had thrown the raucous party on President Kennedy's forty-sixth birthday. One Sunday afternoon at the end of May, it was a beautiful, warm spring day in Washington, and the president decided it would be a nice evening for a dinner cruise. He made a bunch of calls, rounding up fourteen guests to join him and Mrs. Johnson on the *Sequoia*. With very little notice, the White House kitchen had to prepare a full dinner for sixteen and transport it to the yacht.

We arrived at the pier at around five o'clock, and once everyone was aboard, we set off for a leisurely cruise down the Potomac. I was standing on the outer deck as cocktails and appetizers were being served when I overheard one of the president's aides tell him that Prime Minister John Gorton of Australia had arrived, as expected, at Andrews Air Force Base, and he and his party were being transported to Blair House.

"Well, let's invite them to join us," the president said. "The more the merrier."

Are you kidding me?

Of course the prime minister accepted the invitation, along with the rest of his party, and suddenly the leisurely cruise turned into an all-hands-on-deck operation as I scrambled to make arrangements for the Australians to board the yacht mid-cruise, while the kitchen staff was left to deal with the problem of ten additional people for dinner.

Using the yacht's radio—this was long before cell phones—we arranged to have the Australians board a presidential helicopter on the Ellipse and be flown to the Hunting Towers apartment complex near the Potomac River in Alexandria, Virginia. This little jaunt required the Ellipse to be secured for the helicopter to land, and the fire department to be there in the event of fire; vehicles had to be arranged to bring the party from the landing point to a nearby marina; and then one of the Secret Service boats would bring them to the *Sequoia*.

At 7:45 p.m., the ten Australians boarded the *Sequoia*, dinner was served at 8:10, and by 9:45 we were back at Pier 1 where we had started. I have no idea how the Navy stewards managed to serve twenty-six people for dinner when they had prepared for sixteen, but somehow they made it look effortless, and everyone had a wonderful time.

President Johnson had invited Prime Minister Gorton to visit the LBJ Ranch, so several days later we were back in Texas. At some time in late 1967 or early 1968, a couple named Ernest and Teet Hobbs had opened a motel on the outskirts of Johnson City, and what a difference that made for the agents. The entire motel consisted of ten basic rooms adjacent to the Hobbses' living quarters, which meant most of the agents had to sleep two to a room, but the best part about the Hobbs Motel was that it didn't require an hour-and-a-half commute back to Austin at the end of an exhausting day's work.

President and Mrs. Johnson stayed at the ranch for the next several days, with houseguests coming and going, touring the ranches, and looking for deer. When storms broke out one day, the president turned to me and asked, "Is it sunny over at the lake?"

I checked, and the weather was indeed clear and sunny, so we left immediately by helicopter for the lake. There was no such thing as sitting still or remaining inactive for President Johnson.

On June 3, after a long day of visiting the neighboring ranches, we departed Texas at 9:40 in the evening and headed back to Washington, arriving at Andrews Air Force Base shortly after one o'clock in the morning. It was nearly two by the time I got home to bed—just enough time for about four hours of sleep. As it turned out, that would be the most sleep I'd get for several more days to come. Tragedy was about to strike again.

TUESDAY, JUNE 4, was a typically long and busy day that began with an 8:20 a.m. departure from the White House to Glassboro, New Jersey, where President Johnson made a commencement address. The enthusiasm of the crowd and his reaction to it made it feel like a campaign rally, despite the fact that he was not running for office. When we returned to the White House at around eleven, the South Grounds were prepared for a noontime military arrival ceremony for the president of Costa Rica, so the helicopter landed on the Ellipse.

A large crowd had gathered outside the White House fence to watch the arrival ceremony, and when the presidential helicopter landed right in front of them, the people started cheering and clapping. We had cars positioned to take the president immediately to the South Grounds, but when President Johnson stepped out of the chopper and heard the people cheering and calling his name, it was like the force of a magnet pulling him toward the adoration, and instead of getting into the waiting limousine, he walked straight into the crowd.

He was smiling as big as could be, shaking hands, and waving—acting very much like a presidential candidate. As the other agents and I formed a protective envelope and gradually got him through the Southwest Gate onto the White House grounds, I couldn't help but wonder if he was having second thoughts about running. If there was one thing I had learned about Lyndon Baines Johnson, it was that anything was possible.

It was almost the end of the presidential primaries for 1968, and it so happened that voting was taking place that day in South Dakota, New Jersey, and California. Up until a few weeks earlier, most predictions had Kennedy winning all the primaries and thereby sewing up the Democratic nomination. But Senator Eugene McCarthy had taken Oregon and Vice President Humphrey had won Pennsylvania, and it appeared that Kennedy's campaign might be in trouble unless he was able to win California.

When I went home that night after the state dinner, I turned on the television to get some election results. It appeared that Robert Kennedy was winning, and I retired for the night.

At 3:50 a.m. I was wakened by the ringing of the White House phone next to my bed.

"Clint Hill," I answered.

The Secret Service agent on duty was on the other end of the line.

"Mr. Hill," he said. "Senator Kennedy has just been shot in Los Angeles."

Oh my God. I hung up the phone, jumped out of bed, and went down to my basement to turn on the TV. All three networks were broadcasting— something that, at that time, was highly unusual at this hour of the morning—

and details about the shooting were still coming in. I was so stunned, I could hardly believe what was being said. Bobby Kennedy shot.

He had just finished making a victory speech in the ballroom of the Ambassador Hotel to an enthusiastic crowd of supporters and was exiting through the kitchen, thanking the kitchen staff, when a man approached and fired a gun at point-blank range. Bobby's wife, Ethel, pregnant with their eleventh child, was by his side as he lay bleeding on the floor, while pandemonium broke amid calls for medical assistance.

My mind swirled with the memories of that dreadful day in Dallas, four and a half years earlier: bracing myself on the back of the car; President Kennedy's bleeding head in his wife's lap, his eyes fixed. At that time I knew almost immediately there was no hope for him, and now, I prayed that Bobby Kennedy's wounds would not be fatal. I knew the horror Ethel was experiencing, and how this would bring the memories right back for Jacqueline Kennedy. It was almost beyond belief that this had happened again to the same family. It felt like our country was unraveling at the seams.

I knew Senator Kennedy had a former FBI agent working with him handling security, but it was a pretty loose operation. One man, no matter how good he is, without additional help, cannot really be effective. At that time the Secret Service did not protect presidential candidates, but I was certain that was about to change. The thought of such a massive operation, to be undertaken instantly, without adequate preparation, gave me a cold sweat. There was no going back to sleep, so I shaved, showered, made myself a little breakfast, and headed for the White House.

As I walked down the West Drive toward the entrance to the West Wing, I had a million thoughts running through my head. Personally, I was shocked and saddened for the Kennedy family. From a professional standpoint, I realized the security ballgame had changed, and the Secret Service would be at the forefront of that change.

By the time I arrived at my office, President Johnson already had the wheels in motion. He had telephoned Director Rowley as soon as he'd learned of the shooting and requested Secret Service personnel be assigned to all the candidates immediately. Within hours, Rufus Youngblood was in the president's office briefing him on all the assignments. Hubert Humphrey currently had Secret Service protection as vice president, and agents had already been dispatched to protect the other candidates—Nelson Rockefeller, Harold Stassen, Richard Nixon, Eugene McCarthy, and George Wallace. A short time later Ronald Reagan was added to the list. Youngblood made sure I was kept in the loop on all the activity, because this sudden increase in the number of protectees resulted in a manpower drain on the entire organization—manpower that we relied on whenever we took the president on any movement outside the White House perimeter.

At the same time, we were trying to get as much information as possible on the shooter, a twenty-four-year-old recent immigrant from Jordan named Sirhan Bishara Sirhan, who had been wrestled to the ground by witnesses and was now in police custody.

Was he in our files? The answer came back no. Like Lee Harvey Oswald, Sirhan Sirhan seemed to have emerged out of nowhere, and now the life of yet another national figure—another Kennedy—hung in the balance. Sirhan had fired eight shots in a matter of seconds, and along with Senator Kennedy, six bystanders were wounded.

President Johnson spent the day on the phone, receiving updates on Robert Kennedy's condition and making calls to members of Congress prodding them to act swiftly on new legislation authorizing the Secret Service to protect presidential and vice presidential candidates. I remained at the White House all day and into the night, making sure we had every possible thing covered.

At 8:50 p.m., we got a call from our Los Angeles office with information that Robert Kennedy's heart was getting weaker, and a doctor who was only to be called if the situation became very critical had arrived at the hospital. Five minutes later, our L.A. office reported that all members of the family had been asked to gather at the hospital. It seemed it was just a matter of time.

At 1:25 a.m.—now the morning of June 6—I was in the command center when President Johnson called from the residential quarters. He wanted to make sure we were fully staffed and were receiving the latest intelligence information.

"I need you to stay on top of this, Clint," he said. "And keep me advised of any late developments."

"Yes, sir, Mr. President," I said.

"I'm going to eat dinner and then go to bed. Let me know if anything new develops."

I hadn't eaten dinner myself, and since there wasn't much more I could do at that point, I decided it was best for me to go home and get some rest. Despite how exhausted and mentally drained I was, I had trouble sleeping, wondering how Mrs. Jacqueline Kennedy, Caroline, and John were coping.

At 5:00 a.m. the White House phone rang. "Sir," the on-duty agent said, "We have just received word that Robert Kennedy has died."

We had been receiving updates on his condition throughout the previous day, so while the news did not come as a surprise, to hear it said aloud still tied my stomach in knots.

"Has the president been informed?" I asked.

"Yes, sir. Mr. Rostow delivered the news just before I called you."

"Thank you. I'll be there as soon as I can."

THE FLAG OVER the White House was already at half-staff when I arrived. President Johnson had directed that American flags on all U.S. government and military installations at home and abroad be lowered until after Robert Kennedy's burial on Saturday. Sunday, he proclaimed, would be a national day of mourning.

A somber mood enveloped the White House as the press and staff began arriving. No one said much. We were all in a state of disbelief.

One of President Johnson's first calls was to Senator Ted Kennedy, who was in Los Angeles at the hospital where his brother had just died. The president expressed his condolences and offered the Kennedy family anything they needed—planes, vehicles, no request was too big or too small. Despite the long-standing hostility between Lyndon Johnson and Robert Kennedy, the two staffs worked together to assist the grieving Kennedy family in every possible way.

JetStars, Secret Service agents, and government vehicles and drivers were made available for the Kennedy family members spread around the country. The president had offered to send one of the presidential jets to Los Angeles to fly the family and the body of Robert F. Kennedy back to New York

City, where funeral services would be held at St. Patrick's Cathedral, and the family gratefully accepted.

A few hours later, we got word that Mrs. Jacqueline Kennedy, Caroline, and John would be on board the aircraft with the casket, and Mrs. Kennedy had requested that it not be the same plane that was used for President Kennedy. When I heard that, a wave of vivid memories crashed into my mind—calling the funeral home in Dallas to order the casket for President Kennedy; signing for it; squatting in the back of the hearse with Dr. Burkley and Mrs. Kennedy on the silent ride back to Love Field; struggling with the other agents to lift the heavy casket up the stairs to the door of Air Force One; and then the breaking point, when we realized the door of the presidential plane was not wide enough.

Oh God. I immediately got on the phone to Rufus Youngblood, who was working with Tom Johnson on the president's staff to make all the arrangements.

"Ruf," I said. "The casket. If they want it to go topside, they have to make sure it's narrow enough to fit through the door of the aircraft. Remember . . ."

"Thanks, Clint," Rufus said. "I'll get the measurements of the doorway and let them know as soon as possible."

WITHIN HOURS OF President Johnson's request the previous day for legislation authorizing Secret Service protection for major candidates, both Houses of Congress passed a joint resolution doing just what the president had proposed, and at 6:30 on the evening of June 6—less than forty-eight hours after Senator Kennedy had been shot—I was among those present with Director Rowley, Deputy Director Youngblood, and other Secret Service officials as President Johnson signed the resolution into law.

President Johnson realized that in the midst of this national anguish, he had a window of opportunity, which he used to persuade Congress to take action on a many-faceted crime-control bill that included a ban on mail-order sales of handguns—a bill he had been unsuccessful in getting passed due to powerful opposition. Once again, it was Lyndon B. Johnson at his best—making swift decisions in the midst of a crisis, and then, because of his long-standing relationships with members on both sides of the congressional aisle and his unmatched knowledge of the political process, new legislation got passed.

But with two assassinations of national figures in two months, just four years after the assassination of our president, the bigger question on all Americans' minds was: *What is happening to our country? And where do we go from here?* It felt like hatred and violence had taken the helm, thrusting our civilized society into a downward spiral. Hoping to find answers and lasting remedies, President Johnson quickly formed a committee to look into the "Cause and Prevention of Violence and Assassination."

SENATOR KENNEDY'S BODY lay in state at St. Patrick's Cathedral all day Friday, June 7, as people came from all over the country to pay their respects. The Requiem Mass was scheduled for the following day, June 8, at ten in the morning, after which the body of Robert Francis Kennedy would be taken by train to Washington for burial at Arlington National Cemetery.

The president had decided to take a JetStar to New York instead of the presidential jet, and because of its limited capacity, Deputy Director Rufus Youngblood accompanied the president while I flew ahead with a group of agents to be on the ground for the president's arrival.

As our motorcade proceeded slowly through the streets of Manhattan, the scene was eerily reminiscent of November 25, 1963. Thousands of people lining the city streets, somber, silent, weeping.

I had been concerned about seeing Mrs. Jacqueline Kennedy at the funeral—what would I say? How would she react to seeing me? It turned out that with Youngblood there, he accompanied the president inside the cathedral while I stayed outside, supervising the agents on the perimeter, and while I saw Mrs. Kennedy from a distance, there was no opportunity for us to speak to each other.

As soon as the funeral service concluded, we flew back to Washington and carried on with normal business, while the Kennedy family traveled by train from New York's Penn Station through New Jersey, Pennsylvania, Delaware, and Maryland. An estimated two million people lined the tracks— they were black, white, young, old, rich, and poor, their faces hollow with shock and sorrow for the family that had endured so much tragedy—and you could see the desperation in their eyes, wondering, as nearly every American was: *Why?*

The funeral services were scheduled to take place in the late afternoon, but the train trip took more than four hours longer than had been anticipated and didn't arrive at Washington's Union Station until after nine that evening. We brought President Johnson to the train station so that he and Mrs. Johnson, along with Vice President and Mrs. Humphrey, were there to greet the Kennedy family as they arrived.

I was standing immediately next to President Johnson as the narrow, flag-draped casket was moved from the train to the hearse. As President Johnson spoke briefly to Ethel, Teddy, and Robert Kennedy Jr., I saw Mrs. Jacqueline Kennedy emerge from the train with John and Caroline. Our eyes met, and she walked toward me.

"Hello, Mr. Hill," she said. "How have you been?"

She was wearing a black dress—was it the same one she had worn for her husband's funeral?—with a black veil that covered her hair and hung down softly against the sides of her face. And her eyes—oh, her eyes. They revealed the depth of her grief—unbearable grief. And yet she had the grace to inquire *How have you been?*

"Hello, Mrs. Kennedy," I said. "I am so very sorry for your loss."

She closed her eyes for the briefest of moments, and when they opened, glistening with pain, she replied, simply, "Thank you."

At that point, the president was moving toward the waiting limousine. Much as I would have liked to talk to her longer, to find out how she and the children were doing, I needed to move with the president.

"It was nice to see you, Mrs. Kennedy," I said as I tried to muster the semblance of a smile, and then I turned and walked away.

I rode in the front seat of the presidential limousine—we were the fifteenth car in the motorcade procession—and as we slowly made our way down Constitution Avenue, I was filled with an overwhelming sense of loss. Darkness had long since fallen, and the monuments—the sparkling white marble tributes to past presidents—were lit up against the rainy black sky. As the motorcade turned in front of the majestic memorial to Abraham Lincoln—another leader slain by an assassin—and headed onto Memorial Bridge where, up ahead, the eternal flame at President Kennedy's gravesite flickered on the hillside, my heart was heavy with grief, but also deep concern. Our leaders were being gunned down. Every day we were informed of new threats against President Johnson, and the anger directed against him on college campuses across the nation had become explosive. I shuddered at the thought of what another assassination would do to our country. We simply couldn't let it happen. *I* couldn't let it happen.

The other agents and I walked with President and Mrs. Johnson as they joined the Kennedy family around the gravesite where forty two year-old Robert Kennedy would be laid to rest, a stone's throw from where his brother had been buried four and a half years earlier. As the solemn ceremony proceeded, I stood several paces behind President Johnson, surrounded by Kennedys and Shrivers and Smiths—and it was hard to remember the times before the world changed, before our innocence was shattered. My heart ached for Ethel and her children, for Mrs. Kennedy, Caroline, and John standing with them in sad solidarity, and it was all I could do to focus on surveying the crowd, keeping my mind on the reason I was there.

But when Robert and Ethel Kennedy's older children took their younger siblings by the hands and solemnly knelt to kiss the flag-draped casket of their father, the memories came rushing back—Mrs. Kennedy and Caroline in the rotunda, the heart-wrenching sight of John's three-year-old salute, Robert Kennedy holding the hand of his brother's widow at the lighting of the eternal flame—and I was thankful for the darkness and the misty rain gliding down my cheeks.

President and Mrs. Johnson knelt and prayed with the Kennedy family, and when the services were over, we moved them away from the crowd and promptly departed the cemetery. As it turned out, my brief encounter with Mrs. Kennedy at the train station in the shadow of Robert Kennedy's casket would be our last meeting. I would never see or speak with Jacqueline Kennedy again.

28

Loyalty

As we rolled into the summer of 1968, racial tensions simmered just below the boiling point, American casualties in Vietnam mounted, antiwar demonstrations multiplied, and, with the assassinations of Martin Luther King and Robert Kennedy still raw wounds, Americans were desperate for hope.

President Johnson had become a virtual prisoner in the White House, and one of the few things that gave him joy was his grandson, "Lyn"—Luci and Patrick Nugent's son. The president delighted in bringing the infant into the Oval Office and onto Air Force One, and when he was with his little namesake, it was as if all the burdens of the office evaporated.

Meanwhile, Lynda's husband, Marine Captain Chuck Robb, had begun his tour of duty in Vietnam at the end of March, and shortly thereafter the White House announced that Lynda was pregnant. Having a son-in-law in Vietnam—with another grandchild on the way—seemed to make President Johnson even more determined to find a peaceful solution to the war that was ripping the nation apart. Captain Robb provided the president with firsthand details of what it was like for the soldiers on the ground, giving him information that sometimes differed from what his military advisors were telling him.

Even though President Johnson had publicly declared that he would not run for another term, there were signs that perhaps he was indeed still thinking about it—especially now that Robert Kennedy was no longer a factor. I was definitely keeping my ears open for anything that might indicate he was changing his mind.

One day in early July, we were at the LBJ Ranch when something unusual happened. The president's tailor, Irving Frank, had come to the ranch to deliver some clothes he had made for the president. He'd been a guest for lunch, and then had the president try on the clothes to make sure they fit. I was in the Secret Service office when I got word that the president wanted to see me out by the pool.

As I rounded the corner of the house, I saw the president standing in the doorway that led from his bedroom to the pool area, while Mr. Frank was just outside, his tape measure slung around his neck.

As I approached, President Johnson turned to Mr. Frank, pointed at me, and said, "Measure him."

Without hesitation, Mr. Frank began measuring my shoulders, chest, sleeve length, waist, and inseam, scribbling down the numbers on a pocket notepad. The president was watching intently with a mischievous grin on his face, and when the tailor was finished, Johnson looked at me and said, "You can go now, Clint."

There was no explanation, and I had no idea what this was all about. There was no more mention of it for the rest of the day, and that evening we departed the ranch and headed back to Washington.

ONE OF THE results of Robert Kennedy's death was that the Secret Service was now protecting major presidential candidates, and in order to meet the added responsibilities, the White House Detail—of which I was the SAIC— had been cannibalized. Because of the stamina required on the campaign trail, we had moved many of the experienced, younger agents to the candidates' details, and replaced the President's Detail with older agents who had plenty of experience but weren't necessarily as fit or agile. The theory was that the new protective details would be much more active because they were constantly on the go, while the president, presumably, wouldn't be traveling so much. This was true, but it concerned me—especially as we headed into the Republican and Democratic conventions with a severe shortage of manpower.

The Secret Service was protecting four Republican candidates when the Republican convention opened on August 5 in Miami Beach, Florida. At the same time, Democratic candidates Hubert Humphrey and Eugene McCarthy were being protected, as well as George Wallace, the American Independent Party candidate. Meanwhile, the replacement agents I had with President Johnson were agents who had worked on the White House Detail with Presidents Roosevelt and Truman, and alongside me with Eisenhower, and were now back doing a job meant to be done by much younger men. They were hanging in there, but the long hours and extended periods of travel not to mention Johnson's unpredictability—were taking their toll.

President Johnson remained at the LBJ Ranch during the Republican National Convention, and other than a couple of trips to San Antonio for his annual physical examination and tests, there was only the usual ranch activity with guests flying in and out and tours of the ranches and the birthplace. On August 8, the Republicans named their ticket for the upcoming presidential election: Richard Nixon for president and the governor of Maryland, Spiro Agnew, as his vice presidential running mate. Shortly after the official announcement, President Johnson invited Nixon and Agnew to the ranch for a briefing on foreign relations.

Johnson was still working tirelessly for a peace agreement with North Vietnam—it was his greatest hope that he could bring a successful conclusion to the conflict before he left office—and plans were under way for peace talks in Paris. There had been speculation that Nixon would try to undercut the negotiations as a campaign tactic, but in his acceptance speech at the convention, he promised not to say anything during the campaign that might destroy a chance for peace.

On August 10, when I arrived at the Secret Service security office, I was handed a package that had been delivered, addressed to me. Inside were a pair of tan gabardine pants and a Western style shirt, identical to the ones President Johnson wore around the ranch. The mystery of the tailor measuring me by the pool was now solved.

After an early morning swim, the president came out of the house with Tom Johnson and secretary Marie Fehmer, headed for his white convertible, and said, "Goin' for a drive."

I didn't mention the clothes I'd received, but at some point during the drive, President Johnson said, "Clint, did you get that package I sent you?"

"Yes, Mr. President," I said with a smile. "I received it this morning. Thank you very much."

"Well, sometime this afternoon I want to see you in those clothes and make sure they fit. I'll make a Texan out of you yet."

This was the day that Richard Nixon and Spiro Agnew were coming, as well as all of the president's top advisors. I did not think it was a good day for the president and me to be dressed in matching outfits.

We got back to the main house just in time to greet Secretary of State Dean Rusk, Director of the CIA Richard Helms, and Cyrus Vance—one of the negotiators at the Vietnam peace conference in Paris—as they landed on the runway in a JetStar. About an hour and a half later, a helicopter carrying Richard Nixon and his party arrived at the landing strip. Accompanying Nixon were Governor Spiro Agnew, a couple of Agnew's aides, and three of Nixon's aides: Dwight Chapin, H. R. "Bob" Haldeman, and Ron Ziegler.

It was a hot August day, and President Johnson—dressed in his casual ranch clothes—was very much at ease on his home turf as he welcomed the Republican entourage, all of whom were wearing traditional business suits with starched shirts and ties. As LBJ escorted the group from the landing strip toward the main house, he pulled Nixon aside and said, "While they get settled, let's you and me go on a little drive. I'll show you around the place."

I motioned to one of the other agents to get into the follow-up car, and I jumped in the right front seat just in time to tail behind as President Johnson sped off in the convertible with Richard Nixon. Of course we had no idea what his intentions were—how far he'd be going or for how long—but on this occasion he just made a quick twenty-minute tour around the ranch, showing Nixon his birthplace and then looping back to the house.

The others had already gathered in the living room, and as soon as the president and Mr. Nixon arrived, the serious briefing began. The mood lightened during lunch, which was served in the family dining room as President Johnson held court, telling humorous stories and sharing memories of his long political career. If you didn't know any better, you might have thought these were a bunch of lifelong friends at an annual reunion rather than political rivals.

The visit lasted only about two hours, but before the guests departed,

President Johnson once again pulled Nixon aside and walked him to the porch outside his office for one last private chat.

I stood nearby as President Johnson escorted the Nixon entourage back to the runway, memorizing faces and mannerisms and taking mental note of who was who and the apparent pecking order as they boarded the helicopter; for although the election was still three months away and anything could happen, there was a good chance that Richard M. Nixon would be the next President of the United States of America— and in all likelihood, I would be in charge of his protection. I knew very little about Nixon, other than what I had observed when he was vice president under President Eisenhower, and since then he had brought in many new staff members. On that August day in 1968, I could not have imagined what lay ahead, and the turmoil these men would eventually bring upon themselves, the nation, and, yes, even me.

LATE THAT AFTERNOON, after all the guests had left, I received a message in the command post.

"Clint, the president is requesting you put on your new ranch clothes. He's in the pool, and he wants to see how they look on you."

Oh jeez. I had hoped that the visit with Mr. Nixon might have made him forget about the gift he'd given me. No such luck. I had no choice but to put on the outfit.

I put on the shirt and pants in the security room while my fellow agents were laughing and making smart remarks about me becoming a permanent resident of the Texas Hill Country.

"It's meant to be, Clint!" they said, laughing, "Fits you like a glove."

It was true, the tailor had done a fine job, and I had to admit the clothes were pretty comfortable. But still, it was damn embarrassing.

I walked out to the pool area, where the president and his secretary Marie Fehmer were in the pool cooling off from the intense heat of the late afternoon sun, and modeled the uniform.

"Look at that!" President Johnson exclaimed. "Doesn't he look fine, Marie?"

"Oh yes," Marie said with a grin. "You look mighty fine, Mr. Hill."

Ken Gaddis, one of the presidential stewards, happened to be nearby, and he made some smart remark about how the president's tailor must be a miracle worker if he could make a Secret Service agent look like a rancher.

After everybody had a good laugh at my expense, I said, "Okay. The fashion show's over. Time to get back to work."

As soon as I got back to the security room, I changed into my regular clothing and folded the ranch clothes neatly back in the box. I couldn't imagine myself wearing them—and being Johnson's twin—but I realized the gift was his way of saying I had finally been accepted, that despite his initial doubts about my loyalty, I had proven to be worthy of his trust and confidence.

A short while later the president went driving around touring the ranches—I am not kidding; this was a daily, often twice daily activity—and at one point as I got out to open one of the gates, he said, "Clint, where are the ranch clothes?"

Think fast, Clint.

"I didn't want to get them dirty on the first day, Mr. President," I responded. He could see right through me, but he grinned and said, "Good idea. Take good care of them and they'll last a long time."

Later that evening, former presidential assistant Marvin Watson and his wife arrived by plane. Although Watson had accepted a new job as postmaster general, it appeared to me that he was still the president's man in the political arena, and I couldn't help but wonder if something was brewing.

We stayed at the ranch for nine more days, and on August 19, with little notice, the president informed me he was flying to Detroit to speak at the National VFW convention. A few days earlier, he had pulled a similar stunt, informing us at the last minute of a quick in-and-out trip to Houston. With many of the field offices drained of personnel to cover the presidential candidates, this no-notice-surprise-visit philosophy was getting riskier all the time. Fortunately, both the Houston and Detroit field offices stepped up to the challenge, but it was not without a great deal of anxiety for the Secret Service.

The day after we returned to Washington, President Johnson got a hand-delivered note from the Soviet ambassador with a message from Premier Kosygin that the Soviet Union was invading Czechoslovakia. The president held meetings well into the early morning hours and released a taped statement urging the Soviet Union to withdraw its troops. It seemed like every time he turned around, another crisis dropped into his lap. With all of this going on, I was surprised when President Johnson suddenly decided to go back to the LBJ Ranch on Friday, August 23, three days before the start of the Democratic National Convention in Chicago.

Something is going on.

I was aware that Marvin Watson and some of Johnson's other political advance men had been sent to Chicago, while at the same time President Johnson was taking two speechwriters with him to Texas. Additionally, the president's birthday was coming up on August 27, in the middle of the convention, and while I was sure there would be a tribute to Johnson at some point, knowing him as I did, I thought the possibility of his flying to Chicago and appearing at the convention was a real one. He had been keeping his speaking appearances very close to the vest, not letting anyone know exactly what his intentions were, and on top of all this I had never dismissed the notion that LBJ might actually reconsider running again.

I decided to fly to Chicago to snoop around, putting my Assistant SAIC, John Paul Jones, in charge of Johnson's security at the ranch, and telling him to keep his eyes and ears open on that end.

Agent Dave Grant—one of the agents on the White House Detail—was originally from Chicago and knew Mayor Richard Daley and his special events director, Jack Riley, so I had him accompany me to make sure we had all the information we needed and could make our own plans in the event President Johnson decided to make a surprise visit to the convention. Deputy Director Rufus Youngblood and Assistant Director Lem Johns were already in Chicago dealing with candidate protection, and while they had informed us of some intelligence reports that caused grave concern, when I arrived and saw what was actually happening I knew we were in for some serious trouble.

Chicago's black gangs were reportedly stockpiling weapons in apartments near the International Amphitheatre—the convention site—with the intention of stirring up violence in the streets, and an informant had tipped off police that one of the gangs was planning on gunning down Vice President Hubert Humphrey and Senator Eugene McCarthy. Meanwhile, anti–Vietnam War groups had promised to bring in 150,000 protestors and agitators, and they were already arriving by the busload as part of a coordinated effort to disrupt the convention, assembling in Lincoln and Grant Parks. Equally disturbing were rumors that a pro-Nixon group, partially funded by Richard Nixon's close friend Bebe Rebozo, was headed to Chicago to incite disorder.

To combat the expected demonstrations, Mayor Daley had orchestrated unprecedented security arrangements: 12,000 Chicago police officers were on twelve-hour shifts; 7,500 U.S. Army soldiers were posted at strategic points in and around the city; 5,600 National Guardsmen were on standby; and 1,000 federal agents would be guarding hotels and mingling with the crowds. The Secret Service's Chicago Field Office was already spread thin, and while the local agents would automatically assist us if President Johnson made a last-minute drop-in visit, we simply didn't have the bodies to adequately protect the President of the United States in such a contentious atmosphere.

The International Amphitheatre was located in the Chicago Union Stockyard area on Chicago's South Side, while the majority of delegates were staying in downtown hotels. We had rooms in the Conrad Hilton on Michigan Avenue, directly across from Grant Park, which just so happened to be one of the main gathering places for the demonstrators. On Monday night, the first night of the convention, police clashed with a large group of protestors right in front of our hotel. I could hardly believe my eyes when I looked down at the street below and saw police officers swinging their billy clubs at protestors who refused to leave the premises. In the next instant, there was a series of loud pops, and then plumes of tear gas filled the air, sending people running and screaming in a panicked herd. The windows were closed, but the gas was so strong it seeped into the hotel.

Meanwhile, I was keeping in touch with the agents at the ranch on an hourly basis to make sure I was aware of what the president was doing at every moment. I knew we would have only about three hours of flight time—ranch to Austin to Chicago—to get things in place, and the more notice I had, the better. We had selected an aircraft arrival point, planned a motorcade route, and identified a concealed entry point to the convention location. It wasn't going to be easy, and there were plenty of things that could go wrong, but at least I felt comfortable knowing we had a plan.

On Tuesday, August 27, the president spent the morning of his birthday in his bedroom at the ranch making phone calls, and then went out to the pool, where he swam and had lunch with Mrs. Johnson, Luci, and his grandson, Lyn. Around three o'clock in the afternoon, Agent Jones called me.

"Clint, he's been on the phone with Marvin Watson in Chicago and George Christian for the last half hour. I don't know what's being discussed, but I'll keep you posted."

An hour later, Jones reported, "He's called Watson again, and he just got off a conference call with Mayor Daley. But so far, no movement from the house."

At about 4:45, Jones checked in again. "He just got off the phone with Humphrey and advised us to get the helicopter ready. He says he's going to Luci's residence."

Yeah, right.

"Okay," I said. "I'm not going to jump to any conclusions just yet, but the minute he veers off that plan, you let me know."

As it turned out, the president did actually go to his daughter Luci's house in Austin, with the press in attendance, and then returned to the ranch to welcome Lynda and some other guests who were arriving by plane. The president spent the rest of the evening with his guests in the living room, watching the convention on television. There were still two days left in the convention, though, so we weren't out of the woods just yet.

The turbulence within the city continued to escalate to the point that the streets of Chicago looked like a battlefield with armored vehicles, troops armed with assault rifles, and tear gas fired when the crowds couldn't be controlled. Inside the convention hall, tempers flared as the splintered Democratic Party struggled to nominate their candidate, delegates complained about overzealous security, and speakers railed against Mayor Daley and the "Gestapo tactics" going on outside. Members of the news media were caught in melees both inside and outside, and as the horrifying images splashed across America's television screens, protestors chanted, "The whole world is watching! The whole world is watching!"

It was a goddamn mess.

Despite what seemed at one point to be insurmountable differences within the party, Vice President Hubert Humphrey won the nomination and selected Senator Ed Muskie of Maine as his running mate. In the end, President Johnson did not show up at the convention, and when it concluded,

I took a flight to Austin and drove out to the ranch. I never told President Johnson I had been at the convention standing by in case he decided to attend, but just as I was monitoring his every move, his people were reporting back to him, and I am sure he knew.

WE RETURNED TO Washington in early September, and as the presidential campaign of 1968 got into full swing, President Johnson continued to be mired in the problems that had plagued him all year. Despite the impressive amount of legislation he had passed during his administration, it appeared that his legacy was going to be his failure to negotiate a resolution in Vietnam. Still, he worked tirelessly, and while many presidents would be winding down at the end of their administration, he continued at the same frenzied pace.

On several occasions, I arrived at the White House in the morning to find out that the president had requested the agents on the midnight shift take him to St. Dominic's Catholic Church in southwest Washington in the middle of the night. He would sit and talk with one of the priests or friars for fifteen minutes or up to an hour, and then return to the White House in deep reflection. No one but the Secret Service knew about these midnight visits. It was clear President Johnson was searching for guidance, and these secretive visits exemplified the tremendous burden he bore on his shoulders alone.

By this point, having been around President Johnson for nearly four years, I had come to realize that although he was a challenging boss—in so many different ways—he valued those who were loyal to him, and he tried to show his gratitude in his own way.

September 30 was a typical day at the White House, with back-to-back meetings, a quick trip to the Sheraton Park Hotel for a speech, a bill signing for a project on the Colorado River, and the usual multitude of phone calls and briefings, but on this day the president made time to attend two events to express his personal appreciation and affection. Early that afternoon, he attended the Arlington Cemetery funeral for a twenty-three-year-old Navy lieutenant who had been a groomsman at Luci's wedding and had been killed in a training accident in Arizona, and the family was deeply touched by his attendance. This day also happened to be White House staffer Tom Johnson's twenty-seventh birthday.

Now, Tom Johnson, originally from Macon, Georgia, had come to the White House three years earlier in 1965 as the first White House Fellow, and had proven his loyalty to the president by working long days in the press office—often sixteen-, eighteen-, or twenty-hour days—without complaint, and with tremendous attention to detail. Because of the hours, and the fact that he and his young wife, Edwina, had relocated to Washington for the job, he had few, if any, friends outside White House circles. Like those of us on the White House Detail, the demands of his job precluded having a social life.

Edwina wanted to have a dinner party in their small apartment to surprise Tom on his birthday, and being somewhat naive, she invited President and Mrs. Johnson—and to her amazement, they accepted. So Edwina called her mother for an appropriate recipe, and spent the exorbitant sum of $25— equivalent to a month's worth of groceries out of Tom's entry-level government salary—on a decorative white serving dish with a swirled gold rose on top for the shrimp and rice casserole she planned to prepare. On the evening of September 30, everything was perfect; the casserole was in the oven, and at the appointed time of 7:30, two of the invited couples arrived. The only people missing were President and Mrs. Johnson.

Seven-thirty came and went. Eight o'clock. Nine o'clock. Finally, Edwina came to the conclusion that the president was not going to show up, and she had better serve dinner to her other guests.

Now at the time, I had no idea that President Johnson had accepted this birthday invitation. I was at the White House, and at 10:10 that evening, I got a call that the president was going out to dinner and to get the car ready. So we took the president and Mrs. Johnson, along with George Christian, and drove to Tom and Edwina's one-bedroom apartment in Alexandria.

As I waited outside the door, I heard laughter, the clanking of wineglasses, and a rousing rendition of "Happy Birthday," and it sounded like everyone was having a marvelous time. The Johnsons stayed until 11:45, and then we drove them back to the White House, after which I went home for the night.

I didn't learn Edwina's side of this story until 2014—forty-eight years later—but she remembered the details like it was yesterday: how LBJ showed up three hours late, unapologetically, and expected dinner, and all she had to serve at that point was a room-temperature overdone casserole, but you know what? He kept his word. And even though he had the weight of the world on his shoulders, it was important to him to attend the birthday celebration of a loyal friend. That was typical of Lyndon B. Johnson.

SOMETIME IN MID-OCTOBER I got a telephone call from Jack Walsh, the head of the Kennedy Protective Detail.

"Clint," he said. "It's Jack."

"Well, hello, John Francis Michael Walsh," I said as a smile spread across my face. Jack was a good Catholic from South Boston, with a great sense of humor, and I had specifically chosen him to be with John and Caroline when I was still with Mrs. Kennedy in 1964. He was great with the kids, and now he was in charge of the small detail of agents that protected Mrs. Kennedy and the children.

"How are things in New York City?"

"Well, Clint, that's why I'm calling. There are going to be some big changes, and although the announcement isn't going to be made until the last possible minute, I thought you should know."

Before he could get the words out, I knew what he was going to say. I'd been hearing rumors, but I honestly couldn't believe she would do it.

"Mrs. Kennedy is going to marry Onassis," Jack said. He paused, waiting for my response.

I took a deep breath. "When?"

"The twentieth of October. In Greece—on his island. We're flying with the kids a few days before. Making all the arrangements now. Her mother will make the announcement after we're airborne."

"Thanks for letting me know, Jack. I really appreciate it."

I never discussed this with Mrs. Kennedy, so I don't know whether she truly loved Aristotle Onassis. It wasn't any of my business. I do know that he offered her something that few men in the world could provide her—security, both personally and financially—and in the aftermath of the assassination of her brother-in-law, I'm sure she was terrified that she or her children might be targets. Onassis had his own island, his own airline, and homes and apartments all over the world, and I'd seen the power he had to get what he wanted.

All I wanted for Mrs. Kennedy was for her to be happy.

THERE HADN'T BEEN much to be happy about thus far in 1968, but shortly after midnight on October 25, President and Mrs. Johnson's daughter Lynda Bird Robb gave birth to a healthy baby girl named Lucinda Desha Robb. News was immediately dispatched to Lynda's husband, Chuck, at his post in Vietnam, and later that morning, President Johnson handed out cigars to the press people who had convened at Bethesda Naval Hospital.

On the last few days of October, there had been a lot of unusual activity at the White House, and while I didn't know exactly what was going on, I knew something was up. When I arrived at the White House on the morning of October 29, the on-duty agent said, "Mr. Hill, something happened overnight that I think you should know about."

"What happened?" I asked.

"Well, shortly after two o'clock in the morning, we got a lot of high-level visitors."

At two o'clock in the morning? This was very unusual. "Who?"

"Secretary of Defense Clifford, General Wheeler, General Taylor, General Abrams, Director Helms . . ."

"The National Security Council? At two in the morning?"

"Yes, and the president joined them in the Cabinet Room at two-thirty."

Something on the international front was definitely going on, and, clearly, the president and his top advisors were keeping it close to the vest. Over the next two days, the members of the National Security Council were constantly coming and going, and all through the West Wing you could hear the sound of typewriters.

On October 31, I finally found out what was happening, several hours before the rest of the world would learn the same news. I was in the Secret Service office when I heard three buzzes, indicating the president was moving from the West Wing. I went up the stairway to the Oval Office level and learned that the president was going to the theater with several of his top aides to view a portion of a speech he had taped late the evening before, and to add an additional portion that had been rewritten today.

I accompanied the group along the colonnade past the swimming pool and the flower shop, through the mansion, and to the theater. Each of them found a seat, while I stood inside the doorway. The lights dimmed and the film rolled. On-screen, President Johnson was seated, looking directly into the camera.

"Good evening, my fellow Americans. I speak to you this evening about very important developments in our search for peace in Vietnam.

"We have been engaged in discussions with the North Vietnamese in Paris since last May. The discussions began after I announced on the evening of March 31st in a television speech to the nation that the United States— in an effort to get talks started on a settlement of the Vietnam War—had stopped the bombing of North Vietnam in the area where ninety percent of the people live."

He explained that the talks had been deadlocked for many weeks.

"Last Sunday evening and throughout Monday," he continued, "we began to get confirmation of the essential understanding that we had been seeking with the North Vietnamese on the critical issues between us for some time." His tone was somber, his voice hoarse from a nagging sore throat and chronic lack of sleep.

"Now, as a result of all these developments I have now ordered that all air, naval, and artillery bombardment of North Vietnam cease as of eight a.m. Washington time Friday morning. I have reached this decision on the basis of the developments of the Paris talks, and I have reached it in the belief that this action can lead to progress toward a peaceful settlement of the Vietnamese War."

The president noted he was making this decision with the concurrence of his top military and diplomatic advisors, but he cautioned that "arrangements of this kind are never foolproof" and that the new phase of negotiations did not mean a stable peace had yet come to Southeast Asia.

The men in the room agreed that the speech was good, and watched as President Johnson taped one last segment. He appealed to the presidential candidates to support their government and our men in Vietnam with a

I was standing just behind Agent Roy Kellerman in the doorway as Lyndon Johnson took the oath of office on Air Force One with Mrs. Kennedy by his side. It was surreal—and crushingly sad. *John F. Kennedy Presidential Library & Museum/Boston*

Flight crews run for their aircraft at the LBJ Ranch after notification that President Johnson wants to fly somewhere without prior notice. A typical occurrence. *LBJ Library photo by Yoichi Okamoto*

President Johnson discusses Vietnam situation with Joint Chiefs of Staff around picnic table on front lawn of LBJ Ranch. Clockwise from LBJ: Sec. of Defense Robert McNamara, a military assistant, Gen. Curtis LeMay, Gen. Earle Wheeler, Deputy Sec. of Defense Cyrus Vance, Gen. Harold Johnson, Adm. David McDonald, and Gen. Wallace Greene. Dec. 22, 1964. *LBJ Library photo by Yoichi Okamoto*

I walked alongside the left rear of presidential limousine SS-100-X—the same car in which JFK was assassinated—in Johnson's 1965 Inaugural Parade. *LBJ Library photo*

In a secret meeting at Andrews Air Force Base, President Johnson conferred privately with former President Eisenhower on board a Jetstar aircraft. Oct. 5, 1965. *LBJ Library photo by Yoichi Okamoto*

LBJ stands out of the Mexican presidential limousine with President Díaz Ordaz as agents try to control the surging crowds in Mexico City, April 1966. I'm making a request of a Mexican official immediately in front of the car. *LBJ Library photo by Yoichi Okamoto*

Making preparations for a presidential movement in Honolulu. Left to right: Lem Johns, me on the radio, Dick Johnsen, and an unidentified agent. May 1966. *LBJ Library photo by Yoichi Okamoto*

A light moment on Air Force One. Left to right: LBJ, Sgt. Robert Duffey, me, Agent Bob Taylor, and SAIC Lem Johns (foreground). *LBJ Library photo by Yoichi Okamoto*

As LBJ climbs out of the car into the overwhelming crowd in Honolulu, I stand in the follow-up car, scanning the scene and obviously upset by the president's risk-taking. Oct. 17, 1966. *LBJ Library photo by Frank Wolfe*

Protestors in Melbourne, Australia, throw paint at the president's car. Agents Lem Johns, Dick Johnsen, and Rufus Youngblood bear the brunt of the attack. Oct. 1966. *AP Photo*

It was a special occasion for the senior agents on the White House Detail and our wives to be invited guests for dinner at the LBJ Ranch. Dick Johnsen, myself, Peggy Youngblood, LBJ, Rufus Youngblood, and Betty Godfrey in foreground. *LBJ Library photo by Yoichi Okamoto*

Gwen and I pose with President and Mrs. Johnson at the LBJ Ranch. Dec. 1966. *LBJ Library photo by Yoichi Okamoto*

Rev. Billy Graham and President Johnson greet an enthusiastic crowd at the White House, as I remain close. June 14, 1967. *LBJ Library photo by Kevin Smith*

Russia's Premier Aleksei Kosygin and President Johnson (Russian interpreter between them) meet at a quickly arranged summit at the home of Glassboro College's president. Soviet Ambassador Dobrynin on right. June 23, 1967. *LBJ Library photo by Yoichi Okamoto*

I stand on the rear of the jeep as President Johnson and General Westmoreland inspect the troops during a surprise visit to Cam Ranh Bay, Vietnam. Dec. 23, 1967. *LBJ Library photo by Yoichi Okamoto*

I remain close to President Johnson as he shakes hands with the soldiers at Cam Ranh Bay, Vietnam. Dec. 23, 1967. *LBJ Library photo by Frank Wolfe*

I accompanied LBJ to retirement ceremony for Sec. of Defense McNamara at the Pentagon—a day when almost everything went wrong. Feb. 29, 1968. *Clint Hill personal collection*

President Johnson admonishing me for something as we disembark Marine One on the South Lawn.
LBJ Library photo by Yoichi Okamoto

President Johnson on phone receiving information on the assassination of Martin Luther King Jr. as members of the staff watch news reports on three TVs in the Oval Office. *LBJ Library photo by Mike Geissinger*

Robert F. Kennedy's burial at Arlington National Cemetery. Left to right: Ethel and Ted Kennedy; foreground: President Johnson; Deputy Director Rufus Youngblood and me. June 8, 1968. *Getty/Michael Ochs Archives*

President Johnson hosts Republican presidential candidate Richard Nixon and his staff for a briefing at the LBJ Ranch. Left to right: Spiro Agnew, CIA Director Dick Helms, Ron Ziegler, Nixon, President Johnson, Cyrus Vance, Bob Haldeman, Jim Jones, Tom Johnson, and Dean Rusk. Aug. 10, 1968. *LBJ Library photo by Yoichi Okamoto*

It was embarrassing modeling the custom-made ranch clothes LBJ gifted me. The president and secretary Marie Fehmer comment from the pool as Ken Gaddis laughs. Aug. 10, 1968. *LBJ Library photo by Yoichi Okamoto*

Meeting comedian Jack Benny with White House press aide Tom Johnson standing in the background. May 1968. *LBJ Library photo by Yoichi Okamoto*

Judy Agnew, President Johnson, incoming Vice President Agnew, and Mrs. Johnson at the White House on Inauguration Day 1969. I'm standing lower right by the car. *AP Photo*

I was riding in the right front seat of SS-100-X, as the other agents reacted to anti-Nixon demonstrators hurling rocks and other debris during the 1969 Inaugural Parade. *Richard M. Nixon Library*

I stood behind Vice President Agnew and his wife, and former President and Mrs. Johnson observing the launch of the Apollo 11 moon shot at Cape Kennedy. July 16, 1969 *Clint Hill personal collection/NASA*

The press had a field day with President Nixon's uniform design for the White House police division of the Secret Service. I thought they were ridiculous. *U.S. Secret Service Photo*

Agents Chuck Zboril and Don Gautreau scan the crowd as President Nixon stands out of the roof amid swarming crowds in Manila, Philippines. *AP Photo*

Vice President Agnew visiting my mother, Jennie Hill, in Minot, North Dakota. My cousin Olga's husband, Paul Froeming, is in the background. *Clint Hill personal collection*

Secret Service agents Ham Brown (rear) and Gary Jenkins with President Nixon during his predawn excursion to the Lincoln Memorial to talk to antiwar protesters. *AP Photo*

We ringed the White House complex with buses as hundreds of thousands of antiwar protesters amassed in Washington, DC, in May 1970. *AP Photo*

Secret Service agents Bill Duncan and Bob Taylor try to ensure President Nixon's security when he gets on top of the car in Berlin, Germany, just weeks after taking office in 1969. *AP Photo*

The day Elvis Presley showed up—unannounced—at the White House with a letter to President Nixon offering his services as a "Federal Agent at large." *Nixon Presidential Library & Museum*

united voice in this critical hour, adding that although he did not know who would be inaugurated as the thirty-seventh President of the United States, he would continue to do all he could in his last few months to move toward peace.

An hour before the speech was to be aired, several press photographers were allowed to snap some photos of the president and his top advisors in the Cabinet Room where this decision had been made. As they were leaving, Walt Rostow, the national security advisor, commented, "This is the most sustained day-and-night effort I've had since the Cuban Missile Crisis."

The speech aired at eight o'clock that evening—broadcast simultaneously on all three networks—and almost immediately there were accusations that the move was purely a political ploy to improve Vice President Humphrey's chances at election. There was no doubt in my mind that that was not the case. President Johnson knew Vietnam had become his war—his Cuban Missile Crisis—and he wasn't going to leave office without giving it his all to find a resolution. I had witnessed the toll it had taken on him over the past four years. I had seen the deep pain in his eyes as he shook the hands of the young men he was sending into battle, and I knew he hadn't slept more than four hours a night for the past year—with a call to the Situation Room the last thing he did each night, and the first thing each morning. No one wanted an end to Vietnam more than Lyndon Johnson, and Lyndon Johnson wanted to be the man to end it.

It would not happen that way.

On November 5, 1968, Richard M. Nixon was elected as the next President of the United States. During the next few weeks, President Johnson and his staff met with President-elect Nixon, Vice President–elect Agnew, and their staffs, preparing them for the transition in January, while Rufus Youngblood and his deputies had the challenge of reassigning agents.

It would be my third presidential transition, and as the SAIC of presidential protection, I had every reason to believe my job would remain the same.

It would not happen that way.

Helping to clear a passageway for President Ford to exit a speech site in Chicago when I was assistant director.
Courtesy Gerald R. Ford Presidential Library

President Ford visits Secret Service headquarters shortly after taking office. (Left to right) myself, Dep. Dir. Pat Boggs, President Ford, Asst. Dir. Burrill Peterson, and Agent Bob Snow. *U.S. Secret Service Photo*

I was very pleased when we
finally allowed women to
become agents in December
1971. Director James J. Rowley with the first five: Holly
Hufschmidt, Laurie Ander-
son, Phyllis Shantz, Sue Ann
Baker, and Kathryn Clark.
U.S. Secret Service Photo

Vice President Spiro
Agnew exits the Baltimore
Courthouse flanked by
Secret Service agents Jerry
Parr and Jimmy Taylor
after admitting guilt to
tax evasion charges, and
announcing his resignation
as Vice President. Oct. 10,
1973. *Bettman/Corbis*

I was among the many members of the
White House staff who watched as President
and Mrs. Nixon departed the White House
for the last time. Nixon daughters Julie and
Tricia with their husbands in the background. *Nixon Presidential Library & Museum*

I was in the East Room of the White House to witness the
swearing-in of Gerald R. Ford as the 38th President of the
United States. Finally "our long national nightmare" was
over. Aug. 9, 1974. *Courtesy Gerald R. Ford Presidential Library*

29

Last Days with LBJ

On November 13, we flew to El Paso, Texas, where President Johnson and President Díaz Ordaz of Mexico jointly pushed a button causing a diversion dam to be destroyed and allowing waters of the Rio Grande to flow through a diversionary channel. This changed the official boundary between Mexico and the United States, giving Mexico about four hundred acres of new land, while also providing a protective measure against flooding.

There were large crowds along the motorcade route, and near the site of the ceremony the crowds were so enthusiastic that they nearly overpowered the security barriers. President Johnson was reaching into the crowd, shaking as many hands as he could, and at one point I had to grab him from the rear for fear that he was going to fall right into the crowd. He was relishing the adoration, enjoying every last minute of what it was like to be President of the United States—apparently oblivious to his own vulnerability.

At some point during the previous year, funds had been approved for a new presidential limousine to replace SS-100-X, and it had been delivered in late October. The twenty-one-foot-long Lincoln Continental had a bomb-proof steel body and a bubbletop roof made of bulletproof glass panels that opened so the president could stand up during parade situations—a function President Johnson had insisted upon. After the election, however, the car was sent to New York City, where President-elect Richard Nixon had his base of operations, and where it would be used for his movements.

On November 19, President Johnson had been invited to a dinner reception for the National Urban League in New York, but he wanted it completely off-the-record. He had a full day of meetings, and it wasn't until 8:30 p.m. that we finally departed the White House grounds in Marine One, and then flew from Andrews by JetStar to New York's LaGuardia Airport. Since we had the new presidential limousine there in New York, we arranged to have it waiting to transport President Johnson from the airport to the function in midtown Manhattan.

As we drove to the Hilton, I was sitting in the right front seat, and President Johnson began commenting about the number of vehicles in the motorcade and the large number of police officers he was seeing. He raised this issue every time we came to New York.

"Clint, how many cars are in this motorcade?" he asked.

I was not certain of the exact number, but I replied, "There is a Secret Service car out in front and about eight New York City police cars preceding us, Mr. President."

"You sure know how to attract attention and let everyone know I'm in town," he said with a snarl. "Didn't I tell you this was supposed to be off-the-record?"

Then he began to ask questions about the new car.

"How thick is this glass? Must be at least an inch thick."

"Yes, Mr. President; more than an inch—enough to give you the protection you need."

Apparently that satisfied him. He turned to Tom Johnson, who was seated next to him, and said, "Tom, you better let the Krims know we are coming."

Mr. and Mrs. Arthur Krim—wealthy friends of President and Mrs. Johnson and big Democratic contributors—were supposed to meet the president on arrival and escort him to the ballroom where the dinner was being held.

Tom said, "Clint, can you get ahold of the advance agent at the Hilton and have him track down the Krims to let them know President Johnson is almost there?"

I got on the radio and transmitted the request to the advance agent, using code names. A few minutes went by, and the advance agent responded that he was having difficulty locating the Krims. He didn't think they'd arrived yet.

When President Johnson heard this, he flew into a rage and ordered the driver to take a longer route to delay our arrival. Then he began to take it out on Tom. "Why aren't they there, Tom? What happened? Did you screw up again?"

"Mr. President," I interjected. "It's not Tom's fault. It's my fault."

"Well, why did you make that mistake? What is wrong with you?" he screamed.

"There was some confusion transmitting the information, but now everything has been resolved. Don't worry. The Krims will be there to meet you."

That seemed to satisfy the president, and nothing more was said. The agent had found the Krims; they were there by the time we arrived; the dinner went well; and afterward we took the president back to the Hotel Pierre, where Mrs. Johnson had been staying. As we were walking up to her suite, he said, "Clint, I'm going to a party for Mrs. Johnson at Jeanne Vanderbilt's, but I don't want the whole goddamned world to know about it. Let me know when the press has left, and get a small car for us to use. I want this to be as discreet as possible."

"Yes, Mr. President," I said. "We'll take care of it."

I got on the radio to the New York Field Office and had them deliver an unmarked sedan. After a while, the press that had gathered at the hotel assumed the president was in for the night—it was already eleven o'clock—and as soon as they were gone, we put him in the sedan and drove to Mrs. Vanderbilt's residence. The party was wrapping up, so he stayed for only an hour, and we got him and Mrs. Johnson back to the hotel around midnight. It had been another exhausting day, but fortunately the press hadn't gotten wind of his activity, and we all flew back to Washington the next morning.

NOVEMBER 22, 1968, marked the fifth anniversary of President Kennedy's assassination. Senator Ted Kennedy and several members of the Kennedy family made a private early morning visit to President Kennedy's grave at Arlington Cemetery, and to the newer grave, just yards away, of Robert Kennedy. And while in each of the previous years since the assassination President Johnson had attended a church memorial service—we had always been in Texas—this year he was in Washington and made no public acknowledgment of the anniversary. Instead, he sent two military aides in his place with a wreath to place at the gravesite.

The following morning, President Johnson invited about sixty members of the Secret Service to meet him on the White House South Lawn for a formal farewell. It was a crisp, sunny day, and with invited members of the press looking on, all the agents and Secret Service staff gathered around the president, with the White House in the background, for a formal photo.

I was standing immediately to the president's right, and when the photos were finished, President Johnson stepped up to a microphone and gave a short speech.

"Mr. Secretary, Director Rowley, members of the Secret Service, ladies and gentlemen," President Johnson began. "I asked you to take a few moments this morning to come out here so I could say something to you that I have thought for eight years and have rarely expressed."

Squinting into the sun, he said he didn't think the country fully recognized or appreciated the means by which we protect the president and his family.

"Your protection is given by preparation and weary, backbreaking hours of hard work. I have seen it all over the world. There is no greater testimony to your efficiency than the recent trip we took when we were in the air fifty-nine hours and on the ground fifty-three hours, and conferred with more than a dozen heads of state in that many countries," adding that several representatives from those countries told him, "Mr. President, what an extraordinary group of men accompany you."

Speaking slowly and with sincerity, President Johnson's voice turned somber when he said, "I will never forget that day in Dallas when a great big, husky roughneck from Georgia threw 185 pounds of human weight on me and said, 'Down.' And there wasn't any place to go but down, because he was on top of me. His life was being offered to protect mine."

He talked about how grateful Mrs. Johnson was for us and for the protection we provided to Luci and Lynda, and then he got personal.

"A lot of things you have had to live through with me. If I could rewrite them, I would change a lot of them, because I have abused you, I have criticized you, I have been inconsiderate of you and of all those things that you know better than I do."

I could hardly believe what I was hearing. President Johnson was apologizing to us.

"I have spent more of my time telling you what you did wrong than what you have done right." He recalled the incident in Australia and how he "just couldn't keep back the tears" when the agents were splattered with paint, "but their chins up and their president safe."

And then he told a story about me.

"Night before last, I was giving Tom Johnson the dickens for a mishap when I was going to drop in on a group of directors of the Urban League. . . . I said, 'Notify them we are coming.' Tom passed on the instruction, and Clint Hill executed it in his usually intelligent way by code."

He paused, moving his glance across the group. "The fellow on the other end just didn't understand all of the code. He came back and said, 'I can't find that party here out of 300 or 400 in three or four seconds.'"

The president continued, "So Hill said, 'I am not sure they have arrived yet, Tom,' and we had to drive around the block a time or two. By that time, I became impatient."

I stood there listening, perplexed at why he was telling this story in front of everyone, and in front of the press. What was he getting at?

"I felt a little sorry for myself that late in the evening," President Johnson continued, "and I said, 'Tom, why do you do this to me?' Then, characteristically, Clint Hill, before Tom could answer, said, 'Mr. President, that is my mistake—my error.'

"I said, 'Well, why did you make it? What is wrong with you?' And he said, 'I communicated a code and we didn't understand it.'

"So before any more time passed, I started feeling sorry for Clint instead of myself. I was grateful that I had a man who had integrity enough to step up and face the music and say it was his fault, because that is the kind of a man that we all admire."

He looked at me, and everyone began clapping. It was embarrassing to me, and while I couldn't have been more surprised at his remarks, I realized this was President Johnson acknowledging, in his own way, that he appreciated everything I did for him.

He continued by pointing out what a huge burden had been placed on us after Robert Kennedy's assassination, when we suddenly had to protect all the candidates.

"You received this assignment in, oh, as I recall, three o'clock in the morning—you took up your posts of duty. You shifted your assignments. You left your families. You adapted yourselves to unprecedented demands, and as usual you carried out your job with quiet heroism and with the dedication for which you have become very famous."

And then he surprised Director Rowley by presenting him with the President's Award for Distinguished Federal Civilian Service—for more than thirty years of dedication. He had pointed out Rufus and me and a few others specifically, but I was glad he was acknowledging all the agents—for none of us did this job alone.

In closing, President Johnson added, "I did say to President Nixon the other day: 'You will have many problems. Of course, you will have a lot of friends when you come in. But the best friend you will have when you come in'and when you go out will be an organization—that will be the Secret Service of the United States.'"

At some point in late November, Rufus Youngblood requested a meeting with me at Secret Service Headquarters, which were then located at 1800 G Street N.W. He didn't give me any indication what the meeting was about, but I presumed it had something to do with the changeover from Johnson to Nixon.

When I arrived at his office, Assistant Director Lem Johns was also in the room, and after a few minutes of small talk they got down to business.

"Clint," Rufus said, "We need to discuss what your role will be when the new administration takes over. You have been an outstanding SAIC, and President Johnson says nothing but good things about how you've handled his detail."

"But," Lem Johns chimed in, "we think there could be some problems if you are assigned to Nixon."

Problems? A feeling of dread started to creep over me—the same sort of feeling I had had eight years earlier when I was sitting in Chief U. E. Baughman's office.

"What kinds of problems?" I asked.

"The fact of the matter is that you were close with the Kennedys and with Johnson," Rufus said. Then, breaking into a smile, he added, "And, well, Nixon hates both of them."

"I won't deny that," I said with a chuckle.

"We know you're a professional," Lem added, "but we have decided that Bob Taylor would be a better fit as Nixon's SAIC, since he was with Nixon when Nixon was VP during the Eisenhower administration, and Nixon trusts him."

"I agree," I said. It made sense. Bob Taylor had clashed with Johnson and had been moved off LBJ's detail into an administrative position, but he was a good agent with a lot of experience, and I knew he'd do a good job. *But where does that leave me?*

"So, Clint," Rufus said, "we want you to head up the Vice President's Detail."

The Vice Presidential Protective Detail—the VPPD—was obviously a demotion in status, and I also knew that previous SAICs of VPPD had been no higher than GS-15. I was already a GS-16. My mind was racing as I contemplated what this meant, and I realized that, in this moment, I had an opportunity to make some changes to the organization—changes that needed to be made—and from where I was sitting, I had some leverage.

"Okay," I said. "But I have some conditions."

"Sure," Lem said. "Tell us what you need."

"One," I said, holding up my right thumb, "I want to keep my GS-16 pay grade."

"No problem. We've already considered that," Lem replied.

"Two," I said, as I stuck out my index finger, "I want the detail expanded. More personnel." I was well aware that the agents on Vice President Humphrey's detail had had to work an inordinate amount of overtime because they didn't have enough manpower, and the agents were burned out.

"We can do that," Rufus said. "Tell us how many agents you want, and we'll make the necessary administrative changes."

"Three," I said as I added my middle finger to the count, "I want to pick the agents on my detail. I get first choice."

"Okay," Rufus said with a bit of hesitation. "I'm sure we can work that out."

Looking both men straight in the eyes, I added my ring finger. "Four—I want a dedicated physician to the vice president." As much as vice presidents have traveled in the past, I fully expected the new vice president would be no different, and I didn't want to be stuck in someplace like New Delhi or Montevideo with a sick or injured vice president and no doctor.

"That can be done. No problem," Lem replied.

I had saved the biggest request for last. But it was a deal breaker.

"And five," I said, my hand now fully opened, "I want a dedicated Air Force aircraft, exclusively for the vice president's use."

Rufus and Lem looked at each other. I could tell they had not anticipated this, but I wasn't going to back down. The guys on Humphrey's detail had told me how there had been many times when the vice president was going on an official trip and a plane had been authorized, only for them to get to the hangar and find out that President Johnson had denied the request. Not only was it humiliating for the vice president but it also left his staff and agents scrambling to find an alternative means of transportation. After four years of being on the president's detail, where an aircraft was always available, I wasn't about to be put in that predicament. If I was to be responsible for the protection of the vice president, I needed the tools to be able to do my job effectively.

"You're absolutely right, Clint," Rufus said. "The vice president needs to have a dedicated aircraft. We'll get it authorized."

We decided I would finish up with President Johnson through the holidays and begin the transition to Vice President–elect Spiro Agnew shortly before the Inauguration. It was undoubtedly a step down from being SAIC of the Presidential Protective Division, but knowing that I'd get to pick my own team and have a dedicated aircraft at our disposal, I wasn't as disappointed as I otherwise might have been. It wasn't for my personal benefit that I'd made the demands; it was because I'd seen how quickly things could change—how the vice president could become the president in a heartbeat—

and as the person first in line to the presidency, the vice president deserved proper security and respect befitting the responsibility.

PRESIDENT JOHNSON HAD been meeting with various members of President-elect Nixon's staff throughout the week, and on the evening of December 16, after the annual lighting of the national Christmas tree, he had scheduled a meeting with Vice President elect Agnew. I greeted Mr. Agnew and brought him to the Oval Office, where he and the president sat and talked for about an hour, before the president decided to take him upstairs to the residential quarters of the White House.

I was waiting at the elevator when they came down from the residence at 8:30 p.m. and walked with the two men to the South Portico.

After saying good-bye to Agnew, President Johnson turned to me and said, "Clint, let's go upstairs. I want to talk with you."

"Yes, sir," I said.

As we walked into the West Hall, he motioned for me to sit on one of the sofas, while he took a seat in a wing chair immediately next to me. Now, I had been upstairs in the residence a number of times, but this was the first time I had ever sat down alone with the President of the United States in the family's private quarters, and I had no idea what the president wanted to speak to me about.

"Clint," he said, "I'll be moving back home to the ranch next month, and I want to make sure I have people around me I can really trust."

He was looking me straight in the eyes, and as he continued he leaned forward in his chair, his arms resting on his knees.

"When you were assigned to me, I questioned whether I could trust you because of your previous assignments, but you have proven your loyalty."

"Thank you, Mr. President. That means a lot to me."

"Now, I know that many of the agents don't appreciate all the time we spend at the LBJ Ranch, but I have never once heard you complain about it, and in fact, I can tell you feel comfortable there."

Oh no. I hadn't seen this coming at all. Once again, President Lyndon Johnson was about to throw me a curveball.

"Wouldn't you enjoy spending some time away from the stress of Washington?" he asked. Without waiting for an answer he said, "I'd like you to move down to Texas and be in charge of my detail when we leave the White House. Would you consider that, Clint?"

I paused, not knowing what to say. I was truly flattered. But while I had learned to deal with his idiosyncrasies—had taken the poke of his finger to my chest more times than I could count after a cabinet meeting in which I had no idea what had been discussed, knowing that he just needed to vent to someone—and had become skilled at anticipating his movements, I could not imagine spending an indefinite number of years on the LBJ Ranch, driving around looking at cattle and taking guests on tours of his birthplace and boyhood home.

Finally, I said, "Thank you Mr. President, for the trust you have placed in me. I am honored you want me to run your detail." He knew the "but" was coming, and I daresay I saw a tinge of dejection in his eyes.

"But, Mr. President, I think it would be better for me to remain in Washington." And then, suppressing a smile, I added, "I don't think my career path runs along the banks of the Pedernales River."

His eyes crinkled, and he broke into a big grin. "Oh, I know. You just want to sit in some big office up here with a pretty secretary on your lap."

"Oh, I doubt that will be the case, Mr. President."

We both laughed—we really had become comfortable with each other, and nothing he said could shock me anymore—and then he stood up, a signal that our meeting was over, and said, "Let me know if you change your mind, Clint."

"Yes, sir," I said as I stood with him. "But I don't think that will happen, Mr. President." I wanted him to know that there would be no changing my mind so that he could move on and find someone more suitable for the job of running his detail.

"Good night, Clint," he said.

"Good night, Mr. President," I replied as I turned to walk toward the elevator.

"Oh, and Clint . . ."

"Yes, sir?" I turned back to see what he wanted.

"Thank you again. I meant everything I said."

• • •

JUST BEFORE CHRISTMAS President Johnson received word that the eighty-two crew members of the *Pueblo* who had been held captive in North Korea for eleven months were finally being released. And while the North Koreans refused to return the ship itself, the fact that the crew would be returning home to their families in time for the holidays was joyous news.

President and Mrs. Johnson decided to stay in Washington to celebrate their last Christmas in the White House. It was also a nice treat for all of us on the White House Detail to be able to spend at least part of the holiday at home with our families.

Two days later, I was on Air Force One with President and Mrs. Johnson, heading back to Texas for New Year's. It would be my last visit to the LBJ Ranch, and while I had grown fond of the Texas Hill Country over the past four years, as we went about the daily routine of driving from ranch to ranch, I knew that when I'd declined President Johnson's offer to head up his post-presidency detail, I'd made the right decision.

A Gallup poll taken at the end of the year asked the question *What man, living today in any part of the world, do you admire most?* Dwight Eisenhower was number one; Lyndon Johnson number two; Edward Kennedy came in third, and Rev. Billy Graham was fourth. Richard M. Nixon, the man who would in twenty days be inaugurated as the thirty-seventh President of the United States, came in fifth.

1968 would go down in history as one of our nation's most tumultuous years ever, and as we turned the calendar to 1969 there was a feeling of trepidation across America. Were our best days behind us? What lay ahead? Would we see an end to the Vietnam War? Could Richard Nixon save our country?

On January 10, I bid farewell to President Johnson. It was bittersweet, but I was looking forward to the challenges of the new administration with Richard Nixon and Spiro Agnew. And oh how challenging it would be.

PART FOUR

With Presidents Nixon and Ford

The presidential election of 1968 was like the year itself—unpredictable and scarred by violence. When Richard M. Nixon took office, America was a nation divided, with turbulence in our cities, ongoing protests against the Vietnam War, and still reeling from the assassinations of two more of our leaders. As president, Nixon's first priorities were to resolve the Vietnam situation; better our relations with the Soviet Union; and return American society to a civil and harmonious union.

President Nixon would have some major accomplishments and would be reelected in 1972 in a landslide victory in which he carried forty-nine of fifty states. Two years later, he would leave the Office of the President in disgrace, and the country that elected him in trauma.

Suddenly, Gerald R. Ford would become the most powerful man in the world, under such extraordinary circumstances that Americans were in utter disbelief that this could have happened in our country.

30

Vice President Spiro Agnew

After four years with President Johnson, protecting Spiro Agnew was a welcome change of pace. From the moment we met and had a chance to talk, we got along immediately, and unlike my inauspicious beginning with Johnson at the LBJ Ranch, I got the feeling Mr. Agnew was pleased to have me in charge of his detail. As I explained our procedures, he was very attentive and interested, and it was obvious the members of the Elect Detail who had been with him for the past few months had done an excellent job.

I had received everything asked for when accepting the position as SAIC of VPPD, and even though the changeover happened just ten days before the Inauguration, it went very smoothly. I chose my leadership team—John Simpson, Sam Sulliman, and Win Lawson—and we kept many of the same agents who had been on the VPPD Elect Detail as well as adding most of the agents who had been on the small detail protecting Vice President Humphrey, so we had an experienced team that jelled well from the beginning.

Born in Baltimore, Maryland, Spiro Theodore Agnew was of Greek descent and had an affable personality. Like Johnson, he was tall—standing about six feet two inches—and at fifty years of age he was quite energetic and athletic, preferring to take the stairs instead of an elevator whenever possible, which I considered good not only for him but for me and the other agents as well.

When Nixon chose him to be his running mate in August 1968, Agnew was relatively unknown to most Americans. Before taking on my assignment, I got a background file on him and learned that he had graduated from Johns Hopkins University and the Baltimore School of Law, and after being drafted into the Army served as an officer in World War II and the Korean War. He'd only gotten into politics in 1962, when he was elected Baltimore county executive; four years after that he was elected governor of Maryland.

In the wake of Martin Luther King's assassination in April 1968, Agnew had invited black civic and religious leaders to a meeting in Baltimore to discuss the riots and civil rights in general. The meeting failed, however, as Agnew could not withhold his contempt for the more militant leaders, calling them, in the first official style of name-calling for which he would soon become infamous, "circuit-riding, Hanoi-visiting, caterwauling, riot-inciting, burn-America-down type of leaders." Not surprisingly, the group walked out on him. Liberal critics felt Agnew had alienated the African American community that had turned out for him at the voting booths just two years before, but there were many who agreed with his opinion that too many pardons and concessions had been made to looters and arsonists during the riots. This news-making event brought Governor Agnew to the attention of the leadership in the Republican Party—especially Richard Nixon. Subsequently Agnew was selected as the running mate on the Republican presidential ticket in the fall of 1968, just two years after becoming governor.

During the campaign, Agnew came across as a stern disciplinarian father figure, a law-and-order type, but he also had a cringing habit of putting his foot in his mouth. The opposition and the press jumped on him for insensitive comments like "If you've seen one city slum, you've seen them all"; calling Polish Americans "Polacks"; and even referring to one Asian reporter as "a fat Jap." His gaffes were fodder for comedians, and the word "bumbling" often preceded his name in newspaper articles.

Agnew and his wife, Judy, had four children—two of whom were still living at home—and until January 7, they'd been living in the governor's residence in Annapolis, Maryland. The U.S. government did not provide a residence for the vice president—a practice I objected to, because the Secret Service had to secure each new vice president's residence at a significant cost—so when the Agnews came to Washington, they had to find a place to live. They ended up moving into a nine-room suite in the apartment section of the Sheraton Park Hotel in northwest Washington, and although the Sheraton Park was well accustomed to high-profile residents—Presidents Eisenhower and Herbert Hoover, Vice President Johnson, and Chief Justice Earl Warren had all lived there at one time or another—it was still a challenge to secure the portion of the hotel in which the Agnews were residing.

In the days leading up to the Inauguration, antiwar demonstrators were organizing to create disruptions, which gave us some cause for concern. On Sunday, January 19, a group of about five thousand marched down Pennsylvania Avenue in a "counterinaugural parade" wearing Nixon masks, holding up effigies, and carrying signs that labeled Nixon a criminal, just as we were bringing Vice President–elect Agnew to a reception in his honor at the History and Technology Museum. We got him in without incident, but a group of the protestors swarmed around the entrance jeering and throwing stones, bottles, and firecrackers as people arrived for the function. Fortunately, the mounted police were able to move the group away before anyone got hurt, but when the guests had to traipse through the grass to a different entrance, one woman snapped to a reporter, "The hippies have the sidewalk and the establishment has to walk in the mud."

THE SECURITY FOR Richard Nixon's Inauguration had been in the planning for months, but even with tens of thousands of law enforcement officers on the ground, undercover in the crowd, and observing from the air, those of us immediately surrounding the president and vice president knew anything could happen at any moment. In our job, every day was game day, but this—this was the Super Bowl, the final game of the World Cup, and the deciding inning of the World Series all wrapped into one.

The morning of January 20, 1969, we picked up Mr. and Mrs. Agnew at the Sheraton and drove them to the White House to join President and Mrs. Johnson, Vice President and Mrs. Humphrey, and President-elect Nixon and his wife, Pat, for coffee in the Red Room before going on to the U.S. Capitol for the swearing-in ceremony.

It was cold—not quite freezing, but almost—and dark gray clouds covered the sky, threatening rain. Still, hundreds of thousands of people had come to witness the pageantry and history of the transition of power from one president to the next. The trip from the White House to the Capitol was uneventful, and everything was moving smoothly and on schedule as the pomp and circumstance was about to begin.

Rows of tiered seats had been set up on the inauguration platform, on the east side of the Capitol behind the podium where Richard M. Nixon and Spiro T. Agnew would take the oaths of office. Each seat was numbered and assigned by long-standing tradition to members of the House and Senate, state govenors, the cabinet, special invited guests, and family members of the outgoing and incoming president and vice president. Several minutes before the ceremony was to begin, I walked out to the platform and down the steps to my assigned seat, five rows behind the podium on the center aisle, while Rufus Youngblood and SAIC Bob Taylor took their seats directly in front of me in the third and fourth rows. From this vantage point we had a clear view of the hundreds of thousands of people on the ground below, and would be within a step or two of our protectees, while several other agents were standing at strategic posts on the platform—all of us on high alert and ready to react in a heartbeat.

As the band struck up ruffles and flourishes and "Hail to the Chief," President Johnson made his way down the stairs to the front row—it was the last time he would hear these strains in his honor—followed shortly by Vice President Humphrey, and then Vice President–elect Agnew and President-elect Nixon, and the ceremony began. The moment Richard M. Nixon finished the oath of office—with his left hand on two leather-bound family Bibles, and his right hand up by his ear—uttering the words "so help me God," the transfer of power was complete.

As President Nixon stood at the podium and spoke to the crowd—and to the millions watching on television around the world—I must admit I did not pay much attention to what was being said, for my mind was focusing on the people, my eyes constantly scanning from back to front, from one side to the other, looking at hands and faces and body language for anyone who looked out of place, or who made a sudden unusual movement.

When the speech was over, there was a lunch in the Capitol, and then it was time for the parade.

Leading the Inaugural Parade was the brand-new fully armored presidential limousine, SS-800-X, with President and Mrs. Nixon riding in the backseat, waving from behind the bulletproof windows. Six agents surrounded the vehicle—four walking alongside and two standing on the rear footsteps—while two follow-up cars manned with more than a dozen more agents trailed a few feet behind.

I had a clear view of the president's vehicle from my position in the right front seat of the next vehicle in the parade—the limousine containing Vice President and Mrs. Agnew. As fate would have it, this was the same Lincoln limousine used in Dallas on November 22, 1963, but now renovated and armored, top enclosed, and painted black rather than midnight-blue—the same car I had walked alongside four years earlier during President Johnson's Inaugural Parade.

Three notable dates in history—two Inaugurations and one assassination—with three different presidents, and there I was, a part of each one, all in that same car: SS-100-X.

Thousands upon thousands of people lined the wide avenue between the Capitol and the presidential residence at number 1600, and for the most part it was a friendly, exuberant crowd, kept well under control by the unprecedented show of police and military security forces. As the motorcade started, I requested the driver of our car to leave a wider than usual gap between us and the cars ahead so that the president's vehicle would stand out more prominently, as well as to provide us more room to maneuver should the need arise.

Police from the District's Special Operations stood shoulder to shoulder, their backs to the motorcade, with billy clubs firmly in their hands at certain points along the route where protestors had gathered. All of a sudden there was a commotion in the crowd on the right-hand side of the street, and I saw some objects hurled toward the president's vehicle.

"Close the distance to Halfback," I instructed the driver. There was nowhere else for us to go, and I wanted to shorten the gap so we were a unified, compact group.

Up ahead there was a big sign in the crowd that said BILLIONAIRES PROFIT OFF G.I. BLOOD! and as we came near it, a beer can and a couple of rocks flew toward our car. The driver accelerated slightly, forcing the agents alongside into a run in order to stay in position, while the two agents on the back of the car grabbed for handholds to keep from falling into the street.

In the side-view mirror, I could see Agent Win Lawson struggling to maintain his balance while ducking from the incoming missiles as the car lurched forward. All of the agents maintained composure, as they'd been trained to, bravely guarding the occupants inside even as objects continued to be hurled.

The protestors were mostly concentrated in that one area, and once we moved past them, the people were again friendly and cheering. As we neared the glassed-in viewing stand in front of the White House from where the Nixons and Agnews would watch the rest of the parade, President and Mrs. Nixon suddenly emerged through the opening in the roof of the car. The crowd erupted into a thunderous cheer as their new president stood, waved, and then raised both arms up, filling himself with the adoration. I tensed, my eyes scanning the crowd while keeping him firmly in my sight, willing him to get back in the damn car.

I didn't know if he had done this spontaneously or if he'd asked the agents if it would be okay and they felt comfortable enough with the crowd and the security at this point to allow him, but in either case, his actions showed me that this president—like all the others I'd seen thus far—had an ego that needed to be stroked so badly that the man was willing to take calculated risks—risks that might cost him his life.

An armored limousine with bulletproof glass surrounded by Secret Service agents willing to risk their own lives becomes useless when the protectee stands up, exposing his head and body above the car roof. Fortunately, it worked out all right this time, and we got everyone into the viewing stand to watch the rest of the parade.

Two and a half hours later, the parade over, it was time to change into black tie for the evening round of Inaugural Balls. Six of them. We had to be careful of our timing at the balls because the plan was for the president and vice president to attend each one at different times, meeting at the last one for a grand joint appearance.

The top bands of the country performed at the various balls—Lionel Hampton, Sammy Kaye, Lester Lanin, Meyer Davis, Guy Lombardo, and

Duke Ellington—but the ballrooms were so jammed with people dressed in tuxedos and sparkly full-length evening gowns that it was difficult to move, much less dance. Still, Vice President and Mrs. Agnew were enjoying the festive mood, greeting old friends and donors who had helped bring them to this point as we made the rounds. It was early on the morning of January 21 when we finally tucked them into their Sheraton Park Hotel suite, while President and Mrs. Nixon went to their new home, the White House.

TRADITIONALLY, THE VICE president had offices in the U.S. Capitol and the Executive Office Building (EOB), located next to the White House, and that is where Mr. Agnew spent most of his time. My office, and the rest of my staff, was now in the EOB as well, and while I missed being in the center of the main activity, I quickly realized that the VPPD was going to be a lot less stressful than my previous jobs had been.

The vice president is automatically a member of the National Security Council, and also serves as president of the U.S. Senate, for which he is called on to vote only in the event of a Senate deadlock. Agnew took the job of presiding officer at the Senate quite seriously, and, lacking previous congressional experience, he studied with the Senate parliamentarian to make sure he knew the correct procedures. For the first few weeks of the Nixon administration, Agnew presided over the Senate almost every day it was in session—something that had not been the standard practice of preceding vice presidents—and it annoyed some of the senators—even those in his own party, because the Senate is a "closed club" and Agnew was an outsider. Over time he got the message and began to spend less and less time on the Hill.

In the first few months of his presidency, President Nixon focused on international issues and made a highly publicized trip to Europe to meet with his counterparts in Brussels, London, West Berlin, and Rome, as well as a stop in Vatican City to meet with the pope. Meanwhile, Vice President Agnew's schedule was filled with trips to New York City; Cincinnati and Toledo, Ohio; and Stuart, Florida, where he spoke to groups like the Women's National Republican Club and the Conference of Mayors, and handed out the winner's trophy at the Bob Hope Desert Classic golf tournament in Palm Springs.

President Nixon traveled on USAF 26000—the aircraft used by both Presidents Kennedy and Johnson, and on which I had traveled the world— but shortly after he took office, Nixon requested the interior be completely refurbished. Whereas President Johnson had established an open floor plan during his administration, President Nixon had the interior gutted and reconfigured into compartments. The largest section of the aircraft was a two-room suite for use by the president, his family, and invitees. The first room was a lounge area with a desk, easy chairs, and a sofa; and the second room—which Nixon used most frequently—had a desk, two single beds, and a couple of chairs. Directly behind the presidential suite was an area set up as work quarters for his staff, with desks and typewriters. There was a small compartment for the Secret Service in the front of the plane, while seating for additional staff, guests, and the media was aft of the presidential compartment. The new configuration gave President Nixon the privacy he desired.

Meanwhile, the dedicated aircraft the Air Force provided for the vice president's domestic travels was a Lockheed JetStar—known as Air Force Two as soon as the vice president was aboard. Much smaller and far less plush than the Boeing 707s in use by the president, the JetStar had a limited range, but it was fast and small enough to land on most runways, which made it ideal for short trips. Knowing we always had a plane available made life a lot easier for all of us.

From the first trip I went on with Agnew, I realized traveling with him was going to be an entirely different experience than I had been used to with Johnson. As soon as we were airborne and had leveled off, the vice president stood up, holding a deck of cards, and said, "Clint, do you play pinochle?"

"No, Mr. Vice President—sorry, I've never played pinochle before."

"How about gin rummy?"

I shook my head. "No. I guess I never had much time to play cards."

"Well, come on and I'll show you. We're going to be spending a lot of time together. Might as well have some fun along the way."

So that became the routine. Once airborne, the vice president would engage me or his doctor, Bill Voss, in a game of cards to pass the time, and then, just prior to landing, if he were scheduled to make a speech upon arrival, Agnew would go over the speech and make any notes or changes.

When we were in Washington, if the opportunity presented itself, the vice president would request we drive him to Little Italy in Baltimore for dinner at Sabatino's—his favorite restaurant. He loved this traditional, family-owned Italian restaurant, where he knew the owners would keep his visit quiet, so he could meet with friends and associates away from the glare of lights and cameras. We would take him in the back door and up some stairs to a private dining area. The privacy gave him the opportunity to really enjoy himself and relax.

On one occasion, as I was checking the restaurant before Agnew came in, I encountered Frank Sinatra.

"Good evening, Mr. Sinatra," I said. "I'm Clint Hill from the Secret Service. I used to talk with you by phone during the Kennedy administration."

He looked at me with a glimmer of recognition and then broke into a smile and said, "Yes, of course. Clint, great to see you. I wondered whatever happened to you."

"I'm still around. Doing the best I can," I said.

"Keep it up," he said with a nod. "You're one of the best."

It was certainly a nice compliment coming from one of America's favorite entertainers.

THE AGNEW FAMILY also enjoyed going to Ocean City, Maryland, where they would stay with their longtime friends Mr. and Mrs. Harry Dundore, and Agnew could play golf with friends and enjoy a sense of anonymity. I quickly learned that golfing was one of Vice President Agnew's favorite activities, and once again I found myself spending lots of time on the world's most picturesque golf courses—never playing, only observing—reminiscent of my days on President Eisenhower's detail.

On March 2, 1969, President Nixon was returning to Washington after his eight-day trip to Europe, and an official arrival ceremony had been planned at Andrews Air Force Base, with Vice President Agnew heading the welcoming delegation. The president wasn't scheduled to land until just before ten in the evening, and I thought it was strange that the White House had organized all this fuss when it would be well after dark. I could not recall Eisenhower, Kennedy, or Johnson ever having such a formal arrival ceremony in the United States at night. On top of the late hour, the weather was miserable. It had been blustery all day, with periods of sleeting rain as temperatures hovered around the freezing point, and after sunset it just got colder.

Everyone was bundled up in coats and scarves, trying to stay warm and dry, while the military troops were all lined up in formation awaiting the president's arrival. People cheered as Air Force One landed—it is a spectacular sight—and as soon as it came to a stop, the steps were moved to the doorway, and President Nixon emerged to more cheers and the band playing ruffles and flourishes, and "Hail to the Chief".

Vice President Agnew was waiting to greet President Nixon at the foot of the stairs, and after walking through a short reception line, Nixon and Agnew walked together to inspect the troops. I was following Agnew, a few paces behind, when all of a sudden, as he turned at the end of the row, his feet hit a spot of ice and down he went—face-first. I jumped toward him, trying to avoid slipping myself.

"Mr. Vice President, are you okay?"

He moved to sit up, and I saw that his face was covered in blood.

His nose was badly cut and scraped, but his pride was hurt more than anything else. I helped him get up and called for the doctor. Dr. Voss wiped the cut with antiseptic, but the only first-aid material he had was a bandage about four inches square. After the large white bandage was applied to the vice president's nose, Agnew looked like a penguin with the bandage as his beak. The press had a field day with it, and although Nixon still made the headlines, Agnew's stumble and the photo of him with that bloody bandage on his nose stole some of the president's thunder.

Shortly after the 1969 Inauguration, Nixon decided that instead of going to church, he would hold nonsectarian Sunday services in the White House. Whenever a president attends church, he argued, it is extremely disruptive to the congregation with all the media attention and security precautions that must be taken. Raised a Quaker, Nixon was deeply religious, and he used the services to encourage Americans to attend church and to remind members of his own administration that "we feel God's presence here, and that we seek his guidance here." He would invite cabinet members, Supreme

Court justices, Diplomatic Corps members, congressmen, business leaders, military officials, ambassadors, and friends—sometimes having as many as three hundred in attendance. A wide variety of clergy from different faiths would conduct the services—people like Billy Graham, Norman Vincent Peale, and Terence Cardinal Cooke—and getting an invitation to a White House Sunday service soon became something of a status symbol. There was some complaining about the White House being used as a church, but most Americans praised the services, asserting that they testified to Nixon's faith. We in the Secret Service were pleased that the president and his family didn't need to leave the safe confines of the White House.

ON FRIDAY, MARCH 28, 1969, we were informed that seventy-eight-year-old former president General Dwight D. Eisenhower had died at Walter Reed Army Hospital. Although his death did not come as a shock, considering his age and history of heart problems—the first heart attack in 1955 in Denver, and four more in a five-month period in 1968—still, a sense of loss and mourning swept across America. I was saddened to learn that this great American, the military hero who became president and became one of America's greatest ambassadors, had succumbed to his failing heart. He had suffered so much with heart disease, and it had finally taken him. I had such fond memories of my time with President Eisenhower: seeing how beloved he was and how graciously he accepted the applause and accolades of his adoring fans as we traveled around the world; observing him playing golf, shooting quail, and fishing for trout, and how much enjoyment those activities brought him. I had such a personal connection, having been in the Secret Service office in Denver where Mrs. Eisenhower's mother lived and where the Eisenhowers spent a great deal of time. I recalled those many nights I spent at the Doud residence, reading from President Eisenhower's vast collection of Western novels to pass the time. I respected him, as did all the agents, and we tried to make his time as president safe and secure, enabling him to do his job. I had the satisfaction of knowing we accomplished that for him and the Office of the President.

President and Mrs. Nixon went to Walter Reed immediately after re-

ceiving word of his death to visit Mrs. Eisenhower, and preparations for
the state funeral got under way. It would be another major security undertaking for the Secret Service, because President Nixon, Vice President
Agnew, former President Johnson, and Mamie Eisenhower would all be
participating. It was an even larger problem for the U.S. State Department
Diplomatic Security unit, whose responsibility at that time was the protection of foreign heads of state. Many were coming to pay their respects to this
international hero.

President Eisenhower's body was taken to the Gawler funeral home and,
on Saturday, March 29, to the Washington National Cathedral for a brief
prayer service in the Bethlehem Chapel, attended by family and close friends.
I was there with Vice President Agnew and watched solemnly as Mamie
Doud Eisenhower—Ike's wife for fifty-two years—led the tight-knit Eisenhower family into the chapel. Upon conclusion of the private prayer service,
the public was then admitted to pass by the flag-draped casket at a rate of
approximately one thousand per hour. The following day the body was taken
in a procession to the Capitol to lie in state.

All of this ceremony brought back the still vivid memories of those four
days in November 1963, just five years earlier: the funeral procession with
the president's casket on a horse-drawn gun caisson; a riderless horse with
boots in the stirrups, reversed; the slow cadence of the marching military
band. And there I was, once again, standing in the Rotunda with the President of the United States, the vice president, and members of Congress with
the flag-draped casket of a former president in the center of the room directly under the Capitol dome. "Hail to the Chief" played at a very slow
tempo, the military honor guard, the eulogies—all reminiscent of President
Kennedy's funeral.

IN 1961, PRESIDENT Kennedy had initiated legislation that gave the Vice
President of the United States the role of chairing the National Aeronautics
and Space Council (NASC). Lyndon Johnson—vice president at the time—
had been deeply involved with the space program during his time in the
Senate, so it seemed appropriate, while also giving the space program the

high-level attention Kennedy thought it should have. When Johnson was president, I accompanied him to the NASA Manned Spacecraft Center in Houston, where we got briefings and demonstrations with some of the astronauts training for the missions, and saw the Apollo space suit the astronauts would wear.

Now Vice President Agnew had the role of chairing the NASC, and lucky for me, it just happened to be during what was one of the most exciting times in those early days of space exploration.

The first launch I attended with Vice President Agnew was Apollo 9 in early March 1969. It was the first test of a crewed lunar module orbiting the Earth, and as we watched the fiery rocket launch from the control center at Cape Kennedy, it was both breathtaking and nerve-racking. Just two years earlier, in January 1967, I had attended the funerals of two of the three astronauts who had been killed when fire swept through the command module on the launchpad during a preflight test. Launching a manned spaceship was anything but routine.

The Apollo 9 mission was successful, and all three men returned safely. Two months later, we were back at Cape Kennedy for the launch of Apollo 10. This would be the dress rehearsal for the Apollo 11 landing on the moon.

Vice President Agnew had been invited to have dinner with the astronauts—Tom Stafford, Eugene Cernan, and John Young—in the astronauts' quarters the night before the launch, and our advance agent, Johnny Guy, had arranged for me to be a guest as well. I was one of a very small number of people in attendance, and it was an honor I will never forget.

The Apollo 10 mission was successful, and the Apollo 11 launch was scheduled for July 16 that same year. Several weeks prior to the launch, astronauts Neil Armstrong, Mike Collins, and Buzz Aldrin invited President Nixon to dine with them the night before the launch, just as Vice President Agnew had with the Apollo 10 crew, and President Nixon happily accepted. Shortly thereafter, word leaked to the press that one of the NASA physicians was extremely upset by President Nixon's plans to have dinner with the astronauts the night before this critical mission because he might be carrying germs that could affect their health during the flight. There was a lot of discussion, and in the end President Nixon decided to cancel his attendance at the dinner because, if there were any medical issues, he sure as hell didn't want to be blamed for them. Instead, he telephoned them as they were having dinner and sent a telegram that said:

ON THE EVE OF YOUR EPIC MISSION, I WANT YOU TO KNOW
THAT MY HOPES AND MY PRAYERS——AND THOSE OF ALL
AMERICANS——ARE WITH YOU . . . IT IS NOW YOUR MOMENT.

An estimated one million people had gathered in the Cape Kennedy area to view the launch, and the rest of the world would be watching on live television. Once again, I was with Vice President Agnew, and this time we watched from an outdoor viewing area that was set up for five hundred special guests that included heads of state from around the world. Former President Johnson and his wife, Lady Bird, had come to view the launch, along with President Johnson's press secretary, Tom Johnson. We all sat together in the bleachers, squinting into the morning sun as the powerful Saturn V rocket blasted off in fiery brilliance with the three astronauts inside the Apollo 11 module at its tip. The ground shook with the thunderous roar of the liftoff as the world held its collective breath. It was spectacular. Even though I was there on duty, I was thrilled to be present—another historic occasion I was privileged to witness.

Four days later, the entire world watched together, through the magic of television and the remarkable advances made as a result of the space program, as Neil Armstrong stepped onto the surface of the moon and uttered those humble yet profound words, "One small step for man, one giant leap for mankind."

From the Oval Office, President Nixon spoke to the astronauts 250,000 miles away by telephone.

"I can't tell you how proud we all are of what you have done for every American. This has to be the proudest day of our lives. . . . For one priceless moment in the history of man, all of the people on this earth are truly one."

After speaking to the astronauts, President Nixon called President Johnson at the LBJ Ranch and reportedly said, "I thought we ought to share this great moment."

I couldn't help but think how elated President Kennedy would have been to see this day. Eight years earlier, just four months into his presidency, Kennedy had stood before a joint session of Congress, and in a stirring speech filled with passion and substance requested an enormous increase in funding for the space program.

"I believe that this nation should commit itself to achieving the goal, before this decade is out, of landing a man on the moon and returning him safely to the Earth," he said. "No single space project in this period will be more impressive to mankind, or more important for the long-range exploration of space; and none will be so difficult or expensive to accomplish."

There had been much skepticism and criticism—how could we put so many resources into the unknown when millions of Americans were living in poverty? Yet his vision inspired an entire industry as scientists, engineers, test pilots, medical researchers, and businesspeople embraced the challenge to beat the Soviets to the moon.

I had to believe that President Kennedy was right there with Neil Armstrong as he stepped onto the surface of the moon, and he was proud. We had made it to the moon. Now, we had to return the men safely back to earth.

President Nixon had planned an international trip to the Pacific and Southeast Asia, which he and his staff managed to coordinate with the return of the Apollo 11 astronauts. After first stopping in San Francisco—during which he and his wife, Pat, made a spur-of-the-moment decision to ride a slow-moving cable car up and down the steep city streets—Nixon flew on Air Force One to Johnston Island in the mid-Pacific, which put him in position to helicopter to the USS *Arlington*, a communications cruiser. From there he took another helicopter flight to the USS *Hornet*, which was the recovery ship for the astronauts. President Nixon watched as the module splashed down into the ocean at 6:50 a.m. on July 24, and when the capsule was brought aboard the *Hornet*, Nixon had the opportunity to speak to Armstrong, Aldrin, and Collins as he peered through a sealed glass window into their isolated protective chamber.

"Boy, what a moment! Great! Great!" he exclaimed. "This is the greatest week in the history of the world since Creation."

President Nixon had wanted to do something dramatic in conjunction with the moon landing, but it was not without criticism. The telephone call from the Oval Office—which was broadcast on live television—was an unexpected technical issue the astronauts had to deal with in the midst of worries about fuel and oxygen, and space officials later admitted they would have preferred not to have had this additional problem.

The *New York Times* bitterly criticized Nixon's attempts to "cash in" on the moon landing and wrote in an editorial that it was only an "accident of the calendar" that put President Nixon in position to view the realization of the efforts of his two predecessors—Presidents Kennedy and Johnson.

"President Nixon has had the least responsibility for the massive program," the *Times* said, and his "attempt to share the stage with the three brave men of Apollo 11 when they attain the moon appears to us rather unseemly."

AFTER MEETING THE astronauts, Nixon embarked on his trip to Asia, stopping first in Guam, where he held an informal press conference. There had been speculation that the president would likely make a surprise visit to Vietnam, although it was not on the schedule, and Nixon addressed that by saying, "There are no changes in the schedule to announce. I have no present plans to go to Vietnam."

When a reporter asked about the future of the United States and its military relationships in Asia, Nixon answered, "I believe that the time has come when the United States, in our relations with all of our Asian friends, be quite emphatic on two points: One, that we will keep our treaty commitments— our treaty commitments, for example, with Thailand under SEATO; but, two, that as far as the problems of internal security are concerned, as far as the problems of military defense, except for the threat of a major power involving nuclear weapons, that the United States is going to encourage and has a right to expect that this problem will be increasingly handled by, and the responsibility for it taken by, the Asian nations themselves."

This was the crux of the message he was going to give to the leaders of the countries he visited on this trip: We, the United States, will support you, but you must fight your own battles in protecting your homeland. No more Vietnams. This would become the basis of the "Nixon Doctrine."

The next day, having been joined by Mrs. Nixon in Guam, the president flew on to Manila, the first stop on this multination tour. The armored presidential limousine SS-800-X had been flown to Manila and was being used for the arrival motorcade. Enthusiastic crowds lined the parade route, waving American flags. The reception was so warm and friendly that Nixon requested the sliding section of the roof be opened.

During the motorcade, about half a million people viewed the president as he stood and waved, exposed from the chest to the top of his head, along the five-mile motorcade route to the Malacañang Palace, as the agents jogged anxiously alongside.

The next day, it was reported that several hours before Nixon arrived, a man was killed in a gun battle with police near the Intercontinental Hotel, where Nixon was scheduled to speak. A homemade .22-caliber pistol, a smoke grenade, and a rough pencil sketch of the ground floor of the hotel were found on the body of the man. There was no concrete evidence of an assassination plot, but police said "you could surmise that."

Meanwhile I was in Seattle with Vice President Agnew, who was attending the Western Governors' Conference and voicing Nixon's position on the Vietnam War. When I saw the photo of Nixon standing out of the car and read about the scene in the newspapers, all I could do was shake my head.

PRESIDENT NIXON FLEW from Manila to Jakarta, Indonesia, where he met a smaller-than-expected but enthusiastic crowd upon arrival and had a meeting with President Suharto to emphasize the Nixon Doctrine. From there he flew to Bangkok.

This was the jumping-off point to go to South Vietnam. On July 30, 1969, Nixon made an unannounced visit to Tan Son Nhut Air Base and helicoptered to the Independence Palace in Saigon to confer with President Nguyen Van Thieu about the new U.S. policy and the withdrawal of American troops from Vietnam. The visit lasted five and a half hours.

After short stops in New Delhi and Lahore, India, Air Force One landed in Bucharest, Romania. It was the first time a U.S. president had ever made a state visit to a Communist capital, and the stakes were high. Nixon was hoping the visit would lead to East-West breakthroughs without provoking the Soviet Union.

Romania's president Nicolae Ceauşescu had invited President Nixon, and the government had assured a large turnout by letting workers cut short their Saturday half day of labor. Close to a million people lined the twelve-mile parade route, cheering, waving Romanian and American flags, and shouting "Hoo-rah! Nix-on, Nix-on!"

The two presidents rode in the host country limousine—an open-top Mercedes convertible—waving back to the thunderous crowd nearly the entire way. It was the largest, most exuberant reception he received on the entire trip, and by the end of the twenty-seven-hour visit, he and Ceauşescu were arm in arm.

Nixon's trip concluded with a stop in Great Britain to meet with Prime Minister Harold Wilson before returning to Andrews Air Force Base late on Sunday night, August 3, where once again I was there with Vice President Agnew for the formal arrival ceremony in, as luck would have it, a torrential downpour.

Throughout the president's trip, I devoured the news reports and watched the television coverage with mixed feelings. In the seven months I had been with Vice President Agnew, we had developed a very good relationship. He was extremely respectful to our team of agents, and he trusted us to the point that if we made a recommendation or told him not to do something, he complied without question. President Nixon, on the other hand, was much more distrustful of the agents, and clearly he was taking risks that flew in the face of Secret Service recommendations.

Still, even with the stress and anxiety that came with being on the president's detail, I couldn't help but be jealous of the guys who were there. That's where the action was, and that's where I wanted to be.

SPIRO AGNEW, HAVING been born and raised in Baltimore, was a huge fan of the Baltimore Colts football team. As we were heading into the fall of 1969, Vice President Agnew's assistant Art Sohmer and his advance man J. Roy Goodearle came to me one day and asked if I had any concerns about taking the vice president to a professional football game.

"I don't see any problem with that," I said. "As long as we have plenty of time to advance the situation. We'll just make sure we have agents strategically placed."

With my nod of approval that it wouldn't be a security problem, they sat down with Agnew, and as they went through the hundreds of events for which he had received invitations to speak, any event in a locale that happened to coincide with the Colts' schedule got priority.

We watched the Los Angeles Rams beat the Colts in Baltimore, and the next week we saw another crushing loss to the Minnesota Vikings in Minneapolis. But as the season went on, Don Shula's team gained momentum. And so it was that I happened to see thirty-six-year-old Colts quarterback Johnny Unitas set a National Football League record with sixteen straight pass completions in a victory over the New Orleans Saints at Tulane Stadium—in a game that, by chance, was the same weekend the vice president had agreed to speak at a Republican fund-raiser in New Orleans.

As we were flying to New Orleans, playing a game of cards, Agnew asked me, "Clint, have you ever been to Brennan's?"

"Brennan's?" I asked. "Doesn't sound familiar."

"Oh my God," he said with a look of astonishment. "The best shrimp creole you have ever eaten in your entire life."

I accompanied Vice President Agnew to Brennan's restaurant in New Orleans, where they knew what he wanted when he walked in the door—a double order of shrimp creole. That's where Spiro Agnew introduced me to Cajun food, and I've loved it ever since.

It was around this time that Vice President Agnew started garnering a lot of attention for his rather unique choices of words during some of his speeches—speeches he was urged to make on behalf of the administration so President Nixon could remain above the fray. Spiro Agnew was a good speaker, and along with the talents of speechwriters William Safire, Pat Buchanan, and Cynthia Rosenwald, he came up with some memorable lines that really caught people's attention as he went on the offensive against Nixon's detractors. It all started that weekend in New Orleans.

Anti–Vietnam War sentiment had continued to escalate, and on October 15, on college campuses and city streets across the nation, one million Americans—most of them students and people in their twenties—staged the largest protest against the war to date, calling it Moratorium Day. More than 20,000 marchers descended on New York's Bryant Park; 15,000 in Philadelphia; 10,000 in Minneapolis; 15,000 in Cambridge, Massachusetts; and over 20,000 in Washington, D.C.

Agnew was disgusted by the demonstrators. In his speech at the fundraiser in New Orleans, he said, "Education is being redefined at the demand of the uneducated to suit the ideas of the uneducated. The student now goes to college to proclaim rather than to learn. The lessons of the past are ignored and obliterated in a contemporary antagonism known as 'The Generation Gap.' A spirit of national masochism prevails, encouraged by an effete core of impudent snobs who characterize themselves as intellectuals."

On November 3, President Nixon addressed the nation in a live television broadcast in which he explained, in basic terms, the complexities of the Vietnam War he had inherited and his plan for peace. He gave a name to those who were not speaking out against the war—"the great silent majority" and asked for their support. In the hours and days following the speech, telegrams and letters of support poured into the White House by the tens of thousands. The response from the public was overwhelmingly positive. But the television news networks and newspaper editorials were lukewarm at best. The speechwriters went to work.

On November 13, in a speech in Des Moines, Iowa, Vice President Agnew castigated the national news media and challenged people to stand up to the powerful news outlets like the *Washington Post* and the *New York Times*.

"In the United States today," he said, "we have more than our share of nattering nabobs of negativism. They have formed their own 4-H club—the hopeless, hysterical, hypochondriacs of history."

After that speech, Agnew began to develop something of a cultlike following, and the media had a field day. People could hardly wait to hear what was going to come out of his mouth next. No longer did anyone ask "Spiro who?"

In the late fall of 1969, I was consulted about the vice president making a trip to the South Pacific and Southeast Asia, with stops in Hawaii, Guam, the Philippines, Vietnam, Taiwan, Thailand, Nepal, Afghanistan, Malaysia, Singapore, Indonesia, Australia, New Zealand, and a return stop again in

Hawaii. We decided a pre-advance trip needed to be done, so a team was put together with me representing the Secret Service, along with a representative each from the military aide's office, WHCA, the vice president's staff, and press advance. The State Department would be represented in each location by the ambassador.

We departed Andrews Air Force Base on an Air Force 707 and stopped at each location except Vietnam. That part of the trip was kept secret for security reasons. It was a quick, exhausting survey trip, but we had few difficulties. When we returned to the United States we submitted our report and recommendations. Our biggest concerns were, not surprisingly, the anti-American factions against the U.S. role in Vietnam, but we believed we could provide adequate security for the vice president.

As a result of the pre-survey, the official trip was sanctioned, so my staff and I put together the necessary advance teams, and they were dispatched immediately. The twenty-six-day trip would begin the day after Christmas 1969 and would encompass 37,000 miles to eleven countries plus Guam and Hawaii, returning to Washington on January 19, 1970.

It would be my third time visiting the region during the Vietnam War, and I knew anti-American sentiment had only grown more fervent. Fortunately, because of my demand for more agents on the Vice President's Detail, we had a terrific team already in place that worked extremely well together, and most important, we had a very good relationship with Vice President Agnew. I had confidence that we could keep Agnew safe, but I also knew that we couldn't possibly predict what might happen. One thing I didn't anticipate was having my name appear on the front page of the newspapers again, with the words "bomb" and "assassination" in the headlines.

31

Beware Greeks Bearing Gifts

The purpose of the vice president's trip to Southeast Asia was to further the Nixon Doctrine—urging Asian nations to develop economic balance and self-sufficiency without relying on the United States to bail them out—but at the same time reassuring Asian leaders that the United States intended to stand by its treaty obligations. In addition to the typical staff and press people on the trip, Vice President Agnew had invited Apollo 10 astronauts Eugene Cernan and Tom Stafford, and their wives, to join him. As head of the space program, Agnew and his wife, Judy, had become good friends with some of the astronauts and their wives—several times we had taken the vice president to backyard barbecues at the Cernans' home—and it was thought that bringing the astronauts along would add some star power to the trip.

On a personal level, I was fortunate to be able to spend quite a bit of time with both Cernan and Stafford on this extended trip, and it was truly an honor and a privilege.

We departed from Andrews Air Force Base on December 26, 1969, and, after a refueling stop at Travis Air Force Base, headed to Hawaii for an overnight stay, then on to Guam, finally landing in Manila, Philippines, on Monday, December 29. The trip coincided with the inauguration of Philippine president Ferdinand Marcos, who had recently been reelected for a second term. There was a large contingency of detractors who despised Marcos's connection to the United States, however, and there had already been a number of threats to Marcos's life. Vice President Agnew's planned attendance at the inauguration only added fuel to the fire.

I had vivid memories of the last time I was in Manila with President Eisenhower in June 1960, when four million people lined the motorcade route and nearly overwhelmed us with their exuberance. President Eisenhower was a hero to the Phillippine people, and America was held in the highest esteem. Now, less than a decade later, the world had changed dramatically. Anti-American protestors had come to be expected almost everywhere we went—be it in the United States or abroad. And just six months earlier, in this same city, a potential assassination attempt on President Nixon had been thwarted. Everyone was on the highest alert.

The advance agent did an excellent job of keeping the airport crowd restricted to a few hundred people, and after Agnew made a brief statement, we got into the prepositioned cars and headed to the presidential Malacañang Palace, where the vice president and his party would be staying. The crowds were relatively small, with hundreds of Phillippine police and security agents out in force.

We had time for just a brief rest and a change of clothes before it was time to go to the evening event—a formal reception in honor of Vice President Agnew at the U.S. Embassy. Meanwhile, a group of about one hundred protestors had gathered outside the embassy and were awaiting the vice president's arrival.

It was a two-mile drive between the palace and the embassy, and I rode in my standard position—in the right front passenger seat—with Vice President Agnew directly behind me in the rear of the car. We had insisted on closed-top cars—no convertibles—and knowing Agnew as well as I did, I was not concerned that he might try something like Nixon had.

As we got closer to the embassy, we could hear chanting: "Agnew go home! Go home!" and soon we came upon the crowd, many of them carrying signs that said: AGNEW GO HOME—YOU'RE NOT WELCOME HERE! and AGNEW—CROCODILE OF THE U.S.

Just as we approached the embassy gate, I heard an explosive noise that came from behind. My head whipped around toward the noise, and I saw a plume of white smoke about fifteen feet behind our car.

"Get inside, fast!" I said to the driver. At the same time, the agents in the follow-up car jumped out and surrounded our car and ran alongside until we got inside the embassy gate.

It turned out to be what they called a Molotov "bomb"—a glass bottle filled with powdered explosive material (as opposed to a Molotov "cocktail," which contains liquid explosives)—and while it had given us a jolt, even if it had hit the car, it would not have caused significant damage. The vice president was unfazed, and fortunately no one was hurt. But most of all, I was pleased with the way our agents had handled the situation.

The U.S. press made it seem like a much bigger deal than it actually was, with headlines like: "Agnew Eludes Assassins at Manila Inauguration" and "Filipino Hurls Bomb at Agnew's Auto."

Some of the articles—written by reporters who knew me well—mentioned me by name: "Secret Service agent Clint Hill sat in front of Agnew. Hill, in charge of U.S. security for the Agnew visit, is the man who jumped on the convertible of President John F. Kennedy when he was assassinated in Dallas in 1963."

I certainly didn't want any publicity, and I hoped this incident was not indicative of what we could expect for the rest of the trip.

The security at President Marcos's inauguration was extremely tight and well executed. There were five thousand people in the crowd, and when Vice President Agnew was introduced, there was polite clapping. Moments later, Apollo 10 astronaut Eugene Cernan was presented to the crowd, and the place erupted with a thunderous roar of applause, whistles, and cheers.

That turned out to be the case everywhere we went. Cernan was with us on the first leg of the trip, and Stafford would join us a few days later; and every time they appeared, they were a big hit. The astronauts had brought trunks full of gifts along with them—unique gifts straight from space. For each country's leader, slivers of moon rock were encased in plastic bubbles mounted on wooden stands that contained the recipient country's flag. They'd also present a photo of the country taken from space, and each time it was given, Cernan would quip, "If you look closely, you can see your house." The leaders loved it. No doubt about it, the astronauts were major diplomatic assets.

• • •

As the calendar turned from the 1960s to the 1970s and people around the world were celebrating with champagne and kisses, I was on Air Force Two, headed to Saigon, South Vietnam, with Vice President Agnew. While en route, we received the weekly casualty report: in the last week of 1969, 86 Americans had been killed and 557 wounded. That number pushed us over a sobering milestone—in the past ten years that the United States had been involved in the Vietnam conflict, 40,000 Americans had died. It was hard to fathom. One could only hope that Nixon's plan would get us the hell out of this mess.

On arrival at Tan Son Nhut Air Base, Vice President Agnew immediately boarded a helicopter and we flew to meet with President Thieu at Independence Palace. From there we were scheduled to fly by helicopter thirty-seven miles northwest to Firebase Kien—the first gun base operated jointly by U.S. and South Vietnamese troops under President Nixon's "Vietnamization" plan as part of the Nixon Doctrine. But while the vice president was meeting with Thieu, I received information that there had been sniper fire in the area around the base. I gathered as much information as I could, and when Agnew came out of the meeting, I pulled him aside.

"Mr. Vice President, we have substantiated reports of sniper fire near Firebase Kien, where we were planning to go next. Now, I am not too concerned, but I wanted to make sure you are fully aware of the situation. Do you want to proceed as scheduled?"

"I'll leave it up to you, Clint," he said. "If you think we can go, let's go."

"Yes, sir. Let's play it by ear. I'll stay on top of the situation, and if we need to turn back at the last minute, we can do that." That was typical of my relationship with Agnew. He trusted my judgment and never questioned my decisions.

We went ahead as planned, and fortunately didn't run into any trouble. Agnew remained upbeat, and he clearly enjoyed talking with the servicemen.

"People back home are pretty darned proud of you and what you're doing over here," he said to one group. "Don't be misled by what you might read in some publications. It just doesn't reflect the feeling of the American people about the job that's being done by American fighting men in Vietnam."

The young men, in general, seemed in high spirits, but at one point as the vice president was shaking hands with a group of GIs, one of them looked at him earnestly and asked, "Mr. Vice President, when will we be going home?"

I took a deep breath and squinted, looking away, as I waited to hear how the vice president would answer. How many had asked the same question— if not directly, in their minds or in their prayers? Forty thousand of them hadn't come home. I didn't want to think how many of these soldiers would die here too.

Agnew didn't try to lie to the young man. He looked him directly in the eye and said, "I hope for your sake you'll be out soon. But I don't know what soon means." The soldier nodded, and the vice president moved on down the line.

We stayed for just fifty minutes and then flew to Fire Base Patton, where Agnew told the troops of the 25th Infantry Division, "I hope this year is the end of this."

Meanwhile, President Nixon had flown to his coastal residence in San Clemente, California, to spend a quiet New Year's Eve with his family, followed by a two-week working vacation at the Western White House. Four thousand people had been waiting in the rain for hours to greet him at the El Toro Marine Corps Air Station. For nearly fifteen minutes, he and Mrs. Nixon shook hands with an exuberant crowd, and when a reporter asked him what his hopes were for the New Year, he said, confidently, "I expect peace in Vietnam before another Christmas."

In the past ten years, four presidents had tried to find a way to resolve the situation peacefully and with honor. None had struggled more than President Johnson. But now President Nixon was in the hot seat, and the eyes of the world were on him.

THE REST OF our trip through Asia went well, without any major incidents. From Taipei to Bangkok and on to Nepal, moon rocks were handed out at every stop, and the astronauts continued to be immensely popular.

From Nepal we flew in a propeller-driven DC-6 to Kabul, Afghanistan. This was a nostalgic moment for me, as I remembered arriving at the same airport in 1959 with President Eisenhower on his multination tour, driving on the same roadway past similar crowds of Afghan people in turbans and bright-colored robes. The airport and roadways built with the aid and assistance of the Soviets. There was a smattering of anti-American, antiwar demonstrators—one held up a sign that said: STOP KILLING VIETNAM PEOPLE—but very few. Everything looked the same as it did in 1959, with the exception of a new Intercontinental Hotel—a plush oasis in the center of rather primitive surroundings.

From the cool remoteness of Kabul we flew three thousand miles to tropical Kuala Lumpur, Malaysia. It was nighttime as Air Force Two descended into the modern, prosperous Malaysian capital, and with the tall buildings all lit up, it seemed like we had passed through a time warp from Nepal and Afghanistan.

We had recognized during the pre-survey trip that security in Kuala Lumpur would need to be extremely well planned and orchestrated in light of some strong anti-American sentiment there. In the days leading up to the vice president's arrival, left-wing political groups circulated pamphlets attacking Agnew's visit and U.S. policy in Vietnam. Some of the language was very harsh, demanding revenge for the death of a Chinese man shot during anti-American protests when President Johnson visited in 1966. Additionally, riots between the Malay and Chinese factions had been ongoing for the previous seven months, and 1,200 citizens had been killed.

Throughout the trip, I had been pleased with the security arrangements made by the advance agents, and in Kuala Lumpur once again they had done an outstanding job. The sixteen-mile motorcade into the city was well secured, with armed military personnel lining the route and helicopters flying surveillance and cover overhead as we drove from the airport to the Merlin Hotel.

The official activities started early the next morning and included a visit to the Malaysian Rubber Institute for a tour. The vice president's attempt to slice open a rubber tree to watch the oozing of the latex failed, but astronaut Tom Stafford, who had joined the trip in Nepal, was successful, much to the amusement and pleasure of the Malaysian officials. Agnew appeared to be getting upstaged by the astronauts at every turn, but he didn't seem to mind a bit. He had a great sense of humor, and he knew how much their presence had added to the success of the trip.

From Kuala Lumpur it was on to Singapore for a relatively relaxing one-night stay that included a round of golf with the prime minister, and then to the Indonesian isle of Bali.

During the advance, we realized that everyone would be exhausted by this point in the trip, and, as it turned out, we were. We had scheduled a stop in Bali as an unofficial visit for rest and recuperation purposes—having just visited eight countries in eleven nights—before heading to Australia and New Zealand. The only problem was that it was the weekend of Super Bowl IV—the Kansas City Chiefs vs. the Minnesota Vikings—and there was no coverage in Bali, which was disappointing to the vice president.

On Tuesday, January 13, we left the tropical paradise and had an easy five-and-a-half-hour flight to Canberra, Australia. Prime Minister John Gorton and officials of the Australian government were there to meet the vice president on arrival, as well as a small group of very vocal antiwar demonstrators. We skirted around them with no problems and then drove directly to the Australian War Memorial. Apparently word had gotten out that we would be there, and there were upward of three hundred people surrounding the monument, many of them holding signs that said: AGNEW IS A DIRTY FASCIST PIG, BEWARE OF GIFT BEARING GREEKS, and MOON ROCKS AND MURDER.

As we got out of the car, the agents and I stayed close to Vice President and Mrs. Agnew, who tried to ignore the chanted slurs as they walked into the courtyard of the elegant white stone monument building. The vice president placed a wreath on the tomb and seemed quietly contemplative as he spent some time reading some of the names of those who had been killed in various wars. When we came out of the monument, Vice President and Mrs. Agnew waved to the crowd—which responded with a chorus of both boos and cheers. Suddenly, a small group started throwing tomatoes, and we rushed to get into the cars before anyone was hit by a splattering red mess.

That evening a dinner was held at the prime minister's residence, and we were receiving reports that antiwar groups were bringing in busloads of demonstrators from Sydney, Melbourne, and Adelaide for a protest the next day at Parliament House during the time Agnew was scheduled for a cabinet luncheon meeting there. Fortunately, only about two hundred showed up. They shouted "Go home, you murderer!" at the vice president and "Go home, CIA!" at the agents working the outer perimeter—lots of people confuse the Secret Service with the Central Intelligence Agency, but we are two distinctly different organizations. Vice President Agnew's response to these protests was usually to smile and wave—acting like it didn't faze him a bit— but after a while, I would think that anyone would get tired of being called such terrible names on a regular basis.

We faced similar protests in New Zealand two days later. Large numbers of protestors battled with police near the Intercontinental Hotel in Auckland, shouting and waving signs with creative messages like WE IM- PUDENT SNOBS ARE FOR PEACE, but we managed to get into the hotel without incident. I was informed early the next morning that a man who appeared to be emotionally disturbed had entered the hotel overnight and threatened to kill Vice President Agnew. He was swiftly arrested and taken into custody.

The next day we got a respite from the ever-present protestors as we flew by helicopter across the lush countryside, landing near a town called Whatawhata in the Waikato region, where the Agnews toured sheep, cattle, and stud horse farms. The bucolic reprieve was much appreciated by all of us but short-lived, for the protestors were back in force that evening outside the hotel, chanting "One, two, three, four, kick Agnew, end the war!" as the Agnews attended a state dinner.

The angry mobs and the arduous country-hopping schedule had taken a toll on the entire vice presidential party, and the next day, as we took off in Air Force Two and headed back to the United States, everyone breathed a sigh of relief.

It was always a good feeling when we landed on American soil after a foreign trip, but landing in Honolulu, where they greet you with garlands of flowers, was especially nice. It was the perfect way to start a few days of rest before returning to Washington. The only appointment on the vice president's schedule was a Sunday-morning meeting with Admiral John McCain, Commander in Chief, U.S. Forces Pacific (CINCPAC).

When we got the Agnews checked into the Kahala Hilton near Diamond Head, I discovered that Arnold Palmer and his wife were also guests, and I had an idea.

"Mr. Vice President," I said, "we've learned that Arnold Palmer is staying here this weekend. Would you be interested in playing a round of golf with him if I could arrange it?"

Agnew looked at me with wide eyes. "Of course I'd be interested, Clint. The question is, would he want to play with me?"

"Well, I know he enjoyed playing with President Eisenhower—I got to know him a little bit during my days with Ike—and I'd be happy to make the introduction."

"Wow, Clint," Agnew said. "Sure. That would be a great opportunity."

I contacted Mr. Palmer, and he said he'd be honored to play with the vice president, so a golf game between the two was arranged. They got along so well that Palmer and his wife and the Agnews ended up having dinner together as well.

Despite the consistent protests, the trip had been very successful overall, but to end it with a golf game between the vice president and one of his golf idols was a nice final note.

SHORTLY BEFORE WE had embarked on the Asian trip, I had been advised that when we returned, I was being promoted to Deputy Assistant Director of Protective Forces (DAD-PF), and my office would move to Secret Service headquarters. I had very mixed emotions about this promotion. I recognized it was an acknowledgment of my work, but I was enjoying my position as SAIC of VPPD, and I hated to leave. The Vice President's Detail was like a family. We worked well together, relied on each other for support, and trusted each other implicitly.

During the year I had been with Vice President Agnew, I had seen him go from "Who is Agnew?" to being number three on the Gallup poll's most admired list—just behind President Richard M. Nixon and the Reverend Billy Graham. It seemed people either loved him or despised him.

At the time, Mickey Mouse watches had become very popular, and there was a joke going around that Mickey Mouse wore a Spiro Agnew watch. A creative entrepreneur manufactured watches modeled after the Mickey Mouse watch that had a caricature of Spiro Agnew on the face, with his arms spinning around pointing to the time with red-gloved hands permanently affixed in a "V" sign. The Spiro Agnew watches were hugely popular, and I just happen to have one.

For me personally, I got along very well with Vice President Agnew and his wife, Judy. They were genuinely kind, fun-loving, and family-oriented, and they treated all the agents with a great deal of respect.

That weekend in Hawaii, I tried to stay out of everyone's way, letting my assistant, Sam Sulliman—who would be taking over as SAIC—and his deputy, John Simpson, begin to take charge. I spent most of the time sitting on the balcony of my hotel room overlooking the beautiful waves crashing onto Waikiki Beach, trying not to think about the past, yet wondering what a future behind a desk might hold.

32

A Visit from Elvis

When I reported to Secret Service headquarters at 1800 G Street N.W., Washington, D.C., I was given an office within the Assistant Director/Protective Forces Suite on the eighth floor. It was windowless and measured about eight feet by ten feet. For the first time since I began my career in the Secret Service, I was deskbound. Although the paperwork and continuous workload of my new position gave me plenty to do and kept me busy, sitting there in that enclosed space also gave me plenty of time to think. And the thoughts that started creeping back into my mind were the memories of 1963 and that dreadful day in Dallas.

From the time I left Mrs. Kennedy and went back on the White House Detail with President Johnson there hadn't been time to think about anything but the job, and I had somehow managed to put the vivid memories of the assassination out of my mind. It seemed the more physically active I was, the less I thought about it. Now, instead of being constantly on the move, I was sitting at a desk, figuring out budgets and making recommendations on personnel.

After being on the road and away from home more than 90 percent of the time, now I was able to sleep in my own bed and be home for dinner with my family. But, as it turned out, and was to be expected, my wife and sons had developed a routine without me, so I frequently stayed late at the office.

In my new position, I was answering requests from the various protective divisions to better enable their security capability—requests for manpower, both permanent and temporary; equipment requests; and requests for increased training. Since 1963, the Secret Service had, little by little, become responsible for protecting a much larger group of people—both as directed by Congress and also by presidential decree—and yet Congress had not always provided funding to hire the number of agents required to effectively handle the job. When President Kennedy was assassinated in 1963, the Secret Service had the responsibility of protecting the president and his family and the vice president— and we had fewer than fifty agents to do the job around the clock. Less than nine years later, when I started as the deputy assistant director, the Secret Service had been reorganized, and now we had agents assigned to the Presidential Protective Division (PPD); Vice Presidential Protective Division (VPPD); Johnson Protective Division (JPD); Kennedy Protective Division (KPD); Eisenhower Protective Division (EPD); Truman Protective Division (TPD), and the Protective Support Division (PSD). These were just the protective divisions of the Secret Service. The criminal investigation, intelligence gathering, and technical divisions had all expanded as well.

At the time, I was the only agent in the Secret Service who had the experience of being SAIC of PPD and VPPD—as well as having been the SAIC of the First Lady's Detail and then of the KPD—so I had a good understanding of what was needed. I knew that when requests were being made, it was because the agents were concerned about their ability to protect these individuals under the circumstances. In addition we had personnel and equipment in San Clemente, California, and Key Biscayne, Florida—at the personal residences of President Nixon—and having spent so much time at the LBJ Ranch with President Johnson and at the various residences of the Kennedys, I was well aware of the vast resources required to keep those properties secured.

The Office of Protective Forces also had the responsibility for planning and developing new equipment—including armored vehicles. That took a great deal of time and coordination with the PPD and the Office of the President. We were interested in the protection provided by the vehicle. The Office of the President was interested in aesthetics and maximum exposure of the president to the public. One major problem was that we had to have the cooperation of the president, whoever was the occupant of the office. Sometimes our procedures and their desires were in conflict, which created difficult situations. We did not want the president to have the opportunity to place himself in a dangerous situation—like the ability to stand up out of the roof of a car—making the security situation worse than it already was. Somehow it seemed a president's ego—or the overriding goal of an overzealous staff—resulted in a constant battle to thwart our efforts. I've often said, politics and protection are like oil and water.

In late January 1970, PPD notified my office that President Nixon would be going by train to Philadelphia to attend a concert by the Philadelphia Symphony Orchestra and to present to its music director, Eugene Ormandy, the Medal of Freedom. Normally, the president would take a trip to Philadelphia from Washington by helicopter or plane. In 1962, President Kennedy had flown to Philadelphia by helicopter but returned to Washington from Philadelphia by train, after having attended the Army-Navy football game. I suppose that's where President Nixon got the idea.

President Nixon was at Camp David on the morning of January 24, the day of his train excursion, which would have made the trip much less complicated if he had traveled by helicopter. Instead, he flew by helicopter back to the White House, boarded a train at Union Station, and traveled to the Thirtieth Street Station in Philadelphia, returning to Washington by train that night. It involved more people, disrupting some normal business operations and causing inconvenience to many people, and created more risk than necessary.

We advised against it. The president and his staff overruled.

ONE OF THE larger divisions under the supervision in the Office of Protective Forces was the White House Police (now known as the Uniformed Division), which at the time had about 250 men. Unlike the Secret Service agents on protective details, who typically dressed in business-type suits, the White House Police wore uniforms similar to those of police officers, complete with badge and cap. Fortunately for me, fellow agent Vince Mroz had the responsibility of overseeing that group, and I didn't have to deal with the fiasco that was about to occur.

Apparently when President Nixon had visited Europe earlier in 1969, he and some of his staff were impressed by the ornate uniforms worn by security officers at state residences, and upon returning they made a request for the White House Police to design, and have manufactured, uniforms of similar appearance. Within a few weeks of my arrival at headquarters, Prime Minister Harold Wilson of Great Britain came to the White House on an official state visit, and it was on this occasion that the new White House Police uniforms were unveiled.

The new uniforms consisted of black trousers and a white long-sleeved jacket with two columns of gold buttons—spaced evenly from each shoulder to the waist—and two buttons at the collarbone just below the stand-up collar. Gold braid accented the bottom of the sleeves just above the wrists, and an additional double length of gold braid looped from the right shoulder to the chest, ending in dangling tassels. Combined with the pointed, gold-trimmed cap with a black vinyl brim, the uniforms made the officers look like they belonged to a college marching band.

They were ridiculous.

It wasn't my place to comment on the uniforms, but as it turned out I didn't have to say a word. The press didn't hold back. Reporters said the police looked like "old-time movie ushers," and "extras from a Lithuanian movie," some even going so far as to call them "Nazi uniforms" for "Nixon's Palace Guard."

Chicago Tribune columnist Walter Trohan, a Nixon friend, wrote that the uniforms belonged onstage, calling them "frank borrowing from decadent European monarchies, which is abhorrent to this country's democratic tradition." They had become a national joke. Fortunately, President Nixon heard the message loud and clear, and it was the one and only time those uniforms were worn by the White House Police.

A few months later, a recommendation was made to enlarge the size of the White House Police force and increase its responsibilities within the Secret Service. It would grow from 250 men to 850, and in addition to protecting the executive mansion and its grounds, it would also be responsible for the protection of foreign missions within the District of Columbia; any building in which presidential offices were located; and foreign missions located in such areas of the United States, its territories, and possessions as the president, on a case-by-case basis, might direct. With these increased roles, the name of the division was changed from the White House Police to the Executive Protective Service (EPS).

• • •

AT THIS POINT in Nixon's administration, despite the large antiwar contingent among youth, polls showed that more than 60 percent of the American people approved of the job President Nixon was doing. Still, Nixon believed the press was part of the antiestablishment, and he was always grumbling about how they didn't treat him fairly.

Every year there was a white-tie dinner at the Gridiron Club—an elite dining club consisting of the fifty most prominent newspapermen in Washington—and since its inception in 1895, every president except Grover Cleveland had spoken at this annual event. Throughout the dinner, in between the courses of soup, salad, entrée, and dessert—along with, of course, plentiful cocktails and wine—there would be satirical skits and humorous remarks by politicians to keep the audience entertained. The unspoken rule for the many reporters at the dinner was that what went on at this once-a-year event would not be read about in the papers the next morning. But on March 17, 1970, the members of the Gridiron Club saw a show that none of them would ever forget, and which was so newsworthy that the rule was momentarily broken.

At the end of the dinner, everyone toasted President Nixon, who was in attendance, and it was expected that he would stand up at his table and say a few cleverly written remarks. Instead, the lights went dark, and when they came on again, President Nixon and Vice President Agnew were standing together on stage, under a spotlight. For the next ten minutes they bantered back and forth in a comedy routine that had Spiro Agnew answering meekly to President Nixon's demands—playing the yes-man the press made him out to be. And then the curtain rose behind them, revealing two upright pianos. The president sat down at one and the vice president at the other, and they began to play dueling pianos in which Nixon would start a song and Agnew would chime in, but then, invariably, Agnew would start playing "Dixie." Nixon would get a stern look on his face and begin a new tune. They had the audience roaring with laughter.

Finally, they began playing "God Bless America" in unison, and the roomful of hard-to-impress newsies and politicians rose to their feet in a standing ovation. I don't think any president and vice president before or since have ever given a performance that could top that.

THE ANTIESTABLISHMENT ATTITUDE in the country continued to grow exponentially, and as the United States became more deeply entrenched in Vietnam, the demonstrations and protests grew too. Respect for authority diminished. Government and its officials became the enemy.

On April 29, 1970, President Nixon went on national TV and announced he had authorized U.S. troops to enter Cambodia. This set off a new round of antiwar protests at colleges and universities across the country. On May 4, 1970, after two days of large protests at Kent State University in Ohio, during which an ROTC building was set ablaze, state and local officials called for the National Guard to maintain order. Some eight hundred National Guardsmen arrived, and as they surrounded a group of about five hundred students in a campus yard, some of the students started throwing rocks and harassing the troops. Several of the Guardsmen opened fire and ended up killing four students and seriously wounding a dozen more.

The people of the United States were stunned.

We in the Secret Service were concerned that the tragic killings could spark a backlash against the government, and we fully expected bigger and more violent confrontations. We were most worried about the president and vice president because they were often out in public, and it was the positions they took on policy matters that antagonized the protestors. Former President Johnson was also of concern, because it was during his administration that the Vietnam situation escalated. We notified every protective division and the Executive Protective Service to be even more vigilant than ever. Reevaluated the various strength levels. Made sure that everyone was provided the latest intelligence and all were on high alert.

The shock over Kent State had turned to anger, and we learned that a large antiwar demonstration was now planned for the weekend of May 8–10 in Washington. I was involved in multiple meetings with local and federal law enforcement agencies, as well as the military, about how we could prepare for what was expected to be hundreds of thousands of highly emotional, passionate, and potentially violent protestors in close proximity to the White House.

It was decided to ring the White House with buses—parking them bumper-to-bumper—to prevent any intrusion into the White House complex. Federal troops were assigned to various government buildings but were instructed to remain out of sight unless needed. We even had military units positioned inside the Executive Office Building poised to protect the White House complex. A twenty-four-hour command center was established in the EOB to monitor the situation, manned by members of the Secret Service and the EPS, with direct telephone lines to the Metropolitan Police command center. With President Nixon the center of the protestors' anger, we were not taking any chances when it came to protecting the president and the White House.

On the morning of May 9, 1970, I left my home and went directly to the command center in the EOB. Just as I arrived, the midnight–8:00 a.m. shift of the president's detail walked in from the White House.

Agent P. Hamilton "Ham" Brown was one of the agents with whom I had worked closely since the Kennedy administration, and he looked mad as hell.

"What's going on, Ham?" I asked.

"You are not going to believe this one, Clint," he said. "We've just come back from having breakfast at the Mayflower Hotel."

"What?" I asked incredulously. I knew there hadn't been an official function planned this morning. *Why would the president suddenly decide to go out for breakfast?*

As Ham proceeded to tell me the shocking details of what had occurred over the past few hours, he proved to be right; I could hardly believe what I was hearing.

"It all started around four thirty this morning, when President Nixon called and asked for a car," Ham said.

"At 4:30 in the morning?" I interrupted. "Where the hell did he need to go at that hour?"

Ham looked at me and said, "The Lincoln Memorial."

"Oh shit," I said. That was completely outside the security perimeter we had established, and right in the area where many of the demonstrators were spending the night.

"Yup. He wanted to go and have a little discussion with the youngsters," Ham said. "He had Manolo with him"—Manolo Sanchez was Nixon's long-time valet—"and Doctor Tkach"—Dr. Walter Tkach, the president's official physician—"and everyone was trying to talk him out of it, but he insisted."

"Go on," I said.

"So we took him to the Lincoln Memorial, and of course there were kids all over the damn place. He gets out of the car and starts climbing the steps, and points out the carved inscriptions on the wall to Manolo, and by this time a bunch of kids realize it's him and they start gathering around. So what does he do? He sits down on the steps, right in the middle of a bunch of 'em. Asking where they are from. Turns out they're college kids from Syracuse. So he starts talking about the damn football team."

Ham was really getting worked up, and his use of profanity increased as the commentary went on. "The kids aren't here protesting the damn football team!" he exclaimed. "So then he starts rambling on about Winston Churchill, and he's trying to explain what we're doing in Vietnam, but he's making no sense at all, and the kids are just looking at him in disbelief. By this time there's about fifty goddamn kids around, so I finally said, 'Mr. President, we should get back to the White House. Let's get back in the car.'" Ham looked at me. "Well, I'm sure you know how well that went over."

I rolled my eyes, shaking my head. President Nixon did not take kindly to the Secret Service telling him what to do.

"He tells the kids how he remembers what it was like to be their age, and he finally stands up and we get him back into the car."

"And then he wants to have breakfast at the Mayflower?" I asked.

"Oh no, no, no," Ham said. "Now he wants to go to the Capitol. He wants to show Manolo his old stomping grounds in the Senate."

"Oh, for God's sake," I said. I thought I had seen everything with LBJ, but this was really over the top. And the more I heard, the angrier I got. We had taken extraordinary precautions to keep the president and his family safe within the confines of the White House complex, and here the president himself had circumvented the security plan on a whim. It boggled the mind.

By this point, Ham said, a couple of Nixon's aides had shown up and were following in a separate car. When they got to the Capitol, the Senate doors were locked, so they went to see his old House of Representatives seat, but that door was also locked.

A member of the cleaning staff happened to be there and allowed the president into the chamber as Manolo and the agents followed. SAIC Bob Taylor had now arrived on scene and joined the group. Nixon found the seat he had occupied as a House member, then ordered Manolo to go sit in the speaker's chair and deliver a speech. Manolo reluctantly complied. Finally, they persuaded the president to leave and return to the cars. By this point, senior Nixon White House staff members Haldeman, Chapin, and Ziegler had arrived. No one could convince the president to return to the White House—and now he was hungry and wanted to have breakfast at a restaurant. They found that the Mayflower Hotel on Connecticut Avenue, four blocks north of the White House, was open, so the whole entourage went in to have breakfast.

"Then," Ham continued, "he's finished his eggs and hash. He's happy as can be. Now, he wants to walk back to the White House."

"You have got to be kidding," I said. But he wasn't.

Fortunately, they were able to convince the president that that was a very bad idea; they got him into the car and finally back inside the security perimeter. The agents on the detail were, of course, relieved that nothing had happened to the man they were sworn to protect, but all of us were disgusted with the attitude of the president for placing himself in such a vulnerable position.

That day, some 100,000 demonstrators marched through the streets of the nation's capital, some of whom had experienced a one-on-one confrontation with the man whose policies they were here demonstrating against. It was just one more example of the unpredictable situations that develop in presidential protection.

In September 1970 I received a call from agent Bill Berkshire of the VPPD.

"Mr. Hill," he said, "I am in Minot, North Dakota, doing the advance for the vice president's visit. The vice president asked me to contact you because he remembered that your mother lives in Minot and he would like to pay her a visit."

This came as a complete surprise to me, but I thought it was very nice of Vice President Agnew to think of it. What a thrill for my mother to be paid a visit by the Vice President of the United States.

"Let me check on her status and get back to you," I said. "But let the vice president know I hope we can make it work out."

Several years after my father died, my mother had sold our house in Washburn and had moved to Minot to be closer to some of her other relatives, but she now lived in a very small apartment. I was concerned that she wouldn't feel comfortable entertaining the vice president there. One of my cousins, Olga Froeming, and her husband owned a nice home in Minot, and they had a close relationship with my mother, so I gave Olga a call.

"Olga, this is Clint," I said when she answered.

"Oh, Clinton!" she exclaimed. "How are you? It's wonderful to hear from you."

"Thank you, Olga. Listen, I'm calling from Washington, and I've just learned that Vice President Agnew is going to visit Minot and he would like to stop by and see my mother. You know she lives in a very small apartment, and I am wondering if it would be possible for her to be at your home to receive the vice president there?"

"That would be fine, Clinton. Anything you want is fine with us. You know we are all so proud of you."

"Well, thank you, Olga. I wish I could be there. It's been a long time. I sure miss all of you, and I miss North Dakota."

The vice president did go see my mother at the Froeming residence and spent considerable time there, with photos being taken by the local newspaper.

It was a lasting, memorable occasion for my mother and an honor for me to have the Vice President of the United States single out my mom and take the time to visit her while he was busy campaigning.

WE IN THE Office of Protective Forces had been having a discussion over the previous few months about how to improve the Secret Service. One idea that had been floated was employing female officers or agents. Most major cities throughout the United States had female officers within their police ranks, and we had finally realized that females could be tremendous assets to our organization as well. I was involved in a few of the discussions and made the point that when I was with Mrs. Kennedy, it would have been beneficial to have had a female agent working with me.

In September 1970, the first female officer was sworn in to the Executive Protective Service. Six additional women soon followed. It was my intention to push to make some of these female officers full-fledged agents, but I realized I couldn't push too hard. This was a 105-year-old male-dominated organization, and I had seen that change worked best when it was introduced gradually.

The election of 1970 was fast approaching, with many gubernatorial and congressional seats on the line. It appeared the Republicans might be in difficulty partly because of the war in Vietnam, so Nixon decided to do some campaigning all across the United States in an effort to bolster their chances. He campaigned vigorously during the three-week period leading up to the November 3 election, canvassing twenty-two states and hitting big cities like Newark, Kansas City, and Baltimore, and smaller towns like Grand Forks, North Dakota; and colleges like Ohio State and East Tennessee State. In Miami Beach, facing a vocal group of demonstrators at the speech site, he said, "I have news for you. They are not the majority of young Americans, and they will not be the leaders of the future of America."

He had large, responsive crowds in Rochester, Minnesota, and when he heard their cheers, President Nixon decided to climb on top of a car so his adoring fans could see him better.

It had been just seven years since the assassination of President Kennedy, but at times it seemed like everyone had forgotten. Every time I saw a photo like this in the newspaper, my stomach knotted up. A firecracker exploded in my head, my heart raced, and then, the image that never disappeared.

ON OCTOBER 29, 1970, Nixon flew from Omaha to San Jose, California, and was confronted with a large, vociferous, obscenity-shouting crowd of demonstrators as he spoke at a rally in the Civic Auditorium with Governor Ronald Reagan. The antiwar protestors had attempted to force their way into the auditorium but were kept out by security personnel. I was at head-quarters at the time, but when the agents returned they gave me the details of what had happened.

"When he left the auditorium," one of the agents told me, "the president climbed up on the limousine and thrust his arms skyward, making the 'V' sign with his fingers. He was clearly taunting the protestors, and they reacted."

The crowd began throwing rocks, eggs, and bottles. They surged into the street, making it difficult for the vehicles following the president to leave. A few people, including a newsman, cameraman, and an agent, were injured, but fortunately the injuries were minor.

I just couldn't fathom what made a person behave in this way. To this day, I don't understand the ego that must drive someone to risk his life and those of others for a few moments of adoration. Yet the violence in San Jose gave the president great fodder for his speeches over the next few days in Phoenix, Albuquerque, Las Vegas, and Salt Lake City.

"The terrorists of the far left would like nothing better than to make the President of the United States a prisoner in the White House," Nixon said to a group of supporters. "Let me set them straight. As long as I am president, no band of violent thugs is going to keep me from going out and speaking with the American people."

He added, "It is nonsense to suggest violent dissent is caused by the Vietnam War, police repression, or poverty. There is no romantic ideal involved. Let's recognize them for what they are—not romantic revolutionaries but the same thugs and hoodlums that have always plagued good people." People cheered as he railed against the "terrorists" who had the nerve to harass him as they did.

"Those who carry a peace sign in one hand and a bomb or brick in the other are super-hypocrites!" he shouted.

Campaigning in Chicago, Vice President Agnew echoed the president's line: "The only way to sweep that garbage of demonstrators out of society is the election of tough law-and-order candidates."

The election was held on Tuesday, November 3. Nixon voted in San Clemente, California, and Agnew in Baltimore, Maryland. When the results came in, they showed that in the House of Representatives the Republicans had lost twelve seats, while in the Senate the Democrats had lost three seats but still remained in control, 54 to 44, with one Conservative Party member and one Independent party member. The governorships ended up with a gain of eleven for the Democrats. It appeared that the intense campaigning by both Nixon and Agnew had been futile.

IN EARLY DECEMBER I was summoned to Director James J. Rowley's office. He said he had an urgent matter to discuss with me. Even though I had worked my way up the ranks of the Secret Service and Rowley and I had a mutual respect for each other, whenever the director wanted to see me, I couldn't help but wonder what I might have done wrong. When I walked into the director's office, though, he immediately made me feel comfortable and gestured for me to take a seat.

"Clint, have you ever heard of the Federal Executive Institute?"

"Yes," I said. "But to be honest, I really don't know exactly what it is."

"It's a program that provides executive and management training for federal government employees—a stepping-stone to additional responsibility and a higher position in government service."

I wondered why he was talking to me about this. I had just been promoted from SAIC to the deputy assistant director position within the past year.

"The next class begins January 3, 1971, and we have selected you to attend. You have been doing an excellent job, Clint, and we think this will further enhance your career."

I was stunned and didn't know quite what to say. Finally, I said, "Thank you, Mr. Director."

As I walked out of Rowley's office, I wondered what they had in mind in terms of my career. Before becoming the deputy assistant director, I had attended a four-week executive seminar in Kings Point, New York, and there wasn't much further I could go in the Secret Service. It had been ten years since I entered that same office, back when U. E. Baughman was the chief, fearful of being fired, only to be given the assignment to protect Mrs. Jacqueline Kennedy. The world had changed completely, and so had I.

• • •

ON DECEMBER 21, 1970, I was sitting in my office when my secretary, Eileen Walsh, came to the door.

"Mr. Hill," she said. "You won't believe the information I just received."

"What's that?"

Eileen started laughing. "Elvis Presley just showed up at the Northwest Gate, unannounced, requesting to meet with the president."

"You gotta be kidding me. Was it really him?"

"Apparently so. He dropped off a six-page, handwritten letter complete with all his contact information while he's here in Washington."

Sure enough, it was the real Elvis. His letter, written on American Airlines stationery—back when they used to hand out things like that in First Class—read as follows:

Dear Mr. President

First I would like to introduce myself. I am Elvis Presley and I admire you and have Great Respect for your office. I talked to Vice President Agnew in Palm Springs 3 weeks ago and expressed my concern for our country. The Drug Culture, the Hippie Elements, the SDS, the Black Panthers, etc do not consider me as their enemy or as they call it, the Establishment. I call it America and I love it. Sir, I can and will be of any service that I can to help the country out. I have no concern or motive other than helping the country out. So I wish not to be given a title or an appointed position, I can and will do more good if I were made a Federal Agent at Large, and I will help best by doing it my way through my communications with people of all ages. First and foremost I am an entertainer, but all I need is the Federal Credentials. I am on the plane with Sen. George Murphy and we have been discussing the problems that our country is faced with. So I am staying at the Washington hotel Room 505-506-507. I have 2 men who work with me by the name of Jerry Schilling and Sonny West. I am registered under the name of Jon Burrows. I will be here for as

long as it takes to get the credentials of a Federal Agent. I
have done an in depth study of Drug Abuse and Communist
Brainwashing Techniques and I am right in the middle of
the whole thing. Where I can and will do the most good I
am glad to help just so long as it is kept very Private. You
can have your staff or whomever call me anytime today
tonight or tomorrow. I was nominated this coming year as
one of America's Ten Most Outstanding Young Men. That
will be in January 18 in My Home Town of Memphis,
Tenn. I am sending you the short autobiography about
myself so you can better understand this approach. I would
love to meet you just to say hello if you're not to busy.

Respectfully,
Elvis Presley

P.S. I believe that you Sir were one of the Top Ten Out-
standing Men of America also.

The White House Police took the letter to presidential assistant Egil "Bud" Krogh, and after some back-and-forth with Haldeman, a meeting for 12:30 p.m. that same day was arranged. The thirty-five-year-old entertainer showed up in a purple velvet suit and presented President Nixon with a World War II Colt .45 pistol encased in a wooden chest, as well as some autographed photos of himself, while the president's staff arranged to give Elvis an Honorary Federal Bureau of Narcotics and Dangerous Drugs Agent badge, and that seemed to satisfy him.

As 1970 ended, I wondered what the next year would bring. I had just settled into my job as deputy assistant director, and now I would be gone for two months while attending the Federal Executive Institute in Charlottesville, Virginia. I was concerned about being out of the loop for that length of time.

A lot could happen in eight short weeks.

33

1971

The Federal Executive Institute (FEI) had been established in 1968 during the Johnson administration in an effort to provide leadership and managerial training to the top executives in the federal government. The campus was very close to the University of Virginia in Charlottesville, and although it was just a two-and-a-half-hour drive from downtown Washington, the beautiful retreat set amid the rolling hills of Albemarle County was a world away from the political bubble.

I reported to the FEI on Sunday, January 3, 1971, with about thirty other attendees from various federal agencies. We were housed, ate, slept, and socialized within the confines of the institute, listening to lectures and seminars on a wide variety of topics, following up with discussions in which we described our organizations and the specific challenges we encountered. It was interesting, but I missed the camaraderie of my fellow agents, and being so far removed from the day-to-day activity of the White House made me uneasy. Back then there was no Internet, no cell phones, and I knew that the little information I gathered from the newspapers was never the whole story. I was glad when the training was finished, and as soon as I received my certificate of completion on Friday, February 26, I headed straight to my office in Washington, eager to find out what had happened while I was away at school.

The new armored limo program was in process, with some haggling over the roof of the vehicle. The president's office wanted a hole in the roof so the president could stand and be seen, similar to the one in the 1968 model. We were against it, but in the end the White House staff prevailed, and a sliding panel became part of the roof configuration. It certainly was not in the best interests of security.

During my private conversations with fellow headquarters personnel, the most interesting information I learned was that a taping system had been installed in various locations, at the president's request, to capture conversations. Previous administrations had also taped conversations and telephone calls, but what was surprising was how elaborate this system was, and especially the fact that most of it was voice activated. That was new. I was one of very few people who knew about the taping system, and, as with all types of similar privileged information, it was kept very private, limited to people on a need-to-know basis only.

I also learned that while I was away at the FEI, Jacqueline Kennedy—now referred to as Mrs. Onassis—Caroline, and John had attended a private dinner with President and Mrs. Nixon in the upstairs residence of the White House on February 3. Artist Aaron Shikler had completed a full-length portrait of Mrs. Kennedy, and the Nixons had invited Mrs. Kennedy and the children to see the painting as soon as it was hung in the White House, before it was made available for public viewing.

While I was away, a transition in the secretary of the treasury had also occurred. Back in December, President Nixon had announced that David Kennedy would be resigning the post and John B. Connally, former governor of Texas and a Democrat, would be taking over in February. At that time, the Secret Service was a part of the U.S. Treasury Department, so this put Governor Connally—who had been wounded while riding in the motorcade with President Kennedy on November 22, 1963—in the position of approving the budgets for the Secret Service.

WHEN I RETURNED to work at Secret Service headquarters on Monday morning, March 1, I was told by my supervisor, Assistant Director Lilburn E. "Pat" Boggs, not to get too comfortable, because we were leaving for New York City. President Georges Pompidou of France was visiting the United States, and while in Chicago the previous day, ten thousand pro-Israel demonstrators had shown up to speak out against France's policies in the Middle

East. Mrs. Pompidou had been spat upon, and President Pompidou had threatened to cut his trip short due to the inhospitable environment.

President Nixon was thoroughly embarrassed by the way Pompidou had been treated in Chicago, so he ordered the Secret Service to get to New York—Pompidou's next stop—immediately to evaluate the security arrangements provided by the Department of State. Assistant Director Boggs, Assistant Director of Investigations Burrill Peterson, and I flew to New York and observed the operation around President Pompidou. It was our opinion that the protective coverage provided for the president of France—and presumably it was the same for all visiting heads of state—was ineffective and needed to be strengthened.

The aftermath of the incident led Congress to authorize the U.S. Secret Service to take over responsibility for the protection of visiting heads of state and other distinguished foreign visitors to the United States, as well as being required to protect representatives of the United States performing special missions abroad at the president's direction. All of a sudden our protective responsibility had increased dramatically, without an increase in budget or manpower. We were told simply to absorb the new responsibilities.

That same morning, March 1, I learned that an explosive device had been detonated at 12:30 a.m. on the ground floor of the Capitol on the Senate side. No injuries had occurred, but walls on the west front appeared to have cracked.

President Nixon, who had flown to Des Moines, Iowa, to address the state legislature, called the bombing "totally deplorable—it was a shocking act of violence which will outrage all Americans."

But later, when asked again about the bombing, he had changed his tune. "We get these warnings all the time," he said. "Tourists going through the White House could drop a bomb in a receptacle and the place would blow, but those are the risks you take to have an open society. The important thing is that these great buildings not be closed to the public."

Once again, the politician's perspective was far different than those of us in law enforcement. While we appreciate and understand the necessity and need to keep public buildings open and accessible, we want access controlled and the safety of those utilizing the buildings assured.

Nixon's four-and-a-half-hour visit to Des Moines was marred somewhat by about two thousand demonstrators protesting a wide variety of causes. Hard-hat construction workers worrying about an attempt to cut their wages; members of the National Farmers Organization with signs that read WE WANT PRICES—NOT PROMISES; and some obscenity-chanting youths opposed to the Vietnam War throwing rocks and snowballs. It didn't seem to bother the president, and when confronted by reporters, he said, "The snowballs were fun."

These demonstrations, although small, were just an indication that no matter where in the United States President Nixon traveled, he was going to find antiadministration and antiwar protestors. One of the rallying cries of the protestors was "Old enough to fight. Old enough to vote." At the time, the voting age was twenty-one, and students especially were outraged that they were "adult enough" to be sent off to war at the age of eighteen, yet they didn't have the right to vote. This reasoning influenced the members of both the House of Representatives and the Senate, as well as governors and state legislators around the country, to adopt a proposal to lower the voting age from twenty-one to eighteen for both federal and state elections. The proposal was ratified in record time and became the Twenty-sixth Amendment to the Constitution on July 1, 1971.

Since taking office in 1969, President Nixon had reduced the number of U.S. troops in Vietnam to about 330,000—down from more than 500,000 at the time of his Inauguration—in the process of fulfilling his plan to reduce the number to zero. Still, the antiwar demonstrators persisted.

A coalition of antiwar, civil rights, and welfare organizations formed an alliance to demonstrate in Washington, D.C., in late April, with civil disobedience gradually escalating to a climax on May 5 with a nationwide moratorium against the war. The protestors intended to shut down Washington by blocking bridges and surrounding government agency buildings so no business could be conducted, and in preparation the federal government organized Task Force Potomac—ten thousand federal troops ready to be deployed as needed.

The demonstrators managed to litter bridges with debris, nails, tacks, and garbage to hinder vehicular traffic, but they were unsuccessful in shutting down the city.

Backed by the troops, the District police and U.S. Park Police arrested nearly nine thousand demonstrators, who were taken to a football practice field, confined to the outdoors, and processed in the courts by one of eight judges presiding around the clock.

Fortunately, President Nixon didn't try to leave the White House complex for any middle-of-the-night discussions with protestors, and we were pleased with the way the situation was handled.

THE NATIONAL SECURITY advisor to President Nixon at this time was Dr. Henry A. Kissinger. Originally from Germany, Kissinger spoke with a heavy accent and was thought of as a brilliant diplomat. He was deeply involved in all negotiations regarding the Vietnam War, the Strategic Arms Limitation Treaty (SALT) talks, opening the diplomatic door to China, and improved relations with the Soviet Union, as well as other national security matters. He traveled extensively in this capacity, and because he was receiving increasing numbers of threats on his life, President Nixon decided to request that the Secret Service provide Kissinger with protection.

This now came under my jurisdiction, so we formed a small detail that accompanied Kissinger everywhere he went. It was a manpower drain for us, but we had to abide by the president's request. Because of Kissinger's strong personality, it was important to assign the right agents to him, and we chose Jack Ready—who I knew to be steady, diligent, and experienced—as the detail leader. Agent Ready had been on the follow-up car in Dallas when President Kennedy was assassinated, and although we had never talked about it, I knew it was always in the back of his mind—just like it was in mine—and he would do anything in his power to keep from losing another protectee.

In early July 1971, Ready came to my office and said, "Clint, I need to talk to you."

"Sure, Jack," I said. "Come on in and have a seat."

As he sat down across the desk from me, I could see he was really struggling with something. "I've got a real problem," he said.

"What is it, Jack? You can tell me anything, you know that." I couldn't imagine what could be bothering him to this extent. He was the kind of guy I never had to worry about because he was self-motivated and didn't miss even the slightest detail.

"Well," he started, "I'm filling out my expense voucher, and there are some expenditures that I don't quite know how to handle."

"What do you mean, Jack? You've filled out thousands of expense reports."

"Yes, but we did something no one knows about, and they want it to be very secret."

"For God's sake, Jack, what did you do?"

"We flew from Peshawar, Pakistan, to Beijing, China, and spent a few days there, with Kissinger conferring with the leaders of the Chinese government."

This was a surprise to me, but the mission was so secret even the State Department had been kept in the dark. It was the first I knew about the administration's intention to open up diplomatic ties with China, which would eventually lead to President Nixon's historic visit to the country the following year.

"Just give me a list of what you spent and I'll get payment arranged," I told Jack. "No one needs to know where you went."

In 1970, we had begun to select personnel and plan for the 1972 presidential election campaign. In the aftermath of Robert Kennedy's assassination in 1968, we were now obligated by law to protect candidates for president. The law stated that the Secret Service had to protect major presidential and vice presidential candidates and their spouses within 120 days of a general presidential election. After consulting with an advisory committee, the secretary of the treasury would make the determination as to which candidates were considered "major." The Secret Service has no role in determining who is considered a major candidate.

By 1971, the selection process and training for the 1972 presidential campaign had accelerated. This protective responsibility involves every person within the Secret Service, whether they are on a specific detail, in a field office, or at headquarters. When it begins, it is a twenty-four-hour-a-day, seven-day-a-week operation. Presidential campaigns unfortunately require agents to be away from their families for extensive periods of time. In addition to making sure our own people were properly trained and equipped to do the job, we had to bring in agents from other federal investigative agencies to bolster our forces, and provide training for them as well.

Over the previous year, the women who had been made officers in the Executive Protective Service had worked hard and had proven themselves. They'd been trained in hand-to-hand combat, marksmanship, first aid, human relations, communications, and search and seizure. On December 15, 1971, five female members of the uniformed EPS—all of them between the ages of twenty-four and twenty-seven—took the oath and were sworn in as Special Agents of the U.S. Secret Service. The female agents would receive the same pay as the men, and would be required to do the same jobs the male agents did. They were a tough bunch of women—five of them among the more than 1,100 men in the Secret Service at that time—and I was delighted to see this addition to the agent corps, knowing the value they would add.

IN 1971, DEPUTY Director Rufus Youngblood decided to retire, and my immediate supervisor, Assistant Director Pat Boggs, was promoted to the deputy director position. Secretary of the Treasury John Connally and Secret Service Director James Rowley decided to promote me to assistant director of the Presidential Protective Division. I was honored, humbled, and nervous about my being able to handle this new responsibility. The activity of all protective forces would now rest on my shoulders. The mere thought of it was daunting, but I vowed to do my best.

What most people didn't know was that I had been having a difficult time concentrating on the job since being moved to headquarters. At some point after President Kennedy's assassination, the Secret Service had begun using the Zapruder film in training classes for new agents. This amateur color movie, taken by Abraham Zapruder in Dealey Plaza, captured the moment President Kennedy was killed, and when run in real time shows how quickly everything happened. After I was promoted from the detail and moved to headquarters, every so often I would be asked to attend these training sessions. It was surreal for me to see myself on the film, to see the horror from a different perspective. And they'd play the film over and over, sometimes in slow motion, so I had to relive it over and over and over. It was excruciating.

The events of November 22, 1963, were ever present in my mind and affected everything I thought or did. The emotional trauma caused my body to react physically, so I was having physical problems as well. I kept being referred to different doctors, and at that point I was seeing a gastroenterologist, a neurologist, and an internist. Pills were prescribed, but nothing seemed to work or help. I was providing financially for my family, but emotionally I was not there as a husband or a father. There's no doubt about it now: I was going through post-traumatic stress disorder—PTSD. But in the 1970s there was no such diagnosis. I was no longer on a protective detail, and I found that when I got home from the office, a Scotch and soda helped me deal with the transition from problems at work to problems at home. I'm not proud of how I handled my issues. But that's how I dealt with it—and it only got worse over time.

34

1972: The Beginning of the End

Not long after Jack Ready had come to me with his unusual expense report problem, President Nixon went on national television and announced his plans to visit the People's Republic of China.

"Good evening," President Nixon began. "I have requested this television time tonight to announce a major development in our efforts to build a lasting peace in the world.

"As I have pointed out on a number of occasions over the past three years, there can be no stable and enduring peace without the participation of the People's Republic of China and its 750 million people. That is why I have undertaken initiatives in several areas to open the door for more normal relations between our two countries."

President Nixon revealed the secret trip taken by Kissinger and how it resulted in an invitation from Premier Chou En-lai for President Nixon to visit China—which Nixon accepted with pleasure.

Fully aware that the U.S. relationships with our allies in Southeast Asia might be jeopardized by this announcement, he said, "Our action in seeking a new relationship with the People's Republic of China will not be at the expense of our old friends. It is not directed against any other nation. We seek friendly relations with all nations. Any nation can be our friend without being any other nation's enemy.

"I have taken this action because of my profound conviction that all nations will gain from a reduction of tensions and a better relationship between the United States and the People's Republic of China."

The United States had had no direct relations with China for over two decades. We had no embassy there, and no diplomatic personnel whatsoever. In 1972, there were no products imported to the United States with "Made in China" stamped on the back. The announcement was a stunning surprise. The next day the *Washington Post* wrote: "If Mr. Nixon had revealed he was going to the moon, he could not have flabbergasted his world audience more."

From the moment the trip was announced, the Presidential Protective Division began working with WHCA and the White House staff on what would be the most complex arrangements for any presidential trip ever. Agents who went on the initial survey trip came back and told me, "You just can't even believe it. Being in China almost felt like we had landed on a different planet."

Despite the distrust between the Chinese and the Americans, everyone who was working behind the scenes to make this trip happen wanted it to be successful. Months of planning and negotiation came together, and on February 21, 1972, President and Mrs. Nixon—with an entourage of three hundred staffers, press, communications, and Secret Service personnel—departed for Peking.

The thought of accompanying the detail to China had crossed my mind, but with the new responsibility of being assistant director, I needed to concentrate on all of our protective activity not just that for the president. Deputy Director Boggs had a closer relationship with Nixon White House staff members than I did, and he wanted to go, so I gladly remained on duty in Washington.

For a whole week, through the magic of television, Americans got to travel with President and Mrs. Nixon on this remarkable journey, which President Nixon said was "the week that changed the world." And indeed it had.

EARLY ON THE morning of May 15, 1972, I woke up and found my wife, Gwen, in bed, her face contorted and her jaw frozen shut, unable to speak. I immediately called our doctor.

"See if you can get some orange juice into her mouth," he advised. "I'll send an ambulance."

I hurried to the fridge, poured some orange juice into a glass, raced back to the bedroom, and tried to slowly pour some into her mouth. But her teeth were clenched so tightly together that most of the juice flowed down her chin and onto her nightgown. I tried to force her mouth open to get the juice in, but I physically couldn't do it. I had never seen anything like this, and I didn't know what to do.

Our sons Chris, fifteen at the time, and Corey, who was eleven, had heard the commotion and came to see what was going on. They took one look at their mother and realized that we had a serious problem.

"You know your mom is a diabetic," I said as I continued to try to help release her jaw, "and this apparently has something to do with that. Don't worry. An ambulance is on its way. Your mom's going to be all right, but I need you guys to get dressed to go to the hospital with me."

The ambulance arrived, and the attendants immediately gave Gwen an injection. Once she was stabilized, they put her onto a stretcher, took her out to the waiting ambulance, and sped away, sirens blaring. The boys and I jumped into my government car and raced to Alexandria Hospital.

When we got there, Gwen was sitting up, drinking orange juice with Dr. Bazo at her bedside.

"Clint, we have her stabilized," he said. "She's going to be fine. The problem was a mixup in the medication she is taking. We've straightened it out, but I want to keep her in the hospital until tomorrow to make absolutely sure."

"That is a relief," I said. "She can stay here as long as necessary."

I notified my office about what had happened and called the schools to let them know why Chris and Corey hadn't shown up. After being at the hospital for most of the day, finally at around four in the afternoon the nurses suggested we go home and let Gwen get some rest.

I was driving, with Chris in the front seat and Corey in the back, and as usual I had the official Secret Service radio on. We were a mile or two from our house when I heard the Candidate Command Center respond to a radio transmission that I could not hear. All I could hear was the command center response, and I thought it sounded like there was a problem with one of the candidate details.

I picked up the handheld radio and said, "Command Center, this is Dazzle. Do we have a problem?"

Special Agent Johnny Grimes was the operator on the other end, and he simply said, "Yes, sir. We have a big problem."

"I'll two-two you from my residence." That meant I would call on a telephone landline from my home. I didn't want to tie up the radio getting an explanation of the problem.

When I got home, I picked up the direct line to the WHCA switchboard and asked for the command center.

Johnny Grimes answered.

"Johnny, it's Clint. What's going on?"

"Candidate Governor George Wallace has been shot."

"How bad is it?" I asked.

"Wallace is in the hospital in critical condition."

"Oh God," I muttered under my breath as Grimes continued.

"Agent Zarvos was also shot, and one of the Alabama state troopers, as well as a Wallace campaign worker."

"I will be there as soon as I can."

My sons were listening to all this but could hear only my end of the conversation. I explained briefly what had happened and told them I was going to have to go into work.

One of our neighbors was an army sergeant who worked at the White House, so I ran over there and knocked on the door. Fortunately, his wife, Agnes, was home. After explaining everything that had just happened— Gwen, Governor Wallace—I asked if she could look after my sons for a while because I needed to get to the Secret Service command center. She gladly agreed, so I jumped back into the car and sped away.

Of all the candidates we were protecting in 1972, Alabama governor George Wallace—the outspoken segregationist—was the one we worried about most. His rhetoric riled people up—both for his views and against them—and knowing that he could be a target of violence, he traveled with a three-sided bulletproof lectern that was so heavy it required at least two men to move. Wallace had just finished speaking at a rally in a supermarket parking lot in Laurel, Maryland, and as he turned away from the crowd, heading to a waiting vehicle surrounded by Secret Service agents and Alabama state troopers, a man called out, "Hey, George! Aren't you going to shake my hand?"

Wallace immediately turned around, smiling, unable to resist connecting personally with the voters, and walked toward the exuberant crowd. People clamored to get closer, shouting, "Over here! Over here!"

Near the front of the pack was twenty-one-year-old Arthur Bremer, from Milwaukee, Wisconsin. Before anyone knew what was happening, Bremer whipped out a gun and started firing at point-blank range. The agents reacted as fast as humanly possible, throwing their bodies on top of the governor, but in the blink of an eye the gunman had fired off multiple rounds.

The assailant was in custody, and the three victims had been taken to Holy Cross Hospital in Silver Spring, Maryland. As assistant director of Protective Forces I felt responsible, in a sense, that this had happened on my watch. I asked the same questions I had asked myself almost nine years earlier in Dallas. *Where did we go wrong? What could, or should, we have done differently to prevent this?* The answers would not come easily.

It was late by the time I returned home that night, and after making sure the boys were okay, I collapsed into bed.

Gwen was released from the hospital the following day and had recovered completely, now with a better understanding of her medication for her diabetic condition and strict adherence to the medical instructions.

I went to see Wallace as he was recovering in the hospital, representing Director Rowley and the entire Secret Service. I extended my regrets for what happened and apologized for not being able to prevent this tragic event. He was partially paralyzed, and it really made me sick to realize he would never be the same as he was prior to 3:55 p.m. on May 15, 1972. The Secret Service had agents assigned to Wallace in 1968 after the Robert Kennedy assassination, so the agents knew the governor, his family, and his staff very well. This time it didn't go as planned, and I felt awful.

Agent Nick Zarvos was in the same hospital, and when I went in to visit him, it was tough to see the results of his heroic actions, with his wife there by his bedside. He had been shot in the throat and was unable to talk. Ultimately he recovered, but with a much-changed voice pattern.

President Nixon flew down from Camp David, paying calls on both Governor Wallace and Agent Zarvos, and when Wallace was well enough an Air Force aircraft with medical staff on board was used to transport him back to Montgomery, Alabama.

The agents assigned to Wallace accompanied him back to his home state, and out of respect I joined them.

IT DID NOT take President Nixon long to request additional Secret Service protection for *every* candidate running for the office of president, including those who had not previously qualified under the established guidelines and were not considered major candidates. Among them were Representative Shirley Chisholm from New York, Congressman Wilbur Mills from Arkansas, and Dr. Benjamin Spock. President Nixon added one noncandidate to the list as well: Senator Ted Kennedy. We quickly put new protective details together, carefully selecting the leadership. I was quite concerned about the Kennedy Detail, and a very senior, experienced individual was made the Agent in Charge. Three weeks later the senator himself requested the protective detail be terminated, and on June 5, 1972, we discontinued coverage of Senator Kennedy.

Around this time President Nixon was about to depart on a trip that included a historic visit to the Soviet Union. I was scheduled to go, but because of the Wallace shooting and the additional protective details we had just formed, I told Director Rowley it was not the appropriate time for me to be gone. I suggested Deputy Director Boggs go in my place, and he did.

IN SEPTEMBER 1972, I received a telephone call from Alex Butterfield, one of President Nixon's key aides, advising me that the administration was so concerned about Senator Kennedy that they wanted the Secret Service to resume his protection. They wanted to make sure the best agents were assigned, and they requested a specific agent be added as the detail leader.

I informed Mr. Butterfield that we would put the same detail back with Senator Kennedy—they were all well qualified and already had a good rapport.

"The detail leader will be the same," I said. "He is one of our best agents."

Butterfield did not seem satisfied with my response, but finally he hung up. A short time later I received another telephone call, this one from Eugene

Rossides—assistant secretary for law enforcement at the U.S. Treasury Department; Rossides reported directly to the secretary of the treasury.

"Clint," he said, "I understand you have spoken with Alex Butterfield about protection for Ted Kennedy."

"Yes, sir, that is correct."

"Let's get one thing straight," he said. "The White House wants a certain agent assigned to the Kennedy Detail."

I didn't like the tone of his voice, and I did not like someone who knew nothing about protection trying to tell me how to put together a security detail—especially for someone as high-risk as Ted Kennedy. If anything happened to him, the burden would lie on my shoulders, not Eugene Rossides's.

"Mr. Secretary, we have already selected the detail personnel, and they are preparing to begin covering Ted Kennedy as we speak. This is not a good time to change leadership. We do not need anyone else."

There was a slight pause, and then Rossides said, "You apparently don't get the picture, Clint. This is not a request, it is an order."

I heard it as an ultimatum and felt that if I wanted to keep my job, I had no choice.

"If that is what you believe is necessary," I replied with disgust, "we will do as you request."

It sickened me to realize that the president could sink so low as to insist that our organization, which was providing him with protection and enabling him to function as president, place an informant on a protective detail. There was no question in my mind that this was what was happening. I had always held the Office of the President in extremely high regard. This request, although it did not come directly from the president, obviously emanated from him. It sullied the office and gave me an insight into the character of the man in it.

I KNEW I couldn't keep the Ted Kennedy situation to myself—I had to talk to someone I could trust. Deputy Assistant Director for Investigations Jim Burke had the office next to mine, and I knew he would be a good person with whom to discuss the ramifications of this troubling situation. The office of criminal investigations manages Secret Service employees and operations in the various field offices throughout the world, and this is where the majority of Secret Service personnel are located. When we in protective forces need additional personnel, we go to that pool of agents to make up the protective details.

I explained the conversations I had just had with Butterfield and Rossides. And then I added, "Jim, it is obvious to me why Nixon wants this specific agent on the Ted Kennedy detail. He is known to be close to some of the top Nixon staff, and may be indebted to them for some reason. I believe the president wants him as a spy within the Ted Kennedy entourage."

Jim shook his head with disgust. "Let's take care of this right now."

The agent, Robert "Bob" Newbrand, was originally from New York City. He was experienced in investigations as well as protection. He had worked undercover on a number of cases and knew how to handle himself in various situations.

Burke picked up the phone and called the agent at the field office where he was presently assigned.

Burke explained the situation to him and added, "Clint just got this request from both Butterfield and Rossides. It appears the White House is trying to set you up as an informant on the Ted Kennedy Detail."

Agent Newbrand laughed and said, "I'll take care of that."

"What do you mean?" Burke asked.

"I'll lie to them and provide plenty of useless information," Newbrand replied.

Mr. Burke turned to me and said, "Don't worry, Clint; the situation is taken care of."

I was relieved but still disgusted by this unethical demand from the administration.

A few days after Agent Newbrand became part of Senator Kennedy's detail, Burke called me into his office.

"I just got a call from Newbrand," Burke said.

"Oh really? What did he have to say?"

"He said, 'Clint was right. They are requesting all kinds of information about the senator and his activities.'"

It came as no surprise. "Exactly what I thought would happen," I said.

"Yeah, he's got it all under control, but he's really pissed off that Nixon

and his staff would think that he would betray the Secret Service under political pressure," Burke said. "You know Bob—he just laughed and said he'll
use the opportunity to have a little fun with them."

Bob Newbrand continued on the detail protecting Ted Kennedy until it
was disbanded. We never saw any indication that any information the administration was seeking was passed to the White House by this agent. He
finished his protective assignment and returned to his field office, maintaining the Secret Service pledge to be worthy of trust and confidence.

WHEN I WAS selected to be assistant director, I needed to choose a deputy.
I needed someone I could trust, someone who had the best interests of the
Secret Service at heart, someone willing to put in the long, tedious hours
required. One agent had always been there when help was needed—my old
pal Paul Rundle. During the summer of 1962, when I was the only agent
with Mrs. Kennedy, he had stepped in and assisted, working overtime just
to help me. And then, that awful morning, knowing I had been to hell and
back, Rundle was waiting there on the steps of the North Portico when we
brought President Kennedy's body back to the White House. I would never
forget him asking, "Clint, is there anything I can do?"

Now Rundle was the SAIC in Denver, Colorado, and while I knew he
and Peggy were happy there, I hoped I could convince him to return to
Washington. I picked up the phone and dialed his number.

"Paul, it's Clint. How are things going?"

"C.J.! How the hell are you?"

"I'm doing fine, Paul, and you? How are Peggy and the kids?"

He gave me some line about how tough it was out in the field. The perfect opening.

"Well, that's why I'm calling. Just want to make your life a bit easier.
Would you be willing to move back to D.C. and fill the Deputy Assistant
Director of Protective Forces job? I could really use your help."

He knew as well as I did that this would not, as I had facetiously said,
be an easier job. Especially in an election year. It was likely he'd be away
from his family for weeks, if not months, at a time. It was, however, a nice
promotion.

"Gee, Clint," he said. "I don't know. We love it back home here in Colorado. I don't know if I want to leave just now, but I tell you what. Let me think about it, talk to Peggy, and I'll call you back."

"Of course, Paul. See what Peggy says." And then, I added once again, "I sure could use your help."

We hung up, and I anxiously awaited his call. A few hours later, he called back.

"Clint," he said. "Peggy says she is willing to make the move, so count me in."

I was so relieved. I really did need help. I wasn't coping well, and I needed someone who had my back. "Thanks, Paul. I am really looking forward to having you join me at headquarters."

The first job I had for Paul was to head up the security arrangements for both the 1972 Republican and Democratic National Conventions. Initially the Republicans had selected San Diego for their convention site, partially because it was close to San Clemente, Nixon's Western White House. Meanwhile, the Democrats selected Miami Beach. Then a problem developed with San Diego. A newspaper report claimed that a large corporate donation to help fund the convention in San Diego was linked to political favors from the Nixon administration, and three months before the convention, after months of planning, the Republicans switched the site to Miami Beach.

This last-minute change actually made it easier for us in the Secret Service: both conventions in the same city, using the same facility, just at different times. The Democrats would go first, from July 10 to 13, followed by the Republicans, from August 21 to 23. We didn't know for sure what to expect. Would there be riots like at the Democratic convention in Chicago in 1968? Would the antiwar protestors show up for the Republicans? Or the Democrats? Intelligence was working overtime to get as much information as possible, but it was difficult to predict what might happen.

BY MID-JUNE, WE seemed to have things pretty well under control after the chaos following the Wallace shooting and the additional protective assignments that had been thrust upon us. We had more candidates to protect than truly needed it, but someone else made that decision, not us. We simply had to ensure the implementation of securing all of them.

In the early morning hours of June 17, I was asleep in my bedroom in Alexandria when the White House phone next to my bed started ringing.

I picked up the receiver, and the voice on the other end said, "Mr. Hill?"

"Yes, this is Clint Hill."

"Sorry to bother you, sir," said the agent on duty, "but a situation has developed we thought you should be aware of."

"Okay, what is it?"

"The D.C. police have arrested five men for breaking into Democratic chairman Larry O'Brien's office."

"Okay. Good. Glad they got them. What does this have to do with the Secret Service?"

"Well," he responded, "one of them had some identification on him that indicates he is affiliated with the Nixon reelection committee."

"Do you have the names of the men?"

"Yes, sir. The names are Bernard Barker, Virgilio Gonzales, Eugenio Martinez, Frank Sturgis, and James W. McCord."

I didn't recognize any of the names, but I said, "Okay, let me see what I can find out. Thanks for letting me know."

I got out of bed, lit a cigarette—that was always the first thing I did when I got up in the morning—and then walked into the kitchen, wondering if I should call anyone at this hour. The sun wasn't up yet, so I decided to wait for a while and then call Pat Boggs. He had a close relationship with White House staff members and would know if the burglary or any of the men involved should be cause for concern.

When I got him on the line, he answered in a grumpy voice, "Boggs."

"Pat, it's Clint."

"What's happening?" he asked, knowing I wouldn't call at that hour if it wasn't something important.

"I received a call from the duty agent a short while ago. There has been a break-in and attempted burglary of Larry O'Brien's office at Democratic Party headquarters in the Watergate. Five men have been arrested."

"What has that got to do with us?" he asked.

"I have the names of the five men and I don't recognize any of them, but one of them was apparently carrying a Committee to Re-Elect the President ID on him."

I read him the names, and as soon as I said the last one, James W. McCord, Boggs erupted with a flurry of obscenities.

Jim McCord happened to be the security director for the Committee to Re-Elect the President—commonly referred to as CREEP. He was former CIA and FBI, and was presently running his own private security firm. That rang a bell, and then I remembered that I had been introduced to McCord one time by Al Wong, our technical security Agent in Charge. As far as I was concerned, I had passed off the information to the appropriate person, and I couldn't see how the incident would relate to my department, or me, at all.

I turned out to be wrong.

MY FOCUS RETURNED to the conventions. The Miami Beach police force at that time had only about twenty-five officers, but the chief, Rocky Pomerance, was affable and cooperative, as were the other agencies in the area. Rundle and the SAIC in Miami coordinated a formidable force between the Miami Beach police, the Miami police, the Dade County Sheriff, the Florida State Police, and the Florida National Guard to ensure that we had adequate law enforcement should any unforeseen situations arise at either of the conventions.

First up was the Democratic National Convention. It was a typical madhouse, as thousands of banner-waving, crazy-hat-wearing people from all over the country filled the Miami Beach Convention Center. There was minimal disruption by antiwar protestors, and the end result was that Senator George McGovern of South Dakota was selected as the presidential nominee, with Senator Thomas Eagleton of Missouri as his vice-presidential running mate.

Within a few weeks, however, it was revealed that Eagleton had had a number of psychiatric episodes and treatments, and McGovern wanted him off the ticket. Eagleton withdrew, and the McGovern people selected Sargent Shriver—Eunice Kennedy Shriver's husband. This meant another adjustment for the Secret Service as we pulled our detail off Eagleton and assigned a new one to Shriver.

I had some concerns about what might happen at the Republican convention, so I decided to go down there ahead of time and see how things were shaping up. I wanted to see firsthand how well we had planned for all the contingencies. When I was down there, I found a good deal on a short-term rental apartment, so I flew Gwen and the boys down so they could have a mini-vacation on the beach while I was working. I remained at the hotel and convention site nearly the entire time, but managed to get away one night to go out for a nice steak dinner with the whole family.

The Republicans had more demonstrators to contend with than the Democrats, but fortunately there were just some minor skirmishes. The various protestors tried to disrupt the events, and while it was much less contentious than the Democratic convention in Chicago in 1968, they were ultimately unsuccessful, thanks to the precautions set up by Rundle and his team. The ticket of Nixon-Agnew prevailed, and we in the Secret Service were relieved that the national conventions were finally over, leaving the number of candidates we had to protect down to a manageable four. Only about twelve more weeks before the 1972 political season would be behind us.

As President Nixon and Vice President Agnew campaigned around the United States, demonstrations against the Vietnam War continued unabated, despite the fact that the number of troops we had in Southeast Asia had diminished dramatically. In the past two years, as a result of the Nixon Doctrine, troop levels were reduced from 334,600 in 1970 to 156,800 in 1971, and at the time of the election there were just 24,200 troops in Vietnam. The withdrawal corresponded with an increase in U.S. air strikes against the North Vietnamese, and this progress was clearly resonating with the voters.

On November 7, 1972, the American people voted overwhelmingly in favor of Nixon and Agnew, giving the Republicans nearly 61 percent of the popular vote, with less than 38 percent going to McGovern and Shriver. It was an extremely large margin of victory, with the Democrats winning just one state—Massachusetts—and the District of Columbia.

At that moment, it was utterly inconceivable what was about to unfold.

35

A White House in Turmoil

Two reporters from the *Washington Post*, Bob Woodward and Carl Bernstein, had been following the developments from the Watergate break-in, and their stories indicated that there might be some association between some members of the White House staff and the men being indicted. The question of large sums of money being paid to people to remain quiet was also being raised. In addition to the five men caught in Larry O'Brien's office, two others had been arrested—G. Gordon Liddy and E. Howard Hunt. I still didn't have a firm grasp on how this was going to play out. All I knew was that we, the Secret Service, had no part in it.

In December 1972, we were notified by the SAIC of the Truman Protective Division that eighty-eight-year-old former President Harry S. Truman, who had been suffering from ill health for some time, had been hospitalized near his home in Independence, Missouri. Director Rowley was the SAIC of the White House Detail during the Truman administration and had been quite close to both President and Mrs. Truman, so I notified him immediately.

The morning of Tuesday, December 26, 1972, we got word that President Truman had died. The Truman family wanted the funeral services to take place in Independence and to be subdued and kept rather private. Truman had been known as a plain speaker, and a state funeral was not his style.

In 1948, when Truman ran against Republican Tom Dewey, a campaign supporter shouted out at a rally, "Give 'em hell, Harry!" To which Truman replied, "I don't give them hell, I just tell the truth about them, and they think it's hell." He was also known to have said "The buck stops here" and "If you can't stand the heat, get out of the kitchen."

President Nixon flew to Missouri on December 28, and after placing a wreath at the casket of former President Truman, he paid his respects to Mrs. Truman, daughter Margaret and her husband, Clifton Daniel, and their children.

It was around this time that Vice President Agnew, after living in a hotel for four years, bought a new home in Kenwood, Maryland. This meant we would have to secure that residence—which required a great deal of money that had not been budgeted for that fiscal year. I still thought the government would be better off purchasing a nice home on a nice piece of property in the Washington area that could serve as the permanent residence for the Vice President of the United States. As it was, we had to do a survey and provide an estimate of everything that needed to be done to make this new residence meet our security standards.

THE JANUARY 20, 1973, Inauguration was fast approaching, and the Presidential Protective Division and the Vice Presidential Protective Division had their advance personnel working with the Inaugural committee and its staff. One advantage the Secret Service has is that every four years this event is pretty much a reproduction of what transpired four years prior. There are not many changes in schedule or activity, and in the case of an incumbent president taking the oath again, everything is much simpler, with no transition necessary. One unique feature at this Inauguration, however, was that because it had been less than thirty days since the death of President Truman, the flag at the top of the Capitol was still flying at half-staff.

On January 19, the night before the Inauguration, President Nixon and his family attended a concert at the Kennedy Center; then, on January 20, there was the usual swearing-in at the Capitol; a luncheon; an Inaugural Parade; and Inaugural Balls—five of them—that evening. In my position as the AD, I stayed in the Secret Service command center so I could oversee all the operations and make adjustments if needed.

Once again antiwar demonstrators posed a problem. Even though much had been done to withdraw from Vietnam and it was a steady work in progress, the antiwar crowd never seemed satisfied and wouldn't be until all the troops were withdrawn, all bombing stopped, and hostilities ceased. About sixty thousand protestors were kept well away from the parade route, but a small group managed to get close, and when President and Mrs. Nixon rode by, standing halfway out the roof of the limousine, the protestors hurled oranges and apples and other debris at them. Fortunately, none of the fruit met its mark.

TWO DAYS AFTER the Inauguration, the SAIC of the Johnson Protective Detail called and advised me that former President Johnson had died at his home on the LBJ Ranch in Texas of an apparent heart attack. I knew he had been having some health difficulties and he wasn't taking good care of himself, but I was still shocked and saddened by the news. He was just sixty-four years old.

There was a public viewing at the LBJ Library in Austin on January 23 and 24, and then President Johnson's body was flown to Andrews Air Force Base aboard USAF 26000, the same plane on which he had taken the oath of office in 1963 and subsequently in which he traveled the world. A motorcade brought the body to Constitution Avenue, south of the White House, and there it was transferred to a horse-drawn caisson for the slow march to the Capitol.

The president's body lay in state in the Capitol Rotunda overnight as thousands came to pay their respects. At the formal funeral services in National City Christian Church in Washington the next day, I stood in the back and looked around the room, seeing many familiar faces—people whom President Johnson would have been humbled to know had come to pay their respects: Mrs. Mamie Eisenhower, Robert McNamara, numerous civil rights leaders, members of Congress and Supreme Court justices, and so many others who had served loyally with him. President and Mrs. Nixon and the Agnews sat in the front row on one side, while Mrs. Johnson, Luci, Lynda, their husbands, and five-and-a-half-year-old Lyn Nugent—the little boy who brought so much joy to President Johnson during some of his darkest days—sat across the aisle.

I flew with the family aboard Air Force 26000 to take the body back to Texas, where LBJ was placed in his final resting place, in the family cemetery at his beloved LBJ Ranch. Following the interment, Mrs. Johnson had a reception in the house, and I was pleased to be able to express my condolences to her personally, as well as on behalf of the entire U.S. Secret Service.

I had intended to return to Washington by commercial aircraft later that night or early the next morning. When I was at the ranch, however, I happened to be talking with the crew of the JetStar assigned to the vice president and learned that they had flown some officials to Bergstrom Air Force Base from Washington, and were returning to Washington with no passengers aboard.

The pilot said, "Why don't you ride back with us, Clint?"

I gladly accepted. Then a strange thing happened. Jack Valenti, who had been LBJ's assistant at the White House and was at that time president of the Motion Picture Association of America, approached me.

"Clint," he said, "I'm trying to find a ride back to Washington. I had hoped to be able to fly back on the big jet, but I was told that the only way they could accommodate me would be on the JetStar."

And then humbly he added, "And they said that you needed to provide authorization for me to accompany you, since you are the highest-ranking U.S. government official and you have control of the aircraft."

It was indeed an ironic situation. Jack Valenti, once one of the most influential men at the hand of the President of the United States, was now in the position of needing a favor from me. It turned out that one of President Johnson's devoted secretaries, Juanita Roberts, also needed a ride, so we flew back to Andrews Air Force Base that evening, just the three of us and the crew aboard the JetStar. It was a quiet, comfortable flight.

In a sad coincidence, President Nixon announced that an agreement had been reached for a cease-fire in Vietnam the night after Johnson died. Two months later, the last U.S. combat troops would leave South Vietnam and the remaining American prisoners of war would be freed, thus ending our direct intervention in the conflict, and the man who would have felt the impact of it deepest of all had not lived to see it come to pass.

As it turned out, ending the Vietnam War would not be Nixon's legacy either.

• • •

Less than a week after President Johnson's funeral, G. Gordon Liddy and James McCord were convicted of conspiracy, burglary, and bugging the Democratic Party's Watergate headquarters. Five other men who were indicted with Liddy and McCord had pleaded guilty early in the trial to all charges against them.

Shortly thereafter, McCord wrote a letter to Chief U.S. District Judge John J. Sirica stating that there were others involved—people who had not yet been named, and that there had been political pressure and perjury in the trial. This sparked the U.S. Senate to create the Select Committee on Presidential Campaign Activities, which became known as the Watergate Committee. Its task was to thoroughly investigate the activities related to the 1972 presidential election campaign.

By the end of March, Alexander Butterfield, deputy assistant to the president, had resigned his White House post to become the Federal Aviation Administrator, and it was revealed that two top White House staffers, John W. Dean III and Jeb Stuart Magruder, appeared to have had advance knowledge of the Watergate affair. Behind the scenes, Dean, who was the White House legal counsel, started working with prosecutors in an effort to get immunity. He claimed that he was a scapegoat and that the people who were most deeply involved were some of the men closest to the president.

Ever since the Watergate break-in had occurred, Nixon had repeatedly denied that he or any of his staff were involved. Then, on April 30, 1973, President Nixon fired Dean and accepted the resignations of his chief of staff, Bob Haldeman, chief domestic advisor John Ehrlichman, and Attorney General Richard Kleindienst.

As soon as I got word that this was going to happen, I assigned an around-the-clock detail to guard the files in the Executive Office Building. No one was to bring anything in or take anything out. I had seen the way Nixon's staff operated, and I knew that if they had the opportunity, they would be shredding files like crazy.

Meanwhile, Nixon had appointed L. Patrick Gray to replace J. Edgar Hoover as FBI director. Hoover had died in May 1972, but Gray failed to receive Senate confirmation and withdrew his name from consideration.

Nixon then appointed an interim FBI director, William D. Ruckelshaus. The White House was in complete turmoil. It appeared that everyone was running for the woods to get as far away from the burgeoning scandal as possible.

President Nixon finally reached out to Clarence Kelley, a retired FBI agent who was serving as the chief of police in Kansas City, Missouri. Kelley was easily confirmed and became the new director of the FBI on July 9, 1973.

By this point, the Watergate hearings were being broadcast on television. It had become a national drama, a real-life soap opera, unfolding day by day. I was sitting in my office on July 13, 1973, when Deputy Director Boggs came in and said, "Clint, today's testimony is something you need to watch."

"What's going on?" I asked.

"They've just announced a surprise witness. Alexander Butterfield is about to testify."

I raised my eyebrows and said, "Thanks, Pat."

I turned on the television in my office just as Butterfield was being sworn in.

Well, this should be interesting.

Butterfield sat in front of the Senate committee, hands clasped together, as the questioning began.

"Mr. Butterfield, are you aware of the installation of any listening devices in the Oval Office of the president?" Fred Thompson, the chief minority counsel, asked.

I waited as Butterfield sat there in silence for a few moments.

"Yes, sir, I was aware of listening devices. Yes, sir," Butterfield replied.

"When were those devices placed in the Oval Office?"

Butterfield said he didn't know exactly, but recalled that it was sometime in the summer of 1970, as was a similar taping system in the president's office in the EOB. I was sure Butterfield had his dates wrong, because I remembered that the installation was done while I was at the Federal Executive Institute in January and February 1971. He went on to explain how the system operated and that the Secret Service had installed it at the president's request. It was voice-activated, and few people knew it was there.

"My guess is that Haldeman and Ehrlichman did not know," Butterfield answered at one point.

"And how would you go about obtaining what was said?" Thompson asked.

"In the obvious manner," Butterfield said, calmly "To obtain the tape . . . and play it."

I knew of the taping system but had not even given a thought to what this could do to the Watergate hearings. It was like a house of cards that had started to come down slowly, and we were all holding our breath, waiting, knowing that at some point the whole thing was going to come crashing down.

AROUND THIS SAME time I received an urgent message to report to the director's office, along with my deputy, Paul Rundle. Whenever I received this type of summons I got a queasy feeling that something unpleasant was about to happen. We went to the director's office, and after being seated and exchanging pleasantries, Director Rowley said, "Gentlemen, I have a request from the White House that I want you to execute. The president wants a change in leadership at the top of the White House Detail."

I was stunned. I thought things were going along relatively well, considering everything else that was happening.

"Bob Taylor and Bill Duncan were specifically mentioned," Rowley said. "Nixon wants them replaced."

Again I was shocked. Duncan had been with Nixon since the campaign in 1968 and seemed to be well liked. He was one of the very best. I knew Taylor had had some run-ins with Haldeman, so that didn't surprise me as much, but still. What was going on?

There was one more—Art Godfrey, a solid agent, a great guy who had been on the White House Detail longer than anyone else, and we were told to replace him as well.

"You make the selection on replacements and get it done as soon as possible," Rowley said.

Rundle and I went back to my office, closed the door, and had a long discussion about who would best fit the slots. We finally came up with Richard Keiser for SAIC and Robert Burke for Deputy SAIC.

Giving people bad news is never fun, or easy. But telling Bob Taylor, Bill Duncan, and Art Godfrey that they were being transferred was extremely difficult. Paul Rundle knew the history I had with these guys and he offered to be the one to break the news. He couldn't tell them that the president wanted them off the detail, and I think they thought it was Rundle's decision. There were lots of rumors—all unfounded—because no one knew the truth except Director Rowley, Rundle, and me.

IN THE MIDST of all this turmoil, there was a tragic accident. On May 26, 1973, I received a telephone call I never wanted to receive. A helicopter transporting agents assigned to PPD crashed near Grand Cay, the Bahamas, and one of the agents was killed. Clifford Dietrich, married and a father of two girls, drowned when the Army helicopter crashed into the ocean and he was trapped inside. I tried to do everything I could for the widow and her children. I went to the funeral in Connecticut and spent time with her, her daughters, and her mother and father. President Nixon was on his way to Iceland to meet with French president Pompidou and could not attend, but Mrs. Nixon and Julie came to the funeral and spoke with the family. I took it personally. He was one of my men. Such a tragic loss.

THERE IS ONE bright memory I have during the chaotic summer of 1973. I was advised that a group of government officials were flying on a chartered Air Force plane to visit the Truman Library in Independence, Missouri. I had a limited interest in going to the library, but thought it would be productive to visit and inspect the Truman Protective Detail. So I notified the detail of my intentions and soon received a response that surprised me. Mrs. Truman had been made aware I was making this trip, and she requested I come to her residence for tea. I gladly accepted, and the arrangements were made. When I boarded the aircraft at Andrews Air Force Base, I found myself among high-level government officials, including John Eisenhower, son of the former president. They were not aware of why I was making this trip, and I didn't tell them.

When we arrived at the Kansas City airport, the Truman Detail SAIC met me with a car and drove me to the Truman residence, while the others went on their way to the library.

Mrs. Truman met us at the front door, and after the agent introduced us, he politely excused himself.

"Mr. Hill, it is such a pleasure to finally meet you," she said. "Please come in and have a seat."

I sat down in a well-worn wingback chair as Mrs. Truman went to the kitchen and made tea for us. We had an interesting conversation about the agents who were assigned to her and how much she thought of them. She said that, really, they were family. We talked about the White House, and I explained how things had changed over the years, and she reminisced about the people she remembered from her years in the presidential residence. We sat there talking, very comfortably, almost like we were old friends, for nearly an hour. It was a memorable afternoon.

On the return flight, one of the officials asked me, "Mr. Hill, what did you do in Independence?"

"Mrs. Truman asked to see me, so we spent the afternoon having tea and reminiscing," I said matter-of-factly.

They were speechless. None of them had ever met the Trumans. I had the honor of having met President Truman as a former president, and now Mrs. Truman. Pretty special.

IN AUGUST 1973, President Nixon traveled back and forth from the White House to Camp David on an almost daily basis by helicopter. When he was at the White House, most evenings were spent having dinner on the yacht *Sequoia*, cruising along the Potomac. Later in the month he flew down to Key Biscayne for a few nights, and then spent the rest of August in San Clemente.

Most of the top staff Nixon brought to the White House in 1969 had now departed. Vice President Agnew, meanwhile, found his name appearing in the news alleging he had engaged in illegal activity, and a criminal investigation was under way. He held a news conference and charged Attorney General Elliot Richardson and U.S. Attorney George Beall of leaking information about the investigation to the media. The situation with Vice

President Agnew grew worse each day. I did not have any proof that Nixon's people were behind the seething investigation that delved into Agnew's finances prior to his becoming vice president, but knowing how they operated, I wouldn't have put it past them.

On October 10, 1973, Paul Rundle and I received word that Vice President Agnew was in court in Baltimore, Maryland. He was going to plead guilty to a criminal charge against him and resign the vice presidency. He had informed Sam Sulliman, the SAIC of his detail, what he was about to do and had requested no one other than Sulliman and a very few others be made aware of what was about to transpire. The information was not even provided to his staff. Rundle and I were caught unaware and quickly had to create a new protective unit: as soon as Vice President Agnew resigned, the speaker of the House of Representatives was next in the line of succession to the president. It was embarrassing not to have had advance knowledge, but I respected Agnew's decision and also the SAIC for not informing anyone.

Agnew pleaded no contest to tax evasion charges, admitting that he did not pay taxes on some taxable income back in 1967, when he was an elected official of the state of Maryland. It was disheartening to hear this news, because I had grown to like the vice president a great deal. Two days later, Nixon announced that his choice for vice president was Congressman Gerald R. Ford of Michigan.

At some point during that terrible week, Mrs. Agnew called me in tears. She was such a lovely woman, and had been so giving and kind to all the agents.

"Clint," she said, "how did this happen? I don't understand it. Can you please explain it to me?"

I tried my best to explain as well as I understood the situation what the charges were about, but I didn't have all the details, and I didn't want to speculate on what I thought had really happened. But if there was one thing I had learned in the past fifteen years, it was that politics was a damn dirty business.

Now the Watergate investigation was heating up, with more information being revealed and more accusations about White House participation being made. Back in May, Nixon's new attorney general, Elliot Richardson, selected Archibald Cox to be the special prosecutor to investigate the Watergate matter. After Alex Butterfield revealed the existence of the secret taping system, Cox issued a subpoena asking for copies of any tape recordings that had been made in the Oval Office. Nixon refused to comply.

On Saturday, October 20, 1973, Nixon ordered Richardson to fire Cox. Richardson refused and resigned. Then Nixon ordered William Ruckelshaus, who was now deputy attorney general, to fire Cox. Ruckelshaus refused and resigned as well. Solicitor General Robert Bork was the remaining senior Justice Department official. Nixon ordered him to fire Cox, and he did. This all happened on one night, and the news media promptly labeled it the "Saturday Night Massacre."

A few days later, Director Rowley called a staff conference. The deputy director, assistant directors, and our deputies all gathered in the conference room.

Mr. Rowley came in smiling and said, "Gentlemen, I have made a decision and want to advise you of it. I will retire at the end of this month."

Shocked silence filled the room. I don't believe any of us, except perhaps AD Burrill Peterson, Rowley's closest advisor, had had any inkling this was coming. Mr. Rowley expressed his appreciation for our loyalty to him and the organization and for the hard work we each had exhibited over the years. He then wished us well and left the room.

What is going to happen now? Who will the next director be? There had been so many changes in such a short time period, it was astonishing.

Within days, George Shultz, who was at that time secretary of the treasury, submitted a list of people his office wanted to interview in connection with the director's position. My name was on the list.

I was surprised, but also flattered and humbled. There could be no bigger honor. To be the director of the Secret Service would mean I had reached the pinnacle of my career.

When I walked into the office for the interview, I was offered a seat, but I remained standing.

"Mr. Secretary," I said, "thank you for giving me this opportunity. But I am here to ask you to please take my name off the list. I am not physically or emotionally capable to be considered for the position."

36

The Unraveling of a Presidency

T aking myself out of consideration for the director's position was one of the most difficult decisions I had ever had to make, but I knew there was no other choice. I explained that I was having physical problems brought on by the emotional trauma I had been going through since November 22, 1963, and while I was capable in my current role, I felt that there were a number of men who were far more qualified than me to hold this important position. The secretary thanked me for my candor, and then asked for any recommendations I might be willing to provide. I gave him a few names—people I knew were well qualified and highly deserving—and walked out of the office.

I have never regretted that decision. I knew that I was in no condition to take on that important job. Not long thereafter, the assistant director for administration, H. Stuart Knight, was selected and sworn in as the new director of the U.S. Secret Service.

THE APPOINTMENT OF Gerald Ford to the position of vice president was the first time a vice president had been selected following the ratification of the Twenty-fifth Amendment. Even though Ford had not yet been confirmed by both houses of Congress as required, we believed he needed protection and decided to treat him like a qualified presidential candidate, promptly selecting personnel for the Ford Detail.

On November 27, 1973, the Senate voted 92 to 3 to confirm Ford as Vice

President of the United States. On December 6, the House of Representatives voted 387 to 35 in Ford's favor, and that same day he was sworn in before a joint session of Congress in the House chamber by Chief Justice Warren Burger.

It just so happened that Vice President Ford lived in Alexandria, Virginia, not far from my house. My oldest son, Chris, and his youngest son, Steve, were classmates at T. C. Williams High School. Chris and Steve both attended T. C. Williams during the time the school went through some highly publicized racial turmoil as segregation in the Alexandria school system was ending. The turmoil affected the football team and was later commemorated in the movie *Remember the Titans*. When our sons graduated in the spring of 1974, Vice President Ford gave the commencement speech.

After many years of debate and discussion, it had finally been decided that the government needed an official residence for the vice president— something I had been urging for years—and a bill was passed to that effect. There was a beautiful home on the property of the U.S. Naval Observatory that had been used by the Chief of Naval Operations since 1923. It certainly seemed more important that the vice president have a designated residence, so the Chief of Naval Operations was asked to leave, and the residence began undergoing renovations to make it a secure residence for the vice president and his family.

In the meantime, the Secret Service needed to secure the modest Ford family residence at 514 Crown View Drive in Alexandria.

The garage was converted into a room for use by the Secret Service, numerous phone lines were installed, bulletproof glass was placed in the master bedroom windows, and steel rods were placed under the driveway to support the armored limousine.

THE CHRISTMAS SEASON approached, and indications were that the Nixons would spend it in Key Biscayne. The president went to Camp David a few days before Christmas and returned to the White House on Christmas Eve. We had not been informed of any change in plans, but I found out on Christmas Day that he was planning to depart on December 26 for San Clemente, and he intended to fly commercial.

Are you kidding me?

The press office pitch was that the president wanted to set an example for conserving energy, so he gave up the use of Air Force One for this trip and flew on a United Airlines flight from Dulles to Los Angeles. But it wasn't just the president. It was him; his wife, Pat; daughter Tricia; the doctor; two military aides; and a number of Secret Service agents, along with 107 surprised regular passengers. No press were aboard, because they were not told until after the plane left.

Now, I knew that the military would be flying an aircraft out to El Toro Marine Corps Air Station to stand by to bring the party back or in case of emergency. That burns fuel too. What really got me was that he had been flying back and forth to Camp David on a daily basis by helicopter rather than just staying there. This stunt was strictly eyewash for political reasons, and we were left scrambling to ensure his protection on a coast-to-coast commercial flight.

Nineteen seventy-three had been a year that defied the imagination. So much had happened that no one could have foreseen: the resignations of the presidential staff and members of the cabinet; the conviction of a sitting vice president of criminal charges, and his subsequent resignation; and the swearing-in of the first nonelected Vice President of the United States. Like 1963 and 1968, 1973 was a year I was glad to see come to an end. Unfortunately, I didn't have a good feeling about what was ahead.

On February 17, 1974, once again I was awakened in the early morning hours by the ringing of the White House phone next to my bed.

"Mr. Hill?"

"Yes?"

"Sir," the on-duty EPS officer said, "sorry to disturb you, but a helicopter is buzzing the White House. We have identified it as a stolen Huey from Fort Meade. He is attempting to land on the South Lawn." Calmly he added, "Do we have authorization to shoot at the helicopter?"

Without hesitation I said, "If it is threatening, you are authorized to shoot. Try to hit the rotors and keep it away from the house."

I told the officer to give the command and keep the line open.

By this time, the chopper had flown away from the White House and was being pursued by police helicopters trying to force it down.

Then, suddenly, the officer said, "Sir, he's returning to the White House."

I heard the sound of gunfire as the EPS officers began shooting at the intruding helicopter.

"Chopper down, sir. Officers and agents on scene."

I immediately drove to the White House and was pleased to see how the officers and agents had handled the situation. Fortunately, President and Mrs. Nixon were in Indiana at the time attending to their daughter Julie who had undergone emergency surgery. The pilot was injured only slightly and was taken into custody. We discovered the helicopter was piloted by Robert K. Preston, a disgruntled Army private first class who had flunked out of pilot training. He had been reassigned to helicopter maintenance and was doing this to prove his piloting capability. He was arrested and charged with wrongful appropriation and breach of peace, and was eventually found guilty and sentenced to one year in jail and a $2,400 fine. A few days after the incident President Nixon had some of the EPS officials and officers, as well as Maryland State Police officers who had pursued the helicopter, into the Oval Office to thank them for keeping him and his family, and the White House, safe.

IN EARLY MAY 1974, my sister Janice called to tell me that our mother, Jennie Hill, who was in a nursing home in Northwood, North Dakota, was quite ill. She had been in the nursing home for about a year, and at seventy-eight years of age was deteriorating rapidly. I was preparing to go see her when on May 19, Janice called again to tell me mom had died. Janice agreed to make the arrangements, and we decided on a funeral in Minot, North Dakota, where Mom had moved after our father died and where we had many relatives, which would make it convenient for everyone. After the funeral services, we would bring her back to our hometown of Washburn so she could be buried next to Dad.

I notified Director Knight of the situation and told Rundle what my plans were, but did not ask for any assistance. I flew from Washington to

Minneapolis, alone, and had to change planes to go on to Minot. Waiting for me in the Minneapolis terminal was the SAIC of our Minneapolis office, Art Blake. He was going to accompany me to North Dakota. Resident agent Kent Jordan from Aberdeen, South Dakota, met us in Minot. They had everything arranged for me, and I was so very thankful to have friends and associates like these two men. Secret Service agents were supposed to be tough—and we were—but when your mother dies, even the strongest of men need someone to lean on.

As soon as the Watergate Committee had learned about Nixon's secret taping system, they had been trying to get Nixon to release the tapes. It had gone back and forth, back and forth, playing out on television in the living rooms of America. Back on November 17, 1973, in a televised question-and-answer session with four hundred Associated Press editors, the president maintained his innocence in the Watergate case and promised to supply details and more evidence from tapes and presidential documents. He defended his record, and when he proclaimed he had never profited from his public service, he uttered words that would haunt him for the rest of his days.

"In all my years of public life I have never obstructed justice," he said. "People have got to know whether or not their president is a crook. Well, I'm not a crook. I have earned everything I've got."

By July 1974, Nixon had finally consented to release incomplete transcripts of the tapes, but he still refused to turn over the actual tapes. On July 8, 1974, I could hardly believe this was happening in our country, but the U.S. Supreme Court began hearings in the case *United States of America v. Richard M. Nixon*. Our president was a defendant in a case being prosecuted by the Justice Department.

On July 24, 1974, the Supreme Court ruled that President Nixon must turn over the tapes by seven o'clock in the evening. At 8:00 p.m., there was a vote on whether to impeach President Nixon.

Three days later, the House Judiciary Committee adopted rules of impeachment against Richard Nixon. Before the full House of Representatives could vote on the matter, Nixon announced his resignation. On August 5,

President Nixon admitted he held back evidence from the House Judiciary Committee, keeping it a secret from his lawyers and not disclosing it in public statements. And, he revealed, there were more tapes.

In taped conversations with Bob Haldeman on June 23, 1972, six days after the Watergate break-in, it was evident that Nixon clearly had directed the cover-up. The tapes did not implicate him in the burglary, but just as important, they contradicted what he had been claiming to be the truth.

On August 8, 1974, Nixon addressed the nation on live television and announced that he would resign the Office of the President of the United States at twelve o'clock noon on August 9. Vice President Gerald Ford would then be sworn in—the first person to become President of the United States not through the process of election but rather as an appointee.

I was among those standing on the lawn as President Richard M. Nixon and his wife, Pat, exited the Diplomatic Reception Room through the South Portico. Accompanied by Vice President and Mrs. Ford, they walked through a cordon of uniformed military personnel, rifles held at attention in salute, and approached the military helicopter.

Finally, President Nixon walked up the steps of the helicopter, and then turned around and threw his arms skyward with his fingers in his trademark "V" for victory sign. This time there was no cheering, no applause, no tribute—only tears from friends and staff who had gathered for the farewell. It was the sad end of an administration that had gone beyond the laws of the land and tried to cover it up. President Nixon was leaving the White House for the last time, and this time it was in disgrace. At Andrews Air Force Base he boarded Special Air Mission (SAM) 27000 to fly west to San Clemente, and at noon, as the aircraft passed over the heartland of America, the aircraft call sign changed from Air Force One to plain old SAM 27000.

37

History Takes Its Toll

At 12:03 p.m. on August 9, 1974, Gerald R. Ford was sworn in by Chief Justice Warren Burger as the thirty-eighth President of the United States in the East Room of the White House. Standing there in the same room where President Kennedy's body had lain in repose, now crowded with television cameras, members of Congress, staff, and Ford's wife, children, and friends, I was witness to yet another unprecedented event in our nation's history.

After taking the oath of office, President Ford stepped up to the podium. "The oath that I have taken is the same oath that was taken by George Washington and by every president under the Constitution. But I assume the presidency under extraordinary circumstances never before experienced by Americans. This is an hour of history that troubles our minds and hurts our hearts."

He proceeded with what he said was not an inaugural speech, but "straight talk among friends."

"I am acutely aware that you have not elected me as your president by your ballots. So I ask you to confirm me as your president with your prayers."

It was a heartfelt speech lasting less than ten minutes, and at times President Ford choked back tears. "As I begin this very difficult job," he said, "I have not sought this enormous responsibility, but I will not shirk it."

Toward the end of his remarks, he looked up from his notes and said with confidence and defiance, "My fellow Americans, our long national nightmare is over. Our Constitution works; our great republic is a government of laws, not of men."

Just as I had witnessed Lyndon B. Johnson taking the oath of office after another national nightmare in the small, crowded cabin of Air Force One less than twelve years earlier, this transition seemed surreal. But it was, as Gerald Ford noted, a testament to our Constitution that the transfer of power could occur peacefully and seamlessly. Men may die or fail, but our country would survive.

TRADITIONALLY, THERE WAS a swift transition between administrations, and on the same day that one presidential family moved out of the White House, the next one moved in. But because of the unexpected nature of this transition, President and Mrs. Ford gave the Nixons plenty of time to move out, and the Fords ended up spending the first ten nights of his presidency at their home in Alexandria. The agents on the detail said President Ford would come out the front door in the morning, still in his pajamas, and pick up the newspaper before heading back in to prepare his own breakfast of orange juice and an English muffin. And that was indicative of the character of Gerald Ford.

He had been in Congress for a long time and was highly respected. He hadn't campaigned to be president, and I'm not sure he ever envisioned himself as president. But there he was.

Born in Omaha, Nebraska, Gerald Rudolph Ford grew up in Grand Rapids, Michigan, in a close-knit family. A gifted athlete, he played football for the University of Michigan and was voted the Wolverines' most valuable player in 1934. Upon graduation, Ford was offered professional football contracts from both the Detroit Lions and the Green Bay Packers, but he opted instead to pursue a law degree at Yale University, where he graduated in the top 25 percent of his class.

He served in the U.S. Naval Reserve during World War II, was elected to Congress in 1948, and eventually became the minority leader of the House of Representatives during the Johnson administration.

The feedback I got from the agents on the Ford Detail was that Ford was a great guy—humble, respectful, and kind. He loved to play golf and was an avid downhill skier—the Ford family typically spent holidays skiing in Colorado—so we had to make sure we had agents who could keep up with the new president on the ski slopes.

On August 19, President Ford had a scheduled speech at the Veterans of Foreign Wars' annual convention in Chicago. As this would be his first trip outside Washington as president, and his first trip aboard Air Force One, I decided to accompany the PPD to observe the agents in a real-life situation on the road. I was pleased to see the good working relationship the agents had with the Ford staff, and I returned to Washington knowing the detail was doing an excellent job.

That same day, President Ford nominated Nelson Rockefeller, the sixty-six-year-old former governor of New York, to be vice president, but he still needed to be confirmed by Congress. In the interim, we had to provide protection for the person next in the line of succession to the president, Carl Albert, Speaker of the House of Representatives.

On the morning of Sunday, September 8, one month after Ford had taken the Oath of Office, I was at home when I got a call informing me that the president was about to appear on television from the Oval Office. I was as surprised as the rest of the nation when he announced that he was granting "a full, free, and absolute pardon unto Richard Nixon for all offenses against the United States which he, Richard Nixon, has committed or may have committed or taken part in . . ."

The presidential pardon meant that the judicial system now had no choice but to withdraw from any possible criminal legal action against Nixon.

President Ford's reasoning was that a trial would reopen the wounds that were already in the process of healing and would cause "prolonged and divisive debate" while exposing Nixon to "further punishment and degradation" after he had already paid the high price of relinquishing the highest elective office of the United States.

Reaction was swift and severe on both sides. Some agreed that it was the right thing to do in order to close the door on Watergate, while others called it an abuse of presidential power and an insult to the American people. One thing was for sure: Ford's honeymoon period had come to an end, and from that point on, he would be the target of outrage and protests—an additional challenge for the agents on his protective detail.

Meanwhile, we still didn't have a vice president. The largest controversy during the congressional hearings was Rockefeller's wealth. That caused the hearings to go on for four months. He offered to establish a blind trust but Congress chose not to push the issue and didn't require that be done. Finally in December a vote was taken, and Rockefeller was confirmed.

The residence that had been the home of the Chief of Naval Operations at the Naval Observatory off Massachusetts Avenue in northwest Washington was finally finished being renovated and was now the official residence of the Vice President of the United States. It was music to my ears, a dream come true. No more extra costs for a temporary VP residence. The Rockefellers, however, owned a large estate on Foxhall Road in northwest Washington, and they chose this to be their official residence. They ended up using the new official vice president's residence merely for social events. My dream bubble burst—proving yet again that no matter how much you plan, you must always be willing to adjust for unforeseen obstacles and politicians with their own resources, ideas, and agendas.

ON CHRISTMAS NIGHT, in the early morning hours of December 26, 1974, I was once again awakened by the sound of the White House phone ringing next to my bed. A man had crashed his car through the Northwest Gate of the White House, had driven up the driveway almost to the North Portico, and then stopped the car, got out, and stood wearing what appeared to be explosives attached to his outer garments. He wore a hooded sweatshirt and stood with his arms outstretched, with what appeared to be a detonator in one hand. He just stood there, making no attempt to enter the mansion.

I hurriedly drove from my home to the White House to see for myself what was going on. By the time I arrived, Metropolitan Police and Fire Department personnel had responded and were standing by. Chief Earl Drescher of the Executive Protective Service began to talk with the man and eventually convinced him to surrender. The man, twenty-five-year-old Marshall Hill Fields of Silver Spring, Maryland, was taken into custody and then to St. Elizabeths mental hospital for observation. There were no injuries, just a piece of rusted metal gate lying on the White House lawn. Fortunately, President and Mrs. Ford were in Vail, Colorado, for the holidays.

Now, we had been asking for a sturdier, more secure gate for *years*, but our budget proposals were always denied. Guess what? After this incident, the gate was replaced with a very heavy, hydraulic-operated gate—exactly like the kind we had requested.

PRESIDENT FORD TRAVELED to five different countries in his first five months as president: Mexico, France, Korea, the USSR, and Japan. This was the first visit to Japan by a U.S. president and was made possible due to an enormous security operation by the Japanese authorities in cooperation with the U.S. Secret Service. During these travels outside the United States, there was no sitting vice president. Although confirmed by both the House and the Senate as required by the Twenty-fifth Amendment, Nelson Rockefeller was not sworn in until December 19, 1974. We were then able to discontinue protection for Speaker Albert.

In January 1973, President Nixon had announced that an accord had been reached that would end the Vietnam War and "bring peace with honor." Our combat troops had come home, but several thousand civilian U.S. Department of Defense employees had remained in Saigon. The North and South resumed fighting later that year, and in the spring of 1975 the North Vietnamese were advancing toward Saigon.

An evacuation plan was set in motion, but on April 30, when Saigon fell to the North Vietnamese, more than 1,200 Americans still remained. They were airlifted to ships offshore—along with thousands of South Vietnamese desperate to escape the Communist takeover—in a frantic and dangerous helicopter operation. The attempts by the United States to assist South Vietnam over the past fifteen years in defense of its territory had failed.

The statistics were staggering. America's involvement in the Vietnam conflict spanned five presidents—Eisenhower, Kennedy, Johnson, Nixon, and Ford. More than 58,000 Americans lost their lives; over 300,000 were wounded; and 75,000 returned severely disabled.

BY THIS TIME, my physical health had begun to deteriorate considerably. I spent more time going to and from doctors than on the job. I was fast using up the sick leave I had accrued over the years, and I began to delegate more and more responsibility to my deputy, Paul Rundle. Somehow, I was managing to hold it together at work, although, looking back, I'm sure people around me were well aware that the demons were slowly taking over. Paul Rundle was my saving grace—he was, and is, the epitome of a true friend.

In early 1975, I went to Bethesda Naval Hospital to undergo my annual physical exam. One of the examining physicians was Navy Captain Bill Voss, who had been on the medical staff at the White House and served as Vice President Agnew's physician. We had become good friends during all those flights playing cards aboard Air Force Two. As luck would have it, Dr. Voss had been reassigned to Bethesda.

Upon conclusion of my physical, Dr. Voss came to me with a very sad look on his face.

"Clint," he said, "I'm afraid I have some bad news for you. You did not pass your physical. You are no longer qualified to be an agent."

I was shocked. I could not believe what he had just said.

"What is wrong?" I asked.

"Clint, it's a multitude of things. I hate to be the one to tell you this, but the only way for you to get better is to leave the Secret Service and get away from the stress you have been under."

I left Bethesda in a depressed state and drove to my home in Virginia. Over the next few months I continued to see my private doctors, but I knew the decision had been made. On July 31, 1975, I retired from the Secret Service. I was forty-three years old, but I felt much older. Having grown up around farms and cattle, I felt like I was being put out to pasture, no longer a productive member of the herd.

I cleaned out my office and said good-bye to my longtime administrative assistant, Eileen Walsh. Two Secret Service special officers helped me carry my things to the trunk of what used to be my official Secret Service car. They took me to my home, helped to carry all the files into the house, said good-bye, and returned the car to Secret Service headquarters. Two days later, WHCA arrived and disconnected the direct telephone line from my home to the White House switchboard. And that's when it hit me hard. My career had ended, and I was thrust into a state of extreme depression.

I had to get out of there or I knew it would not end well.

The only place I had to go to was North Dakota. Even after all this time in Washington, North Dakota was still home. That's where my roots were.

Two days later, I flew to Grand Forks. My sister, Janice, and her husband, Oben Gunderson, owned a farm forty miles from there, near McCanna, and they let me stay for a while. I'd get up at sunrise and head into the field, all alone, and for the next twelve hours I'd pick rocks off the summer fallow, preparing the land for seeding. By the end of the day, every muscle in my body ached. But when I was out there in the field, with the wind blowing, it was as if I were sweating out twelve years of grief, remorse, and guilt—feelings I had buried deep within my soul.

Every day I'd come back to the house at sunset, caked with dirt and sweat, covered in the dust of the land, nearly unrecognizable, and Janice would greet me at the door and laugh.

"The only way I know it's you is by the whites of your eyes," she'd say. Her laugh was my connection to my past, and her hugs were what kept me in one piece.

Even as I struggled to deal with the anger and guilt I'd locked away for so long, it felt good to work the land, to be with my sister, far away from Washington and politicians. There was a sense of accomplishment at the end of each day, and I realized how much a part of me that land was. I had been around the world multiple times and met more kings and queens and princes and presidents than I could remember, but nowhere did I feel more at home than on a farm in North Dakota.

On the afternoon of September 5, 1975, I returned to the house, and when Janice greeted me at the door, she had a worried look on her face.

"Clinton, you better come in here. There was just a report on television. Somebody tried to assassinate President Ford."

The details from the TV reporters were limited, as usual—we never told the press everything—but early reports said that Lynette "Squeaky" Fromme, a twenty-seven-year-old follower of murderer Charles Manson, had tried to assassinate President Ford with a .45-caliber automatic as he shook hands with spectators near the state capitol in Sacramento, California. Agent Larry Buendorf had seen the gun and quickly jammed his hand onto it and threw the woman to the ground before the pistol could fire, while the other agents rushed President Ford away from danger.

Good work. Those were my guys. *Were* my guys. I was proud of them, yet I couldn't stand not knowing what had happened. I had always been in the middle of the action and now I was on the outside, looking in. I had been away long enough and it had been so good for me, but I needed to return to my home in Virginia. I had a wife and two sons to support.

I flew back to Washington on September 19, and three days later there was another assassination attempt on President Ford—also by a woman. As President Ford exited the St. Francis Hotel in San Francisco, Sara Jane Moore fired a revolver at the president from forty feet away. Just as the gun went off, a bystander managed to grab Moore's arm, and the shot missed. The agents flung the president into the waiting limousine and sped away, just as they'd been trained to do.

Shortly after I returned to Washington, the Secret Service held a retirement party for me at the Washington Hilton. I had no idea what to expect, and wasn't even sure I wanted to go, but Paul Rundle and his wife, Peggy, picked up Gwen and me at our home, and we all headed to the party.

When I walked into the ballroom, I was stunned. There had to be at least two hundred people standing there, and when they saw me, they all started clapping. All the SAICs in the Secret Service from offices across the country were in Washington for a conference and had come to the party, and as I looked around the room, I saw so many faces of people I never dreamed would show up to a retirement party in my honor.

Seventy-nine-year-old former first lady Mamie Eisenhower had been driven down from Gettysburg by her Secret Service detail; former Vice President Hubert Humphrey was there; former Vice President and Mrs. Spiro Agnew; a few members of the press corps who had become friends; and even Senator Ted Kennedy and Ethel Kennedy. One by one the guests came up to wish me well and to express their gratitude for my service.

Paul Landis and his wife came in from Cleveland, Ohio, to surprise me. I hadn't seen Paul since he left the Secret Service in 1964. It was a wonderful evening, and at the end of the night I was presented with a huge book filled with personal notes from everyone who was there. To top it off, a presidential suite had been arranged for Gwen and me to stay overnight.

When I returned to my home the next morning, it really hit me. The party had been terrific, but it was a final reminder that I was no longer an agent in the U.S. Secret Service.

38

60 Minutes

November 1975

"Can I take you back to November the twenty-second, 1963?"

It was a question I should have anticipated, but it caught me completely off guard. *60 Minutes* reporter Mike Wallace was sitting across from me, one leg crossed over the other, relaxed, oblivious to the cameras and bright lights that surrounded us in a small ballroom at the Madison Hotel in Washington, D.C. Having recently retired as assistant director of the United States Secret Service, responsible for all protective activities, I had agreed to be interviewed about the history I had witnessed spanning five presidents, from Eisenhower to Ford.

Gwen was seated next to me on the sofa, nervously clutching her hands together. A couple of weeks earlier we had been in the same room, wearing the same clothes, and as the cameras rolled, Mike Wallace had asked me all kinds of questions about my career in the Secret Service, how our protective activities had evolved, and, not surprisingly, about the recent assassination attempts on President Gerald Ford. I thought the interview had gone pretty well. A few days later, however, Wallace called and said there had been some technical difficulties and they needed to reshoot some parts of the interview.

Mike told Gwen and me to wear the same clothes as before so they could splice parts of the two segments together without it being noticeable. That sounded reasonable to me, so I agreed. When we arrived at the Madison for the second taping, the same crew was there, set up exactly as they had been the last time, with one new addition. Don Hewitt, the show's notoriously demanding executive producer, had come to oversee the interview. Perhaps there hadn't been a technical problem. Perhaps Don Hewitt expected more than what I had delivered the last time.

Can I take you back to November the twenty-second, 1963?

Before I could respond, Mike Wallace rattled on. "You were on the fender of the Secret Service car, right behind President Kennedy's car. At the first shot you ran forward and jumped on the back of the president's car. In less than two seconds . . . pulling Mrs. Kennedy down into her seat, protecting her."

The scene flashed through my mind just as it had, incessantly, for the past twelve years. I closed my eyes and sucked in my breath, trying to block the memories, but it was no use.

I tapped my cigarette into the ashtray in front of me, and without looking at Wallace brought the cigarette to my lips and inhaled. Smoke swirled around my head as I tried to avoid Mike's gaze, unaware that the cameraman had zoomed in tight on my face, magnifying the anguish welling inside me.

"First of all, she was out of the trunk of that car," Wallace continued.

No, that's not accurate.

"She was out of the backseat of that car," I blurted out, "not out of the trunk of that car." As the words came out of my mouth, I could see her, vividly, as if it were happening right in front of me. That pink suit, splattered with the brains and blood of her husband, her eyes filled with terror.

Wallace cut in. "Well, she had climbed out of the back and she was on the way back, right?"

Nodding, my face contorted as I tried desperately to control the wave of emotions flooding my brain, I could barely form the words to answer him.

"And because of the fact," I said, "that her husband's—part of her husband's head . . . had been . . . shot off . . . and had gone off into the street."

Mike was incredulous. "She wasn't trying to climb out of the car?"

I still couldn't look at him. Shaking my head, I said, "She was simply trying to reach that head . . . part of that head."

"To bring it back?" Wallace asked.

"That's the only thing," I said. My chest heaved, and tears began to well up in my eyes. I was struggling to hold myself together, but the emotions were taking over. No one had ever asked me about this before. No one had dared. And now here I was, on national television, on the verge of losing all self-control. It was mortifying.

"In the twelve years since that assassination," Mike said, "undoubtedly you have thought and thought and thought again about it. And studied it. Do you have any reason to believe that there was more than one gun, more than one assassin?"

Still unable to look at Wallace or the camera, I merely shook my head. *No.*

"Was Lee Harvey Oswald alone, or were there others with him?" Mike asked, trying to provoke an answer from me.

"There were only three shots," I said, shrugging. "And it was one gun. Three shots."

"You're satisfied Lee Harvey Oswald acted alone," Wallace confirmed.

I lifted my head and turned to look directly at Mike to make sure there was no denying my conviction. "Completely," I said. If there was one subject I had analyzed inside and out, it was the investigation of the assassination of President John F. Kennedy.

"You're satisfied," Wallace repeated. He paused, and then asked the question that would finally break me.

"Was there any way, any*thing* that the Secret Service or that Clint Hill could have done . . . to keep that from happening?"

I had asked myself the same question a million times. *What could I have done differently? How did I let this happen?* The smoke from my cigarette lingered, ghostlike, as those unforgettable seconds in Dallas replayed inside my mind. I couldn't look at Mike, I couldn't face the camera, but finally, I spoke.

"Clint Hill . . . yes."

"Clint Hill, yes?" Mike asked, perplexed. "What do you mean?"

"If he had reacted about five tenths of a second faster, or maybe a second faster . . ." I said. Turning to face Mike, I added, "I wouldn't be here today."

"You mean you would have gotten there and you would have taken the shot?"

"The third shot. Yes, sir," I said, pursing my lips.

"And that would have been all right with you?" Mike asked gently, almost as if he couldn't believe what I was saying.

The emotions were overwhelming me. I swallowed hard as tears welled in my eyes. "That would have been . . . *fine* with me," I said.

Mike's eyes were tearing up now too. "But you couldn't—you got there in less than two seconds, Clint. You couldn't have gotten there. You don't— surely you don't—have a sense of guilt about that?"

"Yes, I certainly do," I said, wincing. "I have a great deal of guilt about that."

I paused, took a deep breath, and said, "Had I turned in a different direction, I'd have made it. It was my fault."

My anguish had been buried inside for twelve years, and to admit my failure out loud, on national television, was my breaking point.

Mike could see that I was about to lose it completely. He tried valiantly to rescue me.

"No . . . No one has ever suggested that for an instant," he blurted. "What you did was show great bravery and great presence of mind. . . . What was on the citation that was given you? For your work on November twenty-second, nineteen sixty-three—"

"I don't care about that, Mike," I interrupted.

But he continued on. "Extraordinary courage and heroic effort in the face of maximum danger . . ."

Shaking my head, desperately trying to blink back the tears that were filling my eyes, I said, "Mike, I don't *care* about that. If I had reacted just a little bit quicker . . . and I could have, I guess." Looking down, too humiliated to face the camera, I took a deep breath and said, "And I'll live with that to my grave."

At that point, Mike realized I was on the verge of a nervous breakdown. "Clint," he said. "Let's take a break. Stop the cameras."

And they did. The cameras stopped, and Mike escorted me out to the hallway. Tears streamed down my face, and as I wiped them away with my hands, I apologized. I was beyond embarrassed.

"I'm sorry, Mike."

He put his hand on my shoulder. "Clint, it's okay. I can see that you're struggling. I didn't realize how deeply the events were still affecting you. But it's understandable. It's completely understandable."

"The thing is, Mike," I said as I pulled out my handkerchief, "I've never spoken about this to anyone. Not anyone. Not Gwen, not the other agents. You're the first person I've ever discussed this with."

Mike looked at me with utter disbelief. But it was the truth. Other than my testimony to the Warren Commission in 1964, I had never discussed the details of that horrific day, and the days that followed, with anyone. Now the emotions I had buried twelve years earlier had suddenly surfaced for the whole damn world to see on *60 Minutes*.

It is still hard for me to watch that interview. It is not something I am proud of. I was ashamed that that's how I would be remembered—as the crumbling shell of a man on *60 Minutes* in an episode they called "Secret Service Agent #9." I was forty-three years old when that interview aired on December 7, 1975, and the days would get worse before they got better.

In the months following the airing of the *60 Minutes* episode, I spiraled into a depression that deepened as time went on. I cut off contact with friends and associates and spent the majority of my time in the basement of my home in Alexandria. I drank as a form of self-medication and smoked heavily. It wasn't until 1982 when a doctor friend told me I would have to change the way I was living, or I would die. I decided I wanted to live and so I quit drinking and quit smoking. Gradually I improved, but it wasn't easy and thoughts of the assassination were still prevalent in my mind.

In 1990, I decided to go back to Dallas. I went to Dealey Plaza, and walked the area where the Texas School Book Depository building still stood at the corner of Houston and Elm. For nearly two hours I walked outside, analyzing how everything transpired that awful November day in 1963.

A nonprofit museum dedicated to President Kennedy's life and his death had opened on the sixth floor of the building. I stood at the window where Lee Harvey Oswald had fired those three shots and, in the end, I came away with the feeling that I had done everything I could on November 22, 1963, to protect President and Mrs. Kennedy. I wished I had returned to Dealey Plaza much sooner. I felt better, but instead of spending my retirement years traveling and enjoying life, I continued my reclusive existence, still mired in depression.

In 2009, Jerry Blaine, a friend and former Secret Service agent, was writing a book about the agents on the Kennedy Detail and asked if I would agree to be interviewed by the writer who was helping him. I reluctantly agreed, and so it was that in August 2009 I met Lisa McCubbin for two hours at the Hay-Adams Hotel in Washington.

She was primarily interested in my memories of the trip to Texas by President and Mrs. Kennedy in November 1963. I had a difficult time talking about the assassination, having not done so except to the Warren Commission in 1964 and briefly to Mike Wallace of *60 Minutes* in 1975. As unbelievable as it sounds, in the forty-six years since the assassination, I had never discussed the subject with friends, family, or even fellow agents. It was just too painful.

At the end of the interview, I made one mistake. Lisa asked for my telephone number in the event she needed additional information, and I gave it to her. At first she would call with a question or two, and then, over the next several months the frequency and duration of the calls gradually increased. I began to realize that the more I talked with her about the assassination, the better I felt. She listened with compassion and I trusted her.

Shortly thereafter, I was approached to write a book myself about my relationship with Jacqueline Kennedy, and I agreed to do so with Lisa McCubbin as the coauthor. The result was *Mrs. Kennedy and Me*. The experience of writing and then speaking publicly about the subject was very cathartic and gave me the opportunity to reconnect with fellow agents and Secret Service headquarters staff. In 2013, we delved into the details of the assassination with *Five Days in November*, which was even more cathartic.

Today, my life is once again filled with friends and love. I am closer to my sons and grandchildren than ever before. It is wonderful to be alive again.

PEOPLE OFTEN ASK me, if I had it to do over again, would I become a Secret Service agent? Without hesitation, my answer is always the same. "I'd be working right now, if they'd let me. It was the best damn job in the world."

EPILOGUE

During the period I was in the Secret Service, I had the unique opportunity to witness history in the making, one step away from the most powerful person on the planet. It was a significant time of change in U.S. history, as we moved from the bucolic fifties to the turbulent sixties and seventies.

The five presidents I had the privilege to serve could not have been more different: Eisenhower, the revered general; Kennedy, the charismatic, young intellect; Johnson, the unreserved, deal-making politician; Nixon, the calculating, opportunistic introvert; and Ford, the ordinary man thrust into power. Yet there was one thing they all had in common: an enormous ego.

Each of these men faced challenges they could not have predicted or imagined. I saw how each of them had to dig deeply into their past experience and character to make critical decisions that affected the whole world.

Eisenhower was a visionary with exceptional organizational experience and strategic intelligence without any emotional distractions. He ran the administration with military precision.

Kennedy was rhetorically gifted, an eloquent public communicator with the capacity to inspire. His wise actions in the Cuban Missile Crisis made up for his early blunders in the Bay of Pigs and the Vienna Summit.

Johnson had an intimidating, oversized personality and the political skill to muster support for major domestic policies. But his massive military intervention in Vietnam, combined with an unrealistic vision for ending the war, became his unfortunate legacy.

Nixon had some major first-term successes—an opening to China, accommodation with the Soviet Union, and an end to the U.S. combat role in Vietnam—but his emotional flaws and insecurity led to his disgraceful downfall.

Ford was an ordinary man intent on doing the right thing. But his pardon to Nixon divided the country yet again and cost him a second term.

I saw their strengths and weaknesses as each wrestled with life-and-death decisions.

No one person has all the qualities necessary to be a perfect leader in every situation. America's voters carry the responsibility of choosing the best person to lead our nation, and whoever that person may be, there is one thing for certain: they will face challenges that cannot be imagined at the present time.

As we choose our next commander in chief, we can, and must, learn from the mistakes and successes of our past presidents.

ACKNOWLEDGMENTS

We knew when we began writing this book that it was going to be an enormous undertaking. As with our previous two books, our overriding concern was to present a factual account to preserve history, while also abiding by the Secret Service pledge to be worthy of trust and confidence. We are extremely grateful to retired Secret Service agents Paul Rundle, Dick Keiser, Bill Livingood, Ron Pontius, Win Lawson, Jim Hardin, Johnny Guy, Bob Melchiori, Jim Burke, Walt Coughlin, Tom Wells, Ken Giannoules, Chuck Zboril, Toby Chandler, Ken Wiesman, Rad Jones, the late P. Hamilton "Ham" Brown, the late Jerry Parr; former agents Paul Landis, Jerry Blaine, and Sue Ann Baker; and Army helicopter pilot Pete Rice for graciously providing insight, perspective, and corroboration with Clint's memories.

We offer heartfelt thanks to Tom and Edwina Johnson for relating your own special memories of LBJ and allowing us to include them. We so appreciate your friendship and boundless generosity.

Likewise, we are grateful to Sid Davis and Muriel Dobbin for sharing the wonderful story of the night President Johnson took them up to the Lincoln bedroom. To you and the rest of the esteemed group of former White House correspondents—Bill Sheehan, Marianne Means, George Watson, and Carl Leubsdorf—we sincerely appreciate being honorary members in your exclusive Washington lunch club, and for your ongoing support, friendship, and encouragement.

Our research included visits to several presidential libraries—all of which have wonderful staffs dedicated to the preservation of history. Sifting through the enormous amounts of material would have been impossible without the help of the following people: at the Eisenhower Library in Abilene, Kansas—Tim Rives, Kathy Struss, and Valoise Armstrong; at the Lyndon B. Johnson Library in Austin, Texas—director Mark Updegrove, Margaret Harman, and Christopher Banks; at the John F. Kennedy Presidential Library and Museum in Boston, Massachusetts—former director Tom Putnam, Laurie Austin, and MaryRose Grossman; Jon Fletcher at the Nixon Library in Yorba Linda, California; and Elizabeth Druga at the Gerald R. Ford Presidential Library and Museum in Ann Arbor, Michigan.

We are grateful to our bright, hardworking intern Katie O'Neill, who eagerly helps with a multitude of tasks both big and small. And a very special thanks to Wyman Harris for your ceaseless enthusiasm, keen historical perspective, and generous donation of time.

This book would not have happened at all without the guidance and support of our outstanding team at Gallery Books/Simon and Schuster. To Mitchell Ivers, we can't imagine a more dedicated editor, and we hope you know how much we truly appreciate your willing consultation and advice every step of the way. Thank you to Louise Burke and Jen Bergstrom for believing in us, and to Jen Robinson for your tireless efforts with publicity. To Natasha Simons, Jennifer Long, Theresa Dooley, Susan Rella, Alexandre Su, Lisa Litwack, Ella Laytham, Liz Psaltis, and Akasha Archer, we are grateful for each of your efforts behind the scenes to help make this a book of which we are very proud.

Finally, we would like to thank all of the people around the world who have sent Facebook messages, tweets, and handwritten letters. Your support and encouragement means more than you can imagine.

INDEX